Evagrius and His Legacy

With special thanks to the Dumbarton Oaks Research Library and Collection and the Trustees for Harvard University, Washington, DC.

EVAGRIUS *and* HIS LEGACY

Edited by

JOEL KALVESMAKI *and* ROBIN DARLING YOUNG

University of Notre Dame Press

Notre Dame, Indiana

University of Notre Dame Press
Notre Dame, Indiana 46556
www.undpress.nd.edu

Published in the United States of America

Library of Congress Cataloging-in-Publication Data

Names: Kalvesmaki, Joel, editor.
Title: Evagrius and his legacy / edited by Joel Kalvesmaki and
Robin Darling Young.
Description: Notre Dame : University of Notre Dame Press, 2015. |
Includes bibliographical references and index.
Identifiers: LCCN 2015037517 | ISBN 9780268033293 (pbk. : alk. paper) |
ISBN 0268033293 (pbk. : alk. paper)
Subjects: LCSH: Evagrius, Ponticus, 345?–399.
Classification: LCC BR65.E926 E93 2015 | DDC 270.2092—dc23
LC record available at http://lccn.loc.gov/2015037517

∞ *This paper meets the requirements of ANSI/NISO Z39.48-1992 (Permanence of Paper).*

CONTENTS

ABBREVIATIONS

BHL	*Bibliotheca hagiographica latina antiquitae et mediae aetatis*, SubsHag 6 (Brussels, 1898–1911; new suppl. 1986)
BL	British Library
CCSG	Corpus christianorum, Series graeca
CCSL	Corpus christianorum, Series latina
CD	Corpus Dionysiacum
CFMM	Church of the Forty Martyrs (manuscript collection in Mardin, Turkey)
CH	*Church History*
CPG	*Clavis patrum graecorum*, ed. M. Geerard and F. Glorie (Turnhout, 1974–87) [2nd edition under way, with vol. 3 released in 2003]
CPL	*Clavis patrum latinorum*, 3rd ed. (Steenbrug, 1995)
CSCO	Corpus scriptorum christianorum orientalium
DACL	*Dictionnaire d'archéologie chrétienne et de liturgie*
DSp	*Dictionnaire de spiritualité ascétique et mystique*
ET	English translation
FT	French translation
GCS	Die griechischen christlichen Schriftsteller der ersten [drei] Jahrhunderte
GNO	Hermann Langerbeck, ed., *Gregorii Nysseni opera* (Leiden, 1960)
KG	*Kephalaia gnostika* (Evagrius)
LSJ	H. G. Liddell, R. Scott, H. S. Jones, et al., *A Greek-English Lexicon* (Oxford, 1968)
LXX	Septuagint
MGMT	Mor Garbiel Monastery (manuscript collection)

NPNF	Nicene and Post-Nicene Fathers series
ODB	*The Oxford Dictionary of Byzantium*, ed. A. Kazhdan et al. (New York, 1991)
PG	Patrologiae cursus completus, Series graeca, ed. J.-P. Migne (Paris, 1857–66)
PL	Patrologiae cursus completus, Series latina, ed. J.-P. Migne (Paris, 1844–80)
PO	*Patrologia orientalis*
RB	*Reallexikon der Byzantinistik*, ed. P. Wirth (Amsterdam, 1968–)
SC	Sources chrétiennes
SubsHag	Subsidia hagiographica

ACKNOWLEDGMENTS

The editors of this volume wish to thank the institutions and scholars who kindly made possible the meetings in which these essays were first discussed—the Dumbarton Oaks Research Library and Collection and the University of Notre Dame. At Dumbarton Oaks, Director Jan Ziolkowski and then–Director of Byzantine Studies Alice-Mary Talbot generously agreed to cosponsor a two-year, cooperative workshop on Evagrius and his legacy; when Margaret Mullett arrived as Byzantine director, she graciously and enthusiastically accepted the project.

At the University of Notre Dame, Charles Barbour offered funding from the fledgling Byzantine Studies program, Kenneth Garcia of the Institute for Scholarship in the Liberal Arts helped secure additional support, and the staff of the Department of Theology generously assisted with the workshop. Dumbarton Oaks has long had an interest in the religious literature and monastic institutions of Byzantium, as its publications attest—for instance, the five-volume *Byzantine Monastic Foundation Documents*, its translations of Byzantine Saints' Lives, or its *Hagiography Database*. Notre Dame's Anastos Collection—now housed in the Stavros Niarchos Foundation Reading Room—and growing program in Byzantine studies prompted a cooperative effort, and this volume is one result. Yet an examination of the work and the legacy of Evagrius was a new project for both institutions. Thus the editors and authors offer this volume as an invitation to further explorations into the fascinating thought of Evagrius and his intellectual heirs.

We wish also to thank the participants in the 2012 Roundtable held at Dumbarton Oaks, who helped think through the presentations, along with the respondents to the various sessions there: Elizabeth A. Clark of Duke University, Philip Rousseau and Sidney Griffith of the

Catholic University of America, Susan Ashbrook Harvey of Brown University, and Margaret Mullett. We appreciate the observations of the volume's anonymous reviewers and are grateful to the staff of the University of Notre Dame Press for their work in editing and publishing the book. Finally, we wish especially to recall the kind assistance of the late Remie Constable, former director of the Medieval Institute at Notre Dame. Dumbarton Oaks had been a home in her youth, and she was happy to aid the cooperation between the two institutions. Her memory is dear to her friends and colleagues.

Introduction

The Ornament and Intellect of the Desert

Robin Darling Young & Joel Kalvesmaki

In the early thirteenth century, the learned monk Kirakos of Erzinjan in Armenia completed a large commentary on the *Kephalaia gnostika* of the fourth-century teacher Evagrius of Pontus. Kirakos was a *vardapet*, or religious teacher, and he knew Evagrius's works in those Armenian translations available in his native language for nearly eight hundred years. Learned Armenian Christians, like their Syriac-speaking comrades to the south, had for all that time called Evagrius a holy man and had revered and learned from his works. Kirakos elaborately praised him as "Saint Evagrius, the bodiless man-in-a-body, who is called the ornament and the intellect of the desert."

Kirakos's brief encomium touches on three aspects of Evagrius's presence in that Armenian library—his teaching, his intellectual accomplishments, and his Egyptian asceticism. First, Evagrius was known both in his own day and in later eras as a teacher of monks and a brilliant pedagogue of the soul. He had assembled that pedagogy from the oral traditions of his own monastic teachers and philosophical techniques common to both pagans and Christians in late antiquity, writing a guidebook for an endeavor that Pierre Hadot has memorably called "philosophy as a way of life." By Kirakos's time, Evagrius's pedagogy had proven a reliable form of training for nearly a millennium, and had spread far beyond the Greek culture in whose language it was expressed. In this pedagogy, it was believed, the body's troubles yielded to the direction of a healthy soul.

Second, Kirakos celebrates the noetic goal of that same pedagogy. Its more advanced training aimed to restore a human's natural intellectual powers to allow knowledge and contemplation to grow and, through prayer and the deep understanding of scripture, to guide the mind to union with God.

Finally, Kirakos's encomium praises the Egyptian desert itself, which all medieval monks, from the Atlantic to the eastern stretches of the Silk Road, believed to be the origin of the monastic life. The desert was the source, they thought, of their ascetic traditions and the dwelling place of the fathers of monasticism—Anthony, Ammon, Macarius, and other *abbas* from whom Evagrius himself had learned during his residence in Nitria and Kellia from 383 to 399. In the monks' own historiography, the complex origins of Christian monastic life had been simplified: the "angelic life" of the monks had begun with one founder, Anthony; the first abbot and the first rule had come from there; and pilgrims who wanted to learn how to live that life visited first the early monastic houses of Egypt.

From Kirakos's vantage point, Evagrius was an exemplary monk of the first generations of monasticism; that he was a reliable teacher went without saying. But in the west, over the border and beyond Armenia—in the eastern Roman Empire of the sixth century—Evagrius's work had been condemned, and his more advanced writings had been obliterated. For most Latin and Greek speakers, Evagrius was not "the ornament and intellect of the desert," but a dissident who spread the heresy of Origenism; even during his lifetime, some thought him a bad influence on monks.

For this reason there are two problems that continue to afflict the study of Evagrius and his legacy. The first is that he was not only a monk, even measured by the conventions of his own time; thus his work has been interpreted too narrowly. As a cosmopolitan intellectual and former habitué at the imperial court, his was a thorough and sophisticated education. The second problem is that after the Second Council of Constantinople (553) condemned Origen and his teachings, his supposed follower Evagrius began to be considered a heretic, too, and his works were destroyed, or no longer copied, in their original Greek—or in any place where the edicts of the council had force. Only in churches beyond the borders of the empire could Evagrius's works be copied; but they were usually copied in translation, and those translations were often imperfect. Elementary works survived in Greek, and others, esoteric and advanced, that were still considered too useful to lose, survived under pseudonyms or in fragments.

In the modern study of Evagrius, the first and second problems tend to overlap. Interpreting Evagrius first as a practitioner of monasticism has tended to deprive him of the rich and complex world he inhabited, and restrict his study primarily to a kind of monastic history. This often means that he and his work are compared to an author and monastic founder like Pachomius or to the complex collections called *Sayings of the Desert Fathers*. But the second, interpreting Evagrius as a heretic—or trying to rebut that charge—both reinforces his apparent status as a monastic teacher (misguided or not) *and* diverts attention from the intention and scope of his entire work. Of course, both concerns reflect the customarily ecclesiastical orientation of Evagrian scholars—but just because they predominate in the scholarly literature, categories like "monk" and "heresy" have been just as frequent among those students of Evagrius who have little interest in justifying and preserving church tradition or condemnations.

The present volume cannot avoid having to deal with these two aspects of Evagrius's legacy both because they have formed the body of works that survives to the present and because they have dominated prior scholarly discussion. But the editors and authors hope to contribute to shifting the focus—away from the conventional lines of discussion, and toward a richer appreciation of the influence, despite his condemnation and misinterpretation, of Evagrius the Christian thinker.

To introduce these essays, then, it is useful to understand more deeply the two problems mentioned above. Was Evagrius a monastic founder? Was he a heretic? In both these areas, it is essential to try to investigate how Evagrius's work looked in its contemporary setting, without the benefit, or the drawback, of historiographical retrojection.

The Problem of Retrojection

Because Evagrius used the term *monachos*, or "solitary," to describe himself and others for whom he wrote, it is natural enough to depict him as the member of a community of single men like the monasteries of Pachomius to the south, where monks lived in a large community with an abbot and a rule. But in his own day, Evagrius was not what we have come to think of as a monk of the fourth century. He was unlike those of his contemporaries who were shaping and occupying models of monasticism familiar through their survival in the various cultures of the Christian world. Compared to such communities, the settlements of Kellia and Nitria, where Evagrius lived after donning the monastic schema, allowed for relative autonomy within a weekly cycle. During weekdays, monks lived in freestanding dwellings with one or two companions; they joined other residents on Sundays for the Eucharistic synaxis and for study and discussion. Evagrius composed instructions for both experienced and inexperienced monks—but no rule has survived and he did not mention one.

No doubt the literary elegance of Evagrius's writings, and their usefulness for building a foundation for later forms of the ascetic life, guaranteed their wide reproduction and diffusion in later settings, in the languages of the ancient and medieval Christian monastic world. Presumably at the direction of monastic leaders and teachers, various works were copied and remained available in Latin, Greek, Coptic, Syriac, Armenian, Arabic, Ethiopic, Georgian, and even Soghdian translations. Monks from all these cultures evidently considered Evagrius's works important aids in monastic training and therefore ensured they remained in monastic libraries. Among some monks, portions of Evagrius's writings are used to the present day, and since the appearance of modern translations, even nonmonastic readers have both studied and found guidance in them. Just as later readers could, and do, read the

Bible for instruction and inspiration, they may do so without being limited by the context of those ancient works or the forms of life that inspired and shaped them.

Evagrius's own style has contributed to the situation, too. For the most part, he composed collections of short statements that either gave moral instruction to readers—presumably duplicating oral instruction that he gave to his own students—or provoked contemplative meditation upon scriptural verses or images. His statements—technically, *kephalaia*, or "sentences"—imitate biblical proverbs, and they are meant to linger in the memory as a guide to conduct and thought. Evagrius combined philosophical terminology and biblical language in his kephalaia, as he did in his similarly lapidary glosses on scriptural books—Ecclesiastes, Proverbs, and Psalms. Evagrius also wrote more discursive works, and his letters are elaborate depictions of mutual spiritual guidance among friends. But in all this work, Evagrius reflects not a later monastic setting but the setting of an ascetic Christian philosophical circle—attached to prayer, liturgy, and the spiritual interpretation of scripture, of course—but not enclosed in a monastic setting.

He could not have been so enclosed, for Evagrius lived in a busy exurb of Alexandria. In a period when there were many experiments with the single, ascetic life, the settlements in which he lived were in some ways like the cities whence their inhabitants had largely come and from which their numerous visitors traveled to see the monks. Nitria, his first stop after concluding his visit to the ascetic couple Rufinus and Melania in Jerusalem, had been a tourist or pilgrim site for decades. Its inhabitants lived in pairs or threesomes, in single houses, supporting themselves as tradesmen or merchants. Even the archaeological remains of both Nitria and Kellia, explored in the second half of the twentieth century, are sufficient to indicate that there was no uniform, self-sufficient, and abbatially ruled community in those locations.

In the slightly more remote Kellia, to which Evagrius moved shortly thereafter, there were only hundreds of monks living in this style, instead of the thousands living in Nitria. Here too, it was necessary to work, earn money, and buy the necessities for a life disconnected from that of the nearby agricultural villages. Doubtless, though, pilgrims and would-be students brought contributions, both in money and in kind, and Evagrius's frequent worry about the monks' easy travel and intercourse with wealthy families testifies to Kellia's lack of enclosure. When Athanasius wrote earlier in the century that the monks had made "the desert a city," he may have expressed a lifestyle in addition to an estimated population.

If Evagrius was not a monk in the conventional sense, what was he? Most probably, a Christian philosopher of a more ancient type—a man who aspired to live as a Christian intellectual in a society meant to compete with, and imitate, pagan societies, real and ideal, of the third century. As a student of Gregory of Nazianzus and, before him, of Basil of Caesarea, Evagrius may have heard first about this kind of society from those very men who had, in their youth, tried to live that way. Basil famously appealed to Gregory to live in such a style at their retreat in Pontus. Short-lived as it was, that attempt to live as an ascetic couple devoted to prayer and study is just one example of an experiment in the philosophical life that flourished in the fourth century, and that sometimes survived into the sixth century—for example, in the lifestyle of the monks Barsanuphius and John of Gaza.

But in the fourth century, Evagrius aspired to live as a Christian intellectual in a small society of philosophers, not unlike those of Plotinus in Rome, Iamblichus in Syria, Augustine's group of philosophical friends in Cassiciacum, or Hypatia and her circle (including Christian students) in Alexandria. Even his own guides, Rufinus and Melania in Jerusalem, lived more like members of a devout study-circle than as the leaders of a double monastery, as they are often described; and the same might be said of Jerome and his associates in Bethlehem.

Evagrius was unlike all of them except Basil, though, in his decision—following Melania's advice—to live away from the city. The city had been the customary setting of late ancient philosophers, but Evagrius moved to an exurban retreat, and there he provided the services of an authoritative teacher, a kind of philosophical catechist like his Christian predecessors Clement and Origen, or his pagan analogues Porphyry and Iamblichus or, later, Proclus. He was at once ascetic, didaskalos, and gnostikos—a sage—in the mold of numerous third- and fourth-century writers. Even though he lived as a monachos, he understood that title in the light of contemplation of the metaphysical One (*monas*) and guided like-minded monks who were building a new form of Christian institution. But when, in the fifth century, those monastic institutions settled into now-familiar forms, he began to look out of place—because he was.

Less than a year after he died, Evagrius's community suffered destruction—visited upon it by a leader whose intentions remain puzzling. Theophilus, bishop of Alexandria, marked the beginning of the late-fourth-century Origenist controversy by arranging for the expulsion of those monks who allegedly followed the teaching of Origen. The so-called "Anthropomorphite" monks of Egypt had vociferously objected, in an audience with Theophilus, to the study of Origen, and the bishop temporarily obliged them. Thereafter, Jerome—who had already rejected Origen as an ecclesiastical authority—also named Evagrius and his friends Melania and Rufinus as dissidents.

The details of this controversy have been explored thoroughly elsewhere; for the legacy of Evagrius and his teaching, it is important only to note that this episode was the beginning of the end, both of his style of life and of the development of Origenian theology. It is also important to note that this theology found its opponent in the rise of the great urban bishop in the late fourth century—a development made possible with the decisions of the emperor Theodosius. Bishops often came to regard ascetics as both rivals and resources, and they acted to control them. In the course of this development, the more independent style of teacher that had begun with Clement and Origen came to an end, replaced by episcopal teachers and more isolated monastic schools. Thus, even though Evagrius was by no means merely a duplicate of Origen, the latter's freer style of thinking and teaching in the church was transmitted among Evagrius and his friends.

Origen and his Alexandrian predecessor Clement had crafted, in their own pre-Constantinian era, similar approaches to the Christian life that drew from the training of philosophers developed among Stoics and Platonists—in order to foster a deep appropriation of the Bible as interpreted through grammar and metaphor. Philosophy had been adapted to the Christian life—but without any contemporary provision for monasticism. Perhaps more fatefully, the lifestyle of Clement and Origen made no provision for episcopal supervision, and because its setting was the small group of Christian philosophers-in-training, it was prized among later solitaries and ascetics, but not prized among bishops, who needed different tools for the establishment of Christianity in their sees.

Certainly Evagrius's appreciation of Origen and Clement, and his adaptation of their ideas to his new setting, did not win him friends among their latter-day opponents. But it was not primarily his style of life that made Evagrius problematic, either in his own day or in later centuries. Rather, it was the similarity of some of his teachings to those of Origen that guaranteed his later reputation as a heretic.

The Making of a Heretical Monk

Initially, Evagrius's literary works were not the target of the aggressors in the Origenist controversy of the late fourth century, in which Epiphanius of Salamis and Jerome began to turn against the theology and biblical interpretation of Origen and of those alleged followers Epiphanius had labeled "Origenists" in his compendious heresiological work, the *Panarion*. Their writings led to no official ecclesiastical condemnation. Yet their written attacks found contemporary targets—John, bishop of Jerusalem, Rufinus and Melania, and Evagrius were all known to have studied Origen. Rufinus and Melania continued to read Origen after Jerome rejected him—Rufinus, in particular, to translate and introduce his work for the West.

Ironically, Evagrius was not, primarily, an Origenist—either in the sense that Jerome or Epiphanius meant or in the later sense associated with the sixth-century monks of Palestine. He was an eclectic thinker, like many Christian intellectuals of the fourth century—like Gregory of Nyssa, his contemporary and countryman, for example. He thought in the terms of contemporary philosophy, pagan and Christian, like his countrymen the Cappadocians—and if he is represented accurately in *The Disciples of Evagrius*, purportedly a kind of table-talk assembled posthumously by his students, he knew that pagans drew from his work, too:

> If one of the outsiders speaks a true word, do not be astounded—because this is the result of natural seeds [of wisdom], or from hearing [something said by] one of the saints, or he has heard it from a demon, because often they overhear [the saints] when they teach meditations about practice to their students. (*Disciples of Evagrius* 5 [Géhin, 106–7])

Here Evagrius's approach to pagan philosophy resembles Clement of Alexandria's, and indeed he absorbed Clement's thought and terminology, liberally borrowing Clement's esoteric approach to Christian teaching. Like Clement, he taught that the attainment of gnosis, knowledge, came through diligent study and self-reform; he imitated Clement's use of an eclectic, pagan, and Christian moral and metaphysical philosophy interwoven with "barbarian" wisdom as Clement called it, in other words, the scriptures. Ironically, in the late fourth century, Clement's influence was uncontroversial; his work, eclipsed by the more prominent work of Origen, reflected an esotericism so profound and statements so ambiguous that it avoided the kind of doctrinal daring that would trouble later church authorities. It was Origen who tried to clarify Christian teaching, beginning with his *On First Principles*; and though he, too, presented a simplified form of his views in sermons to larger audiences, Origen was less interested in pagan philosophy, and also less interested in preserving esoteric meaning.

Evagrius's debt to Origen is nonetheless clear, and certain views of Evagrius were increasingly unusual in his own day, if not unorthodox. Most well-known among these is *apokatastasis*, the teaching that all rational beings could be saved eventually, even demons—a teaching that made the increasingly popular teaching of a literal and permanent Hell temporary or less important, at least by implication. Jerome objects to the teaching of *apatheia* (calm, literally passionlessness) as shared by Evagrius with others—he came to identify it with Pelagius's views. Yet Evagrius's teachings were not problematic generally until they became associated with a monastic dispute in sixth-century Palestine that led to the condemnation of Origen in the same century.

Evagrius's opponents took aim less at his program of training in the ascetic life and more frequently and intensely at his ideas about the meaning of certain teachings and scriptural interpretations increasingly elaborated at the end of the fourth century. In particular, these were his conception of Christ and the Christian's relation to him, the nature of providence and judgment, and the relationship of the contemplative's mind to God in the final stages of approach to the divine.

But the most damaging criticisms of Evagrius came in the sixth century—from the Great Lavra in Palestine, under the leadership of St. Saba. The monastic biographer Cyril of Scythopolis gave a detailed account of Origenist monks in the New Lavra, called "isochrists" by their enemies for their aspirations to be Christ's equals in the resurrection. A decades-long struggle between the Origenists and their opponents culminated in a decision requested from, and granted by, the emperor Justinian. His letter to Menas, patriarch of Constantinople, counts Origen as one of the worst of the heretics; a subsequent council in 543, in Constantinople, condemned Origen and received the agreement of the bishop of Rome. But it was in the wake of the Fifth Ecumenical Council, in 553, that Evagrius became linked to Origen on the list of the condemned.

Yet among the monks who lived outside the Roman Empire, particularly in the churches of Syria and Armenia, Evagrius was for the most part not controversial. Numerous Syriac and Armenian manuscripts contain his writings and were, or still are, housed in monastic libraries in the Near East and the Caucasus, and they are the only surviving witnesses to some of his works—those that were destroyed and lost to the Greek tradition. This situation means two things: first, it requires scholars interested in studying Evagrius—either in context or in his reception-history—to master the languages in which much of his most complicated and controversial work survives. Second, it requires exploration and explanation for its own sake. Both of these tasks are daunting, and in different ways. Mastering the languages in which Evagrian texts are extant requires a knowledge not only of the language itself, but of the differing cultural and religious contexts in which each developed, and into which Evagrius's works were received and absorbed.

Such a limitation, imposed by circumstance, has also kept Evagrius's work somewhat isolated from the wider discussion of early Christian thought and made it the province of specialists.

A wider question is why these two cultures, very similar in their theological beliefs to their Greek neighbors, preserved and used the texts of Evagrius with little concern for their alleged heresy. The two branches of Syriac Christianity differed primarily in their description of the union of the divine and human natures in Christ; one of them, the West Syrian, held virtually the same views on the matter as the Armenian. And all three of them were, in the fifth century, adherents of virtually the same traditions as the Greeks' apart from their description of Christ. In fact, there were more differences of custom and expression between Greeks and their Latin-speaking Christian brothers to the west than between Greeks and the easterners. Understanding how Evagrius became a heretic on one side of Asia Minor and a saint on the other requires knowing a considerable amount about the fracturing Eastern Roman Empire of the sixth and later centuries. This, too, acts as a limit on the degree to which Evagrius has been discussed among scholars of late antiquity or of early Christian theology.

Finally, apart from the question of divided judgments about Evagrius's work in the various Christian churches, there is the far larger matter of the unacknowledged reception of those works as the foundational and shaping influence on the very traditions that rejected him overtly—the Latin and Greek (and, by extension, Slavic) monastic thought of late antiquity and the medieval and Byzantine periods. Even after imperial or ecclesiastical authorities condemned Evagrius or proscribed the copying (and therefore the reading) of his works, the main lines of his thought were replicated in other authors. Among Greek speakers, in particular, Evagrius's patterns of thought echo through Diadochos of Photikē, Maximus the Confessor, John Climacus (who simultaneously condemns Evagrius), and other, later authors like Gregory Palamas. It still remains to be explored how this obvious replication of ideas took place, even when it did not necessarily depend upon the copying of manuscripts.

The Present Volume

Thus scholars are left with the question of how and by what means did Byzantine, Near Eastern, and medieval Christian societies receive the complex and challenging work of Evagrius of Pontus even when he was considered dangerous? Evagrius wrote exclusively for male and female solitaries advancing in their life of reading and contemplation, and parts of his work have remained in the monastic curriculum to the present day. What did those later monastics accept of Evagrius's, and how did they use it? That question is among those addressed by David Michelson, who tantalizingly suggests that in the sixth century Evagrius was used to combat Origenism in the Syriac world. This, of course, is the inverse of the Latin world, where Origen's writings survive in translation and Evagrius's do not. The explanations for such divergence are explored by Columba Stewart, who charts the fate of Evagrius's corpus in Latin and Syriac through the medieval period. That later period, marked by Crusades and conflict, would seem to herald cultures equally divergent. But there was interchange, as noted by Anthony Watson, who explores the role of Evagrius's eight temptations in thirteenth-century Syriac writers who traveled extensively in the West.

Between Latin West and Syriac East lies Byzantium, which cannot be dismissed, even after the Fifth Ecumenical Council, for disregarding Evagrius's legacy. Dirk Krausmüller and Julia Konstantinovsky both argue that the circles of Evagrius's thought were alive and well in the sixth and seventh centuries, either in the enactment of praxis plus contemplation or in the theories about the fate of the soul after death. The notion of Evagrius's troubled Byzantine reception is further developed by Gregory Collins and Joel Kalvesmaki, both of whom focus on the middle through late Byzantine reception, either through explicit theological appeals or implicit adoption of literary modes.

Although later associated with solitaries or monks in monasteries, the greater part of Evagrius's life was spent in the company of scholars, theologians, and urbanites, and so his work can be seen as part of a web of conversations among contemporaries in the regions of Asia Minor, Syria, and Egypt, and likewise part of a chain of philosophical commentary from ancient Athens and Alexandria to the fourth century.

The essays that consider Evagrius in his own day bring his thought together with contemporary theologians, as does Brian Daley's essay on the continuities and discontinuities between Evagrius and his Cappadocian teachers. Kevin Corrigan shows how Evagrius uses the concept of "cutting" in his consideration of moral agency, extending a philosophical discussion rooted in the *Phaedo* and the *Posterior Analytics*, with reference to Stoic ideas—showing how deeply Evagrius's thought is rooted in the philosophical tradition he loved, while at the same time is mingled with biblical expressions. Luke Dysinger, writing of Evagrius as a spiritual guide, shows how he understands biblical exegesis as an aid in "reading the heart" and rendering guidance in the "drama of each soul's struggle." In a similar vein, Robin Darling Young discusses the aims of Evagrius's letters, now extant only in Syriac. Guillaumont called them "the workshop of his thought"; possibly meant for wide circulation, they convey his friendship, his guidance (sometimes stern), and his own struggles. And Blossom Stefaniw urges that considerations of Evagrius's condemnation move beyond the discussion of "Origenism" to consider his own high sense of his authority, a sense that made conflict with developing conciliar authority—particularly by the time of Justinian—virtually inevitable.

The essays in this volume can only begin to address the question of how later authors received Evagrius's work. After the sixth century, the church of the later Roman Empire reorganized itself, dividing into smaller groups with differing languages and theological traditions. In some, Evagrius was received as a saintly teacher; in others, he was rejected outright or preserved in truncated or concealed forms. We offer these studies as initial explorations into their reception of Evagrius's works, and his thought.

CHAPTER 1

Evagrius and Cappadocian Orthodoxy

Brian E. Daley, SJ

Most of what we discover about Evagrius seems to challenge earlier assumptions—even our assumptions about his relationships to the people who most deeply influenced his theological thought: Origen and the Cappadocian Fathers. Evagrius is usually identified as the classic "Origenist" whose views colored the posthumous debates that swirled around the name of the great Alexandrian exegete and theologian, from the late fourth century on. Elizabeth Clark, for instance, deals at length with the structure of Evagrius's thought within the "anthropomorphite" controversy of the 390s, and sees him as a major shaper of the highly intellectual tradition of biblical interpretation and personal asceticism associated with Origen, within a late-fourth-century monastic context that was increasingly focused on mystical prayer and spiritual growth.[1] Antoine Guillaumont, in his celebrated study of Origenism in the sixth century, identifies most of the controversial aspects of Origenism—expressed in theses condemned by Justinian and his domestic bishops, and apparently ratified by the Second Council of Constantinople in 553—as coming from the Evagrian tradition of Christological and soteriological speculation rather than from Origen himself.[2] Yet Evagrius's actual theological and spiritual writings are so different from Origen's, in form as well as in content, that it is often difficult to see even a more distant genetic connection. Beyond the fact that he was inspired by some of Origen's own concerns—his instinct to provide a unified, synthetic narrative of creation and redemption, for instance, his spiritualizing tendency, or his rejection of biblical and doctrinal literalism—it is difficult to specify clearly how much Evagrius actually borrowed from his third-century Egyptian predecessor.

The same can be said about his relationship to the three great Cappadocian Fathers: Basil of Caesaraea, Gregory of Nazianzus, and Gregory of Nyssa. There is certainly biographical and historical evidence that they and their wider circle of friends gave Evagrius his start as a churchman and a thinker. But to judge how much he was actually influenced by the content of their theological thought takes a good deal of further reflection because—in a literary as well as a theological sense—his writings are so different from theirs. And yet there are obvious, powerfully attested connections. Sozomen, for instance, tells us that Evagrius, whom he praises for his powers of analytical thought as well as for his rhetorical skill, "had philosophized and studied the Sacred Scriptures" under the guidance of Gregory of Nazianzus.[3] Gregory's *Letter* 3, in fact, which is dated by its editor, Paul Gallay, to 359, is directed to a certain Evagrius, whom Gregory addresses with the respectful title "your reverence" (*hē timiotēs sou*). Evagrius has written to thank Gregory for teaching what we might call "language arts" (*logous*) to his son, also named Evagrius, and Gregory, in his reply, plays down the importance of rhetoric to claim instead that the most important thing he has taught the younger Evagrius is the fear of God and a healthy contempt for "present things" (*tōn parontōn*).[4] Gregory, at this time, was a thirty-something layman, just returned from higher rhetorical and philosophical studies in Athens and himself a committed, if rather gentlemanly, devotee of Christian asceticism. We have no direct proof, but the circumstantial evidence leads us to identify this younger Evagrius with the man Gregory later invited to come to Constantinople as his archdeacon,[5] when he himself had taken over the leadership of the Nicene community there, probably late in 378.[6] The deacon Evagrius was, Sozomen also tells us,[7] a native of Ibora in Hellenopontus, the town nearest to the family estate of Basil, Macrina, and Gregory of Nyssa at Annesoi, where Gregory of Nazianzus frequently fled, in the years just after his return from Athens, for spiritual and intellectual refreshment—and to pore over Origen's exegetical works with his friend Basil. Perhaps it was in those Pontic hills that the young Evagrius's spiritual and intellectual relationship with the Cappadocian Fathers, and through them with the legacy of Origen, began. If Gregory was indeed his boyhood teacher, the younger man would have been about fourteen years old when they first met; the father of the future deacon, according to Palladius,[8] was the local chorbishop in Ibora.

Palladius also tells us that Evagrius the younger was later ordained a lector by Basil for the church at Caesaraea, and that it was after Basil's death, early in 379, that Gregory of Nazianzus brought him to Constantinople and made him his theological and administrative assistant.[9] By this time, Evagrius was about thirty-five: according to Sozomen, a handsome man and a careful dresser, as well as a person of considerable learning and dialectical skill.[10] Gregory left him behind to work for his theologically unsophisticated successor, Nectarius, when he suddenly retired in June 381. In his will, drawn up formally on December 31 of that same year, back in Cappadocia,[11] Gregory expresses his gratitude to "Evagrius the deacon, who has labored much with me and shared in my thinking, and has shown his kindness in many ways," and makes him a generous bequest of a shirt, a colored tunic, two cloaks, and thirty gold pieces as "a little sign of friendship."

Shortly after Gregory returned home, the chroniclers tell us, Evagrius became romantically involved with a married woman of some social prominence in Constantinople; having dreamed that her husband was making arrangements to have him killed, according to Sozomen and Palladius,[12] Evagrius apparently came to realize both the physical and the moral danger of his situation. He fled the capital and settled in Jerusalem, where he seems again to have wavered for a while in his sense of vocation; but after a serious bout of what Palladius calls "the six-month fever," and serious spiritual advice from the elder Melania—the wealthy and strong-minded monastic leader, a friend of Origen's apologist Rufinus, herself now living on the Mount of Olives—to reform his life, Evagrius moved on again to Egypt. He spent the rest of his life among the growing company of ascetics there: first at "the mountain of Nitria" at the edge of the Nile delta, and later in the more remote desert monastic settlement known as Kellia ("the Cells").[13] Following fifteen years of ascetical struggle, study, and simple labor, he died there in 399. The *Sayings of the Desert Fathers* recall little of Evagrius's life in those desert communities, beyond his constant focus on death and the coming judgment, and the rebuke once given to him by the local priest for talking too much theology.[14] Education was not a priority in his new monastic world.

Some Similarities

Identifying theological continuities between Evagrius and his Cappadocian mentors, then, is a plausible project; but such connections are not always easy to make. Part of the problem, of course, is that the theological convictions of those authors—though clearly related, and based on similar church-political concerns and a common education, as well as blood and friendship—often differ in significant ways; the cohesive "Cappadocian theology" for which some have argued[15] tends to vanish from view when one examines their writings closely. Although Basil of Caesaraea, in his debate with the neo-Arian Eunomius, clearly laid the groundwork for a new way of conceiving the substantial unity and hypostatic distinctiveness of the Father, the Son, and the Holy Spirit invoked in the baptismal formula, for example, his own pastoral interests and his diplomatic reticence prevented him from taking theological innovation very far. His friend Gregory of Nazianzus is notably more outspoken on the full and hypostatically distinct divine status of the Holy Spirit than Basil is, and consequently emphasizes the unity of substance and the reciprocal relationships among Father, Son, and Spirit in a bolder and more synthetic way. Gregory of Nyssa, expressing an even deeper penchant for ontological language, carries the discussion of plurality and unity in God further still, towards what has come to be accepted as the classical conception of God as a single, inconceivable Mystery subsisting in a Trinity of hypostases or "persons." How does Evagrius relate to this late-fourth-century theological movement?

What I propose to do here is to discuss what seem to be clear echoes of themes from the Cappadocians in Evagrius's three main doctrinal works (although I will refer in passing to others, as well): his expository *Letter on Faith*, which is usually taken to have been addressed to friends at home in Pontus during Evagrius's stay as Gregory's assistant and (probably) his theological advisor in the capital;[16] his *Great Letter*, sometimes also (but probably erroneously) called his *Letter to Melania*, which seems to have been composed after he had settled at the Kellia in Egypt, in the late 380s or 390s, and which witnesses to his continuing reflection on the central Christian mysteries of faith in their relation to the ascetical and contemplative life; and his *Chapters on Knowledge* (*Kephalaia gnostika*), that collection of tantalizing aphorisms on creatures' access to the divine mysteries and on the knowability of God as the foundation of contemplative union, which presents itself as a means for "the instruction and progress (*lo d'rōshō' wal' tarbithō*; perhaps *eis tēn paideian kai auxēsin*) of monks."[17] I will focus on similarities and differences between Evagrius and his Cappadocian friends and teachers especially in three central areas: Evagrius's way of speaking of *God*, as a single, utterly simple substance that is inseparably (but perhaps not always distinctly) constituted by Father, Son, and Holy Spirit; his way of understanding the *person of Christ*, the Word made flesh, who is for us the model of, and path towards, immersion in this divine mystery; and his understanding of the *created realm*, as both the medium of contact between us, in our present life, and God, and as an occasional obstacle to be overcome in our journey towards him.

God as Trinity

Evagrius emphasizes, in his early *Letter on Faith*, that God is "one, not in number but in nature"—unlike the whole universe, which is "one in number but *not* one in nature."[18] In the *Chapters on Knowledge* (*Kephalaia gnostika*), a work from his later Egyptian period, Evagrius insists that "the holy Trinity is not like a quartet, a quintet, or a sextet: those numerical [constructions] are forms without substance, but the holy Trinity is essential knowledge."[19] The Trinity, he insists, is not simply a numerical structure, formed by the addition or subtraction of insubstantial mathematical units.[20] Rather, as three who constitute a radically single and simple substance, which Evagrius repeatedly characterizes as "essential knowledge" (*gnōsis ousiōdēs*; *idu'thō 'ithyōithō*), Father and Son and Holy Spirit are distinguished from each other simply in the mutual relationships by which they give or receive the divine reality that all of them are. So, in the recently published *The Disciples of Evagrius,* which may represent accounts of Evagrius's teaching recalled by his followers, we find a discussion of the distinguishing marks of the Trinitarian hypostases in terms that could come equally well from Gregory of Nazianzus:

> The Father has, as proper characteristics in his relationship to the Son, the very fact that he is Father and is always Father, Father of one who is unique, and uniquely Father. So, too, the Son has, as proper characteristics in his relationship to the Father, his being "in the beginning" and the very fact that he is Son, only Son and eternally Son. But the Spirit has, as the proper characteristic in his relationship to the Father, the fact that he proceeds. And again, the Father has, as proper characteristic in his relationship to the Son and to the Spirit, his being at the same time Father and first principle. And since our ideas about them are such, we call them "three hypostases."[21]

Another saying in the collection connects this relational distinction in God to the process of human salvation, by which human creatures come to share in the inner life of the Trinity through their free choice to reach out towards contemplative knowledge:

> The Father is at once Father and Principle—Father of the Son, Principle of the Holy Spirit, not in a temporal way but in substance. From these acts of naming we call them three hypostases. This is the reason, too, we can speak of the Holy Spirit; for Scripture says, "Go and baptize in the name of the Father and of the Son and of the Holy Spirit." This holy Trinity, insofar as it is always the creator of what has been formed by it from nonbeing into being, also judges them worthy of adoptive sonship, to the extent that they

> participate freely in knowledge of it [the Trinity], and is said[22] to be adoptive father of intelligent creatures. But the Son, being Son of the Father by nature, has come to be the first adoptive father of intelligent creatures. Even if they do not wish it, he is their creator, but [his] being their father depends on their free choice.[23]

So God, as Trinity, is creator and father of human beings. But the eternal relatedness of Father, Son, and Holy Spirit provides, within this creaturely dependence, the framework for Evagrius's understanding of human salvation, as a process that begins in God's engagement with human freedom and that ends in contemplative union between creatures and God—a point to which we will return.

Evagrius's emphasis on the manifold simplicity of God is surely in continuity with the position being developed by all three Cappadocian Fathers, in somewhat different ways, beginning in the 360s. In response to the philosophically grounded, strongly analytical arguments of Aëtius and Eunomius that the Son and the Spirit, as "generated" and "brought forth" by the Father, cannot be God in the same ultimate sense that the Father is, but must themselves belong to the created realm, Basil, about 363, argued that the transcendent divine reality, which creates and saves the world, is itself eternally constituted of Father, Son, and Holy Spirit in their mutual relationships. With his younger brother, Gregory of Nyssa, and their friend and colleague Gregory of Nazianzus, Basil was really the first to articulate, in clear and consistent terminology, what the church has come to profess as the doctrine of the Trinity.

Gregory of Nazianzus takes this newly formed summary of the central faith of the church as a kind of constant theme, a *basso continuo*, for many of his orations; it seems to have been central to his sense of pastoral preaching, the most urgent point of his catechesis, the symbolic link holding orthodox ecclesiastical life together.[24] In *Oration* 31, for instance—the fifth of his "Theological Orations," in whose composition Evagrius himself may have helped[25]—Gregory insists that Father, Son, and Holy Spirit "are one in their divinity, and the one is three in proper qualities (*tais idiotēsin*),"[26] qualities presumably determined by the distinctive way in which each is the one God. He observes, paradoxically but suggestively, that "each one of them is related to what is united to it no less than it is to itself: by identity of substance and of power (*tō tautō tēs ousias kai tēs dynameōs*)."[27] The threeness of God is due, in Gregory's understanding, not to substantial, let alone to accidental, differences among Father, Son, and Spirit, but to a certain internal, unchanging "motion" (*kinēsis*) within the divine being, a kind of natural structure or rhythm in God's life that is rooted in the distinctive relationships of Son and Spirit to the Father, as their single source. This means that the one Mystery at the heart of all reality is always in a kind of harmonious, dynamic flow; so Gregory writes:

> For us, what is honored is *monarchia* [= singleness of cause]: but a *monarchia* not such as one face might reveal it . . . but such as the rank of a single nature establishes it, and harmony of knowledge, and identity of motion, and a convergence of the things that proceed from it. . . . For this reason, the monad, from the beginning set in motion in the direction of duality, comes to rest in trinity. And this is, for us, the Father and the Son and the Holy Spirit.[28]

Gregory of Nyssa, Basil's younger brother, has also left us a number of short treatises—probably written in the 380s, shortly after Gregory Nazianzus's "Theological Orations" were composed—dealing with the challenge of conceiving of the divine Mystery as both utterly simple and irreducibly threefold. In his essay *To the Greeks, Based on Common Notions*, for instance, this Gregory begins with the assertion that the word "God" signifies not simply a person or role (*prosōpon*), but a substance; therefore "in confessing the single substance of the holy Trinity, we rightly affirm that there is one God, since 'God' is the one name of the single substance."[29] In another, more celebrated essay, however—*On Not Thinking We Should Say "Three Gods," to Ablabius*—Gregory deals with the stubborn problem that always seems to result from this conceptual practice:

> What you are suggesting [he writes to Ablabius] is something like this: Peter and James and John, who are sharers in a single humanity, are said to be "three human beings." And there is nothing

> strange if those who are united in their nature, when there are several of them, should be numbered in the plural by the name of that nature. If then in this case, custom gives such a result, and there is no one who would forbid us to call two "two" and what is above two "three," why—if we confess three hypostases when we speak the language of sacramental teaching and understand no natural difference among them—must we still struggle, in a way, with our confession, saying that there is one divinity of Father and Son and Holy Spirit, and forbidding anyone to speak of "three Gods"?[30]

Gregory advances several arguments to explain why the church's practice in speaking about the Trinity differs from our usual practice of using "nature" terms in the plural when speaking of individuals: that even this latter practice, strictly speaking, bends the logic of attribution, if in a tolerable way; that the "persons" in God are not defined by particular activities, as humans are, but that God's activities are all radically single, even if the three hypostases share in those activities or operations in different ways; and that the need to guard against polytheism must guide our language about God with particular urgency. Finally, Gregory insists that the only enduring difference between Father, Son, and Holy Spirit is a difference between "cause and what is caused":

> But if someone should criticize our argument deceptively, saying that by not recognizing a difference on the level of nature it introduces a kind of mixture and confusion among the hypostases, we will reply to the criticism in the following way: in confessing the unchanging character of the nature, we are not denying a difference with respect to cause and what is caused, the aspect in which alone we understand the one to differ from the other. We believe that the one is cause, and the other is from the cause; and in that which is from the cause, we further understand another difference: the one is immediately from the first, the other is from that which is immediately from the first; so that the name "only-begotten" remains unambiguously with the Son, and there is no confusion about the Spirit's being from the Father—the mediating position of the Son preserving for him the title "only-begotten" and yet not

> preventing the Spirit from having a natural relationship to the Father. In saying "cause" and "from the cause," we do not indicate nature by these words (for no one would define "cause" and "nature" in the same way), but we have signified the difference in *how* they are. . . . It is fully necessary for us first to believe that something exists, and then carefully to work out how what we believe in exists; the description of what exists is thus one thing, that the description of how it exists is something else.[31]

Like many of his theological successors over the next three centuries, Gregory of Nyssa here identifies the distinction between Father, Son, and Holy Spirit as rooted above all in the *manner* in which each of them is God: the origin or "ancestry" of their being—and their acting together as the single divine source of all that is.[32] In a sense, he is articulating a benign, even a doctrinally necessary, form of "modalist" Trinitarianism.

Evagrius echoes the caution of the other Cappadocian Fathers in not interpreting the three hypostases of Father, Son, and Spirit as suggestive of parallel *substances* or even parallel, self-contained instantiations of the same generic substance. Evagrius's own tendency to emphasize the simplicity of God and to downplay distinctness in number, which we have already discussed, seems to be linked to a letter addressed to "Evagrius the Monk," which appears in manuscript collections as *Letter* 243 of Gregory of Nazianzus. Scholars as early as Gregory's Benedictine editors in the eighteenth century recognized, on grounds of style and content, that this cannot be a work of Gregory himself; it was later also published as *Letter* 23 of Gregory of Nyssa,[33] but this attribution is also generally discounted today. François Refoulé has argued persuasively that it is probably a work of the school of Marcellus of Ancyra, representing the more "modalist" side of the Trinitarian debates of the last third of the fourth century, and that our Evagrius, the deacon and later desert monk, may well be its true addressee.[34] The unknown author of the letter argues that predicating three names of God does not damage God's simplicity of substance, but is only "a means towards the good of our souls' salvation"[35]—only reflects, in other words, the ways that God has become involved in history for human good, not God's inner, transcendent reality. This seems to coincide with the general tone of Evagrius's own strongly unitive, even modalist conception of God, at the same time as he takes pains to affirm the three hypostases of baptismal faith; so the author of this letter—whoever it may have been—could possibly have had some influence on Evagrius's early thinking, or at least to have been writing for what he assumed would be sympathetic eyes.

In his early *Letter on Faith*, Evagrius explicitly removes God, even as Father, Son, and Holy Spirit, from those things that are subject to numbering, by an argument significantly different from that of Gregory of Nyssa's letter to Ablabius:

> Number is a property of quantity, and quantity is linked to bodily nature; therefore, number is a property of bodily nature. We have affirmed our faith that our Lord is the fashioner of bodies. So every number designates the things that have been allotted a material and circumscribed nature, but "One and Only" is the designation of the simple and uncircumscribed essence.[36]

Numbering the hypostases of the Trinity, to Evagrius, seems dangerously close to Arian thinking; he continues: "so anyone who introduces number or [the notion of] creature when confessing the Son of God or the Holy Spirit, introduces a material and circumscribed nature unawares."[37] God's unique and simple essence, Evagrius continually stresses, is to be *knowledge* (*gnōsis*) itself, or as he often puts it, "essential knowledge" (*gnōsis ousiōdēs*);[38] he comments, somewhat cryptically, in the later *Kephalaia gnostika*: "God is both knowing and knowable; but it is not as incorporeal nature [= angels? intelligibles? forms?] that he knows, nor is it as nature both corporeal and incorporeal [i.e., finite nature] that he is known."[39] God the Father, as source of all that is God, is "the generator of essential knowledge (*ida'thō 'ithyōithō*)."[40] The Word, on the other hand, has as his role to communicate that knowledge to intelligent creatures, who in turn communicate to each other what they have learned of the Word in his incarnation: "Just as the Word makes the nature of the Father known, so also rational nature makes that of Christ known."[41] In the eschatological future, Christ's saving work will be accomplished by the full realization of his revelation in created minds; quoting Romans 8.29, Evagrius writes:

> In the world [to come] God "will change the body of our humiliation into the resemblance of the glorious body" of the Lord; and after all the worlds he will also form us "to resemble the image of his Son," if the image of the Son is the essential knowledge of God the Father.[42]

Still, as Evagrius makes clear in a number of passages, God—who *is* "essential knowledge" and therefore, at the heart of his being, both knowing and knowable—cannot be known by the ordinary analytical processes through which we know limited, composite creatures; he is not known as an object, or classifiable in terms of genus and species, or form and matter. So Evagrius writes:

> The Trinity is not to be associated with the contemplation of sensible and intelligible things, and it is also not counted among objects; for the first [= contemplation of sensible and intelligible things] is a mixed reality (*muzōgō*), and the latter are creatures. But the holy Trinity is alone essential knowledge (*ida'thō 'ithyōithō*).[43]

In fact, the contemplative study of things in nature around us, which Evagrius and the rest of the early spiritual tradition calls "natural contemplation" (*theōria physikē*), cannot bring us beyond the level of causal explanation, an awareness of the created world's intellectual structure or "formal cause." So Evagrius writes:

> Analysis makes us ascend to [know] the beginnings of objects, and science appropriate to them makes us aware of the wisdom of the Creator. But it is not according to these signs that we see the holy Trinity. In fact, it has no beginning, and we also do not say that the wisdom found in these objects is God—if these beginnings agree, in the contemplation of nature, with the things of which they are the beginnings. In fact, such wisdom is insubstantial knowledge (*ida'thō dlō qnum*), which only appears in objects.[44]

So the mind that is ascending to the knowledge of God as God is—in other words, to an awareness of God as Trinity—passes first through knowledge of the world as created by him, a knowledge that itself is made possible by God's gracious coming to dwell in us. Commenting, in one of the fragments of his *Scholia on the Psalms*, on the phrase "Lord, remember your mercies" (Ps. 24.6), Evagrius writes that with God, such "remembering" is not the recapturing of a mental image, as it is with us:

> The Lord, in fact, is said to "remember" someone in whom he comes to dwell. First, the Lord comes to dwell, by the [created mind's] contemplation of created beings, in those in whom he comes to dwell. But later, it is by knowledge of himself.[45]

In fact, Evagrius distinguishes between the "many names" or concepts by which God is known in the present order of creation and salvation—judge, governor, healer, shepherd, doctor; also door, way, lamb, priest—and what God, as Trinity, *is* eternally in himself: "He is Father and First Principle (*archē*?) even before the beginning of incorporeal beings: Father of Christ, and First Principle of the Holy Spirit."[46] He insists, in his *Letter to Melania*, that the "names and numbers" that are associated with the life of rational beings in the created world—the specific identities that we experience in what he calls "the movement" of time—will eventually cease to matter, and "once the names and numbers that came upon the mind because of the movement have passed away, then the many names by which God is named will also pass away."[47] The Trinity itself, however, is of a different order of reality—it is ultimate. So he assures his reader, a few lines earlier:

> But when it is said that names and numbers of rational creation and its Creator will pass away, that does not mean that the hypostases and names of the Father, Son, and Spirit will be expunged. The mind's nature will be united to the nature of the Father, in that it is his body;[48] likewise, the names "soul" and "body" will be absorbed into the hypostases of the Son and Spirit, and the one nature, three persons of God and of his image will endlessly remain, as it was before the Incarnation.[49]

So, too, Gregory of Nazianzus, in the fifth "Theological Oration," is perfectly willing to assign names to the Son and the Spirit that designate their relationships both to us and to each other, as we have come to know them. But after suggesting a few analogies one might use to imagine the Trinity better, Gregory says he is reluctant to see any human concept or image as an adequate representation of what God is in God's self, besides those fundamental relationships that we designate, for lack of better names, as "Father," "Son," and "Holy Spirit."

> There is nothing [he says at the conclusion of the Fifth Oration] that presents a fixed point to my mind in these illustrations, from which to consider the object which I am trying to represent to myself, unless one is to take only one aspect of an image, with a bit of good will, and throw away the rest. Finally, then, it seems best to me to let the images and the shadows go, as being deceitful and very far short of the truth, and to attach myself to a more reverent way of thinking: to take my stand on few words, using the Holy Spirit as my guide, and to preserve until the end what I received as enlightenment at the beginning, like a "faithful companion" and friend, continuing on this road that cuts across the present world; and to persuade others, as far as I can, to worship Father and Son and Holy Spirit, the one divinity and power.[50]

For both Evagrius and Gregory the Theologian, Trinitarian language is deeply embedded in the tradition of baptismal faith; but the believer must always be on guard against taking it as an adequate explanatory theory of *how* God really is.

The Incarnation and Human Transformation

Like Origen and all the fourth-century defenders of Nicaea, Evagrius insists that Christ, the incarnate Son and Word of God, truly reveals God to us and provides the believer with both a path towards union with God and a model of perfect fulfillment. In *Letter on Faith* 9, he engages the post-Nicene debates on the Son's status head-on, by denying that "the Son is either like or unlike the Father." Evagrius is not a "homoian," as scholars now designate the great majority of mid-fourth-century Eastern bishops because of their unwillingness to move beyond the New Testament's suggestion that the Son is "like" the Father as his perfect image (e.g., Col 1.15; John 14.9), and because they tended to avoid speculative metaphysics. Nor is he an "anhomoian," as the more radical opponents of Nicaea, like Aëtius and Eunomius, have come to be called, for insisting that the Son, as one begotten, is at heart *unlike* the unbegotten God; to be begotten, these writers assumed, is to be produced—but God, as creator of all things, has no creator who produces him. Responding to such a position, Evagrius counters, "The terms 'like' and 'unlike' are used only with respect to qualities, whereas the divine is free from quality."[51] So the existence of the incarnate Son is inherently paradoxical, "both unnatural and natural."[52]

> While being what he is, in his grace [i.e., in the divine plan of redemption] he received at his birth everything that follows, from birth to death. Now these things are not only unnatural to him, but I would even say that they are unnatural to us, too. . . . But he willingly took them upon himself without transgression, since on our own we are unable to rise from them.[53]

The great challenge of Christian theology for Evagrius, it seems, was to integrate his understanding of the personal unity and saving activity of Jesus, the Son of God, with his own understanding of the universe of intelligible creatures; his view owed much to Origen's *De Principiis*, even if it pushed Origen's scheme beyond its original hypothetical status into more assertive, systematic form. Assuming a prematerial creation of "naked intellects" (*logikoi*) or *noes*, Evagrius suggests that the individual we call "Christ" is, in himself, simply the most perfect of these intellects, the one who most closely resembles God: "The mind (*hawnō*) [of Christ], from among of all the *logikoi* (*malilē*) imprinted with a resemblance to their creator, is Christ our Savior; it is he who perfects the rest in knowledge of the Holy Trinity."[54] Christ reveals to us the divine Wisdom that he possesses and has used in creating the material world, "but in knowledge concerning intellectual creatures (*logikoi*) we are instructed about his own substance."[55] What we are, in other words, reveals what he is. Christ's particular role in God's plan is to be the mediator between the Trinity and the present universe of fallen, embodied intellects; he alone is "unmoved" and unfallen;[56] his existence is mysterious, "nameless,"[57] because he "possesses" the unique One—the Son or Word of God—and is therefore himself worthy of adoration.[58] Since he is appointed as creator and savior of the world, and since the Father also dwells in him, Christ brings together in himself a knowledge of the Father and of all beings;[59] the goal of created history, it seems, is for all creatures to be led by Christ to the contemplative knowledge of God:

> When Christ will no longer lend his stamp to various worlds and to all kinds of names, "then he also will be subjected" to God the Father and will delight in a knowledge of him alone, [a knowledge] which will no longer be divided in the world and in the growth of rational beings.[60]

Here and elsewhere, Evagrius clearly distinguishes between God the Word, who is integral to the divine Trinity, and Christ, the created intellect whom the Word makes his own and who leads the rest of creation to contemplative union with God. Christ is the first created intellect, at least in rank if not in temporal sequence;[61] but from the beginning of his existence, the Word has dwelt in him: "There was a time when Christ did not have a body," he writes, "but there was not a time when the Word of God was not in him. It is with his coming to be, in fact, that the Word of God has also dwelt in him."[62] Christ, as the one in whom the Word always dwells, always manifests that divine Word in a limited, concrete, creaturely way; he always has within him—*as* that Word—the "essential knowledge" that is central to the very identity of God, even though he is, as a creature, "not essential knowledge."[63]

It is this indwelling presence of the Word of God in him which gives him the name "Christ," in fact, because the presence of the Word "anoints" him with the gift of "essential knowledge" that he eventually will communicate to the rest of created intellects. Evagrius writes, for example:

> Either "anointing" indicates knowledge of the Unity [= God], or else it designates the contemplation of [created] beings. And if Christ is "anointed more than any of the others" (Ps. 45.7), obviously he is anointed with the knowledge of the Unity. For this reason, he alone is said to be "seated at the right hand" of the Father (Acts 7.56)—the right hand which indicates, here, according to the rule of those who know (*gnōstikoi*), the Monad and Unity.[64]

So Evagrius sets Christ, as receiver of the Word, squarely between the wholly immaterial, eternal God, the undivided Trinity, and the world of created intellects: "The body of Christ is of the same nature as our bodies, and his soul is of the nature of our souls; but the Word that is essentially in him is of one substance with the Father."[65] It is this preincarnate Christ, inhabited by the Word and drawing on the divine Wisdom, who is the appointed creator of bodies and the material world: "God," he writes, "when he created intellects, was not in anything; but when he created corporeal nature and the worlds which come forth from that nature, he was in his Christ."[66]

Here, of course, is another of the principal areas in Evagrius's theological system that would appear stridently unorthodox to many fifth- and sixth-century Christian theologians, especially to those who resisted the Chalcedonian definition. He clearly does not conceive of the divine Logos as the sole subject of the human experiences of Jesus, as Cyril of Alexandria and his followers would soon insist; in different terms, in fact, his understanding of Christ seems—or seemed to the critics of the Chalcedonian definition of Christ's identity—close to that of his contemporary, Theodore of Mopsuestia, and to Theodore's later, less cautious disciple, Nestorius of Constantinople. So in the sixth century, as the Emperor Justinian strove to find a way of reinterpreting the Christological definition of Chalcedon that would make the central, divine identity of Jesus clearer than the council itself had done, in order to build a wider imperial consensus on doctrine, it was not only the Antiochene theologians such as Theodore and Nestorius who received renewed imperial and ecclesiastical condemnation, but also the "Origenists"; these were generally understood to be speculators, intellectuals who (among other errors) "divided Christ" by distinguishing between the second hypostasis of the Trinity, the Word, and the rational creature, Christ, in whom he always dwelt.[67] The eighth anathema of the decree of the Second Council of Constantinople (553) against Origen and the Origenists seems to have the Christology of Evagrius's *Kephalaia gnostika* directly in its sights:

> If anyone does not say that the divine Logos, who is of the same substance as God the Father and the Holy Spirit, who has become flesh and become a human being, is in the proper sense Christ, one of the holy Trinity, but rather is so only metaphorically, because of what they call the *nous* who emptied himself, and that this *nous* is called Christ, in the proper sense, because he is united with the very Word of God; and that because of the latter [Christ] the former [the Word] is called "Christ," and the latter is called "God" because of the former, let that person be excommunicated.[68]

Evagrius's ultimately dualistic conception of the person of Christ the Savior, as the Logos inhabiting a created intellect, in fact, seems to follow logically from his strongly unitary conception of the God who is Trinity: to see the "persons" in God as barely distinguishable poles within a substance of ultimate simplicity almost necessarily implies a conception of Christ as a creature in which God's active Word dwells, but not as the Word himself, who has become a human being.[69]

The purpose of the Incarnation of Christ, who is the *nous* in whom the divine Word always dwells, is—in Evagrius's view—to make present here in the world the transforming knowledge of God, through the Word, that Christ has possessed since his own creation: a knowledge that gives life to all who share it, because it is in fact participation in the inner reality of God. Even as early as his *Letter on Faith*, Evagrius cautiously uses this idea of Christ as teacher of saving knowledge as the key to interpreting his mission. Explaining John 6.57 ("I live because of the Father"), for instance, he there writes:

> He can also mean by "life" that life which Christ lives, in that he has God the Word within himself. And we see that this is so from what follows. "And whoever eats me," he says, "will live through

> me." For we eat his flesh and drink of his blood, becoming communicants of the Word and Wisdom through his Incarnation and physical life. For he calls "flesh and blood" everything to do with the holy secret of his dwelling [among us], and disclosed that teaching (consisting of ascetical, physical, and theological elements) by which the soul is nourished and prepared for the contemplation of ultimate realities.[70]

Through the Eucharist, the believer makes personal, even material contact with Christ, who is identified with the indwelling Word of God; its goal, then, is not simply this contact, but, through Christ's teaching, access to the substantial knowledge which characterizes the life of God.

Christ, the created intellect, becomes fully human, then, in a corporeal sense, to bring about the transformation of all humanity, from its present state of mortal weakness to a share in God's everlasting life. Insisting—as Gregory of Nazianzus also does at length in *Orations* 29 and 30 (the third and fourth "Theological Orations")—that the scriptural texts attributing human limitation to Christ are witnesses not to his diminished ontological status as Son, but to the economy of salvation, by which he freely took on our limits to transform them,[71] Evagrius remarks that "our Lord [presumably in his incarnate state] is not the final object of desire," even though he is "the end and the ultimate blessedness, in consideration of the Word [dwelling within him]."[72] To know Christ in his human form, in other words, is only to pass through a temporary stage of the revelation that leads us to God as its final goal; "for Christ is the first-fruit and not the end, according to rudimentary teaching, which contemplates Christ not in himself, but, as it were, for us."[73] Here Evagrius reminds the reader perhaps most closely of his Latin contemporary Augustine's emphasis that Christ, in his human reality, is the way to what he himself is as God; as a human being, he is not the final object of our contemplation.[74] Evagrius's goal, in any case, in discussing the human reality of Christ is to present it as the core of a transformative process of revelation for humanity, not simply as presenting a paradox for faith: in the traditional exchange-language of Irenaeus and Athanasius, "he became human, that we might become divine."[75]

So Evagrius writes of Christ, in *Great Letter* 61, "He is the leaven of divinity who, in his goodness, has hidden himself in the unleavened lump of humanity. Not only did he not lose his own nature, taste and vitality; instead, he drew the whole lump to all that is his."[76] Here both the image of leaven in dough and the emphasis on the transformation of the whole mass of humanity in Christ parallels most closely the thought of Gregory of Nyssa, whose Christology, as I have argued elsewhere, might best be understood as "a Christology of transformation."[77] In his *Antirrhetikos* against the Apollinarians, for instance—probably written in the mid to late 380s, shortly after Evagrius had left Constantinople for Jerusalem and Egypt—Gregory of Nyssa writes:

> The Logos, who "is in the beginning with God," has "become flesh" in these last days out of love for humanity, by sharing in the humble reality of our nature; by this means, he mingled with what is human and received our entire nature within himself, so that the human might mingle with what is divine and be divinized with it, and that the whole mass (*phyrama*) of our nature might be made holy through that first-fruit.[78]

For both theologians, the very presence of Christ among us, sharing our humanity in body and soul while being uniquely identified with the Word of God, is enough to transform all of those who share the same nature and who follow him. It is salvation by divine nearness—the communication of divine life through common, universal human substance.

For Gregory, too, in fact, the process of human salvation is wholly tied up with the person of Christ and with his life, death, and resurrection. Just as the incarnate Son passed through human weakness and even through human death, and in being raised from the dead brought all his own humanity—the nature shared with us—along with him into the glorious, life-giving presence of God, so each of us, by being joined to Christ in faith and the life of the church, here begins a long transformation—in virtue, in consciousness of God, in ascetical purification—that will end in our almost total absorption, with him, into the boundless divine Mystery. Evagrius, in several passages of his *Great Letter*, speaks of the goal of our individual human histories—unity with God's infinite fullness—in terms of water flowing into the sea.[79] Similarly, Gregory of Nyssa writes, in his *Letter to Theophilus* [of Alexandria] *against the Apollinarians*—also from about 385—of the risen glory of Christ:

> Everything that was weak and perishable in our nature, mingled with the Godhead, has become that which the Godhead is. . . . The first-fruits of human nature, which he has taken up—absorbed (as one might figuratively say) by the omnipotent divinity like a drop of vinegar mingled in the boundless sea, exists *in* the Godhead, but not in its own proper characteristics. . . . But since all the traits we recognize in the mortal [Jesus] we see transformed by the characteristics of the Godhead, and since no difference of any kind can be perceived—for whatever one sees in the Son *is* Godhead: wisdom, power, holiness, freedom from passion—how could one divide what is one into double significance, since no difference divides him numerically?[80]

In our present lives, for both Gregory of Nyssa and Evagrius, this process of transformation begins in our acquisition of virtues, the godlike traits that form us ever more fully in God's image. Virtues, in Evagrius's view, are to the soul what nourishment and breathing are to the body: necessary for survival as what we are. God brings them about in us, in ways that are above our nature and our understanding, because it is proper to his nature to give us a share in his perfection.[81] For Gregory of Nyssa, too, it is the life of virtue here on earth, energized and guided by grace, that first allows us to share in God's glory,[82] and that begins a process that will end in the resurrection and transformation of the body. All of this comes from God, as part of the economy of salvation, because "the divine nature is the source of all virtue."[83]

Salvation of Human Nature

A third area of similarity between Evagrius and the three great Cappadocians is clearly their common emphasis on our present human need to be laboriously purified, in heart and mind, before we are capable of transformation by following the path of Christ, which leads to knowing union with God. The distinction Evagrius elaborates, in his ascetical works and in the whole shape of his literary project, between *praktikē, theōria physikē*, and *theologia* or *gnōstikē*,[84] was, in fact, a scheme reaching back at least to Origen, and is reflected also in Gregory of Nyssa's way of reading the biblical wisdom books ascribed to Solomon.[85] Gregory of Nazianzus begins his five "Theological Orations" with a classic reflection on the dangers of attempting to think and talk about God without "having been tested, and having made progress in contemplation, and—before these things—having been purified in soul and body, or at least being in the process of purification."[86] His second oration in this series, *Oration* 28, actually sketches out an elaborate strategy for seeking to form a conception of God—who is himself beyond all words and concepts—through a loving and attentive contemplation of the mysteries of the natural world (*theōria physikē*), which defy ordinary causal explanation. In *Oration* 28, however, Gregory emphasizes that even such knowledge of God through nature is impossible to achieve in any fullness during this present life,

> not merely to total slackers, or to people whose gaze is fixed downwards, but also to those who are highly exalted, and who love God—indeed for every created nature, for all of whom the darkness of this world and the thickness of this flesh is an obstacle to the full understanding of the truth.[87]

Evagrius, too, distinguishes—in the presumably unmodified Syriac version of the *Kephalaia gnostika* (S2)—between a contemplation of this world (*theōria physikē*), which remains limited by the world's materiality, and a kind that is "intelligible and spiritual," the latter of which is shared only by angels and saints:

> The contemplation of this world is twofold: the one obvious and thick (*'abithō; pacheia?*), the other intelligible and spiritual. The wicked and demons come near to [i.e., make use of?] the first kind of contemplation, the just and the angels of God to the second.

> And just as the angels are more knowing in spiritual contemplation than the just, so also the demons are more knowing in "thick" contemplation than the wicked; so one imagines that they share this with some of those who belong to them. And we also have learned from the Holy Book that the holy angels do this, as well.[88]

Salvation and human fulfillment, in fact, for Evagrius, is usually conceived in intellectual terms, as a God-given share in the "essential knowledge" that characterizes God's very being. So he writes, in the *Kephalaia gnostika*:

> The first of all branches of knowledge is knowledge of the Monad and of the [divine] Unity [the Henad], and spiritual knowledge is more ancient than all contemplation of nature. The former [spiritual knowledge], in fact came forth from the Creator at the beginning, and appeared along with the nature that accompanied it.[89]

At the end of its laborious journey of purification, energized and enlightened by its contemplation of the natural world and instructed by Christ, who bears the divine Word within him, the created mind recaptures God's own "essential knowledge" and becomes himself a temple of divine Wisdom. So Evagrius writes, later in the same work:

> The intelligible temple is the pure *nous*, which now has in itself "the manifold wisdom of God" (Eph. 3.10). The temple of God is the one who gazes on the holy Unity, and the altar of God is the contemplation of the holy Trinity.[90]

For Evagrius, contemplating the ineffable Unity, which God is, and the Trinity, in which that divine Unity is eternally articulated, seem to be two ways of realizing the same unitive gaze. As he writes in a short work *On the Cherubim*, "The contemplation of the Trinity is contemplation of the Unity in the Trinity and of the Trinity in the Unity."[91]

In his *Letter on Faith*, Evagrius urges his reader to "knock at the door of knowledge, that perhaps we may rouse the Master of the house, who gives spiritual bread to those who request it."[92] Even though Christ himself claims not to know the day and the hour of the coming judgment, his ignorance was actually a "dispensation for your weakness," so that humans would not despair about not knowing the time of the end.[93] But this is precisely the knowledge promised the disciples of Christ in their final state:

> The holy disciples of our Savior, once they had come to contemplation (as far as humans may) and had been purified by the Word, yearn for the goal and desire to know ultimate blessedness. This is the blessedness that our Lord asserted that neither his angels, nor he himself knew. For in saying "day," he meant the complete and precise comprehension of God's purposes, and in saying "hour," the contemplation of the One and Only. . . . "Only the Father knows," he says—since the Father himself is the end and ultimate blessedness. For when we know God no longer in mirrors (see 1 Cor. 13.12) or through any of the other intermediaries, but approach him as the One and Only, then we shall also see the final end. For they say that Christ's kingdom is the whole of material knowledge: but the kingdom of our God and Father is contemplation that is immaterial and, if one may say so, contemplation of unconcealed divinity itself.[94]

To know God as God is—to know the Word as Word and not simply as he dwells in the created intellect Christ, let alone in Christ's incarnate state—will be an emancipation of the human faculty of knowing: a "resurrection" of the created mind, parallel to the resurrection of the body, in which "it will be able to approach the unconcealed divinity itself."[95]

For all its apparent difference from the Cappadocian way of speaking about salvation, this kind of direct contemplation of God is also something Gregory of Nazianzus hints at as part of our eschatological future. So he asks, in a curiously Evagrian passage in *Oration* 29:

> What, then, is the substance of God? To ask this is a proof of your ignorance, you who are such a busybody in probing even how [the

> Son] is begotten. For us it would be a great thing, if ever—even in the future—we should come to know this, when the darkness and thickness (*pachutēs*) of our present state is taken away, as the promise of him "who cannot deceive" holds out to us. Let this, then, be the knowledge and the hope of those who are undergoing purification for that purpose.[96]

For now, it seems, all we can really know about God, beyond what is revealed to us in Christ, is what we cannot know.

Some Differences

To point out some of these similarities between Evagrius's conceptions of God and Christ and human salvation, and those of the great Cappadocian Fathers—especially Gregory of Nazianzus—who were his colleagues and family friends, is not to say that he was simply an intellectual or spiritual clone, a faithful member of their putative "school." Let us, then, briefly sum up a few of the ways in which Evagrius's thought and writings obviously differ from theirs.

(1) Surely the form, the scope, and the emphasis of Evagrius's writings are strikingly different from what we find in any of the authentic works of Basil or the two Gregories. As we have said, Evagrius writes largely, though not solely, either in aphorisms or in commentaries or brief, learned scholia on scripture—not in polemical treatises, pastoral sermons, or artistic rhetorical compositions. He writes for his fellow monks and contemplatives or for a more scholarly world of theological readers, not for the church at large. And he writes in a style that is, by comparison to that of the three Cappadocians, modest to the point of plainness, philosophically understated, and often (like that of Clement of Alexandria two centuries before) appearing to be deliberately enigmatic. He writes sentences to challenge the reader and to be reflected on at length, not orations to move the heart.

(2) In the conception of the triune being of God and of the person of Christ the Savior, Evagrius, as we have tried to show, follows in much the same direction as the great Cappadocians: he is intentionally Nicene in his understanding of the Son's being, carefully Trinitarian in

his conception of God's ineffable reality. But he is willing to take more intellectual risks than any of the Cappadocians had been, and does so in a clearly "gnostic" or speculative direction. So his Trinitarian "modalism" and his "divided" conception of Christ, as the intellectual creature with whom the divine Word has uniquely identified himself, the agent of illumination and salvation, appear at least to verge, in the end, on the unorthodox, while theirs do not. Basil and the two Gregories emphasized the mysterious character of God's threeness, which would prevent us from saying they are three "persons" in the same way a human family may be, let alone worshipping "three gods"; the relation of Word to flesh in Jesus may lead to paradox and to the transformation of his humanity, but it is always more than a matter of the indwelling of one in the other. In his quest to see in Christ the pioneer of human initiation into the life of God as "essential knowledge," Evagrius at least anticipated some of the positions that would, in the course of the fifth century, be rejected as "Nestorian" by the mainstream church, even while the Cappadocians—in the subtle differences of their thought from his—came more and more to represent the classical voices of the orthodox tradition.

(3) Far more than any of the three Cappadocians, Evagrius stresses the epistemic or contemplative character of human salvation—much as Origen had done before him.[97] The "Kingdom of God the Father," as we have already seen, is for Evagrius the "contemplation of the unconcealed divinity itself"[98]—not a condition or a place, even in a metaphorical sense, but a relationship of total absorption in God's own being. The reason, as he emphasizes in many of his works, is that God *is* himself "essential knowledge": God the Father, the original source of all things, even of the Son and the Spirit who constitute with him the inner structure of the divine Mystery, is himself the root and the ultimate object of the contemplative knowledge that brings all creation to fulfillment. "The Father is the generator of knowledge of what is," we read in the *Kephalaia gnostika*.[99] "The Father is the one who has a rational nature (*kyōnō' mlilō'*), which is united to knowledge of the Trinity. The Father is the one who has a rational nature, which is united to the contemplation of beings."[100] And that "rational nature," which the Father "has," seems to be the Logos who comes forth from the

Father, and dwells within the *nous* Christ as in a Temple. So in the aphorism just preceding these texts, Evagrius offers a decidedly Christological reflection:

> If "all the nations come and prostrate themselves before the Lord," (Ps 85.9), it is evident that even the nations which seek war will come, as well. And if this is so, all rational nature will prostrate itself before the name of the Lord, who reveals the Father who is in him. This, in fact, is "the name which is above every name" (Phil 2.11).[101]

The "rational nature" who reveals the Father is also, at the end of sacred history, the glorified Lord.

(4) For Evagrius, too, the created world is related to God not simply as a curtain or veil, which conceals while revealing, but as a kind of embodiment in which God the Father expresses himself through creation and the saving works of Christ. Gregory of Nazianzus, too, commenting on Moses's vision of "the back parts of God" on the top of Mount Sinai, interprets them as signifying God's presence in creation: "his greatness in creatures and in the things produced and governed by him . . . ; all the things that in his wake are tokens of him, like the shadows of the sun in water, and the images that reveal the sun to ailing eyes, since they cannot gaze on it directly."[102] But Evagrius, in the *Great Letter*, writes of the created world not simply as a shadow or image, but as a kind of *writing*, a book revealing God's love and power in a direct, explicit way, embodying in concrete terms what God really is. God "inhabits" our created mind through the power of the Word and the Spirit, he suggests, so that just as the body reveals the living and sensitive soul, which in turn reveals a governing *nous*, our own *nous* or mind reveals within itself the empowering Word and Spirit of God, who are sent forth and directed by the Father and so also, in turn, reveal *Him*. The human mind thus functions as a *body* to the originating, creative mind of God, in that "it is receptive of the knowledge of the Father," and it will find its ultimate form in union with him.[103]

(5) As a result, Evagrius seems inclined to speak of the final fulfillment of rational creatures not simply in terms of union with God in dependence and love, but as an annihilation of any ontological differ-

ence between them and God. This unification through knowing is really the goal of mystical contemplation, in any age. The two Gregories, surely, were in their own way mystical theologians. Both also held, like Origen, a theology of *apokatastasis*—of the final reconciliation of all rational creatures with God;[104] and both saw this as a fulfillment of the vision of final unity hinted at in 1 Corinthians 15.28, "God will be all in all." But Evagrius speaks in places of this restoration not simply as the return of rational creatures to an original state of contemplative unity with God and each other, but as an actual abolition of the substantive boundaries separating creature and creator, and even of those distinguishing the persons of the Trinity. "Now it will happen," he writes in the *Great Letter*, "that the names and numbers[105] of 'body,' 'soul,' and 'mind' will pass away, since they will be raised to the order of the mind . . . ; likewise, it will happen that the names and numbers of 'Father,' 'his Son,' and 'his Spirit,' and 'his rational creation'—that is, 'his body'—will pass away, as in 'God will be all in all.'"[106] A little further on, he writes: "When, like torrents to the sea, the minds return to him, he completely changes them to his own nature, color and taste: in his endless and inseparable unity, they will be one and no longer many, since they will be united and joined to him."[107] As so often in mystical theology, human speech and thought here reach their limits in speculating on the direction of human longing for God, and even on the experience of present, anticipatory union with him through the various stages of contemplation. It is here, perhaps, more than anywhere else, that Evagrian mysticism and Cappadocian orthodoxy run the risk of parting from each other.

Notes

1. Clark, *Origenist Controversy*, 61–84.

2. Guillaumont, *Les "Képhalaia gnostica."* See also Guillaumont, *Un philosophe au désert*, 53–64, 77–95; Corrigan, *Evagrius and Gregory*, 21–36. For treatments of the sixth-century "Origenist" controversies, see below, n. 67.

3. Sozomen, *CH* 6.30 (trans. Chester D. Hartranft, NPNF 2.2:368).

4. Gregory of Nazianzus, *Letter* 3.1–2 (Gallay, 1.2).

5. Sozomen, *CH* 6.30; Palladius, *Lausiac History* 38.1.

6. For the date, see McGuckin, *St. Gregory of Nazianzus*, 236–37.

7. Sozomen, *CH* 6.30; Palladius, *Lausiac History* 38.1.

8. Palladius, *Lausiac History* 38.2.

9. Ibid.

10. Sozomen, *CH* 6.30.

11. For a discussion of Gregory's will, see Daley, "Who Is the Real Bishop."

12. Sozomen, *CH* 6.30; Palladius, *Lausiac History* 38.4–7.

13. For details, see Guillaumont, *Un philosophe au désert*, 41–64.

14. *Apophthegmata Patrum*, Evagrius 7.

15. See, for example, the celebrated article of Otis, "Cappadocian Thought as a Coherent System."

16. See Guillaumont, *Un philosophe au désert*, 36, 142–43. Guillaumont observes (36): "Evagre assista donc, vraisemblablement, à l'élaboration, sinon à la redaction, des grands discours prononcés alors par Grégoire. On peut penser que celui-ci, aux heures de délassement et se souvenant de son ancienne profession de rhéteur, ait complété la formation intellectuelle de son disciple." Kalvesmaki, "*Epistula Fidei*," however, argues that Evagrius wrote the *Letter on Faith* to former associates at home, after he had left Constantinople for Palestine, perhaps after he had settled as a solitary in Egypt.

17. *KG*, title (*PO* 28.1:15).

18. Evagrius, *Letter on Faith* 5–6. This work has come down to us, in Greek, as part of the corpus of Basil of Caesaraea, where it usually appears as *Letter* 8. Dom Jean Gribomont, however, has convincingly argued that it is not the work of Basil but of Evagrius, to whom it is ascribed in the Syriac translations; see Gribomont, "Ps.-Basil, Epistula 8." Today, most scholars accept this attribution, and see the work as an early product of Evagrius's thought, reflecting his close association with Gregory of Nazianzus. I have used here the translation of Casiday, *Evagrius Ponticus*, 46–58, here 47.

19. *KG* 6.10 (*PO* 28.1:221). This text, which we have cited, is from the longer version of the Syriac translation of this work, which Guillaumont calls S2; it is found in a single sixth- or seventh-century manuscript in the British Library (Add. 17,167) and was first published by Guillaumont. A somewhat shorter version, already published by Frankenberg (*Euagrius Ponticus*) and republished on facing pages in the *PO* edition, which Guillaumont calls S1, represents, in Guillaumont's view, a later version of the Syriac translation, "cleaned up" in the interest of appearing less radically "Origenist" in its speculations (see Guillaumont, *Un philosophe au désert*, 102–3). Here, the corresponding text in S1 is: "The holy Trinity is not like a quartet or a quintet, etc.; these are

numbers, but the holy Trinity is a unique essence." As Evagrius uses the term "essential knowledge," it seems to refer to ultimate, transcendent reality, to which the created mind only has access through purified contemplation.

20. See *KG* 6.11–13 (*PO* 28.1:220–24).

21. Evagrius, *The Disciples of Evagrius* 22 (Géhin, 124–26). This collection of sayings or chapters is largely based on a thirteenth-century Greek manuscript in the Benaki Museum in Athens (TA 72 [Gr. 53]), which contains 198 of them; several other chapters appear in Greek in other ancient collections, and there are Syriac and Armenian sayings in the same genre. Maximus the Confessor seems to have drawn on the collection in putting together his *Centuries on Charity*. Although it is impossible to judge the actual authorship of each chapter, the teaching seems certainly to reflect Evagrius's ideas, and in many cases, at least, probably his words as well. In two manuscripts of John of Damascus's *Hiera* the collection is referred to as "from the teachings (*mathēmatōn*)" rather than "from the disciples (*mathētōn*)" of Evagrius. See Géhin's introduction, *Chapitres*, 21–41.

22. As divine substance, presumably, and involving all three hypostases.

23. *The Disciples of Evagrius* 29 (Géhin, 134–36).

24. On Gregory's "pastoral dogmatics," centered on right faith in the Trinity, see Beeley, *Gregory of Nazianzus*, esp. 263–70.

25. See above, n. 16.

26. Gregory of Nazianzus, *Oration* 31.9.

27. Ibid. 31.16.

28. Ibid. 29.2.

29. *To the Greeks, Based on Common Notions* (*GNO* 3.1) 19.3–5.

30. *On Not Thinking We Should Say "Three Gods," to Ablabius* (*GNO* 3.1) 38.7–18.

31. Ibid. 55.21–56.20.

32. See Daley, "Nature and the 'Mode of Union.'"

33. PG 46:1101–8.

34. Refoulé, "La date de la lettre à Évagre (P. G. 46, 1101–1108)."

35. PG 46:1105A.

36. Evagrius, *Letter on Faith* 7 (Casiday 48).

37. Ibid. 8 (Casiday 48).

38. See, for example, *Scholia on the Psalms* 43.21.13 (Guillaumont, *Un philosophe au désert*, 341). These scholia, largely identified among passages in the Greek *catenae* on the Psalms by Marie-Josèphe Rondeau, have not yet been published in a single edition. I have made use of translations of them cited by Guillaumont.

39. *KG* 3.80 (S2).

40. *KG* 6.28 (S2); *The Disciples of Evagrius* 30.

41. *KG* 2.22 (S2).

42. *KG* 6.34 (S2).

43. *KG* 2.47 (S2). The word we have translated "mixed reality," Syriac *muzōgō*, is translated "une qualité" by Guillaumont in his *PO* edition. This seems not to capture the sense; the Greek original may have been *mixis*, referring to the interplay of sense-knowledge and knowledge of intelligible forms in ordinary experience. In the (apparently) modified version (S1), this is put somewhat more clearly: "The holy Trinity is not included with the contemplation of sensible and intelligible things, because the former [= sensible things] are corruptible and the latter [= intelligible things] are capable of change. But the holy Trinity alone is essential knowledge." See also *KG* 4.77; 4.87; 5.62.

44. *KG* 5.63 (S2). Evagrius seems here to be following the Middle and Neoplatonic custom of speaking of "knowledge" as both what is in the knower's mind and what is knowable in the object known.

45. *Scholia on the Psalms* 24.6.5 (Guillaumont, *Un philosophe au désert*, 342).

46. *KG* 6.20. Evagrius seems to be referring here to the *epinoiai* or intelligible "concepts" by which Origen and his followers characterized the being and salvific role of the second Person of the Trinity: see Origen, *Commentary on John* 1.22–2.4; cf. Gregory of Nyssa, *On Perfection*.

47. Evagrius, *Great Letter* 24 (Casiday, 68–69).

48. See below, p. 40.

49. Evagrius, *Great Letter* 23 (Casiday, 68).

50. Gregory of Nazianzus, *Oration* 31.33. In referring here to the language of his "enlightenment" (*ellampsis*), Gregory is referring to the baptismal confession, which is of course one of the Christian tradition's primary sources for speaking of God as Trinity.

51. Evagrius, *Letter on Faith* 9 (Casiday, 48).

52. Evagrius, *Great Letter* 56 (Casiday 75).

53. Ibid. 58 (Casiday 75).

54. *KG* 1.77 (S1); here the presumably original Syriac version (S2) simply says, "the *nous* is Christ, who is united to knowledge of [divine] Unity." (*PO* 28.1:52–53).

55. Ibid. 2.2 (S2) (*PO* 28.1:61).

56. Ibid. 2.43; see also anathema 6 of the decree against Origenism associated with the Second Council of Constantinople (553): "If anyone should say . . . that one mind, from the whole so-called Henad of rational creatures, remained

immoveable in the love and contemplation of God, who became the Christ and king of all reasonable creatures, to bring into being all bodily nature, heaven and earth and all between them . . . and that it was not the all-holy and consubstantial Trinity who created the world—and therefore it has come into being—but the Mind, whom they say preexisted as creator of the world, and by giving being to the world itself revealed it is a created thing, let that person be anathema." (For text, see Origen, *Vier Bücher von den Prinzipien*, 826.)

57. *KG* 2.37 (*PO* 28.1:76–77).

58. *KG* 2.53 (*PO* 28.1:82–83).

59. *KG* 6.28–32 (S2) (*PO* 28.1:229–231). These chapters are more than usually enigmatic, however.

60. *KG* 6.33 (S2) (*PO* 28.1:231), alluding to 1 Cor. 15.28.

61. *Scholia on the Psalms* 109.3.3 (Guillaumont, *Un philosophe au désert*, 377).

62. *KG* 6.18 (S2) (*PO* 28.1:225). The "corrected" version, S1, adds a sentence that seemingly points to the pre- and post-incarnate Christ: "But, as soon as he came to be, [the Word] resided in him in a hidden way, and his manifestation was produced at the end of days."

63. *KG* 6.14 (S2) (*PO* 28.1:223).

64. *KG* 4.21 (S2) (*PO* 28.1:145).

65. *KG* 6.79 (S2) (*PO* 28.1:251). Evagrius clearly wants to affirm a Nicene understanding of the Word's relationship to the Father and the Spirit, and also to avoid Apollinarius's approach to seeing the Word as taking the place of a created intellect in Christ. He clearly understands Christ's "soul" (*psychē*; *naphshō*) here to be the vegetative and animal soul of living human beings in the world, but not the eternal created intellect or *nous*, which he names "Christ."

66. *KG* 4.58 (S2) (*PO* 28.1:161).

67. See Daley, "The Origenism of Leontius of Byzantium," and "What Did 'Origenism' Mean in the Sixth Century?" See also Diekamp, *Die Origenistischen Streitigkeiten*. Hombergen, *The Second Origenist Controversy*, disagrees with my suggestion that sixth-century "Origenists" were rejected by their critics more for their critical intellectual style, or for sympathizing with the strongly diphysite understanding of Christ that had also been promoted by the admirers of fifth-century Antiochene theologians, than for holding explicitly Origenist or Evagrian doctrines. Abbot Hombergen believes that sixth-century "Origenists" were probably more sympathetic to monophysite Christology (152), or at least to a Cyrillian reading of the Chalcedonian definition, than they would have been to Theodore of Mopsuestia and a strongly two-nature Christology. While many of Hombergen's points questioning my own

suggestions are well taken, he seems to overlook the fact that Leontius of Byzantium, who is accused in Cyril of Skythopolis's monastic lives of being the archetypal "Origenist," is, in his extant writings, almost exclusively concerned with promoting a straightforward defense of Chalcedon's two-nature, one-hypostasis understanding of Christ. To try to find clues in Leontius's writings to a presupposed Evagrian anthropology of spiritual progress is to read a great deal into the evidence and gives us little help towards understanding what "Origenists" held doctrinally in the sixth century. Abbot Hombergen's reconstruction of the theological struggles of the time, even more than my own, I think, is largely an argument from silence and from conjecture.

68. "Canones XV contra Origenem sive Origenistas," no. 8, in Origen, *Vier Bücher von den Prinzipien*, 828.

69. For an argument attempting to support this thesis at length, see Daley, "One Thing and Another."

70. Evagrius, *Letter on Faith* 15 (Casiday, 50). Evagrius alludes here to the stages of interior purification and enlightenment—moral and ascetical transformation (*praktikē*), contemplation of the inner meaning of created nature (*theōria physikē*), and contemplation of God in God's own self (*theologia*)—which, in many of his works, mark out the path for human ascent, through Christ, to union with God. This classic distinction is already proposed by Origen, in his *Commentary on the Song of Songs*, prologue 3.1; see also Gregory of Nyssa, *Homily 1 on Ecclesiastes* 1; 8–10.

71. See Evagrius, *Letter on Faith* 14–19, 28–29.

72. Evagrius, *Letter on Faith* 22, 23 (Casiday, 52).

73. Evagrius, *Letter on Faith* 24 (Casiday, 53).

74. See, for example, Augustine, *Enchiridion* 35; *De civitate Dei* 11.2.

75. See, for instance, Irenaeus, *Adversus haereses* 5, preface; Athanasius, *Orationes contra Arianos* 2.69–70.

76. Evagrius, *Great Letter* 61 (Casiday, 76).

77. See Daley, "Divine Transcendence," and "'Heavenly Man' and 'Eternal Christ.'"

78. Gregory of Nyssa, *Antirrhetikos against Apollinarius*, *GNO* 3.1:151.14–20; see also ibid. 222.25–223.10.

79. See Evagrius, *Great Letter* 27, 29, 66 (Casiday, 69, 70, 77).

80. Gregory of Nyssa, *To Theophilus*, *GNO* 3.1:126.17–127.10; cf. his *Contra Eunomium* 3.3.68–69 (*GNO* 2.132–33) for the same image of vinegar absorbed in the sea.

81. Evagrius, *Great Letter* 51–54 (Casiday, 74–75). The Syriac word used for "virtues" in this part of the *Great Letter*, *m'yathrōthō*, seems quite clearly

to be a translation of the Greek *aretai*: they are regularly practiced activities that sustain the soul in its being, just as food sustains the body (51); they are natural to the soul, and yet must be carefully and intentionally cultivated (52–53). See the edition of Vitestam, *Seconde partie*, 19–21.

82. Gregory of Nyssa, *Antirrhetikos*, *GNO* 3.1:164.21–24.

83. Gregory of Nyssa, *On the Soul and the Resurrection* (PG 46:104A; trans. in Roth, *Soul and the Resurrection*, 86).

84. See above, n. 68.

85. See above, n. 68; see also Evagrius, *Scholia on the Proverbs* 247, on Prov. 22.20 (Géhin, 342); *Scholia on Ecclesiastes* 1.1 (Géhin, 58); *Praktikos* 1.

86. Gregory of Nazianzus, *Oration* 27. The "contemplation" (*theōria*) he refers to here is presumably *theōria physikē*, such as he describes in the second half of *Oration* 28.

87. Gregory of Nazianzus, *Oration* 28.4.

88. *KG* 6.2 (S2) (*PO* 28.1.217).

89. *KG* 2.3 (S2) (*PO* 28.1.61).

90. *KG* 5.84 (S2) (*PO* 28.1.213).

91. Muyldermans, "*Sur les séraphins*," 375; quoted by Guillaumont, *Un philosophe au désert*, 341.

92. Evagrius, *Letter on Faith* 20 (Casiday, 51). Evagrius is alluding here to Jesus' parable in Luke 11.5–9.

93. Evagrius, *Letter on Faith* 19. Here Evagrius is referring to Matthew 24.36.

94. Evagrius, *Letter on Faith* 21–22 (Casiday, 52).

95. Evagrius, *Letter on Faith* 23 (Casiday, 52). Evagrius expresses this centrally eschatological character of the knowledge of God more simply at the beginning of the *Praktikos*, where he offers a subtle distinction between the Gospel phrases "Kingdom of heaven" and "Kingdom of God." He writes: "The Kingdom of heaven is freedom from passion in the soul, along with true knowledge of the things that are. The Kingdom of God is knowledge of the Holy Trinity, coextensive with the constitution of the mind and exceeding its incorruptibility" (*Praktikos* 2–3; see also *KG* 4.49 [S2]).

96. Gregory of Nazianzus, *Oration* 29.11 (Gallay, *Discours*, 200).

97. See, for example, Origen's comments on the eschatological, contemplative vision of God in *De principiis* 1.1.9; 1.3.8; 2.11.7.

98. Evagrius, *Letter on Faith* 22 (Casiday, 52).

99. *KG* 6.28 (both S1 and S2) (*PO* 28.1:229).

100. *KG* 6.29–30 (S2) (*PO* 28.1:229). This text identifies both *theologia* or *gnōsis* and *theōria physikē* as experiential knowledge of the Trinitarian God.

101. *KG* 6.27 (S2) (*PO* 28.1:229).

102. Gregory of Nazianzus, *Oration* 28.3 (second "Theological Oration").

103. Evagrius, *Great Letter* 16 (Casiday, 67).

104. See, for example, Gregory of Nazianzus, *Oration* 30.6; Gregory of Nyssa, *In Canticum Canticorum, Homily* 15 (*GNO* 6:468.15–469.9); *De hominis opificio* 21 (PG 44:201B–204A).

105. By "numbers," Evagrius seems to be referring to intelligible structures, which make possible naming, counting, and formal identification.

106. Evagrius, *Great Letter* 22 (Casiday, 68).

107. Evagrius, *Great Letter* 27 (Casiday, 69).

CHAPTER 2

Thoughts that Cut

Cutting, Imprinting, and Lingering in Evagrius of Pontus

KEVIN CORRIGAN

One strange feature of Evagrius's theory of eight *logismoi* has, to the best of my knowledge, received hardly any attention. This is the idea expressed in *Thoughts* 7 (1, 7, 10, 19, 20; cf. 31.2), and repeated verbatim in *Letter* 18 (Frankenberg 578.12–22), that thoughts can "cut" or "be cut." What does it mean for a thought to cut (or in Sinkewicz's translation "cut off")[1] and where does such a notion come from? Is cutting related to imprinting, that is, to leaving a (relatively) lasting mark? And is it also related to what appears to be the cognate notion of "lingering" or "persisting"? This is generally (but not exclusively) a negative notion in Evagrius, as in *Thoughts* 22.20–22, where Evagrius observes that "mental representations of sensible things, if they persist, destroy knowledge."[2] The ultimate reason for this is provided by *Prayer* 70. To be concerned with material things or material representations is to cut oneself off from God: "You cannot practice pure prayer if you are interwoven with material things[3] and agitated by continuous mental cares, for prayer is the putting aside of mental representations" (οὐ δυνήσῃ προσεύξασθαι καθαρῶς, πράγμασι συμπλεκόμενος ὑλικοῖς, καὶ φροντίσι συνεχέσι δονούμενος προσευχὴ γάρ ἐστιν ἀπόθεσις νοημάτων). This would seem to imply that all such lingering, imprinting, or cutting is negative, and yet, in Evagrius's view, *logismoi* are not entirely negative. Some are positive (angelic and human thoughts are positive to their core—see *Thoughts* 8) and good *logismoi* have their own "cutting" efficacy. *Thoughts* 7, the principal passage in question, runs as follows:

> Τῶν λογισμῶν οἱ μὲν τέμνουσιν, οἱ δὲ τέμνονται καὶ τέμνουσι μὲν οἱ πονηροὶ τοὺς ἀγαθούς, τέμνονται δὲ πάλιν ὑπὸ τῶν ἀγαθῶν οἱ πονηροί τὸ τοίνυν πνεῦμα τὸ ἅγιον τῷ πρώτως τεθέντι προσέχει λογισμῷ καὶ πρὸς ἐκεῖνον κρίνει ἡμᾶς ἢ ἀποδέχεται. Ὃ δὲ λέγω τοιοῦτόν ἐστιν ἔχω τινὰ φιλοξενίας λογισμὸν καὶ τοῦτον ἔχω διὰ τὸν κύριον, ἀλλ' οὗτος ἐπελθόντος τοῦ πειράζοντος τέμνεται καὶ δόξης χάριν φιλοξενεῖν ὑποβάλλοντος καὶ πάλιν ἔχω φιλοξενίας λογισμὸν πρὸς τὸ τοῖς ἀνθρώποις φανῆναι, ἀλλὰ καὶ οὗτος ὑποδραμόντος κρείττονος λογισμοῦ τέμνεται τοῦ πρὸς τὸν κύριον μᾶλλον ἡμῶν τὴν ἀρετὴν ἀπευθύνοντος καὶ μὴ δι' ἀνθρώπους ταῦτα πράττειν ἡμᾶς καταναγ κάζοντος. Ἂν οὖν διὰ τῶν ἔργων λοιπὸν τοῖς προτέροις ἐμμείνωμεν ὑπὸ τῶν δευτέρων πειραζόμενοι, μόνον τῶν πρότερον τεθέντων λογισμῶν ἕξομεν τὸν μισθόν, διότι ἄνθρωποι ὄντες καὶ παλαίοντες δαίμοσιν, ἀεὶ κατέχειν τὸν ὀρθὸν λογισμὸν ἄφθαρτον οὐκ ἰσχύομεν οὐδὲ πάλιν τὸν πονηρὸν λογισμὸν ἔχειν ἀπείραστον, ἀρετῶν σπέρματα κεκτημένοι. Πλὴν ἐάν τις χρονίσῃ τῶν τεμνόντων λογισμῶν, ἐν τῇ χώρᾳ τοῦ τεμνομένου καθίσταται, καὶ κατ' ἐκεῖνον λοιπὸν τὸν λογισμὸν ὁ ἄνθρωπος κινούμενος ἐνεργήσει.
>
> ———
>
> Among thoughts some cut; others are cut. Bad thoughts cut good ones and are in turn cut by good ones. The Holy Spirit therefore pays attention to the thought posited first and condemns or approves us in relation to that. What I mean is something like this: I have a thought of hospitality and this I have because of the Lord, but this thought is cut when the tempter comes along and suggests offering hospitality for the sake of my reputation. And again: I have a thought of hospitality for the sake of being seen by people, but this is cut when a better thought comes up that directs our virtue instead to the Lord and constrains us not to do this because of people.

> If then by our actions we stay henceforth in the former thoughts even while being tempted by the second thoughts, we will receive the reward only of the thoughts posited earlier, because since we are human beings and occupied in the struggle with demons, we do not always have the strength to hold to the right thought incorruptible, nor again are we able to hold the bad thought untested, since we have acquired the seeds of virtues. However, if one of the cutting thoughts lingers, it becomes established in the place of the thought that is cut and henceforth the individual will be moved to act in accordance with that thought.

What does Evagrius mean? In what sense do thoughts cut or get cut by other thoughts? Is this more or less a special instance in one chapter, or does it relate more broadly to other elements in Evagrius's thought?

To cut or be cut can mean many different things. One can cut a line, angle, surface;[4] prune vines, branches, corn, fruit trees, which means giving old or new shape to structures; this appears to bear some similarity to "cutting into shape" or cutting pathways and roads, dividing rivers or mountains (for many examples see LSJ 1775), like empowering or articulating a form or alternatively deforming a structure; one may cut away (as opposed to cauterizing in medical usage) a secondary or pathological growth in favor of a healthy primary cut; or again, as an ax cuts wood, form cuts matter, or vice versa; and productive form or *logos* in a human being cuts or articulates an organic structure (or is correspondingly deformed by misuse—though how this is possible is a good question), perhaps as a sculptor molds a statue and permits or fails to permit different form-possibilities to emerge. Everyone knows then what it is to cut or to be cut, but the abundance of meanings and contexts makes it hard to pin down a precise meaning or to *visualize* thoroughly what Evagrius means; and the transference to thought problematizes our experience further (though everyone knows what it is *like* for thought to "gnaw" at or prick us). How does thought really cut anything? How does a thought cut its "object" by its very activity? How do positive and negative thoughts occur concretely in the same being, and why should self-love cut hospitality? Evagrius gives us a simple example that everyone recognizes and yet its many meanings, despite the simple examples from the commandments, yield no single objective referent but rather provoke the hearer to meditate on several levels simultaneously—and to more questions.

Although there are no hints about these difficulties in either Géhin's edition or Sinkewicz's notes and translation,[5] Sinkewicz's translation of *temnein* as "to cut off" implicitly signals the difficulty of determining precisely what Evagrius means. Does one thought cut off another in the sense that it stops it from registering or imprinting?[6] If so, then if a thought cuts, cuts off, or splits (another possible translation) another thought, does it thereby imprint itself and, by its imprint, prevent the second thought from registering, or does it simply cut or split the thought in two? It would seem, from the above passage, that it cannot simply be a case of cutting off or cutting in two, since the "good" thought ("because of the Lord") in some sense articulates or manifests the healthy state of the soul, that is, insofar as good thoughts are "posited earlier," namely, insofar as they express God's creation in us in relation to "the seeds of virtues" (or the potential healthy flourishing of the soul) and to the degree that we stay or remain in them.

Lines 13–21 implicitly set up a contrast between "staying" or "remaining in the former, good thoughts" and "lingering" or "spending time" in the place of the thought that is cut. The former implies an abiding or indwelling (not unlike the Neoplatonic *monē*) and the latter implies, from the perspective of time, the possible establishment of both good and bad thoughts as motive forces for future action (as in *Praktikos* 6.7–8 of both good and bad thoughts perhaps: "Whether or not all these thoughts trouble the soul is not within our power; but it is for us to decide if they are to linger within us or not and whether or not they stir up the passions"; and *Thoughts* 22.1 and 22.21 of bad or impure thoughts).[7]

All of this seems to imply the following: First, cutting and being cut, while immediate on one level for ordinary experience, naturally bear many meanings, complicated further by the transference to thought. All of these meanings—including the apparent incommensurability between various forms of physical cutting and thought, I suggest—are operative (or at least some for each different listener), and none should be eliminated from this meditation. Second, while these primary thoughts are not imprints in the sense that secondary thoughts (cf. *Thoughts* 7.13–14) as "representations of sensible objects" are, they nonetheless articulate, manifest, or reinforce the healthy structure of the psyche, and their cutting or splitting capacity seems to be an essential property of their nature as created by God. Third, it is a powerful and striking observation that thought not only leaves traces or deposits but cuts or splits creation positively or negatively, for it provokes the addressee not only to a deeper sense of the significance of moral agency but also to a practical meditation upon the co-creativity ("with the Lord") or destructive character respectively of all human action. Thought has real effects for good or ill in us and in the world—it is not something purely "private," and we are effectively in the position of either agent-doctor or patient.

As Shakespeare's Macbeth asks so poignantly of the doctor in *Macbeth*, act 5, scene 3: "Canst thou not minister to a mind diseased; pluck from the memory of a rooted sorrow; raze out the written troubles of the brain; and with some sweet oblivious antidote cleanse the stuff'd bosom of that perilous stuff which weighs upon the heart?" To which the doctor replies: "therein the patient must minister to himself." Or again, and even more pertinent, Macbeth's famous soliloquy instantiates precisely the negative or privative power of this theme in Evagrius:

> Is this a dagger which I see before me
> . . . .
> Art thou not, fatal vision, sensible
> To feeling as to sight? Or art thou but
> a *dagger of the mind, a false creation*
> Proceeding from the heat-oppressed brain?[8]

And later (act 3, scene 2, line 36), Macbeth confesses to his wife: "O, full of scorpions is my mind, dear wife!"

The medical analogy is, I believe, not accidental,[9] for this is precisely what doctors do: they cut and cauterize (cf. Plato, *Gorgias* 479a–480c); and part of the cause of disease, according to the Hippocratic tradition and especially Galen, is an imbalance in the humors caused by the lingering or festering of a wound[10] or the persistence and lingering of food instead of its swift and effective passage through the system;[11] or again, sepsis gets worse as a result of bad juices lingering in the body.[12] Evagrius's use of *chronizein* and *temnein*, therefore, may well bear a subsidiary medical resonance, a natural practical application given Galen's mapping of the tripartite soul (an immortal substance, in Galen's view despite his agnosticism about the "substantiam animae")[13] onto the body's three principal systems: brain and nervous system; heart and arteries; and liver and veins. Something of this is summed up in *The Disciples of Evagrius*.[14] The doctor as doctor possesses the art of medicine, and even when he is not practicing he is related to that art: "for first he cuts (*temnei*) and second he heals (*therapeuei*); in the case of God it is similar."[15] Unfortunately the text is corrupt at this point after line 3, but the analogy is relatively clear: God's creative act is like the doctor cutting, while His care is like healing.

While Shakespeare's *Macbeth* emphasizes the *physical* effects of mind's disease or thought's anxieties, Evagrius's notion of cutting or splitting may seem at first sight purely metaphorical or restricted at least to the soul; but Evagrius's image has a psycho-physical immediacy, for, first, it concerns action as well as thought, and, second, the lingering or festering thought establishes itself in "the place" of the cut thought (τῇ χώρᾳ), which, as we know from *Prayer* 72–73, is not only the "mind" but also "a place in the brain" (τοῦ κατὰ τὸν ἐγκέφαλον τόπου)[16] that can be physically manipulated by demons. Evagrius's "cut" therefore is a vivid image for a psycho-physical reality (precisely as in Shakespeare) and it is presented in a down-to-earth fashion that brings home the often overlooked real possibilities of ordinary experience.

Are this chapter and its principal images Evagrius's own invention? I think for the most part they may be, but this should not prevent us from seeing other dimensions of thought behind them, and in the chapter itself, that add significant nuances to Evagrius's expression. Some of these dimensions are "Platonic," "Middle Platonic," "Neoplatonic," as we shall see, but these are just convenient, or inconvenient, terms from much later ages that can hide the obvious fact—in a preintellectual-property world—that ideas always transgress, flow into each other, and belong exclusively to no one. Plotinus is taken to be the "father of Neoplatonism" and the originator of the "three ones." Yet is he really so in any meaningful sense? He himself emphasizes his almost entire dependence upon the prior tradition and, like just about everyone of his time, he distrusts "innovation." Indeed the "three ones" theory antedates Plotinus, going back either to Moderatus (perhaps, but since this is from Porphyry's account in Simplicius, we have to be wary)[17] or to the Sethian Gnostic texts of the Nag Hammadi Library, some versions of which were read in the "school" of Plotinus. The famous being-life-mind triad with its sophisticated enneadic articulations, thought to be post-Plotinian, predates Plotinus in those Gnostic texts and can only be called exclusively "Platonic" with some difficulty.[18] So the term "Platonist" is fraught with problems. Jonathan Barnes has argued in his recent translation and commentary of Porphyry's *Isagogē* that "there is no reason why the hot air should be Platonic rather than Aristotelian, why it should be Plotinian rather than Alexandrian gas. . . . Porphyry was a Platonist. The *Introduction* is compatible with Platonism. But the *Introduction* is not, and was designed not to be, a Platonist document."[19]

With this caveat in mind, let me look at some of the other dimensions of thought that by their presence or absence add significant nuances to an account of Evagrius's thought. In a recent book,[20] I suggested that the use of the term *chora* shows that Evagrius is thinking perhaps of Plato, just as *energēsai* shows the Aristotelian side of his thinking. This looks entirely circumstantial—even unlikely, in the light of what I have said above, though *orthos logismos* also points to Plato—and to Plotinus (see, for example *Ennead* 6.8[39].2: εἰ δὲ λογισμῷ μετ' ὀρέξεως, ἆρ' εἰ καὶ πεπλανημένῳ τῷ λογισμῷ; Ἢ τῷ ὀρθῷ λογισμῷ καὶ τῇ ὀρθῇ ὀρέξει). But the very notion of cutting probably owes something to Iamblichus, I also argued, for whom while gods "cut through" matter and separate with divine power, there is a class of apparently non-evil demons that is strictly limited to a single function and, devoid of reason and judgment, such demons either divide or bring together in this strictly limited fashion, "just as the function of a knife is to cut" (*De mysteriis* 4.1; 5.12). Iamblichus puts it as follows: "Even as the function of a knife is to cut, and it does nothing else but this, so also, of those spirits that are distributed about the universe, according to a particular natural necessity, one divides while another brings together things in the realm of becoming."[21]

The image of the pruning knife, it has been suggested,[22] may come from *Republic* 1.353a ("a knife to cut a vine-twig"— αχαίρᾳ ἂν ἀμπέλου κλῆμα ἀποτέμοις), but Iamblichus probably derived it from several sources. First, perhaps, from the divided line and its "cuts"—*noesis*, *dianoia*, *pistis*, and *eikasia* (511d–e), the last of which, *eikasia*, or guesswork, is precisely characteristic of demons (in Evagrius). The lowest "cut" on the divided line lacks the clarity of its related "cuts" in the whole soul (cf. 509d9), and possesses a limiting and limited motive power. Second, and more important, Iamblichus probably derived it from the form of dialectic we find in Plato's *Phaedrus* (265d–266b), collection and division (cf. above—"one divides while another collects"), as is also shown by Iamblichus equating *temnein* with diairesis. *Synagein* also recalls the highest function of dialectic in the *Republic*, that is, to be *synoptikos* (537c7).[23]

While the broader context of Evagrius's thought about demons' guesswork and limited power (by contrast with the truly kardiognostic power of God) bears some resonance with Iamblichus, *Thoughts* 7 is very different from Iamblichus. Evagrius will distinguish angelic, human, and demonic thought in *Thoughts* 8, but here in chapter 7 he focuses concretely on human thought and its power to cut or be cut. This, I suggest, must ultimately be related to Plato's *Phaedrus* for two major reasons. First, it is the human function of dialectic, according to Socrates, "to see together and bring into one form items that are scattered in many places, in order that one can define each thing and make clear whatever it is that one wishes to instruct one's audience about on any occasion" (265d3–5: εἰς μίαν τε ἰδέαν συνορῶντα ἄγειν τὰ πολλαχῇ διεσπαρμένα, ἵνα ἕκαστον ὁριζόμενος δῆλον ποιῇ περὶ οὗ ἂν ἀεὶ διδάσκειν ἐθέλῃ); and then to be able "to cut it up again, form by form, according to its natural joints, and not try to break any part into pieces, like an inexpert butcher" (265e1–3: Τὸ πάλιν κατ' εἴδη δύνασθαι διατέμνειν κατ' ἄρθρα ᾗ πέφυκεν, καὶ μὴ ἐπιχειρεῖν καταγνύναι μέρος μηδέν, κακοῦ μαγείρου τρόπῳ χρώμενον). The contrast between the good, dialectical cutting and the bad butcher is not unrelated to Evagrius's good and bad *logismoi*. So too is the idea that dialectic follows and articulates the proper organic structure of things.

Second, a locus classicus for *chronizein* is surely *Phaedrus* 255b7 (and the analogy of the charioteer and horses likened to human psychological drives). The "beloved," Socrates says, in the process of falling in love with the lover, realizes that nobody else has "anything to offer by way of affection in comparison with the friend who is divinely possessed (ἄλλοι φίλοι τε καὶ οἰκεῖοι μοῖραν φιλίας οὐδεμίαν παρέχονται πρὸς τὸν ἔνθεον φίλον). And when he spends time doing this (ὅταν δὲ χρονίζῃ τοῦτο δρῶν) . . . then it is that the springs of that stream which Zeus called . . . desire (ἵμερον) flow in abundance upon the lover. . . . So he is in love, but with what, he does not know; and he neither knows what happened to him, nor can he even say what it is, but like a man who has caught an eye disease from someone he can give no account of it, and is unaware that he is seeing himself in his lover as if in a mirror" (255b5–d6). Evagrius, I suggest, has changed the erotic context into Christian hospitality (*philoxenia*) in *Thoughts* 7 and transformed the love of God implicit in Plato's account of the experience of the love of the other into the two greatest commandments. And though the stream of desire in Plato looks potentially pathological, it is, in fact, finely balanced in the sequel, just as in *Thoughts* 7:

> If the better elements of their thought [cf. Evagrius: "the former thoughts"] get the upper hand by drawing them to a well-ordered life and to philosophy, they pass their life here in blessedness . . . and when they die they become winged and light. . . . But if they turn to a coarser way of life [cf. Evagrius: "second thoughts"], devoted not to wisdom but to honor, then . . . the licentious horses in the two of them catch them off their guard . . . and once having done so, they continue with it, but sparingly, because what they are doing has not been approved by *their whole thought* (ἅτε οὐ πάσῃ δεδογμένα τῇ διανοίᾳ πράττοντες). (*Phaedrus* 256a8–c7)

A similar structure, however transformed by scripture, is to be found in Evagrius. First, the struggle in both is between real virtue or philosophy, on the one hand, and desire for honor, on the other. Second, our whole thought does not approve vice in Plato while the wicked thought cannot remain untested in Evagrius, because our whole thought does not approve it: we have acquired the seeds of virtues. There is, in my view, a reasonable parallel here—and I wonder if Evagrius's use of καθίσταται in his closing statement ("if one of the cutting thoughts lingers, it becomes established in the place of the thought") signals briefly Aristotle's notion of the establishing or coming to stand of universals in, for example, *Posterior Analytics* 2.19, for it is characteristic of Aristotle's view that the universal becomes established in the soul from perception, memory, and many memories (100a–b): "a fresh stand is made among these (rudimentary) universals, and the process does not stop until the indivisible, that is, the [true] universals are established" (Mure, 100b1–2: πάλιν ἐν τούτοις ἵσταται, ἕως ἂν τὰ ἀμερῆ στῇ καὶ τὰ καθόλου).

For Evagrius, by contrast, all universals are *not* indivisibles (as we shall see implicitly further below), for we have to be much more wary about what comes from perception and memory, since all these things are cuttable, that is, they can lead to fragmentation, and we risk by an uncritical approach giving a pathology or diseased frame of behavior the status of universality not only in our *actions* (*erga*) but in our *characteristic activity* (*energeia*). True universality, implicitly, for Evagrius is guaranteed only "if . . . by our actions we stay henceforth in the former thoughts," that is, in a steadfast, stable disposition, still susceptible of better calibration through testing, not an oscillating state between positive and negative.

We have then in the *Phaedrus* and *Posterior Analytics* some further context for situating Evagrius's use of terms, but scripture is still in *Thoughts* 7 the *entire* context despite these other parallels. It is as if Evagrius thinks of these different traditions holographically (everything is present in even the smallest bit) yet the scriptural senses pervade them all. In the case of *chronizein*, Evagrius's scholion 68 on Proverbs 5.20; 82 to 6.27 (negative usage); and 377 to 31.21 (positive) are small but significant examples of this. In the case of *temnein* and other related terms, that I think go to the heart of Evagrius's thought, this is more difficult to uncover, and I am compelled to tease this out by taking the long route through "Platonic" thought to scripture to sketch a story or "likely tale" of what I mean. I shall do this by focusing upon four contexts for understanding *temnein* and cognates: first, a logical model; second, a metaphysical-cosmological model of demiurgic creativity; third, a complex individual, but highly concrete model for understanding agency; and fourth, a theological-biblical model.

First, the logical usage, implicit in Platonic dichotomous dialectic, is the cutting of genera into species and so on into individuals (uncuttables), as in Porphyry's *Isagoge* where *temnesthai* is used in the sense of "divide" (e.g., at 5.3; 10.10; 14.19) and as a stylistic variant for *diairein*. *Temnesthai* is not found in the logical sense in Aristotle (who does use *atomos*), but this becomes popular in later common usage.[24] It comes from Plato,[25] of course, from the *Phaedrus* as above,[26] where it is given a metaphysical application and later in the same work a psychological and rhetorical application: "someone will not be able to make speeches as a whole in a scientific way until he becomes capable of defining the whole by itself . . . and knows how to cut it up again according to its forms until it can no longer be cut, and until he has reached an understanding of the nature of soul itself along the same lines, discovering the form which fits each nature, and so arranges and orders his speech" (*Phaedrus* 277b–c: ὁρισάμενός τε πάλιν κατ' εἴδη μέχρι τοῦ ἀτμήτου τέμνειν ἐπιστηθῇ, περί τε ψυχῆς φύσεως διιδὼν κατὰ ταὐτά, τὸ προσαρμόττον ἑκάστῃ φύσει εἶδος ἀνευρίσκων, οὕτω τιθῇκαὶ διακοσμῇ τὸν λόγον). Thought is what cuts here—that is, thought articulating a *logos* or speech that can address and persuade different souls in different ways. A question immediately presents itself in relation to Evagrius's thought (and Plato's later thought): What are the uncuttables? Species? Individuals? But if it is a property of thought to cut, and cutting can go on *eis apeira* as in the *Parmenides*,[27] what is truly uncuttable? I shall return to this below.

Second, in the *Timaeus*, *temnein* enters the cosmological sphere in two principal ways: the geometrical cutting by the Demiurge of what is in between the indivisible and the divisible in the making of the World Soul (36a2: μοίρας ἔτι ἐκεῖθεν ἀποτέμνων καὶ τιθεὶς εἰς τὸ μεταξὺ τούτων; 36b6: ἐξ οὗ ταῦτα κατέτεμνεν) and the cutting quality of fire (57a2–3: so that it cuts whatever it meets), perhaps akin to the thunderbolt of Zeus in Iamblichus's *De mysteriis*. The world's soul is mingled from the indivisible and divisible and then divided and cut proportionately (35a–36d: ἤρχετο δὲ διαιρεῖν ὧδε). And this demiurgic creativity is reflected on every level all the way down: (1) in the active and passive elemental cutting, namely, in earth being dissolved by fire's sharpness or being cut by its angles, a dividing power that cuts bodies into small pieces (*Timaeus* 56d–57a; 61e–62a: *kermatizein*), and in active pungent particles cutting everything that comes in their way (65e–66c: τὸ προστυχὸν ἀεὶ τέμνει); (2) in the secondary gods "cutting air channels leading to the lung" for the proper psychosomatic function of the heart in its context (70b–d: διὸ δὴ τῆς ἀρτηρίας ὀχετοὺς ἐπὶ τὸν πλεύμονα ἔτεμον, καὶ περὶ τὴν καρδίαν αὐτὸν περιέστησαν οἷον μάλαγμα, ἵν' ὁ θυμὸς ἡνίκα ἐν αὐτῇ ἀκμάζοι, πηδῶσα εἰς ὑπεῖκον καὶ ἀναψυχομένη, πονοῦσα ἧττον, μᾶλλον τῷ λόγῳ μετὰ θυμοῦ δύναιτο ὑπηρετεῖν); (3) in the causes of respiration, and of nourishment that comes from the blood whose color is contributed to by the "cutting action of fire" (80c–81a: ἡ δ' ἐρυθρὰ πλείστη περὶ αὐτὰ χρόα διαθεῖ, τῆς τοῦ πυρὸς τομῆς τε καὶ ἐξομόρξεως ἐν ὑγρῷ δεδημιουργημένη φύσις); (4) in the connection between soul and body from birth to old age and the possibility of the release of soul at death in the cutting quality or dullness over time of the triangles from which meat and drink are composed (81b–e); and (5) in the assimilation, finally, of the tripartite soul and its noblest part to "the thoughts and revolutions of the all" (90a–d), as cut originally by the Demiurge (35a–36d). In other words, according to the language and thought of the *Timaeus*, the creative power of the Demiurge is a form of *diairesis* and *tmēsis* that seems to be reflected throughout the whole of nature, from the world's body and soul down into the cutting power of the elements and up into the complex physiology of the body-soul relation and the tripartite soul that most directly links or harmonizes the individual living creature, through the power of thought, with the revolutions of the all. In this context, then, demiurgic thought is *diairetic*, that is, a creative articulation of what comes to be, and this is reflected physiologically and psychosomatically in the action or passion of every particle. I suggest then that this is one major context for understanding the cutting power of thought, first, in its demiurgic function and, then, in its psychosomatic, physiological, and stoicheiological applications.

This usage, in fact, sets the scene for thoughts as cuts that we find explicitly for the first time—I think—in the *Chaldean Oracles*[28] and for cutting as an essentially demiurgic activity. Fragment 53 (from Proclus, *In Timaeum* 2.61.22–25) reads as follows: "Thus, even the Oracles call the divisible intellections of the Demiurge 'thoughts'" (οὕτω δὴ καὶ τὰ λόγια τὰς μεριστὰς τοῦ δημιουργοῦ νοήσεις διανοίας προσείρηκε); "After the Paternal Thoughts I, the soul, dwell, animating the All with heat" (μετὰ δὴ πατρικὰς διανοίας Ψυχὴ ἐγὼ ναίω θέρμη ψυχοῦσα τὰ πάντα); and fragment 22 (*In Tim.* 3.243.16–21): "for the Intellect of the Father said for all things to be cut into three (εἰς τρία γὰρ νοῦς εἶπε πατρὸς τέμνεσθαι ἅπαντα), governing all things by the Intellect <of the very first> eternal <Father>. He nodded his assent to this and immediately all things were cut."[29] Here we are, of course, in an entirely different world from that of Evagrius—no intelligible world or intervening "hypostases" for a start, but the deeper structure of thought already anticipates Plotinus, Porphyry, and Iamblichus to the degree that the Highest God (or "Once Transcendent") exists as an indivisible unity (without form or imprint, frags. 144 and 145 *amorphōtos*), whereas the Second God begins the process of "cuttings," "lightning bolts" (frags. 35 and 37) that leads to creation (intelligible) and generation (sensible).[30] So too in Plotinus, in the approach to mystical union there is a moment of non-imprinting (*Ennead* 5.3[49].11.12: ἀτύπωτος ὄψις) or non-shaping (*Ennead* 6.7[38].33).[31] At least analogous in Evagrius is the formlessness of God, "formless even beyond the incorporeal" (*The Disciples of Evagrius* 1), formless in the purest prayer (ibid., 39) and non-imprinting (*Thoughts* 41: Τὸ τοίνυν νόημα τοῦ θεοῦ οὐκ ἐν τοῖς νοήμασιν εὑρεθήσεται τοῖς τυποῦσι τὸν νοῦν, ἀλλ' ἐν νοήμασι τοῖς μὴ τυποῦσι διόπερ τὸν προσευχόμενον δεῖ παντάπασι χωρίζεσθαι τῶν νοημάτων τῶν τυπούντων τὸν νοῦν). The ultimate cut or "separation" for Evagrius is to cut away everything that imprints the mind (a little like Plotinus, *Ennead* 5.3[49].17: Ἄφελε πάντα).

Cutting or division, therefore, seems to be a function—in both Platonism and Evagrius—of divine creative power as manifested, and actively manifesting itself, in both incorporeal and corporeal reality, on the one hand, and yet, on the other, to leave room for a non-imprinting power in all experience (from scripture to consciousness) that goes beyond both conceptual imprints and other representations derived from sense-experience.

Third, how does this relate concretely to individual agency? An application of the cutting–being cut theme, crucial for understanding the hidden background to *Thoughts* 7, is to be found in the Aristotelian context of what we mean by a single activity that can be looked at from two different points of view, namely, as an activity or *energeia* like cutting and as an affection or movement like being cut. This application locates both sides of an activity in the same being. How then are we to distinguish the two? In his criticism of Aristotle's categories and of what I take to be minimalist interpretations of Aristotle's single activity theory[32] (*Ennead* 6.1[42].19—part of his massive treatise on the genera of being, 6.1–3[42–44]), Plotinus uses what is clearly a kind of category-tradition example to think through his own theory. Are certain activities "incomplete" in the Aristotelian sense that they are movements, Plotinus asks, or are some self-originated and others produced in the moving things by the agency of others, and the self-originated movements are activities, whether they are directed to other things or independent, but those which come from others are passivities. And he thinks through these questions in the following way:

> For cutting, the cutting which comes from the cutter and the cutting which takes place in what is being cut, is one, but cutting and being cut are different. But perhaps even the cutting originating from the cutter and the cutting going on in the cut are not one, but what cutting is is the process in which, from an active actuality and movement of this particular kind, another successive movement comes to be in what is being cut. Or perhaps the difference does not lie in the actual being cut, but in something else, the subsequent movement, feeling pain for instance. (*Ennead* 6.1[42]19.1–20)

Plotinus is effectively working through the activity or movement of cutting (and subsequently in the chapter—making and writing) in relation to a complex view of agency. Are cutting and being cut a single activity of a single unitary being or two kinds of activity of a more complex, unitary being, namely, cutting as an active energy and being cut as something occurring "in the thing cut" (cf. *Thoughts* 7: ἐν τῇ χώρᾳ τοῦ τεμνομένου), which is a movement or passive affection in the thing or compound being but not strictly speaking in the active agent? If they are one from one perspective, but two from another, then implicitly the active energy is different from the compound thing as compound or from the subject-substrate that undergoes the affection—but both are agents in different ways, though the active agent is primary. And implicitly again, this explains how there can be a single activity and yet different aspects of agency in the complete living being that allows for the double action of thought in the same being having such different outcomes.

If we reposition this now from the perspective of the Christian appropriation, through Origen and Didymus the Blind, as outlined by David Brakke,[33] of related Stoic ideas,[34] particularly on the need for discernment (*diakrisis* [judging or cutting through]—in the assent or rejection of proto-passions or first movements) and in the use of oppositional techniques such as replacing vicious temptations with less vicious ones (as in *Praktikos* 58: "driving out a nail with a nail")[35] or using scriptural passages for defense, consolation, and so forth, as in Athanasius's *Letter to Marcellinus* or Evagrius's *Antirrhetikos*—if we place Plotinus in this broader context, then we have a subtle model of agency from which to see Evagrius's practical concerns in *Thoughts* 7 to "stay henceforth in the former thoughts (διὰ τῶν ἔργων . . . τοῖς προτέροις ἐμμείνωμεν)," namely, thoughts as activities and susceptible to degrees of impassibility, "even while being tempted by the second thoughts," namely, thoughts as movements (but still susceptible of being purer energies), in the realization that "since we are human beings and occupied in the struggle with demons, we do not always have the strength to hold to the right thought (ὀρθὸν λογισμὸν) incorruptible, nor again are we able to hold the bad thought untested, since we have acquired the seeds of virtues." To be in the position of failing and of having to test our experience and inclinations is not necessarily failure; it can be the awakening of a new vista in experience. A biblical use of *logos*, for instance, seems to be the purpose of Evagrius's *Antirrhetikos*, which provides 492 brief biblical texts (normally of one or two verses) to be used as remedies against different manifestations of the eight principal *logismoi* (from gluttony to pride). "In such and such case, these words are to be used." Evagrius emphasizes the contradiction of demons and their operations in his definitions of *antirrhēsis* in the prologue to the *Antirrhetikos* and in *Letter* 11, but the majority of these verses/*logoi* have a wide range of spiritual application, as Luke Dysinger notes,[36] serving to evoke repentance or compunction, to exhort, to console, and to provide prayers for the afflicted soul. Compunction or *katanyxis* itself involves a *piercing, stinging, or puncturing of the heart* through which one comes to repent and understand.[37] Furthermore, even affliction is itself a conduit to virtue as *Exhortations* 2.11 indicates: "Just as water makes a plant grow, so does affliction make righteousness grow in the soul of the just."[38] So the contradictory *logos* turns pain into pleasure, affliction into virtue, muteness into speech. Even temptation and physical affliction (*thlipsis*) then have a "unique power"[39] to galvanize the soul into a type of prayer characterized by frankness or "freedom of speech" (*parrhēsia*; cf. *Letter* 1.2)[40] despite its own muteness.[41]

So finally, we come to the theological-biblical model. The biblical context, I suggest, provides the crucial transforming perspective upon all the above models.[42] If we ask the Platonic tradition, "what is uncuttable?" we might get different answers but ultimately it is really (and perhaps only) the "One." However, if we ask Evagrius, we get a scriptural answer that has perhaps escaped attention. The first application of cutting, not to *dianoia*, but to *logismos* before Evagrius (as far as I know) is in Philo's *Who Is the Heir of Divine Things* in a commentary on Genesis 15.2–18, and particularly verse 10: "And he [Abram] took for him [God] all these [heifer, goat, ram, turtledove, and pigeon] and divided them in the middle and placed them facing each other, *but the birds he did not divide*" (emphasis added). For Philo the divine Word and our *logismos* are the birds, turtledove, and pigeon, and they are "uncuttables" (ἄτμητοι δὲ οὖσαι μυρία ἄλλα τέμνουσιν. ὅ τε γὰρ θεῖος λόγος τὰ ἐν τῇ φύσει διεῖλε καὶ διένειμε πάντα, ὅ τε ἡμέτερος νοῦς, ἅττ' ἂν παραλάβῃ νοητῶς πράγματά τε καὶ σώματα) that together in synergy cut or articulate the whole universe. The universe, though divided in an infinite manner, into an infinite number of parts (εἰς ἀπειράκις ἄπειρα), is divided, distributed, and supported by the power of these "uncuttables."[43]

This is almost exactly the thought of Evagrius but in a different key. In *The Disciples of Evagrius* 93, Evagrius's disciples report him as holding the view that "there are three powers of the soul (*thymikon*, *epithymetikon*, *logistikon*) which constitute the rational human being (*to logikon*). These are *atmēta*. But when the common notions begin to come to be in us they are cut [or they cut] (*temnontai*) either to the worse or to the better and so there come to be many conditions (*katastaseis*)." In other words, the tripartite soul is an uncuttable unity as created, but a unity that can cut or get cut in our developmental experience for better or worse. Where is Philo's "Divine logos"? It is absent here but present elsewhere in its scriptural form when Evagrius explicitly links the Old and New Testaments in his interpretation of Matthew 10.34: "I have come to bring but a sword": "Just as the knife circumcizes (*peritemnein*) the sensible Jew, so *praktikē* circumcizes the intelligible Jew; this is what Christ has symbolically named 'the sword which he has brought into the world.'"[44]

What is different in Evagrius from Philo, and especially in *Thoughts* 7, is the concrete presence in and to our thoughts of "the Lord," closer to us, in soul and body, even than Philo's *theios logos*. There is a new intimacy and immediacy in *Thoughts* 7 not caught by any meditation before Evagrius. In our first thoughts we live in Christ and Christ in us. So the notion of cutting, in fact, goes to the heart of Evagrius's scriptural icons, and yet it retains the force of all its varied history and speaks to the reader in *Thoughts* 7 in this deceptively simple, direct, yet simultaneously compressed and saturated way. Thoughts do transfix and cut us for better or worse, but we notice this only occasionally in our most vivid experiences. Evagrius cuts away the background chatter and habitual unconsciousness and shows the simple force of ordinary experience with scriptural iconic clarity—against a much broader thought background hidden in the rest of his work.

In this light, we can also see that Evagrius's powerful use of the supposedly Platonic notion of *chorismos* is deeply related to cutting and dividing. To separate oneself from all mental representations (*Thoughts* 41) or from arrogance (*Disciples* 58) is to live in the one who said, "I am the Life" (Jn. 11.25). At the same time, it is the deepest way of being present to the world: "A monk is one separated from all and united with all" (*Prayer* 124). Similarly, to divide can be a means of *articulating* a unified, more holistic strength: "When we come up against the demon of acedia, then with tears let us divide the soul and have one part offer consolation and the other receive consolation" (*Praktikos* 27, trans. Sinkewicz). Finally, the entire pattern of natural and supernatural life articulates itself as a cutting of various pathways of thought, practice, and meditation. As Evagrius puts it in scholion 247 to Proverbs 22.20: "He who has enlarged his heart through purity will think the words of God, words that are practical, physical, and theological, for the whole doctrine of Scripture cuts three ways into ethics, physics, and theology; and Proverbs follows the first, Ecclesiastes the second, the Song of Songs the third."[45]

In conclusion, I want to make three points. First, the idea that thoughts cut and are cut, which seems at first sight so restricted to the unique expression of *Thoughts* 7, actually reaches into the whole of Evagrius's thought and expresses the latent force of many hidden voices. To cut can be to bisect a line, to cut an angle, surface, or solid (of thought or sensation—along the line of psychosomatic existence); to foster or eradicate a power or privation; to empower a form; to articulate or deform a structure; to cut away a secondary or pathological growth in favor of a healthy primary cut—like God's creation and healing analogous to the medical articulation, maintenance, and restitution of health, and to be contrasted with thought's infective, invasive, and disabling capacities. Thought's cutting power has real psychophysical force since it leaves its mark or deposit "in the ground of what is cut," and there is therefore a direct emphasis upon the existential character of choice and the ambivalent powers of moral responsibility. I have sketched a nuanced late ancient context for situating Evagrius's terms: through Iamblichus I suggested that positive creative cutting is a unitary quasi-demiurgic power of many *logoi*, whereas demonic suggestion operative in human agency is limited to a single reductive function. I linked this to several important perspectives: (1) to the divided line in the *Republic*; (2) to healthy and unhealthy division, like good dialectical cutting versus bad butchery in the *Phaedrus*; (3) to the problematic establishment (for Evagrius) of quasi-universals in thought and practice; (4) to the related logical usage of cutting (genus into species and Platonic dialectic as a cutting through forms); (5) to the cutting of demiurgic thought in the *Timaeus* reflected on every level down into the elements and back up into the tripartite soul's resonance with the cosmic revolutions; (6) to the kind of nuanced agency one finds in the Aristotelian "single activity" of thought, according to Plotinus's critical analysis of cutting and being cut; and (7) in Philo's application of cutting to *logismos* and his interesting thought about "uncuttability," strong resonances of which are to be found in theories attributed to Evagrius. To complicate any simplistic hierarchy of such cuttings, I also briefly sketched important applications: (a) in the cutting/piercing quality of *katanyxis*, (b) in the positive kathartic quality even of affliction and trauma (and abandonment?),[46] (c) in the cutting, separating power from world and all representations, (d) in the symbolic/real power of circumcision, and (e) in the cutting articulation of Evagrius's three ways, *praktikē*, *gnostikē*, *theologia*, by "the whole doctrine of Scripture."

In sum, we have a subtle view of agency in Evagrius with no simplistic distinction between positive and negative thoughts, but with the possibility of positive and negative agency all the way down into sin, repentance, compunction, even affliction and trauma; at the same time, there is a broader distinction among primary causal agency, secondary active agency in the midst of sin and trial in experience, passive-active agency in potentially habitual sinful action, and the negative cutting, or being cut, that complicates and threatens to excise integral agency.

Second, in the context of these many resonating strings, namely, this network of terms—logical, surgical, psychological, metaphysical, geometrical-cosmological, and theological—I want to emphasize that Evagrius has created in *Thoughts* 7 a meditation that is primarily *scriptural*, that is, a compressed iconic word about Christian life rooted in the two greatest commandments, love of God and love of neighbor (*philoxenia*), concretely mediated by the "Lord" but realistically cast into the human condition both of abiding in God and of the ambiguous but prudent knowledge that one cannot remain untested. *Thoughts* 7 is therefore simple, and accessible to anyone, and yet complex.

Third, all of these strings to different degrees make Evagrius's thought possible throughout his work, but terms like "Platonism," "Middle Platonist," and "Neoplatonism" are later abstractions that do not fit Evagrius's capacity (or that of Basil and Gregory Nazianzus) to see what must be discarded in "learning from elsewhere" and what is genuinely useful and requires thought. When we find "Platonic" elements in Evagrius, they are subordinate, however pervasive, parts of complex traditions that have already transformed and continue to transform whatever insights may have given rise to them "originally." Even when these elements are prominent (e.g., the tripartite soul), they do not belong exclusively or even predominantly to "Plato" and are handed on to Evagrius from his "teachers" in the much broader community of creation. As in Plato's *Symposium*[47] and Clement's *Stromata*,[48] so too in Evagrius's *Letter to Melania*,[49] the great ocean into which all streams pour is neither of our individual preference nor at the disposal of the creative power of any individual to determine.[50]

Notes

1. See Sinkewicz, *Evagrius of Pontus*; also Brakke, *Talking Back*, 24–30.

2. *Thoughts* 22.20–22: "τὰ νοήματα τῶν αἰσθητῶν πραγμάτων χρονίζοντα διαφθείρειν τὴν γνῶσιν"; cf. χρονίζειν at *Thoughts* 7.19; 11.17; 14.14; 16.10, 28; 20.8; 22.1, 3, 6, 8, 21; 31.2; and for the reason see Géhin, Guillaumont, and Guillaumont, *Sur les pensées*, 232n5, and Evagrius, *Prayer* 12, 43, 55–57, 67, 68, 70, 112, 115.

3. Cf. 2 Tim. 2.4.

4. See generally LSJ; also Euclid's *Elementa*, passim and book 2, demonstration 1.25, 2.1, 11.1 (*temein*).

5. See also Brakke, *Talking Back*.

6. For "imprinting" see especially *Thoughts* 2, 25, 41; and see Corrigan, *Evagrius and Gregory*, 78–79, 94–100.

7. See also Evagrius, *Scholion* 68 to Prov. 5.20.

8. *Macbeth*, act 2, scene 1, lines 33, 36–39, emphasis added. Even Shakespeare's language is reminiscent of Platonic/Neoplatonic usage. For such usage in Platonism, see Corrigan, *Evagrius and Gregory*, 78–82.

9. Luke Dysinger has suggested (in conversation) that there is, perhaps, a distant reflection here of the ancient Hippocratic Oath's promise: "I will not cut persons laboring under the stone, but will leave this to be done by men who are practitioners of this work." I think that this is quite likely because, as we shall see below, cutting is both positive and negative—and to cut with

divine skill is to follow the natural articulations of God's creation/creative power, even if we find resonances of such cutting, above all, in Plato (on which see below). One might object that medical usage is primarily physical whereas Evagrius's usage is psychological and spiritual or, in modern terms, a physical usage transferred covertly (or metonymically or metaphorically) to the psychological plane. This is a misunderstanding, I think, of the complexities of late ancient usage. In Galen, for instance, there is a natural psychosomatic continuity between psychical (tripartite soul and variants—Aristotelian, Stoic, Pauline, etc.) and somatic (brain, heart, liver) systems, a continuity that one can find in striking ways in the Cappadocian Fathers, especially Gregory of Nyssa (e.g., *De hominis opificio*, and see Corrigan, "Simmias' Objection"). However, I would trace this psychosomatic continuity back to Plato's middle dialogues, for if the *Timaeus* is not late but written after the *Phaedrus*—which I think it is—then a striking psychosomatic continuity can be traced through the *Phaedo*, *Republic*, *Symposium*, and *Phaedrus* to the *Timaeus*, exactly as appears to be Gregory of Nyssa's interpretation of the "middle" dialogues (as one can see in the *De hominis opificio*, for instance) and also in his "eclectic" psychology and physiology (as one sees especially in *De hominis opificio* and *De anima et resurrectione*).

10. Galen, *De methodo medendi*, Kühn, 10:276.13: σημεῖον μὲν οὖν τῆς κακοχυμίας τὸ χρονίζειν τὰ ἕλκη τοῦ συμφέροντος δ' ἡ εὕρεσις, οὐκ ἐκ τοῦ χρονίζειν.

11. Galen, *De usu partium*, Kühn, 3:350.4: ταχέως ἀνάγκη διεξέρχεσθαι τὴν τροφήν, ὡς μηδὲν ὑπομένειν κατ' αὐτὸ τοῦτο μηδὲ χρονίζειν, ἀλλὰ δίοδον εἶναι μόνην καὶ ταύτην ὠκεῖαν.

12. Galen, *In Hippocratis librum iii epidemiarum commentarii*, Kühn, 17a:703.5: καὶ διὰ τὸ χρονίζειν μὲν ἐν τῷ σώματι τὴν κακοχυμίαν ἡ σηπεδὼν ηὐξάνετο.

13. See *De sententiis*: Nutton, *On My Own Opinions*, 78, 12–13.

14. On this generally see Dysinger, *Psalmody*, 104–30; Corrigan, *Evagrius and Gregory*, 43–48, 88–92, 100; see also Gill, *Structured Self*, especially 103–67; and in this volume, Dysinger, 73–95.

15. Evagrius, *Disciples of Evagrius*, chap. 1.1–3 (Géhin, 102).

16. Evagrius, *Prayer* 72: "A man experienced in the gnostic life said that this happens [thinking that one sees God in some aesthetic way and that one has reached the goal of prayer] under the influence of the passion of vainglory and that of the demon who touches a place in the brain and causes palpitations in the blood vessels" (trans. Sinkewicz, 200).

17. See especially Hubler, "Moderatus."

18. See Rasimus, "Porphyry and the Gnostics"; Turner, "Platonizing Sethian Treatises."

19. Barnes and Porphyry, *Porphyry: Introduction*, 141.

20. Corrigan, *Evagrius and Gregory*, 81.

21. Iamblichus, *Iamblichus on the Mysteries*, 4.1 (Clarke, Dillon, and Hershbell, 204.4–7): Ὥσπερ οὖν μαχαίρας ἔργον ἐστὶ τὸ τέμνειν καὶ οὐδὲν ἄλλο ποιεῖ ἢ τοῦτο, οὕτω καὶ τῶν ἐν τῷ παντὶ διῃρημένων πνευμάτων κατὰ φύσεως μεριστὴν ἀνάγκην τὸ μὲν διαιρεῖ, ἄλλο δὲ συνάγει τὰ γιγνόμενα.

22. Ibid., 205n52.

23. Plato, *Republic* 7.537c7.

24. On this and for examples in Ptolemy and Galen, see Barnes and Porphyry, *Porphyry: Introduction*, 112.

25. And, in my view, this is an implicitly "philosophical" but still religious transformation of earlier ritual sacrifice (to cut the sacrificial gift) and practice (*temenos*—the consecration or cutting of a sacred spot).

26. See also Plato, *Sophist* 219e; 221b; 221e; and *atomos* of species at 229d and *atmētos* at *Phaedrus* 277b. Aristophanes' speech in the *Symposium* is all about cutting. For varied usage in the Platonic corpus see Ast, *Lexicon Platonicum*, but the *Cratylus* 387a3–6; *Symposium* 190d7; 190e1; 205c4; *Alcibiades* I, 129c7, 10–11; 129d4; and *Sophist*, *Politicus*, *Parmenides*, *passim*, are central.

27. *Parmenides* 144b4–c1; compare Plotinus *Ennead* 6.2[43].22.13–19 (where *Philebus* 16e1–2 is also cited).

28. Cf. Julianus the Theurgist, *The Chaldean Oracles*, 1–5: a collection of abstruse, hexameter verses purportedly handed down by the gods to a certain Julian the Chaldean or his son Julian the Theurgist (fl. late second century CE), which either indicates Julian's spiritual affinity with the wisdom of the East or Pater Julian's homeland of Chaldea or a Syrian origin, perhaps supported by the *Oracles*' striking parallels with fragments of Numenius (a native of Apamea in Syria); "whatever the mode of transmission, of singular importance is the fact that the *Oracles* were regarded by the later Neoplatonists—from Porphyry (c. 232–303CE) to Damascius (c. 462–537CE)—as authoritative revelatory literature equal in importance to Plato's *Timaeus*" (ibid., 2).

29. For text, translation, and commentary see Julianus the Theurgist, *The Chaldean Oracles* (Majercik, 69 and 56, respectively). See also fragment 179: "And we say that the intelligible is the beginning of every division."

30. Julianus the Theurgist, *The Chaldean Oracles*, 6.

31. Plotinus, *Ennead* 6.7[38]33.34–39: Οὖσα δὲ κάλλους ἀρχὴ ἐκεῖνο μὲν καλὸν ποιεῖ οὗ ἀρχή, καὶ καλὸν ποιεῖ οὐκ ἐν μορφῇ· ἀλλὰ καὶ αὐτὸ τὸ γενόμενον ἀμορφεῖν, ἄλλον δὲ τρόπον ἐν μορφῇ. ἡ γὰρ λεγομένη αὐτὸ τοῦτο μόνον μορφὴ ἐν

ἄλλῳ, ἐφ' ἑαυτῆς δὲ οὖσα ἄμορφον. Τὸ οὖν μετέχον κάλλους μεμόρφωται, οὐ τὸ κάλλος.

32. That is, reductive interpretations of Aristotle such as Boethus of Sidon's materialist interpretation of form. For Aristotle's theory in relation to Neoplatonism, see Lloyd, *The Anatomy of Neoplatonism.*

33. Brakke, *Talking Back*, introduction, 24–30.

34. Such as *apatheia*, *diakrisis*, etc., though they are never exclusively Stoic.

35. This example was suggested by Columba Stewart and Luke Dysinger (in personal conversation). For the proverb, see Palladius, *Lausiac History* 26.4; Evagrius, *Praktikos* 58: κἂν δυνηθῇς τὸ δὴ λεγόμενον ἥλῳ τὸν ἧλον ἐκκρούειν, γίνωσκε σεαυτὸν πλησίον ὄντα τῶν ὅρων τῆς ἀπαθείας.

36. Dysinger, *Psalmody*, 138.

37. See especially *Prayer* 57 and the invaluable work by Hausherr, *Penthos.*

38. Translation Sinkewicz.

39. Dysinger, *Psalmody*, 138.

40. Bunge, *Briefe aus der Wüste*, 211.

41. See *Antirrhetikos* 8.28, ed. Frankenberg, *Euagrius Ponticus*, 540–41, cited in Dysinger, *Psalmody*, 138n28.

42. On this context above all, see Stewart, "Imageless Prayer"; Driscoll, *Evagrius Ponticus*; Dysinger, *Psalmody.*

43. Philo, *Quis rerum divinarum heres* 234–36: ἄτμητοι μὲν οὖν αἱ δύο φύσεις, ἥ τε ἐν ἡμῖν τοῦ λογισμοῦ καὶ ἡ ὑπὲρ ἡμᾶς τοῦ θείου λόγου, ἄτμητοι δὲ οὖσαι μυρία ἄλλα τέμνουσιν. ὅ τε γὰρ θεῖος λόγος τὰ ἐν ῇ φύσει διεῖλε καὶ διένειμε πάντα, ὅ τε ἡμέτερος νοῦς, ἅττ' ἂν παραλάβῃ νοητῶς πράγματά τε καὶ σώματα, εἰς ἀπειράκις ἄπειρα διαιρεῖ μέρη καὶ τέμνων οὐδέποτε λήγει. τοῦτο δὲ συμβαίνει διὰ τὴν πρὸς τὸν ποιητὴν καὶ πατέρα τῶν ὅλων ἐμφέρειαν. τὸ γὰρ θεῖον ἀμιγές, ἄκρατον, ἀμερέστατον ὑπάρχον ἅπαντι τῷ κόσμῳ γέγονεν αἴτιον μίξεως, κράσεως, διαιρέσεως, πολυμερείας· ὥστε εἰκότως καὶ τὰ ὁμοιωθέντα, νοῦς τε ὁ ἐν ἡμῖν καὶ ὁ ὑπὲρ ἡμᾶς, ἀμερεῖς καὶ ἄτμητοι ὑπάρχοντες διαιρεῖν καὶ διακρίνειν ἕκαστα τῶν ὄντων ἐρρωμένως δυνήσονται.

The two natures are indivisible; the nature, I mean, of the reasoning power in us, and of the divine Word above us; but though they are indivisible themselves, they divide an innumerable multitude of other things. (235) For it is the divine Word which divided and distributed everything in nature; and it is our own mind which divides everything and every body which it comprehends, by the exertion of its intellect in an infinite manner, into an infinite number of parts, and which, in fact, never ceased from dividing. (236) And this happens by reason of its resemblance to the Creator and Father of the universe; for the divine nature, being unmingled, uncombined with anything else, and most completely destitute of parts, has been to the whole world the cause of mixture, and combination, and of an infinite variety of parts: so that, very naturally, the two things which thus resemble each other, both the mind which is in us and that which is above us, being without parts and indivisible, will still be able in a powerful manner to divide and distribute all existing things.

44. *KG* 6.6 (trans. O'Laughlin). Compare *KG* 4.12: "the intelligible circumcision is the voluntary rejection of the passions for the sake of the knowledge of God."

45. Ὁ πλατύνας διὰ τῆς καθαρότητος τὴν καρδίαν αὐτοῦ νοήσει τοὺς τοῦ θεοῦ λόγους τούς τε πρακτικοὺς καὶ τοὺς φυσικοὺς καὶ τοὺς θεολογικούς. Πᾶσα γὰρ ἡ κατὰ τὴν γραφὴν πραγματεία τέμνεται τριχῶς εἰς ἠθικὴν καὶ φυσικὴν καὶ θεολογικήν. Καὶ ἀκολουθεῖ τῇ μὲν πρώτῃ αἱ Παροιμίαι, τῇ δὲ δευτέρᾳ ὁ Ἐκκλησιαστής, τῇ δὲ τρίτῃ τὰ Ἄσματα τῶν ᾀσμάτων.

46. See especially for abandonment Dysinger, *Psalmody*, 188–92.

47. Plato, *Symposium* 210d2–e1.

48. Clement of Alexandria, *Stromata* 1.5.

49. Evagrius, *Letter to Melania* 28–30; cf. versions in Parmentier and Casiday.

50. Julia Konstantinovsky asks a good question to which I do not have an answer. Where is the theme of cutting to be found after Evagrius? As far as I know, it does not appear in John Cassian and in Maximus the Confessor it appears only in the *Chapters on Love* 4.48, where it is a question of circumcising (*perikoptein*) or excising (*ekkoptein*) the passions, and in *Questions and Doubts* 41 in the scriptural context of the mind choosing the second best course of Law (simultaneously a very Platonic thought): "And the sacred nous, being angered, cuts this into pieces [the legal worship] and sends them to every border of Israel, to the twelve tribes; that is to say, it divides the commandments of the law and assigns each one to the relevant power of the soul, so that all are set in motion together for the destruction of disorderly thoughts." (Ὁ δὲ ἱερὸς νοῦς ἀγανακτήσας μελίζει [?] ταύτην καὶ ἀποστέλλει εἰς πᾶν ὅριον Ἰσραὴλ εἰς τὰς δώδεκα φυλάς, τουτέστιν τὰς νομικὰς ἐντολὰς διέλει καὶ ἑκάστην ἀπονέμει τῇ ἁρμοζούσῃ τῆς ψυχῆς δυνάμει, ὥστε πάσας συνκινηθῆναι πρὸς ἀναίρεσιν τῶν ἀτακτησάντων λογισμῶν.) These are only the most distant usages. What then about the use of *temnein* and cognates in later Patristic writing (Lampe has no entries for *temnein*, and *apotemnein*, *katatemnein*, and *diatemnein* are invariably negative: decapitate, excommunicate, destroy, castrate), and how does the vivid image of thoughts that cut come to be so vividly and powerfully represented in Shakespeare—apart from the obvious fact that thoughts do cut, gnaw, and pierce through and through, as in *katanyxis*?

CHAPTER 3

Evagrius Ponticus, Exegete of the Soul

Luke Dysinger, OSB

From the Scriptures to the Soul

A striking characteristic of Byzantine liturgical commentaries is their application to religious ritual of categories and hermeneutical methods that in earlier centuries had been employed chiefly in the exegesis of sacred scripture. By means of these methods, the liturgy becomes both a re-enactment of Jesus's life and a paradigm of the believer's spiritual journey towards union with God.[1] An early exponent of this approach is Evagrius Ponticus, for whom biblical exegesis served as the foundation for spiritual guidance. Evagrius believed that biblical texts explicated at the literal or historical level can be of great value to the *abba* or *amma*: his *Antirrhetikos* recommends nearly five hundred different scriptural verses to be employed during specific kinds of temptation. However, Evagrius also practiced a more spiritual, allegorical method of exegesis that he regarded as useful in interpreting the history of the individual who seeks spiritual counsel.

Peter Brown has described the literature of the desert fathers and mothers as representing a cultural shift from exegesis of the sacred text to exegesis of the experience of temptation, a transition from the urban practice of Origenist biblical exegesis by the learned to an "alphabet of the human heart," a contemplation and interpretation of the human soul by the *abbas* and *ammas* of the Egyptian desert.[2] If Brown is correct, then the writings of Evagrius Ponticus reflect a milieu where these two values were held in balance, a context in which the interpretation of scripture and the interpretation of thoughts were viewed not as separate disciplines but rather as mutually dependent studies, each of which benefited the other. Evagrius describes the spiritual guide as a *gnostikos*, a "knower" or sage who was both an accomplished exegete of the biblical text and the human *nous,* as well as a contemplative able to perceive the *logoi* (purposes and meanings of God) within biblical salvation history and in the complex journey of each soul.

Spiritual Progress and the *Gnostikos*

According to Evagrius, spiritual progress occurs in simultaneous rhythms of ascetical practice (*praktikē*) and contemplation (*theōria*). Following Plato and the later Aristotelian tradition,[3] Evagrius considers the soul to be tripartite, ruled (when all goes well) by the *logistikon*, or reasoning faculty, which is chiefly responsible for developing the virtues of prudence, understanding, and wisdom.[4] This faculty rules over the *pathetikon*, the portion of the soul subject to passion and the source of the powers of *epithumia* (desire) and *thumos* (indignation).[5] These powers or energies in turn, "yoked to [the soul] as helpmates,"[6] are intended by God to be used "according to nature"; but they will overwhelm the soul as passions if they are misused or present in excess. When exercised according to nature the *epithumētikon* contributes the virtues of temperance, love, and continence,[7] while the *thumētikon* provides courage and patient endurance.[8] Through the practice of *diakrisis* (discernment) the ascetic or *praktikos* learns to employ these "helpmates" as they are experienced in interpersonal relationships, in dreams, and in thoughts, especially thoughts that occur during prayer.[9] The *praktikos* learns the nature of the different *noēmata* (concepts, ideas) with which the mind is filled, and is able to distinguish between *logismoi*, demonic tempting thoughts of gluttony, lust, avarice, sadness, anger, acedia, vainglory, and pride;[10] as well as to appreciate the beneficial *noēmata* suggested by angels or that arise from neutral sense-perception.[11] The labors of the *praktikē* are rewarded by God with the birth of love and the gift of *apatheia*, "dispassion" or "freedom from compulsion."[12]

Evagrius holds out the hope and even describes to some extent the process by which a Christian *praktikos* can mature into a *gnostikos*, a contemplative and teacher who is able to perceive the divine *logoi*, the inner meanings and purposes of God within creation and history. The *gnostikos* learns to appreciate and make use of a natural movement between the poles of *physikē*, the perception of God's presence and purpose within creation, and *theologikē*, contemplation of the divine nature, often experienced in "pure prayer" transcending all words and concepts.

Although Evagrius thus describes sequential levels or stages of spiritual progress, he is very much aware that it is impossible to completely surmount the *praktikē* and somehow "graduate" from the quest for virtue. On the contrary, the *praktikos* makes spiritual progress and learns to perceive the ongoing (and indeed, never-ending) work of asceticism, *gnostikoteron*, that is from an increasingly contemplative perspective.[13] And since the struggle against certain passions continues until the moment of death, the mature *gnostikos* must always advance in virtue, continuously practicing ascetical vigilance.[14] Thus the journey towards God is not a simple linear ascent beyond ascetical practice into contemplation; rather, spiritual progress entails a gentle oscillation between these two poles in such a way that continuing attention to the changing demands of *praktikē* yields ever-greater contemplative refreshment.[15]

Biblical Exegesis

The *gnostikos*'s principal textbook is the Bible. For Evagrius, biblical exegesis consists chiefly in the search for biblical texts that will be of benefit to the *gnostikos* and those who seek spiritual counsel. The *gnostikos* must be able to "give a word to each, according to their [spiritual] attainment."[16] Thus the frequent plea to the desert *abba*, "give me a word!" should be answered according to the circumstances and spiritual capacity of the questioner. This necessitates a large store of biblical wisdom and a familiarity with the different levels of meaning contained in sacred scripture. For Evagrius, these include spiritual "definitions" of biblical terms[17] and familiarity with both the "customary expressions of scripture"[18] and the rules for allegorical exegesis.[19] Evagrius's underlying exegetical method, which he describes in *Gnostikos* 18, is an application to the scriptures of his schema of spiritual progress:[20]

> It is necessary to search for allegorical and literal passages pertaining to the *praktikē*, *physikē*, and *theologikē*.
>
> [1] If the passage concerns the *praktikē* it is necessary to determine whether it concerns *thumos* and its effects, or *epithumia* and its consequences, or whether it concerns the movements of the *nous*.
>
> [2] If the passage pertains to the *physikē*, it is necessary to note whether it reveals a doctrine concerning nature, and which one.
>
> [3] Or if it is an allegorical passage concerning *theologikē* it should be determined as far as possible whether it reveals the doctrine of the Trinity.[21]

The *gnostikos* is thus instructed to superimpose Evagrius's spiritual schema on the Bible, employing as a hermeneutical principle the utility of each passage in explicating the different levels of spiritual progress and the practices that correspond to *praktikē*, *physikē*, and *theologikē*. Evagrius's extensive biblical scholia and his *Antirrhetikos* (which, taken together comprise the bulk of his literary output) are intended as reference works for *gnostikoi*. They serve as biblical glossaries and sourcebooks in which texts have been assembled and explicated according to: (1) their usefulness in the battle against temptation and the acquisition of virtue (*praktikē*); (2) what they reveal of the inner purposes of God in history and creation (*physikē*); and (3) whether they hint at the ineffable mystery of the divine nature or the transcendent experience of pure prayer (*theologikē*).

Exegesis of the Heart

The close interrelationship between the monastic practice of biblical exegesis and the art of "reading the heart" is readily apparent in Evagrius's letters.[22] *Letter* 25 is particularly illustrative and has the good fortune of being one of the few letters for which a significant portion of the original Greek has survived.[23] Evagrius's sixty-four letters have been translated into German and extensively commented by Gabriel Bunge: some of his comments and suggestions have been incorporated into the following discussion.[24]

Spiritual Diagnosis (*Letter* 25.1)

> *Letter* 25.1. It was always my preference that with the Lord's help you would lead the monastic life, wherein you may "destroy every [tempting] thought and every obstacle that arises against the knowledge of Christ" (2 Cor. 10.4–5). But you imagine that having fled the Praetorians[25]—if, indeed, you really have fled them—you have fulfilled the works of righteousness and even advanced so far as to say, "graciously receive, O Lord, the voluntary offering of my mouth" (Ps. 118.108), as if you had fulfilled everything in the law (cf. Rom. 13.10; Gal. 5.14).

From Evagrius's comments it is clear that the intended recipient of *Letter* 25 was a monk living in Jerusalem who had formerly been a high-ranking imperial official. Gabriel Bunge is convinced that the recipient is the same "Anatolius" mentioned in the Coptic version of Palladius's *Lausiac History*, to whom Evagrius dedicated his trilogy of *Praktikos*, *Gnostikos*, and *Kephalaia gnostika*.[26] While this identification is far from certain,[27] it will help avoid unnecessary periphrasis in the following discussion to refer to the recipient of *Letter* 25 as "Anatolius." Whoever he may have been, he evidently wrote to Evagrius, exulting in the spiritual freedom afforded by monastic life and expressing his joy in the words of Psalm 118.108: "graciously receive, O Lord, the voluntary offering of my mouth." Evagrius's response to this enthusiasm takes the form of a rebuke that reflects a diagnosis of Anatolius's spiritual state based in part on an exegesis of the psalm verse Anatolius employed. This rebuke is comprehensible only in light of Evagrius's exegesis of this verse in his *Scholia on Psalms*:

> 118.108. Accept the freewill-offerings of my mouth, O Lord.
>
> 47. The *freewill-offerings of* our *mouth* are virginity, abstinence from food and drink, and the life of withdrawal into the desert. The law constrains us to perform the commandments: thus one who performs all the commandments can furthermore say publicly, "Accept, the freewill-offerings of my mouth, O Lord." But one who offends against the law lacks the necessary freedom of speech (*parrhēsia*) to say this.[28]

Evagrius considered it inappropriate for Anatolius to have applied this verse to himself. It should only be employed boldly ("with *parrhēsia*") by one who has made great progress in monastic asceticism, who has studied and "performed all the commandments," or as Evagrius puts it in this letter, "fulfilled the works of righteousness." These "works of righteousness" include not only the moral injunctions binding on all Christians, but the interior vigilance and struggle that particularly characterizes the monastic calling. Although Evagrius makes it clear that he had always supported Anatolius's decision to embrace monastic life, he questions whether Anatolius has inwardly relinquished his former status and whether he understands the importance of the struggle with tempting thoughts that is the deeper work of asceticism. Although Anatolius may have renounced the power and wealth of the praetorium, Evagrius will now invite him into a deeper exegesis of his own soul by highlighting the struggle against *logismoi* that is the foundation of the monks' "works of righteousness."

Antirrhesis / "Contradiction" (*Letter* 25.2)

> *Letter* 25.2. But in regard to the other [tempting] thoughts, you fail to understand that they *proceed from the heart* (Mt. 15.19) and soil the *nous*; and if it mentally consents to them, it draws near to sin. And there is a spiritual contradiction (*antirrhesis*) to use against

> them in regard to both sins of intention and of action. For consenting to sin, even in thought, is accounted as sin: and see how Moses teaches you, saying "Do not agree with them!" (cf. Ex. 23.32, Dt. 23.6). And in the Gospel the Lord condemns the *nous* as adulterer that only looks passionately on a woman (Mt. 5.28), as well as one that mentally angers a brother (Mt. 5.22).

Evagrius reminds Anatolius of the moral significance of the interior landscape of thoughts and temptations. This he does through an exegesis of texts from the Sermon on the Mount. He first recalls Jesus's insistence on the importance of the heart and the thoughts that arise from it (Mt. 15.19). He then explicates these thoughts at the level of ascetical practice, employing the method of biblical exegesis he recommends in *Gnostikos* 18, cited above. For Evagius the *praktikē* chiefly consists in learning to properly use the energies of *epithumia* and *thumos*; thus he reminds Anatolius of Jesus's warning against lustful (Mt. 5.28) and angry (Mt. 5.22) thoughts. He describes this against the background of the important monastic practice of *antirrhesis*, the "contradiction" of harmful thoughts, a subject on which Evagrius had written extensively.

Evagrius wrote a handbook based on his exegetical researches intended for use in the struggle against tempting thoughts. The *Antirrhetikos* is unique among Evagrius's writings and was of particular interest to his biographers.[29] It resembles his biblical scholia insofar as it cites and to some extent interprets successive biblical texts, but its purpose is more practical. The *Antirrhetikos* is a collection of bible verses intended for use by those undergoing specific temptations. It contains 492 brief texts from the scriptures,[30] usually consisting of only one or two verses, intended to serve as *antirrhesis* ("contradiction" or "response") to the experience of temptation by the *logismoi* of gluttony, lust, avarice, sadness, anger, acedia, vainglory, and pride. It consists of eight chapters, each concerned with a different temptation: each chapter begins anew at *Genesis* and offers verses from successive books of the bible. This systematic correlation of successive biblical texts with specific *logismoi* affords a unique insight into Evagrius's understanding of the intimate relationship between exegesis of the biblical text and the tempted heart.

Evagrius's art of *antirrhesis* enables the offending thought to be transformed and healed through the application of a specific biblical word or phrase, intended to be memorized, recited, and prayerfully pondered. And here in *Letter* 25 Evagrius offers specific bible verses for Anatolius to ponder. The texts from Matthew 5.28 and 5.22 that he deploys here against lust and anger are recommended for almost the same purpose in *Antirrhetikos* 2.56 ("Against the *logismos* of lust") and 5.35 ("Against the *logismos* of anger").[31] However, *antirrhesis* is more than a method of simply counteracting or "contradicting" the demons. The range of different spiritual functions these verses are meant to serve may be conceived as a spectrum, consisting at one end of what might be termed "direct *antirrhesis*," a kind of exorcism that specifically negates or repels the offending demon or *logismos*.[32] At the other end of this spectrum are brief prayers that are not directed against the demons, but are offered, rather, to God.[33] Between these two extremes lie the majority of Evagrius's antirrhetic texts, which are neither directed against the demons nor offered to God, but are rather intended for the tempted soul.[34] Both in the *Antirrhetikos* and in this letter these verses serve a variety of functions: to exhort, to evoke compunction and repentance, to console, to inform, and often to encourage practice of the virtue opposed to the temptation being endured.[35]

Diakrisis / "Discernment" (*Letter* 25.3)

> *Letter* 25.3. These commandments uproot from the heart consent to lawlessness, and "prepare" in the *nous* "the way for the Lord" (cf. Mk. 1:3). But the ignorant consider it foolish to undertake this path and imagine they fulfill the apostolic path in a single moment, as if keeping the commandments were hindered only by the passions of the body: for the [tempting] thoughts that arise from these are transitory, while jealousy and resentment endure into old age.

Having highlighted Jesus's admonitions against lust and anger, Evagrius now invites Anatolius to consider these temptations at a deeper level by searching out the nature and qualities of his thoughts. Elsewhere in his writings Evagrius calls this the art of discernment (*diakri-*

sis) and careful observation (*paratērēsis*).[36] In his treatises *Praktikos* and *Thoughts*, Evagrius describes this practice in detail, explaining how one can learn to distinguish between: (1) angelic *noēmata* that educate and console the *nous*, leading it to God;[37] (2) neutral thoughts that arise from memory and sense-perception;[38] and (3) demonic *logismoi*, tempting thoughts and fantasies that pervert the natural powers of the *nous* and lead it into error.[39]

Here Evagrius encourages Anatolius to discern or distinguish between the "passions of the body" that arise from the *epithumētikon* and those "of the soul" that have their origin in the *thumikon*. Evagrius treats this subject in some detail in *Praktikos* 35–38. Temptations that invite the misuse of *epithumia* are generally rooted in human physiology, arising from such physical needs as hunger, thirst, and sexual desire.[40] They are the subjects of the virtues of temperance (*sōphrosunē*) and chastity (*enkrateia*), attained through fasting and abstinence. According to Evagrius, these virtues can become so firmly fixed that the "passions of the body" need not persist into old age. On the other hand, resentment and jealousy, "passions of the soul," arise from the *thumikon* and chiefly afflict interpersonal relationships. They can "endure into old age," and remain active even "up to the moment of death."[41] Their remedy is spiritual love, *agapē*. And there are also passions that afflict the highest powers of the *nous*, and it is to one of these that Evagrius now directs Anatolius's attention.

Natural Contemplation: Encoding, Decoding, and Replacement (*Letter* 25.4)

> *Letter* 25.4. Perhaps the [tempting] thoughts of the praetorium do not afflict you; but is it not possible that you are afflicted by [tempting] thoughts of vainglory? Take care that although physically in "Jerusalem" your spirit is distant from "Bethany" through which your tempting thoughts of avarice (cf. John 12.4–8) and its associated failings incline towards shopping, buying and selling (cf Mt. 21.12) salt, vinegar, and bread, while there are starving thousands deserving of daily bread (cf. Mk. 14.7; Mt. 6.11).

Evagrius now invites Anatolius to note the higher, intellectual temptations, especially vainglory, which Evagrius understands as satisfaction with one's accomplishments together with a yearning for human approval and respect.[42] An awareness of having attained virtue or success in monastic observance, to which Anatolius seems to have alluded, can stimulate vainglory.[43] Evagrius offers a remedy in the form of biblical symbolism and allegory, an approach characteristic of all Evagrius's writings, but especially notable in his biblical scholia. As Paul Géhin has noted, the scholia appear at times to be glossaries containing lists of biblical terms together with their spiritual "translation."[44] Columba Stewart has described Evagrius's technique as "encoding" biblical words and phrases with specific allegorical definitions that can then be "decoded" by those familiar with his teachings.[45]

In this instance Evagrius reminds Anatolius of his emphasis on "Jerusalem" and suggests that he should, instead, consider the significance of "Bethany." While the term "Jerusalem" can have a very elevated symbolic significance for Evagrius,[46] it is more probable that he intends it here chiefly in the literal sense of Jerusalem as the geographical locale of Anatolius's monastery. The encouragement to shift his attention from contentment with "Jerusalem" to "Bethany" is an example of Evagrius's practice of "replacement," the substitution of lower thoughts with higher ones, a form of meditation that redirects one's contemplative focus towards more worthy concepts and biblical images. At its lowest (and most controversial)[47] level this consists of replacing particularly vicious temptations with less malignant ones: Evagrius calls this "driving out a nail with a nail."[48] A more elevated application, the one he recommends here, holds the potential for transforming demonic *logismoi* into *noēmata* of the human or even angelic type. Anatolius's enthusiasm for living in the Holy City Jerusalem should be tempered with meditation on the complex metaphor of "Bethany," the village associated both with the house of Mary and Martha where Martha was chided for her concern over food (Lk. 10.39–42), and with the house of Simon the Leper, where Judas's vaunted concern for the poor kept him from appreciating the importance of spending everything to anoint the Lord's feet (Mk. 14.3–7). Evagrius's pejorative reference to "buying and selling" may suggest that Anatolius was *oikonomos* (steward) of his monastery, and that his labors prevent him from attending, like Mary of Bethany, solely to the Lord. However, Bethany is also associated with the themes of resurrection (Jn. 11) and ascension (Lk. 24.50), two images towards which Evagrius will now guide Anatolius.

Exegesis of the Spiritual Journey

To this point Evagrius has offered Anatolius advice at the level of *praktikē*, pointing out the significance of the inner struggle with temptations. He will now invite Anatolius to perceive the matter of spiritual progress in a broader context: first through the vision of his own *nous* as the dwelling place of God, then from the perspective of the whole cosmic drama of reunion with God.

Guided Ascent to Purified Vision (*Letter* 25.5a)

> *Letter* 25.5(a). But forgive me, I beg you. I answered your letter because you wrote me that you dwell in a place receptive of God, "who made heaven and earth" (Ps. 113:23). Know, too, that he dwells "in your midst" as John the Baptist testified (Jn. 1:26). And he awaits you as you progress through your works towards "Bethlehem": through the spiritual vision of your purified nature you become "resurrection" . . .

Anatolius had apparently described Jerusalem as a "place receptive of God," probably in the sense of a place where one is vividly aware of God's presence. Evagrius now draws on Anatolius's description of Jerusalem and uses it to highlight Anatolius's lofty dignity as one who bears God's image. Evagrius invites him to shift his gaze from the physical "Jerusalem" understood as God's dwelling place to that place where God dwells "in your midst"; that is, within the *nous*, the deepest self and the center of personal identity. Anatolius can symbolically progress towards "Bethlehem," Christ's birthplace, by discovering that he is himself the place where Christ is born and seen "through the spiritual vision of your purified nature." In several texts Evagrius describes this "spiritual vision" of "purified nature" as the light or radiance of the *nous*,[49] most clearly in *Thoughts*:

> When the *nous* has stripped off "the old man" and put on that [which comes] from grace (cf. Col. 3.9–10), then it will see its own state at the time of prayer, like a sapphire or the color of heaven, which Scripture calls the place of God that was seen by the elders under Mount Sinai (cf. Exod. 24.20).[50]

In the next sentence, Evagrius describes this vision of the sapphire "place of God" as the consequence of the ascetical practice and successive replacement of thoughts he has recommended to Anatolius:

> The *nous* is incapable of seeing the place of God within itself unless it is raised above all the concepts [*noēmata*] of external objects. But it will not be raised up unless it strips off the passions chaining it down with concepts [*noēmata*] of sensory objects. And as it lays aside passions through the virtues, the more subtle tempting thoughts are laid aside through spiritual contemplations; and these, in turn are laid aside when there appears to it the light that imprints it with the place of God at the time of prayer.[51]

Evagrius elsewhere calls this vision of the *nous* as the place of God "resurrection." In the *Kephalaia gnostika* he describes a threefold resurrection: from vice to virtue ("resurrection of the body"); from subjection by the passions to *apatheia* ("resurrection of the soul); and from ignorance to the state of spiritual knowledge ("resurrection of the *nous*").[52]

The Logoi of Providence and Judgment (*Letter* 25.5b)

> *Letter* 25.5(b). . . . [through the spiritual vision of your purified nature you become "resurrection"] and through understanding the divine *logoi* you become what is called "ascension" and "Mount of Olives."

The vision of one's own *nous* as the "place of God" points towards the final destiny of all created beings: reunion with the God from whom all reasoning beings fell away in the primordial "movement." Evagrius calls the understanding of this eschatological goal "ascension," and associates it with "understanding of the divine *logoi*," the inner purposes, or designs of God that the contemplative can begin to perceive once freed from preoccupation with the inner struggle against temptation. Evagrius understands Christ's "ascension" as the fulfillment of his salvific work, the sign of God's eternal providence and the impulse for all spiritual help and guidance.[53] For the Christian believer, "ascension" is both knowledge or contemplation of "the things which have been and will be" and restoration of the *nous* to union with God.[54]

The details of this eschatology are the subject of two *logoi* Evagrius particularly emphasizes throughout his writings and to which he probably alludes here, although he does not mention them by name, namely, providence and judgment.[55] These *logoi* are part of a hierarchy of contemplative objects that the *gnostikos* must learn to perceive[56] both in the fixed microcosm of the scriptures and in the ever-changing macrocosm of creation. The highest object of contemplation is God; next comes God's creation, that is, the corporeal and incorporeal reasoning natures or *logikoi*, including all the "ages and worlds" of angels, human beings, and demons. But more important than details concerning the ranks or ordering of the *logikoi,* that is to say, the structure of the natural world, are their *logoi*, the inner purposes of God to which they attest. The "*logoi* of providence and judgment" are, for Evagrius, a means of probing beneath the diversity of creation so as to perceive all created things as active participants in the ongoing spectacle of creation, fall, and restoration. Meditation on these *logoi* entails an appreciation of creation from the perspective of its origin and destiny. The variety and multiplicity apparent within creation, "the diversity of bodies and worlds," reminds the *gnostikos* of God's compassionate "judgment," his *krisis,* understood not as disastrous punishment but rather God's placement of every reasoning nature within the body and world that will best facilitate a return to that divine unity from which all have fallen. The complexity and variety of creation thus serves as a reminder of the diverse paths and circumstances that lead to God. The "*logos* of providence" enables the Christian contemplative to bear in mind God's unfailing presence in all human circumstances and to recall that grace is mediated, often by friends, acquaintances, *abbas* and *ammas*, and even angels who facilitate those acts of free choice that enable reasoning beings to make spiritual progress.[57]

Meditation on "ascension" and "the divine *logoi*" will enable Anatolius to discover that the journey towards God is actually a return of the *nous* back to the God from whom it has fallen away. Such contemplation is itself part of the *nous*'s gradual re-ascent to its original *taxis*, its "first rank." However, this return of the *nous* to its primordial state is possible only through Christ. Apart from God's grace the *nous* cannot rise above the world of sin and death to which it is subject. Re-ascent to its first rank is possible because of what God accomplished through the incarnation, death, resurrection, and ascension of Christ.[58] Similarly, the descent of God into death and Christ's ascension to the Father is what makes possible Anatolius's spiritual "ascension."[59] The direct experience of that grace of Christ that makes "ascension" possible takes place in prayer, the subject to which Evagrius now guides Anatolius.

Spiritual Guidance in the Place of Prayer (*Letter* 25.6a)

> *Letter* 25.6a. But if you wish to comprehend the state of your heart, whether it is careful or inattentive, then observe yourself at the time of prayer. With which fantasies is your *nous* confused and distracted; which comes first, impassioned or dispassionate [thoughts]? If it is besieged by the first, then it is inattentive to the commandments of God; and the passions bloom, setting in motion indignation and desire, together with a whole crowd of sufferings. But if it finds itself disturbed by the second, then it is not observant in reading and prayer: rather, it is being utterly ruined through [preoccupation with] various events and new stories, constantly wishing "to say or hear something new" (Acts 17.21).

At first glance, Evagrius appears to have descended from his high eschatological theme and reverted to the mundane subject of temptations and distracting images. However, he is now actually pointing even higher, towards the exalted realm of *theologikē*, for his subject is prayer.

As Columba Stewart has shown, Evagrius's treatises on prayer are among his most advanced works, intended for those who have made considerable spiritual progress.[60] Prayer, "conversation of the *nous* with God," can be an even higher spiritual activity than perception of the divine light within the soul. Having glimpsed a reflection of the divine activity in its own "purified nature," the *nous* that turns to prayer has lifted its gaze from reflected light to the source of light. In prayer the *nous* not only perceives its creator and redeemer but engages in intimate dialogue with God "as with a father"[61] without the need for any intermediary.[62] This conversation (*sunomilia*) or intercourse (*sunousia*) may initially entail the use of words; in the presences of the one who transcends all words and concepts,[63] however, it becomes appropriate to lay aside all thoughts and images. While Evagrius regarded contemplation or *gnosis* as the proper activity of the *nous*, the experience of undistracted prayer towards which he now guides Anatolius is higher still. It is "the highest noetic activity of the *nous*."[64] As Evagrius asks, "What can be higher than conversing with God (*prosomilein*) and being occupied in intercourse (*sunousia*) with him?"[65]

By inviting Anatolius to note the nature and character of his distractions during prayer Evagrius not only encourages him to lay aside thoughts at prayer, he explains how to do it. When confronted by thoughts redolent of temptation, tainted by misuse or excess of *epithumia* or *thumos*, Anatolius should meditate on the commandments. If he finds himself preoccupied with neutral or even elevated "angelic" concepts, he should recover his focus by reading scripture and persevering in prayer. In prayer one should not be distracted by the glory of created things, however clearly they may reflect their creator, rather one should attend to the creator himself. In his advice to Anatolius, Evagrius further condenses his already compact instructions in *Prayer* 52–61. Both impassioned and "pure" elevated thoughts are distractions at the time of prayer because the goal is communion with the God who transcends both. In pure prayer it is possible to move from natural contemplation (*theōria physikē*) to *theologia*; the *gnostikos* can become *theologos*: "If you are a theologian, you pray truly; and if you pray truly, you are a theologian."[66]

Ascent to Vision of the Bridegroom (*Letter* 25.6b)

> *Letter* 25.6b. Nevertheless, "fight the good fight" (1 Tim. 6.12), in order to be "crowned with the wreath of justice" (2 Tim. 4.8) and to behold Christ the bridegroom (Mt. 25.1), whom you now seek through good works, which is in actuality the search for the Lord.

In a final sequence of biblical citations Evagrius concludes his letter by joining the military and competitive imagery of *praktikē* to the contemplative vision of "Christ the bridegroom." This brief catena of three texts, which he repeats verbatim with the same explanation elsewhere,[67] is a coded reiteration of the threefold ordering of both spiritual progress and biblical exegesis: *praktikē*, *physikē*, *theologikē*. The "good fight" of 1 Timothy 6.12 describes *praktikē*, the "fight" against tempting thoughts to attain *apatheia*. The "crown of justice" is a metaphor Evagrius frequently employs as a symbol of contemplation and spiritual knowledge.[68] Since Origen's third-century commentary and homilies on the Song of Songs, "Christ the bridegroom" had become a widely used means of describing the soul's union with God.[69] Despite this increasing popularity of nuptial metaphor among Christian thinkers, however, Evagrius is surprisingly sparing in his own use of spousal imagery: it is only here and in three other places that he deliberately invokes the image of Christ as bridegroom.[70] Of these a close parallel to his use here is *Thoughts* 42, where Evagrius describes the allegorical "eye" of the *nous* that is able at the time of prayer to "contemplate the blessed light of the holy Trinity" and thus "ravish the heart of the bridegroom."[71]

Conclusion: Exegete and Spiritual Guide

Letter 25 clearly exemplifies the close interrelationship between biblical exegesis and spiritual guidance for Evagrius Ponticus. In all of his letters he interweaves spiritual advice with encoded allusions to biblical texts and images that presuppose familiarity with his exegetical approach, the results of which make up the "spiritual glossaries" of his voluminous exegetical scholia. But *Letter* 25 not only illustrates Evagrius's love of encoding advice in the form of biblical symbols and texts, it highlights that the methodology he employs in interpreting the life and situation of "Anatolius" is analogous if not identical with his method of exegesis. In *Gnostikos* 18, cited above, Evagrius states that biblical texts are to be collected and interpreted according to the three categories of *praktikē*, *physikē*, and *theologikē*. Evagrius's analysis of Anatolius's circumstances follows this pattern, even to the extent of reiterating it in coded scriptural form at the end of the letter. It is as if the one who seeks advice is a kind of "book" that can be read by the *gnostikos* who has learned the art of spiritual exegesis. Indeed, Evagrius alludes to this approach in a scholion on Psalm 138.16:

> The *book of God* is the contemplation of corporeal and incorporeal beings in which the purified *nous* comes to be written through knowledge.[72]

Evagrius's approach to both biblical exegesis and spiritual guidance may be summarized as an attempt to perceive and describe everything *sub specie aeternitatis*, in the light of a divine origin and an eternal destiny, or as Columba Stewart has described it, within a "unified vision of everything."[73] As a biblical exegete, Evagrius's *gnostikos* discovers in the scriptures symbols and allegories of the great cosmic drama of fall, incarnation, and the eschatological reunion of all reasoning beings with God. As spiritual guide the *gnostikos* looks up, as it were, from the Bible and perceives in the movements and experiences of each soul a miniature reflection of that cosmic journey towards reunion. Thus the drama of each soul's struggle is illuminated by the sweeping movements of salvation history.

Such a vision of the other as a legible, comprehensible "book" is possible because, for Evagrius, the text of sacred scriptures and the individual who seeks advice are both reflections and bearers of the divine word. In his treatise *On Prayer* Evagrius presents a series of beatitudes that depict both the contemplative potential inherent in the attainment of *apatheia* and the attitude towards one's fellow human beings that must be maintained by those who would offer spiritual advice:

121. Blessed is the monk who regards himself as *the offscouring of all* (1 Cor. 4.13).

122. Blessed is the monk who sees the salvation and progress of all with perfect joy, as if it were his own.

123. Blessed is the monk who regards every human being as God, after God.

The "other" who seeks spiritual counsel is, for Evagrius's *gnostikos,* both a microcosm of salvation history and "God-bearer," one in whom the image of God shines: *hos theon meta theon*—"as God, after God."

Notes

1. This approach is foreshadowed in the catechetical homilies of Cyril of Jerusalem (*Jerusalem Catecheses*) and becomes progressively clearer in the writings of Dionysius the Areopagite (*Ecclesiastical Hierarchies*), Maximus the Confessor (*The Church's Mystagogy*), Germanus of Constantinople (*On the Divine Liturgy*), and Nicholas Cabasilas (*The Life in Christ*).

2. Brown, *Body and Society*, 229.

3. The beginning of chapter 89 of Evagrius's *Praktikos* is modeled closely on an anonymous first-century peripatetic treatise, *On Virtues and Vices,* ed. Bekker, *Aristotelis opera*, 2:1249a26–1251b37.

4. Evagrius, *Praktikos* 89.

5. Evagrius, *S-Ps*. 107.3(1), no. 2, cited according to an unpublished collation of M.-J. Rondeau, based on MS *Vaticanus Graecus* 754, cf. Pitra, *Analecta sacra*, 3:107.3.1.

6. Evagrius, *Thoughts* 17.

7. Evagrius, *Praktikos* 89.

8. Ibid.

9. Evagrius, *Praktikos* 25; *Prayer* 12, 13, 24, 25.

10. These roughly correspond to the divisions of the Platonic tripartite soul, beginning with the ἐπιθυμητικόν, moving through the θυμικόν, and concluding with intellectual temptations.

11. Evagrius most commonly uses the term *logismoi* to designate the tempting thoughts inspired by demons, and νοήματα to describe thoughts which are benign or angelic in origin. However, this distinction does not always apply; and the terms are occasionally used in the opposite sense, i.e., malignant *noe-*

mata (*Praktikos* 42) and neutral or beneficial *logismoi*. Evagrius, *Praktikos* 30; *Eulogios* 8; see also Sinkewicz, *Greek Ascetic Corpus*, 5, 314–15.

12. *Apatheia* does not mean freedom from temptation, since Evagrius emphasizes that certain temptations will continue until death (*Praktikos* 36); rather, it refers to freedom from the inner storm of passions' irrational drives, which in their extreme forms would today be called obsessions, compulsions, or addictions (*Praktikos* prol. 8; 81).

13. Evagrius, *Praktikos* 50, 79, 83.

14. Evagrius, *Praktikos* 36. On the persistence of anger in those who have made considerable spiritual progress: *Gnostikos* 10, 31, and 32.

15. A vivid depiction of the mutually enhancing interrelationship between *praktikē* and *theoretikē* is found in Evagrius, *Thoughts* 17.

16. Evagrius, *Gnostikos* 44.

17. Ibid., 17.

18. Ibid., 19.

19. Ibid., 20–21.

20. Evagrius's approach is based on the exegetical methods of Clement of Alexandria and Origen: Clement, *Stromateis* 1.28.179.3–4 (Stählin, 2:108); Origen, *Commentary on the Song of Songs* Prol. 3.6 (Origen, *Commentaire sur le Cantique des cantiques*, 1:132).

21. Evagrius, *Gnostikos* 18.

22. See in this volume for the discussion of Evagrius's *Letters* by Robin Darling Young, who is preparing an English translation of the letters with commentary.

23. A fragment amounting to the last fourth of the *Letter* 25 has been published by Guillaumont, "Fragments grecs inédits." Of the remaining letters, with the exception of *Letter* 63, the *Letter on Faith* (a theological treatise on the Trinity), only a few fragments of the original Greek survive. The corpus of sixty-four letters is available in Syriac with a Greek retroversion published in 1912: Frankenberg, *Euagrius Ponticus*, 564–611.

24. Bunge, *Briefe aus der Wüste*, 211–83.

25. In the late fourth century the office of "praetorian" no longer referred to imperial bodyguards, as it had in the early Roman Empire. During this period a praetorian was a high-level administrator of an imperial prefecture, or region.

26. Bunge, *Briefe aus der Wüste*, 33–36.

27. Bunge gives as his reasons for this identification inferences in the letter that the recipient was: (1) formerly an important government official; (2) rich; and (3) living in Jerusalem. Ibid., 347–48.

28. Evagrius, *S-Ps.* 118.108, no. 47 (cf. Pitra, 3:118.108.1).

29. Palladius (*Lausiac History* 38.10), Gennadius (*On Illustrious Men* 11), and Socrates (*Ecclesiastical History* 4.23) all mention it; and Gennadius translated the *Antirrhetikos* into Latin.

30. Frankenberg's edition of the Syriac text of the *Antirrhetikos* provides 486 verses, but David Brakke's more recent careful study of the manuscripts has yielded 492: Brakke, *Talking Back*.

31. Evagrius, *Antirrhetikos* 2.56: "For the [tempting] thought that makes one eager to sin by presenting images of men and women: *But I say to you that every one who looks at a woman lustfully has already committed adultery with her in his heart* (Mat. 5.28)." *Antirrhetikos* 5.35: "For the wrathful thought that rises up against a brother out of accedia: *But I say to you that every one who is angry with his brother shall be liable to judgment* (Mat. 5.22)."

32. Evagrius often alerts the reader that a verse is of this type by introducing it with the phrase: "For the demon. . . ." Thirty-two verses of the *Antirrhetikos* are of this type. He evidently regards these ejaculatory prayers as "indirectly" antirrhetic in the sense that they invite the soul to turn towards God and away from the demons, thus "contradicting" not so much the temptation itself as the demonic goal of preventing prayer.

33. Most of these are introduced with the phrase: "For the Lord . . . ." Forty-four verses of the *Antirrhetikos* are of this type. Evagrius believed that temptation and physical affliction have a unique power to galvanize the soul into a type of prayer characterized by *parrhēsia*, frankness or freedom of speech (Evagrius, *Letter* 1.2). However, the struggling soul often finds itself mute; thus these antirrhetic prayers provide the stunned soul with words which may be addressed to God (Evagrius, *Antirrhetikos*, 8.28).

34. The majority of verses (301 of 492) begin with the phrase: "For the [tempting] thought of. . . ." Less than a quarter (116 verses) begin: "For a soul. . . ." or "For a mind. . . ."

35. Evagrius alternately describes these different categories of verses as intended: "For the soul (or 'mind'). . . . ," or, "For the tempting thought. . . ." These two introductory phrases appear to serve a stylistic rather than a taxonomic purpose; their alternate use avoids an endlessly repetitive introductory formula rather than signaling a change in content.

36. Evagrius often employs παρατήρησις as a synonym for διάκρισις. Evagrius's flexible use of this terminology as contrasted with his successors is discussed by Rich, *Discernment in the Desert Fathers*, 39–68.

37. Angelic *noēmata* are characterized by feelings of peace (Evagrius, *Praktikos* 80), and "are concerned with the inner nature of things and with searching out their spiritual principles."

38. Human thoughts are characterized by simple images, unclouded by passion (Evagrius, *Thoughts* 8).

39. Demonic *logismoi* are disturbing or terrifying and incline the soul towards passion and vice (Evagrius, *Praktikos* 51 and 80; *Thoughts* 8).

40. An exception to this is the *logismos* of avarice (*phylargia*), which Evagrius, following Aristotelian/Stoic tradition, also assigns to the *epithumētikon.* That there is no instinctive "physiological" desire for precious metals or money until one has learned to desire it was a subject of much discussion by early monastic theorists of the passions. John Cassian noted that it arises "outside of our nature" (*extra naturam*), *Institutes* 8.1.

41. Evagrius, *Praktikos* 36.

42. Ibid., Prol. 13, 30.

43. Ibid., Prol. 30, 31.

44. Géhin, *Scholies aux Proverbes*, 15–16.

45. Stewart, "Evagrius Ponticus on Monastic Pedagogy."

46. In the *Kephalaia gnostika* "Jerusalem" is a "symbol of natural contemplation" (5.88) and "contemplation of incorporeal beings" (6.49).

47. He particularly recommends this as a means of replacing lustful fantasies with vainglorious contempt for lust: Evagrius, *Eulogios* 21 (Sinkewicz, 48–49, 324–25). Later spiritual authors, such as Barsanuphius of Gaza, strongly disapproved of this approach and considered it dangerous.

48. Evagrius, *Praktikos* 58.

49. Evagrius, *Praktikos* 64: "The proof of *apatheia* is that the *nous* begins to behold the gentle radiance proper to it." *Gnostikos* 45: "those who are also able at the time of prayer to contemplate the light of their *nous* illuminating them." *Prayer* 75: "The angel of the Lord . . . moves the light of the *nous* to undeviating activity." *Antirrhetikos* 6.16: "the intellect also cannot be illuminated while praying without the grace of God." *Reflections* 2: "If any would see the state of their *nous*, let them deprive themsel[ves] of all concepts (*noemata*)[:] and then they will see themselves *like a sapphire or the color of heaven*; (Exod. 24.10) but this cannot be accomplished without *apatheia*, since it requires the cooperation of God who breathes into them the kindred light." Muyldermans, "Evagriana," 38.

50. Evagrius, *Thoughts* 39 (cf. *Reflections* 2).

51. Evagrius, *Thoughts* 40.

52. *KG* 5.19, 22, 25; it is noteworthy that within this chain *KG* 5.21 describes vision of the worlds of Jerusalem and Mount Zion, while 5.23–24 concern the *logoi* of providence, judgment, and the primordial fall ("movement").

53. *KG* 6.76: If "He who has ascended above all the heavens" has "accomplished everything" (Eph. 4.10), it is evident that each of the ranks of celestial

powers has truly learned the *logoi* concerning providence, by which they rapidly impel towards virtue and the knowledge of God those who are beneath them."

54. *KG* 3.42: "Contemplation is spiritual knowledge of the things which have been and will be: it is this which causes the *nous* to ascend to its first rank."

55. Evagrius, *KG* 1.27.

56. Evagrius, *S-Ps.* 72.23, no. 15; cf. Pitra 3:72.23.

57. Evagrius, *KG* 6.43.

58. Evagrius, *Letter to Melania* 57, "But because of his love for us, God was born of a woman . . . in order to give us a second birth—a birth to which blessing and justice belong." Vitestam, *Seconde partie*, 23; Bunge, *Briefe aus der Wüste*, 324.

59. Evagrius, *Letter to Melania* 56 and 58, "(56) he descended and endured all that we had acquired since we stepped out of our nature: that is, everything from conception to death. . . . (58) Since we have corrupted our nature by our free will, we have come to our present conception and birth which are subject to the curse. But he, remaining what he is, by his grace has taken upon himself with birth all that follows birth until death. . . . He frees us from them in that he who had not sinned took these things voluntarily upon himself; for we are unable to ascend above them by ourselves. . . . But not only did he not remain in [things subject to the curse], but he also enables us to ascend out of them; because he, as we said, descended to them in his love—not because of [his] sin." Vitestam, *Seconde partie*, 22–24; Bunge, *Briefe aus der Wüste*, 323–25.

60. Stewart, "Imageless Prayer," 181–86.

61. Evagrius, *On Prayer* 55: "One who loves God always converses (συνομιλεῖ) with him as Father." There exists as yet no critical edition of Evagrius's *On Prayer.* The best available version is that of Tugwell, based on six manuscripts and PG 79:1165–1200; Nicodemus the Hagiorite and Makarios, *Φιλοκαλία*, 1:176–89.

62. Evagrius, *On Prayer* 3: "to stretch out unalterably towards its own Master and converse (συνομιλεῖν) with him without any intermediary (μηδενὸς μεσιτεύοντος)."

63. Evagrius, *On Prayer* 4: "you want to see him who is above all perception and all concepts and converse with him (συνόμιλος αὐτῷ)."

64. Evagrius, *On Prayer* 35: "Undistracted prayer is the highest noetic activity of the *nous* (ἄκρα νόησις νοός)."

65. Evagrius, *On Prayer* 34: Τί γὰρ αὐτοῦ ἀνώτερον τοῦ τῷ θεῷ προσομιλεῖν καὶ τῇ πρὸς αὐτὸν συνουσίᾳ περισπᾶσθαι (Tugwell, 8).

66. Evagrius, *On Prayer* 61: Εἰ θεολόγος εἶ, προσεύξῃ ἀληθῶς, καὶ εἰ ἀληθῶς προσεύξῃ, θεολόγος εἶ (Tugwell, 12).

67. Evagrius, *Letter* 20.1 (Frankenberg, 579).

68. Evagrius, *S-Ps.* 5.13, no. 12: "And the knowledge of God is divided into two parts, practice and contemplation. To practice belongs the *shield of favor*, while of contemplation is *the crown*"; cf. PG 79:1173.8. *S-Prov.* 1.9, no. 7: "here *crown* and *necklace* signify knowledge." *S-Prov.* 4.9, no. 44: "The *crown of graces* and the *crown of delights* are the knowledge of God." *Monks* 27: "An ornament for the head: a crown; an ornament for the heart: knowledge of God." *KG* 3.49: "The *nous* will not be crowned with the crown of essential knowledge, if it has not cast far from it ignorance of the two struggles."

69. Compare Gregory of Nyssa's *Commentary on the Song of Songs*, and the frequent use of texts from the Song by Ambrose and Cyril of Jerusalem in their catechetical homilies.

70. Evagrius, *Virgin*, 11, 43, 52, 55; *Thoughts* 42; *Letter* 20.1; *S-Prov.* 23.18, no. 256.

71. Evagrius, *Thoughts* 42 (Gehín et al., 296–97).

72. Evagrius, *S-Ps.* 138.16(2), no. 8: Βιβλίον Θεοῦ ἐστιν ἡ θεωρία σωμάτων καὶ ἀσωμάτων ἐν ᾧ πέφυκε διὰ τῆς γνώσεως γράφεσθαι νοῦς καθαρός; cf. PG 12:1662.

73. Stewart, "Imageless Prayer," 173–82.

CHAPTER 4

Evagrius and Authority

Blossom Stefaniw

Problematizing a Legacy

Evagrius's legacy is not what he himself would have expected. In his thirties, Evagrius was rising up the ranks of those jockeying to define and enforce correct doctrine, as Christians became more and more able to mobilize imperial authority. From the time of his death about twenty years later, Evagrius's teachings came into disrepute and were eventually condemned in the very city where he had once made such a fine showing as a promising young deacon debating the Arians.[1] It would be easy to explain this clash between his early career and his posthumous legacy by suggesting that Evagrius in fact became less orthodox later in his life. In order to be coherent, such a proposal would require that orthodoxy is an independently existing quality that accrues to certain teachings or beliefs and not others. One could then survey Evagrius's writings and quantify the degree to which they manifest said quality.

Treating orthodoxy as a stable and unified thing-in-the-world is problematic, whether we seek it in Evagrius's own day or in the period of later doctrinal controversy in connection with which he was finally condemned (540–53). What constitutes right belief was never univocally resolved nor consistently enforced, whether among bishops and priests, teachers and ascetics, or lay people. Orthodoxy is neither a state of affairs nor a set of doctrines and practices curated by an institution that always could or always did assess religious belief throughout the empire. Orthodoxy is more aptly treated as an ideological point of reference, a notion of right religion as a constant, unified, and universal truth that served as the discursive condition for combining religious and imperial authority. While this sort of real, true, unchanging, solid orthodoxy never happened in time and space, it is still immensely important to late antique religious history because it is the point of reference around which major religious debates revolve. Casting someone as a divergent individual whose teachings are a threat to right belief can thus be seen less as a diagnosis of an objective state of affairs and more as part of a larger argument about the ownership and use of authority. Evagrius's legacy among those who see themselves as representatives of orthodoxy should not be read as a matter of the lonely genius finding his work misunderstood and rejected by an unyielding totalitarian institution. The clash between Evagrius and representatives of orthodoxy from Theophilus to Justinian was a conflict in which *both* parties considered themselves entitled to define what is true Christianity. If this is the case, Evagrius's condemnation can be reread, and perhaps better explained, not as a mismatch between Evagrius's teachings and orthodox teachings, but as a clash over the ownership of truth.

In the following, I will argue that the long accumulation of anti-Evagrian sentiment eventually leading to his condemnation can be read as a means of undermining his legacy as an authority and thus drawing boundaries around who has the right to articulate religious truth for all Christians. Implicit in this reading is a claim that Evagrius, far from being an otherworldly recluse, wielded religious authority of a type and scope that rivaled the authority of bishops and other representatives of ecclesial authority. This claim can be made plausible by means of an examination of the sort of authority Evagrius cultivated and deployed in his writings, especially his ascetic teachings. Evagrius's authority can be broken down into the claim to teaching authority evident in his practice as a monastic teacher and writer, and the command of logistical resources that allowed for his role in forming the religiously ambitious to proliferate and expand.

This hypothesis may lead to a more satisfactory explanation for Evagrius's orthodoxy being called into question than the most frequently found claim that he was condemned because he was an Origenist.[2] Explaining the condemnation of Evagrius in terms of his "Origenism" is to explain it in exactly the same terms as his opponents, which begs the question: it is not apparent why some of those passing forward ideas derived from Origen are condemned while others are not. There is no necessary causal connection in this period between writing things that seem to reflect a friendly reading of Origen and ending up condemned as a heretic. One might bring to mind cases like that of Rufinus, who was certainly targeted for his sympathy to Origen but who was never condemned. Another exmple is that of Gregory Thaumaturgus, who is treated as a saint by his biographer, Gregory of Nyssa, who promoted his reputation as the founder of Christianity in Cappadocia in his *Life of Gregory Thaumaturgus.* Gregory remains entirely unproblematic for ecclesial authority, despite his close personal ties to Origen and his praise of Origen's exegetical practices and speculative methods as expressed in the *Farewell Address to Origen*. "Being an Origenist" is not an adequate explanation for anyone having been condemned.

A more complicated view of orthodoxy will be necessary to make sense of how Evagrius, who certainly considered himself to be explaining true religion in his later writings, and whose earlier doctrinal positions were indeed in line with those ratified as orthodox at ecumenical councils, can be condemned by the emperor Justinian, who likewise considered himself to be the defender of right religion, and likewise in line with the decisions of ecumenical councils. We must look for something other than an objective decrease in orthodoxy to explain Evagrius's condemnation. One might proceed instead on the hypothesis that, in order to be condemned, one has to do something that is, however directly or indirectly, problematic to the interests and aims of those individuals most persistent and effective in claiming to represent the one true church. Pursuing the question of why aspersions are cast upon

Evagrius's orthodoxy is to pursue the question of how his teachings or writings could have posed a problem for those pursuing an agenda of consolidating their own claim to define right belief.

In mustering my argument, I will draw primarily on the Greek ascetic corpus.[3] These works all manifest the sort of authority Evagrius exercised as an ascetic teacher in the desert, whether he addressed himself to beginner anchorites, monks in community, learned friends abroad, or more advanced monks. Second, I will briefly synthesize this reading with the earliest acts of agitation against Evagrius's followers by the bishop Theophilus of Alexandria in an effort to connect my argument to the earlier period of anti-Origenism between 390 and 410. In order to connect to the period surrounding Evagrius's actual condemnation, an effort will be made to see how Evagrius's conception and exercise of authority, added to his persistent influence, may have conflicted with the religious agenda of Justinian and his associates. It should be noted that this does not constitute a claim that Evagrius's exercise of a certain type of authority *rather than* any specific doctrinal teaching led to his rejection. An explanation in terms of doctrine and one mustered in terms of authority are on different analytical levels, given that putting forward teachings on the nature of Christ, the fate of souls, or the composition of the Trinity are themselves authoritative acts.

I will proceed from an approach to authority informed by neopragmatism and that thus need not be tied to a perfectly disambiguated and universally applicable definition of authority-as-such. Rather, a pragmatist notion of authority concerns itself with how authority works within the specific parameters of a given historical setting and sees authority, like everything else, as a contingent and provisional tool that human beings use (whether by having it or assenting to it or engaging with it) to achieve certain ends and to solve those problems that seem presently compelling.[4] A pragmatist approach raises no claims to identify the nature of authority, but instead examines authority as a tool within a context of experimentation and imperfect information, asking how it was built, and how it worked, and what people were trying to do with it. My examination of Evagrian authority thus focuses on how something more or less like the ability to facilitate the distribution of prime religious resources is implemented, what its terms and structures are, and how it is applied. In the context at hand, the prime resources desired by ascetic Christians around Evagrius are expertise in the spiritual life, exceptional spiritual status, reliable means of protecting and cultivating the soul, and secure attachment to a religious patron able to supply these resources. In fourth-century Egypt and among ascetically ambitious people "gnostics," Manichaeans, philosophers, rabbinic teachers, and diverse Christians all offered accounts of how the soul could be rightly cultivated and guaranteed to be moving in the right direction. Such rehabilitation, cultivation, and refinement of the soul was one valued resource that multiple parties were raising competing claims to command. Inasmuch as Evagrius can provide these resources, as much as he can offer others a dependable way to attain them and be recognized for attaining them, his authority will be stable and valuable in that context.

This way of approaching authority provides an unaccustomed but fruitful alternative to the Weberian heritage in the study of authority and power in religion. Taking a Weberian approach could too easily encourage a pursuit of a definition of the nature or type of authority we see Evagrius exercising, rather than tracing out the terms, modes, and media of his strategies of authority. Given the priority of this latter agenda, it is only of secondary importance whether a person is offering to distribute and ensure prized religious resources from inside or outside an institution, with or without heredity or bureaucracy as legitimation. A natural animosity between charismatic authority and institutional authority does not seem to be the case in the particular historical context of late antiquity. More tellingly, *both* Evagrius *and* the representatives of orthodoxy who oppose him claim all three Weberian types of authority. Evagrius is granted charismatic authority by his immediate disciples and supporters, but had also been ordained, lending him institutional (legal-rational) authority. He also associates himself with recognized leaders including Gregory Nazianzen, Basil, Athanasius, Serapion of Thmuis, and Didymus the Blind as spiritual ancestors, thus also at least putting in a bid for traditional authority.[5] Bishops of his day aspired to manifest the virtues of the ascetic and philosopher, thereby claiming both charismatic and institutional authority, and also conceived of themselves as successors to the apostles, claiming traditional authority.[6] Thus a Weberian typology does not provide a way to differentiate Evagrius from ecclesial authority, but that fact itself suggests that the problem should be sought less in some native animosity between the charismatic monk-philosopher and the institutionally legitimated bishops, and more in the neighborhood of competition and rivalry for the same scale or quality or scope of authority.

Evagrian Authority

Examination of the Greek ascetic corpus yields three broad fields in which Evagrius deploys a claim to authority. In this section, I will examine rhetorical strategies that motivate adherence to his guidance, argue for the value of his authority, or display command of valued spiritual resources. The two most prominent rhetorical strategies are metaphors of peril and armament in discussion of the spiritual life, and claims to knowledge of the really real. These first two strategies can be seen as properly rhetorical and properly generated by Evagrius himself as an author. The third field in which authority is manifested is both rhetorical and logistical and includes material resources and social networks that enable proliferation and universalization. This latter field requires special attention because it negates the traditional perception of Evagrius as living in isolation and brings his authority into contact with ecclesial jursidiction outside of the desert. Because he has not only rhetoric but also material and social resources at his disposal, Evagrius's claim to authority conflicts with that of anyone else, also raising a claim to define and describe religious life in universal terms. Such a conflict can then become an actual confrontation when and where the other party has the capacity to contradict Evagrius's claims in a manner that is public and normative.[7]

Armament and Anxiety

The pervasive agonistic metaphors in Evagrian writings have been duly noted in the literature already and are so lushly distributed throughout his works that it will be necessary to differentiate four subcategories within this rhetoric. In the *Letter to Eulogios* 3, Evagrius refers to the "wrestling school of the desert" and cautions Eulogios against being "caught without training."[8] While such athletic metaphors are frequent, portraying his readers in militant terms as frontline soldiers or as civilians in the midst of a war zone is an even more pervasive trope.[9] Second, Evagrius persistently articulates the peril in which the monk finds himself and reminds his disciples of dangers of all kinds. Third, and well in line with this sense of urgency and danger expressed in his rhetoric, Evagrius also implicitly promises that he can provide the monk with the necessary means of self-defense.

Evagrius also paints stark contrasts between the life of virtue and its opposite, casting the ascetic pursuit of virtue as the means of proper soldierly training and armament against attacks from demons. The sense of danger Evagrius articulates is highly empathetic. Evagrius is working in a religious context in which being attacked by demons was commonly feared, and within a tradition of ascetic life that had long been cast in militant or adversarial terms, as a fight or a struggle, as combat with the body or with demons. Given this context, the repertoire of metaphors at his disposal already tends in an agonistic direction. What is significant for the present discussion is that carrying forward this rhetorical framework and casting himself as someone who can help the beleaguered monk is, precisely because of the heritage he is reinforcing in his rhetoric, part of the foundation for Evagrius's authority.

Evagrius foregrounds the fears and dangers connected to the spiritual life and uses them as an argument for the urgency of engaging in the ascetic battle. In his treatise *Eulogios*, he praises fear as "the beginning of wisdom."[10] Reasons to be anxious are everywhere, not only in the examples of horrible things that have happened even to very senior monks who fell prey to demons,[11] but also in the very high density and quantity of things that are dangerous. Prayer itself is an undertaking subject to invasion by demonic delusions.[12] Even the typical symptoms of sleep-deprivation, which Evagrius describes very aptly as having cold eyelids and a feeling of weight on the top of the head when trying to concentrate on reading, is portrayed as a particularly egregious demon.[13] There is little Evagrius considers it safe to think about. It is dangerous to remember good times with one's family, to wonder how one's siblings or parents are getting on, to get bored, to worry about one's health, or to wish one had something nice to eat.[14] As Evagrius explains especially in the *Praktikos* and *Thoughts*, such preoccupations are *logismoi* and constitute examples of acedia, sadness, avarice, or gluttony. One is not safe even among fellow monks withdrawn from the world, because one is still besieged by the demons through one's own body and mind. Everything is dangerous, even one's own mind and thoughts. The danger of going mad is referred to repeatedly, for example in *Eulogios* 31: "(Satan) promises to sanctify some of those who having received the faith missed the mark regarding the truth and became mentally deranged."[15] Again in *Prayer*, Evagrius admonishes the monk: "Hold no desire to see angels or powers or Christ with the senses, lest you go completely insane, taking a wolf to be the shepherd and worshipping your enemies, the demons."[16] The fear of thus missing the mark makes the need for a competent guide and teacher, like Evagrius, all the more desperate. Without Evagrius, one is left unarmed in the face of grave danger, and one could fail to understand even one's own thoughts and intentions.

Not only is danger ever-present, it is also never-ending. The battle with the demons is unceasing, and the state of the soul is never good enough to allow the monk to slacken his efforts. The monk is to keep watch over himself and report any disturbing internal processes to the master.[17] The unrelenting siege state in which the monk finds himself lays the foundation for constant anxiety and necessitates a corresponding escalation of efforts. It also provides for endless insecurity, as one can never know whether one is actually advancing or merely being persecuted by a demon of vainglory giving the impression of having advanced.[18] Only the teacher, or his proxy in the form of the diagnostic tools laid out in his writings, can ensure that one's progress is legitimate. Since the disciple's perception of his experience in prayer is not reliable, and since his progress must be assessed by the teacher before he can receive more advanced teachings, the success in the spiritual life that is so urgently needed is also hardly attainable.

I argue that the *Antirrhetikos* can be seen as a facility for stockpiling verbal and mental arms in readiness for an inevitable onslaught. Evagrius is equipping people, and, implicitly, asserting his ability to provide the means of self-defense in the face of attacks by demons. The particular set of weapons explicated in the *Antirrhetikos* links to two aspects of Evagrius's claim to knowledge of the really real, which will be discussed below, for it asserts the defining and cataloging authority of the one who knows the nature of the demons and their works, and also the insight into scripture that allows Evagrius the discernment with which to prescribe certain verses of scripture as remedies for specific demonic disruptions. This use of scripture, along with his interpretation of it in terms of his own ascetic ideology, might suggest one reason that allowing Evagrius's authority to be seen as legitimate is a high-stakes question, as it constitutes a rewriting of scripture and an individual claim to know what should properly be done with scripture (a way of bidding for authority by no means originating with Evagrius). The manner in which authority is mustered in this work has already been outlined by David Brakke, and includes not only the claim to expert application of scripture but also claims to be an experienced fighter against demons and self-identification as a representative of a valuable monastic heritage.[19] In the analytical scheme I am using here with regard to the larger ascetic corpus, the latter two claims would fall into the category of armament and special knowledge, because they substantiate Evagrius's claim to be able to supply the monk with legitimate and dependable means of self-defense.

In the second letter to Eulogios, Evagrius gives definitions and descriptions of the vices and virtues in terms of binary oppositions, a common tool for evaluating and directing human behavior in terms that purport to reflect nature and reality.[20] Within Evagrius's own heritage, especially in the paraenetic and two-ways traditions of ethical instruction, we can see this ideological and directive aspect in the use of binary oppositions at work, laying out two incompatible paths or pairing up vices as inversions or perversions of the virtues.[21] Evagrius goes beyond this stripped-down, either-or rhetoric of ethical direction and invests the virtues and vices with qualities and characteristics that motivate the desired relation to them. For Evagrius, the virtues are manly, athletic, controlled, agonistic, and dominant, expressing soldierly opposition and solidarity within the ranks. "Abstinence is a bridle for the stomach, a scourge of immoderation, a balance of due proportion,"[22] and "Chastity is . . . an axe for wantonness, a charioteer for the eyes, an overseer for one's thinking, a circumcision of thoughts,"[23] and again

"Patience is a shield for prudence, a tribunal for anger, a surgery for the heart, admonition of the over-confident, calm for the troubled, a harbour from storms."[24]

The vices are described through metaphors suggesting they are out of control, perverted, and vulgar, and that they constitute a pollution or invasion of the mind. For example, gluttony is "the mother of fornication . . . the relaxation of fasting, . . . a dissolute fawn, unbridled madness . . . weakness of the body."[25] Fornication is "that which softens the heart in advance, a furnace of lustful burning . . . unnatural activity, a form covered in shadows, an intertwining wrought in the imagination, a bed of dreams,"[26] whereas "Anger is a plundering of prudence, a destruction of one's state, a confusion of nature, a form turned savage . . . a mother of wild beasts."[27] While the virtues are conformed to the masculine ideal, the vices are insane, soft, hallucinatory, destructive, and inhuman. In line with Platonic tradition, control of the passions is described on the metaphor of the properly dominated horse:

> A docile horse, lean in body, never throws its rider, for the horse that is restrained yields to the bit and is compelled by the hand of the one holding the reins; the body is subdued with hunger and vigil and does not jump when a thought mounts upon it, nor does it snort when it is moved by an impassioned impulse.[28]

Knowledge of the Really Real

Raising a claim to knowledge of the nature of things is a very simple but very effective means of asserting authority. Evagrius's interest in penetrating to higher realities is, like his agonistic rhetoric, easily recognizable and highly pervasive in his writings. However, the role it plays in manifesting and substantiating his authority is both subtle and potent. Evagrius deploys a claim to knowledge of reality in a variety of ways, including not only facilitating the promised fulfillment of the ascetic life in which the person will be able to apprehend the real directly, but also in his constant defining, describing, and cataloging of how the virtues and the vices work. A claim to have a specialized grip on reality is also implicit in his scriptural interpretation and in his praxis of discernment and diagnosis of others' mental and spiritual condition. Evagrius also defines his followers themselves when he articulates a specific identity for them and tells them who they are.[29]

Evagrius claims expert knowledge of how things work spiritually based on his own experience and learning and his identification with an esteemed monastic lineage. In the prologue to the second letter to Eulogios, for example, he argues for his own identity as a capable teacher of the ascetic life, having "not come to this task because of works that we have done, but having as our model the sound discourses which we have heard from the fathers, we have been equally a witness to some of their deeds."[30] For all his rhetorical modesty, Evagrius is locating himself in a key position as personal witness to the teachings and practices of older fathers and thus as one who holds superior knowledge of the ascetic life.

In the same work, Evagrius deploys the cataloging, defining, and describing techniques that are familiar, in more elaborate form, from Epiphanius in his war on heresy, but Evagrius directs these weapons at the question of vices and virtues.[31] This custom of cataloging mental states or moral problems can also be seen very frequently in both his speculative and his ascetical works, not least in *Prayer*.[32] By defining the causal relations between the *logismoi* that can afflict the monk, Evagrius establishes a moral taxonomy within which the person must understand himself. Evagrius gives several definitions of the monk according to his moral taxonomy in the same work: "A monk is one who is separated from all and united with all," or "A monk is one who esteems himself as one with all people because he ever believes he sees himself in each person." Evagrius instructs his monks through substitute beatitudes, confirming his readiness to assert knowledge of his readers' true identity.[33] *Reflections* likewise provides definitions of the mind, instruction, a demonic thought, an anchorite, and so on.[34]

Regardless of the object at which it is directed, this rhetorical technique necessarily constitutes a claim to authority. This is what some present-day philosophers would refer to as a regime of truth, emphasizing how putting forth a definition as a true account of how things are is an act of power such that any opposing or diverging opinion must appear as just that, a departure from what is obvious and normal.[35] The claim to realism is bolstered up by the rhetoric of definition and further strengthened by the specific procedure that Evagrius employs in his second letter to Eulogios: "In what follows we have set these down in brief as opposed, contrary, and antithetical to one another."[36] This provides Evagrius's account of the virtues and vices with dialectical structure, lending it a logical substance that resists questioning.

The main work of the ascetic life is prayer, and the ability to pray in a sophisticated way is the primary skill that monks are trying to develop. Evagrius provides instruction on advanced forms of prayer, again supplying a desirable resource. The *On Prayer* includes a sequence on the nitty-gritty of the conditions for pure prayer, its mechanics, and problems to expect. Not only do we again find the rhetoric of armament and anxiety seen above ("Be on your guard for the snares of your adversaries," "Stand on your guard") but also advanced technical points on how to assess any perceptions one may experience while progressing towards pure prayer. Using biologizing and diagnostic language, Evagrius points out, for example, how to spot a demon manipulating the mind to produce the impression of having seen God. This can be recognized by stimulation of the brain and "palpitations in the blood vessels." Evagrius goes further and analyzes exactly how this false impression is produced:

> I think that the demon, by touching the spot just mentioned, alters the light around the mind as he wishes, and in this way the passion of vainglory is moved towards a thought that forms the mind heedlessly towards localizing the divine and essential knowledge. . . . (The mind) . . . supposes to be divine the manifestation that arises within it under the influence of the demon, who employs great cunning in altering through the brain the light associated with it and giving the mind a form, as we said previously.[37]

Here Evagrius articulates the very finest fine points of the highest pinnacle of the monastic journey in such a way that he both disrupts any security or satisfaction to be derived from the experience of the contemplative vision of pure light and casts himself in the role of expert diagnostician with knowledge of even the most subtle and insidious demonic manipulations.

In *Thoughts*, the reader is briefed on the mechanisms of the intellect (it is impossible to entertain two thoughts at the same time) and is instructed on how exactly one may discern at precisely which point a demon has infiltrated the mind.[38] One must differentiate between thought, mind, object, and image in order to identify how the demon is gaining traction and ascertain whether one's thoughts are actually produced by "that which is not an object with substantial subsistence, nor the mental representation of an object, nor even the incorporeal mind, but a pleasure hostile to humanity, born of free will, and compelling the mind to make improper use of the creatures of God."[39] Here again there is the expression of special expertise and knowledge of the nature of things. Evagrius knows what is and is not hostile to humanity, and he knows what constitutes proper or improper use of the creatures of God. That is exactly the sort of epistemological bank (creation, human nature, the will of God, reason, reality) that one needs in order to shore up a viable authoritative stance.

In a feedback system of attachment and commitment, the efficacy of Evagrius's advice is conditional upon the quality and purity of the person receiving it:

> But these things [deliberately contemplating the relative role of humans in relation to demons and angels in order to "greatly wound" the demon] work for those who have attained some measure of purification and see to a certain degree the reasons of created beings. People who are impure, on the other hand, do not know the contemplation of these things, and even if they should learn of this from others and repeat it like an incantation, they will not make themselves heard because of the abundance of dust and noise raised in the battle on account of the passions.[40]

Since Evagrius's advice is in line with the nature of things, the only circumstances under which it can fail to be effective is if the person receiving the advice fails to live up to the required moral standard. In fact, Evagrius is inviting the monk to monitor himself according to the same order of the universe that Evagrius himself is presenting, such that assent to his authority is the means of self-preservation in the face of demonic attack. The efficacy of this technique is conditional upon the monk having already ordered himself according to the standard of purity that Evagrius teaches, and also having attained some sense of really real reality, which Evagrius refers to here as being able to "see to a certain degree the reasons of created beings." Evagrius argues again for this sort of internalization and submission to the accurate reflection of reality manifest in his teachings when he says, "My own proof in most cases is the heart of my reader, especially if it possesses understanding and experience in the monastic life."[41] Thus Evagrius's expert knowledge extends into the very heart of his reader.

Evagrius both locates the monk in a condition of immanent danger through demonic attacks and provides the necessary means of self-defense in texts like the *Antirrhetikos*. In the same way, Evagrius both asserts his own expertise in the nature and workings of virtues and vices and the progress of the soul, and provides, in texts like the *Praktikos* especially, the means of engaging with this knowledge as real and urgent by evaluating the actions of the intellect and the passions.[42] This could be understood as more of the desperate-times empowerment of the person seen in the section on armament above, but it could equally well be understood as a medium through which the person is encouraged to assent to and internalize Evagrius's account of the nature of the intellect and the forces acting within it and then to self-administer Evagrius's technique for dealing with those forces. Evagrius is providing a valued resource for managing the problems and dangers of the monastic life.

A good example of this dynamic can be seen in his teachings on impassibility. Using a diagnostic tone, Evagrius encourages the monk to observe himself and watch for certain symptoms. He can then compare his condition to Evagrius's diagnostic criteria and evaluate it accordingly. In the *Praktikos*, a whole work dedicated to instructing the monk on how to achieve impassibility, guidelines for discerning whether one is getting close to an impassible state are set out. For example, "When the mind begins to practice prayer without distraction, then all the warfare is concentrated around the irascible part of the soul by night and by day." Thus if the monk is experiencing increased disruptions of the irascible soul (such as feelings of anger), he can locate himself on a trajectory near the point of breaking through into a higher quality of prayer. In the same way, should awareness of the irascible soul recede altogether, the monk can safely conclude that he has indeed "completed the work of the practical life."[43] In the more advanced teaching text *On Thoughts*, Evagrius gives specific advice on how to interpret one's inner state. If a monk imagines being given the keys of the First City but wards off the thought using the technique that Evagrius has just outlined (thinking about the right order of things instead), then he is being assaulted by demons but is coping correctly. If on the other hand he imagines being given the keys "of just any city taken at random and he works it out in the same way, he is blessed with impassibility."[44] In both this passage and the one preceding it, Evagrius exhorts the reader to focus on correct technique and generalize the examples given to "all the impure thoughts."[45] Through this sort of self-monitoring, the authority of Evagrius over the individual soul can proliferate into contexts where he himself is not present and can be mediated through texts like those under examination here, so that the direct oral teaching of the master to his disciples no longer limits the scale on which this sort of authority can be deployed.

Another forum in which Evagrius asserts knowledge of higher realities can be found in his engagement with scripture. There are three ways that Evagrius's authority is manifested or deployed through his claim to expert knowledge of the Bible. First, Evagrius's demonstration of the ability to perform noetic exegesis and thus to interpret the Bible in a more penetrating and sophisticated way than others is especially significant in a context where the Bible is considered the revelation of the true nature of reality. The person who can cause the text to render up its revelation has privileged access to this knowledge and is in a position to guide others towards it, such that this type of exegesis is frequently found among ascetic teachers.[46] Evagrius's exegetical expertise has been observed in his use of scripture for purposes of self-defense as in the *Antirrhetikos*, and can also be seen in his exegetical works.[47] Second, Evagrius claims for himself the ability to determine who is ready to receive instruction on the noetic content of scripture and who will be taught to master that most advanced exegetical skill.[48] That is, Evagrius claims the right to assess the spiritual and epistemic adequacy of others and the privilege of withholding access to a prized spiritual resource. Third, Evagrius teaches the spiritual life through commentary on the Bible using noetic exegesis, thus making his own area of proficiency (ascetic formation) correspond to the highest meaning of the text.[49] Evagrius is, in the way he relates himself to scripture, banking up a prime resource, and then raising the stakes once more in that he conceals and carefully doses out his knowledge of the reality contained in scripture and how to access it. Evagrius is doing a very competent job of controlling and mediating an extraordinarily valuable resource in the stance he takes up with regard to the interpretation of scripture. Only a highly advanced ascetic can interpret scripture adequately, and only knowledge of the revelation contained in scripture can ensure advancement in the ascetic and spiritual life. This way of structuring access to and competence with scripture is something that Evagrius generates rhetorically and reenforces socially. He must manage this claim in a context in which there are many competing claims by other religious leaders who likewise cast themselves as expert readers of scripture. Further, even the model of scripture as a deposit of divine revelation is contested in the fourth century by those who insist on the sufficiency and value of a surface reading and polemicize about the foolishness of allegorical readings.[50]

Evagrius claims knowledge of the identity of his readers. He demonstrates this through making statements of identity. In introducing the *Praktikos*, Evagrius differentiates monks from "other people," setting them apart as exceptional.[51] One highly articulated case of this can be found in the prologue of the letter to Eulogios:

> Those who hold the land of heaven as their own by means of ascetic labours do not fix their gaze on the stomach, nor on concern for perishable goods, like those who offer prayers for the sake of their own personal profit, "thinking that piety is a means of gain" (1 Tim. 6:5). On the contrary, by means of an intellectual vision they participate in a nourishing light from the highest realities, like the incorporeal beings who are surrounded by the radiance of the light of the divine glory. Therefore, you too, Eulogios, mystic initiate in the virtues, in nourishing your intellectual substance on the brilliance of the supreme realities, strip off the weight of the flesh by

> collecting your thoughts, for you know that the matter of the flesh constitutes the nourishment of the thoughts. Having restrained the wiles of the flesh with the sharp instrument of ascetic labours, you choose me to be the voice of your works against the flesh, and if it were not foolhardy to break an injunction of charity, I would refuse to sail on this voyage.[52]

In effect, Evagrius is telling Eulogios which sort of person he is, how far he has come, and how far he has yet to go. This is done on the basis of an either/or rhetorical structure differentiating "those" to whom Eulogios belongs from people who "fix their gaze on the stomach" or entertain "concern for perishable goods." Evagrius then unpacks the characteristics of those among whom Eulogios is to count himself: they are privy to an intellectual vision of higher realities, they are "like incorporeal beings surrounded by divine glory." This is taken as an argument from which conclusions may be drawn. Eulogios is exhorted to undertake the ascetic life in order to move from being an initiate to being able to enjoy full membership in this spiritual elite. Eulogios is identified as a sojourner struggling for full emancipation from the flesh. This rhetoric sets up a discrepancy between who Eulogios should be and who he is now and problematizes that discrepancy. Evagrius presents himself as the person who is able to provide resolution, to get Eulogios across that telling gap. Not only does Evagrius know who his reader is, he knows what to do in order to make him who he should be. Indeed, by the end of the letter, Evagrius refers to Eulogios as "suppliant of the Holy Trinity," asserting again the tenuous state of Eulogios's spiritual status while suggesting proximity to some final resolution.[53]

The significance of this sort of definition of the person as an act of authority has been articulated most recently in the work of philosophers and other theorists concerned with gender. The act of defining who a person is, and with that, who they should be and should not be, is done in a tone of obvious common sense and is insidious precisely because of that.[54] Evagrius's statements of identity pull his readers off balance and press upon them the task of shedding their ordinary selves (the flesh and everyday concerns) and pursuing a virtually unreachable goal of becoming able to attain knowledge of the highest realities. By disrupting their own self-perception, Evagrius makes his readers and disciples all the more dependent on him for assessment of the degree to which they are or are not adequately becoming who they should be. Further, in identifying monks and other ascetics as exceptional, Evagrius is implicitly identifying ordinary people, unconcerned with higher realities, as inadequate. While this is a familiar trope from exhortations to commit to the philosophical life, it is highly problematic to a church that intends to universalize itself to such a degree that ordinary people have a legitimate place within it.

Proliferation

Evagrius's ability to deploy his authority outside the desert is often obscured by the popular modern image of Evagrius as an otherworldly figure, isolated with his prayers and thoughts in the desert. What I refer to here as proliferation includes both logistical factors like support provided through his social connections and rhetorical factors that tend towards universalizing, that is, asserting the applicability of his teachings not only to monks in his own community but to monks elsewhere and to everyone. This topic will lead us to the problem of incompatibility with the aims of the fifth-century church because Evagrius's willingness to instruct on the right way of life for both monks and ambitious laypeople would tend to constitute a breach of jurisdiction over and against a body that itself wishes to define the true Christian life as it applies to and should be followed by everyone. In his ascetic writings, Evagrius is exercising authority that presupposes his right to form and define legitimate religious people. His diagnostic and mentoring activities are done on a freelance and elective basis and thus may well be an irritant to an institution that asserts its own exclusive right to define persons as religiously legitimate or otherwise, and requires that submission of the self to the sort of diagnosis that Evagrius is so skilled at cultivating be compulsory for everyone.

Far from being an esoteric teacher huddled in a cave with a few loyal souls, Evagrius was a key part of a large and privileged network of religious leaders. This included ascetic scholars like Rufinus and

Melania and the famous fellow monks like the Four Tall Brothers. Evagrius's youthful connections to the Cappadocians may also have continued to play a role in maintaining his reputation.[55] These relationships, especially with the wealthy Melania, gave him access to funding but also, more importantly, a mechanism for circulating and distributing his writings. They also provided several ready-made audiences, whether in the monastic communities around Rufinus and Melania or in circles of urban ascetics commissioning writings from him. After his death, his work also achieved very good distribution through disciples like Cassian and Palladius. Indeed, Evagrius was the first to use the instructional genre observable in the ascetic corpus in written form,[56] and it is significant that, apart from the *Kephalaia gnostika*, his writings are readily comprehensible and aimed at practical application to ascetic discipline. This means that Evagrius has a medium at his disposal (not just writing, but writing that is rhetorically effective and, for those who saw themselves as struggling forward in the ascetic life, a dependable resource for confronting their problems) that has high reception potential. He also has, or is posthumously received into, a distribution system of a caliber and variety that could effectively convey his writings to a large audience.

In thinking of guidance in the ascetic life as a coveted resource for many religious people in this period, one might say that Evagrius both owns and knows how to use the means of production, and he produces very much. This in itself is a potential threat to any contemporary religious institution aiming at homogenizing religious life on its own terms and at consolidating its own claim to authority. Since Evagrius's writings were most widely circulated after his death, and since the proliferation of his teachings went hand in hand with Evagrius's continued popularity and influence into the sixth century, his rival claim to authority and the right to teach all Christians, rather than direct interpersonal conflict during his life, may explain his condemnation and its late date.

The three treatises *Monks*, *Virgin*, and *Exhortations to Monks* constitute a proliferation of Evagrius's exercise of authority, enabled by deposit in writing, through which Evagrius moves his teachings past his own location among anchorites and offers instruction to monks in community and virgins. While it is plausible that these texts were originally solicited by Rufinus, such that Evagrius, as he composed the text, was by no means breaking out of existing social networks or obtruding himself into communities uninvited, in the longer legacy, after Rufinus and Evagrius had both died, the text is still there with teachings directed at monks in community. One might object that Athanasius also addresses himself to both foreign monks and to anchorites and communities in his own region, not to mention instructing other bishops and lay Christians in general, without being (permanently) condemned as a heretic. The important difference in the reception of both sets of writings is that Athanasius is a bishop, and his obtruding himself into monastic life is compatible with the ideas of proper episcopal jurisdiction in the sixth-century church, whereas monks like Evagrius taking on the same role is undesirable.

What must be the most disquieting breach of jurisdiction from the point of view of the church is the alacrity with which Evagrius universalizes his teachings. Evagrius's *Praktikos*, *Gnostikos*, and *Kephalaia gnostika* is not only a curriculum for specialized monastic formation. In his own description of the trilogy, Evagrius calls it a definition of "what Christianity is."[57] Evagrius is arrogating to himself the right to set out how one might achieve the true Christian life. The first two sentences of the *Praktikos* make the goal of Christianity synonymous with the goal of the monastic life: "Christianity is the doctrine of Christ our Savior. It is comprised of the practical, the natural, and the theological," and, "The kingdom of heaven is impassibility of the soul accompanied by true knowledge of beings."[58] If the goal of the monastic life (impassibility) is the same as the goal of the Christian life (the kingdom of heaven), and if Evagrius is a master of the monastic life and in control of the key resources needed to survive in it, then Evagrius is an authority for all Christians, including clergy and monks in community and ordinary people. This sort of claim to explain the true Christian life is not compatible with a picture of Evagrius as a specialized teacher of anchorites out on the margins of the religious world. If his trilogy is intended as a definition of Christianity, then Evagrius is performing exactly the task that numerous other parties in his lifetime and afterwards are also trying to perform, namely, setting down what constitutes correct and legitimate Christianity (and a correct process of Christian formation) for everyone.

Conflict and Condemnation

It remains to relate the quality and scope of Evagrius's authority to the two most probable points in history at which his exercise of authority could have provoked ecclesial leaders. The first period in question is that immediately after his death, and the second is that leading up to his actual condemnation in 553. We can execute this step by first eliminating other possible reasons for Evagrius's legacy to be greeted with antipathy, and then focus on making plausible the case for Theophilus, as the Alexandrian bishop, having initiated the rejection of Evagrius and his associates because of the incompatibility of Evagrius's claims for authority with his own. While it initially seems most feasible and worthwhile to focus on Theophilus, both because he opens hostilities with Evagrius's close associates as soon as Evagrius dies and because he is openly and obviously concerned with consolidating ecclesial authority, there is no hard evidence for animosity towards Evagrius specifically motivating Theophilus's campaign. The second main branch of this argument will focus on the mid-sixth century, seeking to make plausible a conflict between Evagrius's authority as deposited and circulated in his writings and the drive for orthodoxy under the leadership of Justinian in the sixth century.

In a spirit of due diligence, we can first explore whether the hypothesized conflict over authority between Evagrius and the church took place on the level of immediate, local, and personal rivalry between Evagrius and the bishop to whom he would have been beholden, Theophilus of Alexandria. The first reason for Theophilus to be disgruntled with Evagrius would be some manner of direct interpersonal or intercommunal conflict. While explicit animosity towards the clergy is completely absent in Evagrius, his attitude towards the clergy could well have proven offensive to a man with Theophilus's robust view of the appropriate scope of his own authority. Evagrius suggests that the weakness of monks for fantasizing about being forced into the priesthood is an example of vainglory.[59] This could be interpreted as implying either that the priesthood is an illegitimate ambition entailing worldly pride or that the priesthood is a desirable state requiring monks to curb their ambition precisely because becoming a priest is so attractive and valuable. In *Thoughts,* Evagrius is concerned about monks imagining how they will become priests and be admired for healing the sick, suggesting that the priesthood was a desirable honor and its attainment an ambition which had to be controlled.[60] We come closer to an offensive stance towards the clergy at the end of the *Praktikos*, when Evagrius says, "One should love the priests after the Lord, for they purify us through the sacred mysteries and pray on our behalf."[61] Here the attitude towards the clergy that Evagrius encourages among the monks is not one of unmitigated submission. On the one hand, Evagrius advocates a respectful attitude towards the clergy. On the other hand, one reason given for this, as in the above quotation, is the service they render to monks by performing the liturgy: their value is relative to their aid in pursuing the monastic life. Finally, the *Gnostikos* includes a sentence that suggests that the teacher can and should instruct priests, at least those of the "better sort."[62] It is not hard to imagine Theophilus, if he in fact read these works, failing to be amused at the notion of monks adjudicating the quality of his priests and taking it upon themselves to act as their teachers. Even so, Evagrius does not see himself as being at odds with the church and calls down punishment on those who disrupt ecclesial authority: "Fire shall consume one who troubles the church of the Lord; the earth shall swallow one who sets himself up against a priest."[63] In the same way, he is also concerned to shore up orthodoxy, giving warnings against heretics and exhorting his readers to keep the faith.[64] Here of course we must remember that Evagrius himself is ordained and was formed with the best conceivable orthodox credentials from his younger days so there is no need to see an anomaly in his generating this sort of church-friendly exhortation. What is anomalous is how someone so firmly behind the church and clerical authority (albeit as a supplement to his own authority) ends up getting condemned as a heretic.

Is there a reason to see personal antagonism between Theophilus and Evagrius as a motivation for attacking Evagrius's associates? The evidence is not very promising. The two were age-mates, both, like Rufinus, born in or around 345. This might foster a more competitive relationship than that found in a conflict with a significantly more senior or more junior adversary. Both are backed as young men by key figures in the Arian controversy (Theophilus by Athanasius and Evagrius by the Cappadocians). When Theophilus becomes bishop, it is 385, and Evagrius has recently passed through Alexandria to study with Didymus and settle in the desert. Theophilus is also heir to an administrative structure set up by Athanasius, which gives him authority over bishops outside of Alexandria, including those overseeing monastic settlements.[65] Thus Evagrius officially falls under Theophilus's jurisdiction. One might also see fertile ground for jealousy and hostility in the familiar problem of unequal funding. Theophilus is running a large-scale building program in a city whose church is not particularly wealthy, and finds himself soliciting funds in order to pursue these ambitions (some historiographers suggest funding was attained by misappropriation and embezzling).[66] At the same time, Evagrius and other educated ascetics are the benefactors of extraordinarily wealthy patronesses such as Melania and Olympias of Constantinople, thus diverting wealth, albeit substantially smaller sums than those needed to build churches, into ascetic scholarship. Specifically, there is the rivalry between the cities of Alexandria and Constantinople to consider, with Evagrius possibly being perceived as representing a Constantinopolitan connection, which was only strengthened when his associates decamped there, and thus into the jurisdiction of John Chrysostom, after the raid on the monastic settlements shortly after Evagrius's death.[67] From then on, Theophilus's concerns about jurisdiction and the reach of his own authority are well documented as a result of his altercation with John Chrysostom. So there is plenty of circumstantial evidence that would provide Theophilus with a motive, but not the caliber of evidence needed to conclude that Evagrius falls into disrepute because of a personal conflict with Theophilus.

Theophilus never mentions Evagrius by name, and his antagonism towards Evagrius's followers only starts after Evagrius's death and is far more plausibly explained as part of his conflict with Isidore.[68] It is hard to see Theophilus deliberately waiting for the demise of Evagrius before initiating hostilities, as he was by no means averse to direct frontal attacks on his opponents. There is also no substantial evidence that Theophilus took any particular interest in Evagrius at all, although some sort of knowledge of him is probable. So the case for an immediate, local, personal rivalry is not very good, nor is there any clear indication of rivalry between Evagrius and other bishops in this early period. This may serve as a corrective to a reading of Evagrius's authority that might cast Evagrius as a type of angry young man. Had this been the case, local and personal rivalry should show up. While Evagrius has a potent and far-reaching sense of spiritual authority, the empathetic, discerning, and careful tone of his ascetic works also mitigates against over-correcting to an image of him as some manner of rebel.

A conflict between the quality and scope of Evagrius's authority and the interests of the sixth-century church under Justinian can be more feasibly established.[69] Here the terms of rejection are clearly articulated and are not those of personal rivalry but rather of defining the limits of orthodoxy. Where is the conflict between Evagrius's teachings and the agenda of orthodoxy cultivated by Justinian, under whom he was condemned? As the above reading has shown, Evagrius deploys all the arguments for armament against an impending threat and raises claims to expert knowledge of nature, reality, and God, which are key to any viable universal authority. He also has the mentality and the machinery to encourage the reach of his authority to proliferate and encroaches upon ecclesial jurisdiction with alacrity. In addition, he has a strong, influential, and well-funded network, which is able to spread his writings through Palestinian ascetic communities to Constantinople and into the West. By the sixth century, his works continue to be read in Palestine and are also translated into Syriac and were popular among those Christians who, in connection with sixth-century doctrinal controversies, would form the Syrian orthodox church. Further, to the majority of his readers (anyone who did not read the *Kephalaia gnostika* or did not take statements on Christ or the Trinity in that text as statements of doctrine), Evagrius will have appeared to have impeccable orthodox credentials. He performed well in the Arian controversy, was formed by the Cappadocians, and actively advocates avoidance of blasphemy and heresy along with respect for the clergy. From the perspective of an emperor like Justinian, however, all of these points are problematic because they converge to present an alternate claim to define how the Christian life works and who should administer the formation of spiritually ambitious individuals within it. Justinian finds himself confronted with a robust rival claim to religious authority that is still influential during his reign and must find some way to undermine it.

One functional problem, for any representative of the imperial church pursuing a consolidating agenda, with the form of spiritual authority that Evagrius takes up is that it is ungovernable both in its location in a specific individual and in the medium through which it is conveyed, namely the insight, discernment, and intuition of that person. The means of the legitimation of Evagrian authority also resists normalization and regulation. It is a form of authority that is both compelling in its basis in personal attachments and emotional exposure, and energetically anarchic—anyone can practice asceticism and can do so with or without taking an interest in the expectations of the church. Evagrius is a Christian teacher with fine orthodox credentials, a good level of reception in multiple languages, a substantial body of instructional writings that can convey his authority all over the empire, and a command of the rhetoric of armament, anxiety, and appeals to special knowledge of reality. The reason Justinian has to undermine Evagrius is not that he is "the Other," some alien enemy out in the desert cultivating obscure teachings, but rather because he is too close for comfort, and too comfortably doing exactly what Justinian and his associates are trying to do from within institutional structures.

Can we make sense of Evagrius's condemnation as a response to a rival claim to authority? The discourse of orthodoxy within which this occurs is not only a matter of asserting what counts as religious truth, but also of establishing who may legitimately describe the way the religious world is: where souls come from, why and how they must be worked upon, the relations of good and evil, the fate of creation. Answers to these questions are supplied by Evagrius in abundance, and it is a condensed account of this description of religious reality for which he is condemned.[70]

Along with what I have discussed above as Evagrius's assertion of knowledge of the really real, we might also see the acts of enumeration and definition that constitute the conditions of truth according to which Evagrius's followers find themselves examined and diagnosed. The same project of establishing truth conditions, of defining and enumerating the truth about the world, is being pursued by Justinian as well, but with the more far-reaching apparatus of church councils and religious legislation, not least the *Edict on the True Faith* of 551, at his disposal. Evagrius is condemned as part of Justinian's effort to define true Christianity.

The framework of Evagrius's condemnation is something proper to the scope and quality of authority that Evagrius himself practiced. He is condemned because he represents a persistently influential and potent account of religious reality that conflicts with the ambition of the emperor to achieve the same mode of authority on a far larger scale. Both Evagrius and Justinian want for themselves the right to examine, diagnose, and define the thoughts of others, and also to describe and explain reality and administer access to it. Evagrius is condemned on his own terms.

Notes

I am greatly indebted to the response to this essay by Professor Elizabeth Clark, who kindly made her comments available to me in print in the course of making revisions and who, with accustomed graciousness and love for the craft of scholarship, provided both a clarified line of thought and a model of intellectual generosity. Thanks are also due to the participants of the roundtable at Dumbarton Oaks for their comments and suggestions and in particular to the editors of this volume whose critique proved invaluable in correcting my argument.

1. The Fifteen Anathemas of the Second Council of Constantinople in 553 do not name Evagrius explicitly but appear, especially since the edition of the *Kephalaia gnostika*, to be based on a summary of Origenist cosmology and anthropology based on Evagrius's writings.

2. Our evidence for hostility towards Evagrius clusters around two distinct periods, from 390 to 410 and from 540 to 553. There is no demonstrable continuity between the two. In the earlier period, Theophilus may have been opposed to Evagrius, as discussed below, and, although never mentioning Evagrius by name, Theophilus did persecute Evagrius's primary associates and followers shortly after his death. This campaign may also have been aimed at antagonizing John Chrysostom, however, and is thus not strong evidence for an immediate backlash against Evagrius. Also in this early period Jerome decried Evagrius as an Origenist and complained about his anthropology, but did not

denounce him as a heretic directly (see the discussion of Jerome, *Letter* 133.2–3, in Casiday, *Evagrius Ponticus*, 3–7). It is thus misleading to postulate a steady simmering anti-Evagrian sentiment that finally boils over in the mid-sixth century. The only examination of Evagrius's works for which we have evidence and his official condemnation as a heretic take place in this later period. Thus it must be emphasized that the argument in the present essay relates to a persistent influence of Evagrius (as attested by the spread and translation of his works into Latin, Coptic, Syriac, Arabic, Armenian, and Georgian) but not persistent animosity towards Evagrius. Our evidence, patchy as it is, is sufficient only to substantiate a concentrated official rejection of Evagrius in the sixth century.

3. All English translations come from Sinkewicz, *Evagrius of Pontus*, cited below with references to Sinkewicz's edition.

4. For purposes of the present essay, it may suffice to outline the epistemological (and therefore methodologically relevant) tenants of pragmatism as follows. As the name suggests, pragmatists shift the epistemological standard from the discovery of certain knowledge of incontrovertible truth that can be confirmed against some nonhuman measure like God or Reality and instead pursue the best possible functioning explanation given the necessarily limited and contingent resources at hand. Pragmatists also seek to avoid conundrums presented by the Platonist philosophical heritage and its dualisms of reality vs. appearance, essence vs. accident, and found vs. made. Things (like authority) are neither, as in some applications of poststructuralism, reduced to being constructs devoid of all reality and thus somehow insidious nor, as in some applications of essentialism or positivism, are they nuggets of appearance that can be cracked by the historian and made to reveal their real nature. Instead, one is resigned to making do with what one has, namely, language and a human brain. On these terms, one need claim neither that authority is really ("just") the discourse nor that it has some definable essence whose attributes may manifest themselves in the person and work of Evagrius to some greater or lesser degree. Rather, one may assume that both Evagrius and the church are shooting from the hip, so to speak, and building their authority as they go, by doing things and saying things. In the same way, the historian may build a viable account of Evagrian authority not by trying to crack its essence but by seeing how it works and what it is good for. For more on pragmatism as deployed here, see especially Richard Rorty, for example his *Consequences of Pragmatism* and *Philosophy and Social Hope.* For an introductory view of the application of pragmatism to religious studies see Frankenberry and Penner, *Language, Truth, and Religious Belief.*

5. See Young, "Evagrius the Iconographer," 71, regarding this claim in Evagrius Ponticus, *Gnostikos* 44–48.

6. See Rapp, *Holy Bishops*.

7. Identifying a tendency towards proliferation or universalization in a teacher well known for his policy of withholding more sophisticated teachings until disciples have matured appropriately may seem counterintuitive. While Evagrius's pedagogic discernment does limit the total set of people who *can* excel spiritually at any given time, it does not restrict the number of people who *should* embark on the journey towards spiritual excellence or who could eventually reach the required level of maturity to receive more privileged teachings.

8. Evagrius, *Eulogios* 3 (Sinkewicz, 30).

9. Evagrius also proposes a militaristic identity for the anchorites as a sort of elite special forces unit, at the vanguard of a larger struggle against demonic forces. While every person is subject to attacks from demons, "The demons fight directly against the anchorites." *Praktikos* 5 (Sinkewicz, 97).

10. Evagrius, *Eulogios* 23.24 (Sinkewicz, 20).

11. Evagrius, *Prayer* 106–12 (Sinkewicz, 204–5). The attacks of the demons include impersonating a lion and digging his claws "into both sides of the athlete's loins," taking on the form of a dragon who "was chewing off chunks of his flesh and vomiting them back in his face," and using the monk as a ball for two weeks.

12. See among many examples Evagrius, *Prayer* 133 (Sinkewicz, 207): "When you are praying against thoughts, if they should abate easily, look for the reason that this happened, lest you suffer an ambush and because of your mistake deliver yourself over."

13. This is the demon vagabond described in Evagrius, *Thoughts* 9 (Sinkewicz, 159).

14. See for example Evagrius, *Praktikos* 12.

15. Evagrius, *Eulogios* 31 (Sinkewicz, 59).

16. Evagrius, *Prayer* 115 (Sinkewicz, 205–6).

17. Sessions of group and individual counsel of this kind are portrayed in the Coptic *Life of Evagrius* 17 (Vivian, *Four Desert Fathers*, 84–85). The peril of diverging from a state of submission to the spiritual father is discussed, for example, in Evagrius, *Eulogios* 15 and 26 (Sinkewicz, 53).

18. As soon as one progresses in asceticism, it is time to start worrying about pride, as in Evagrius, *Eulogios* 14 (Sinkewicz, 40–41). Vainglory is described as a last-ditch ambush used by the demons as soon as the monk has achieved "some small degree of impassibility," by means of which the demons can reconquer all the territory they have lost: "When all the demons have been defeated, together they augment this particular thought and thereby they all regain their entrance into souls." Evagrius, *Thoughts* 14–15 (Sinkewicz, 162–63).

Here it is precisely the feeling of security and confidence in one's progress which is the most insidious threat.

19. Brakke, *Talking Back*, 30–35.

20. One disruption of such binaries was achieved by Judith Butler in *Gender Trouble*, where the notion of gender as reflecting obvious and natural and real differences that are inherent in bodies was found to reflect ideology rather than the incontestable reality that it claims for itself.

21. The *Teachings of Silvanus* and *Sentences of Sextus* are examples of this earlier tradition of ethical instruction.

22. Evagrius, *Vices* 1 (Sinkewicz, 62).

23. Evagrius, *Vices* 2 (Sinkewicz, 62).

24. Evagrius, *Vices* 5 (Sinkewicz, 64).

25. Evagrius, *Vices* 1 (Sinkewicz, 62).

26. Evagrius, *Vices* 2 (Sinkewicz, 63).

27. Evagrius, *Vices* 5 (Sinkewicz, 64). In the *Chapters 33*, the first sixteen chapters constitute definitions of diseases as passions in terms of the status of uncleanness of certain afflictions as in Deuteronomy and Leviticus. This fits in with the concept of passions or vices as sick and wrong and corrupt (Sinkewicz, 224).

28. Evagrius, *Eight Thoughts* 1.35 (Sinkewicz, 75).

29. At the same time, Evagrius also conveys his expert knowledge to his disciples as a means of equipping them for battle against the demons. As David Brakke has put it, in Evagrius's teaching scheme, knowledge is power. See Brakke, *Demons and the Making of the Monk*, 48–77. Evagrius's authority is, like that of a general in a state of emergency, both domineering and empowering.

30. Evagrius, *Vices* 1 (Sinkewicz, 61).

31. See K. King, "Social and Theological Effects."

32. For example, definitions for prayer found in Evagrius, *Prayer* 3, 14, 15, 16, and 35 (Sinkewicz, 193, 194, 196).

33. Evagrius, *Prayer* 124 and 125 (Sinkewicz, 206).

34. Evagrius, *Reflections* 10–16, etc. (Sinkewicz, 212).

35. This concept of a regime of truth or a regime of the normal has been developed in queer theory and feminist theory, especially by Judith Butler from her early work, *Gender Trouble*, and onwards.

36. Evagrius, *Vices* prol. (Sinkewicz, 62).

37. Evagrius, *Prayer* 51–73 (Sinkewicz, 198–201).

38. Evagrius, *Thoughts* 24 (Sinkewicz, 169).

39. Evagrius, *Thoughts* 19 (Sinkewicz, 166). This is repeated in *Reflections* 15: "A person engaged in the practical life is one who makes proper use of the things given by God" (Sinkewicz, 212).

40. Evagrius, *Thoughts* 19 (Sinkewicz, 166).

41. Evagrius, *Thoughts* 25 (Sinkewicz, 170).

42. See Evagrius, *Prayer* 204–5 (Sinkewicz, 204).

43. Evagrius, *Praktikos* 63 and 66 (Sinkewicz, 109).

44. Evagrius, *Thoughts* 20 (Sinkewicz, 167).

45. At the end of the above passage, Evagrius says, "Similarly, upon examination such a method can be found to apply to the other thoughts. It is necessary to know these things for the sake of our zeal and our strength, so that we may know if we have crossed the Jordan and are near the city of the palm trees or are still continuing in the desert and are being beaten upon by the foreigners."

46. The view of inherited texts which makes exegesis so vital to intellectual and ethical development is discussed in Lamberton, *Homer the Theologian*, and its reception within intellectualist ascetic circles is analyzed in Stefaniw, *Mind, Text, and Commentary*.

47. Evagrius's surviving exegetical works include a commentary on Ecclesiastes titled *Reflections* (*CPG* 2433), *Scholia on Proverbs* (*CPG* 2456), and *Scholia on the Psalms* (*CPG* 2455).

48. Evagrius's elaboration of the role of the teacher in mediating this deposit of knowledge has been discussed in detail in Young, "Evagrius the Iconographer."

49. This can be observed throughout his exegetical works and also in *Chapters 33* (Sinkewicz, 226), where an interpretation of a passage from Proverbs is given in terms of the monastic life. For full discussion of noetic exegesis in Evagrius, see Stefaniw, *Mind, Text, and Commentary*.

50. Examples of hostility towards Origenist exegesis can be found in Jerome, *Letter* 51, and Epiphanius, *Panarion* 4.7–11.

51. Evagrius, *Praktikos* 1 (Sinkewicz, 95).

52. Evagrius, *Eulogios* 1 (Sinkewicz, 29).

53. Evagrius, *Eulogios* 32 (Sinkewicz, 59).

54. This aspect of identification and definition of persons has been articulated in most detail by queer theorists such as Judith Butler in *Gender Trouble*, as noted above, or, more recently in *Undoing Gender*.

55. The reader is referred to Clark, *Origenist Controversy*, for correction of the level of importance attributed to Evagrius in the Origenist controversy

and for full discussion of the social networks in which he and especially his colleague Rufinus and the nearest leading bishop Theophilus were embedded. In particular, Melania and Rufinus link Evagrius to Palestine and to ecclesial and imperial networks in Constantinople, Alexandria's rival city and the site of concentrated quantities of money and power (Clark, *Origenist Controversy*, 20–22).

56. Young, "Evagrius the Iconographer," 54.

57. Evagrius, *Praktikos* prol. (Sinkewicz, 97). In the note preceding the one hundred chapters in which Evagrius also gives instructions to future copyists, he says, "We begin then by the first chapter with what Christianity is and we have proposed defining it as the teaching of Christ our Saviour, comprised of the practical, the natural, and the theological." Placed where it is, at the outset of the first work outlining the practical life, this must lead us to the conclusion that Evagrius considers himself to be outlining the Christian life when he writes on precisely the practical, the natural, and the theological which he has just posited as the definition of Christianity.

58. Evagrius, *Praktikos* 1 and 2 (Sinkewicz, 97).

59. Evagrius, *Praktikos* 13 (Sinkewicz, 100).

60. Evagrius, *On Thoughts* 28 (Sinkewicz, 173).

61. Evagrius, *Praktikos* 100 (Sinkewicz, 113).

62. Evagrius, *Gnostikos* 14, quoted and discussed in Young, "Evagrius the Iconographer," 70.

63. Evagrius, *Monks* 114 (Sinkewicz, 129).

64. Evagrius, *Monks* 124–27 (Sinkewicz, 130). *Monks* 134 (Sinkewicz, 131) also includes pronouncements against specific blasphemes.

65. Norman Russell, in *Theophilus of Alexandria*, 7, points out that Theophilus had up to one hundred bishops in his clientele, over whom he had not just ecclesial authority but also the relationship of patron with all the reciprocal obligations and privileges which that entailed. This relationship sheds some light on the implication of Theophilus's efforts to make Evagrius and several of the Tall Brothers bishops: in so doing, he could bring them unambiguously into a relationship of dependency and obligation to himself. That these efforts were not successful gives us a hint as to a possible personal grudge against Evagrius and his associates and, more significantly, at least one representative of orthodoxy who did see a need to curtail Evagrius's independent form of authority, recognizing its potency and broad reach. On Evagrius and Theophilus, see also Clark, *Origenist Controversy*, 107.

66. Haas, *Alexandria in Late Antiquity*, 207.

67. This raid on monastic settlements by Theophilus is mentioned in Socrates *CH* 6.7. See also Haas, *Alexandria in Late Antiquity*, 259–67.

68. Clark, *Origenist Controversy*, 107–8.

69. While he is not mentioned by name in the surviving documentation from the Second Council of Constantinople, reports on the council persistently cast the anathemata against Origen as including Evagrius and Didymus specifically. See for example Evagrios Scholastikos, *CH* 4.38.

70. The anathemata against Origen are arranged in a sort of cosmogenical chronology from the preexistence of souls, through the creation of the world, to the incarnation, the resurrection, and judgment.

CHAPTER 5

Evagrius Ponticus and Maximus the Confessor

The Building of the Self in Praxis and Contemplation

JULIA KONSTANTINOVSKY

Scholarly interest in Evagrius has steadily increased over recent years as the realization grows of the potency and intricacy of the Evagriana: psychological, theological, and philosophical. This chapter aims to contribute to the increasing fascination with Evagrius and his tradition by tackling his system from the perspectives of theological ethics and metaphysics, which, in premodern thinkers such as Evagrius and Maximus the Confessor, are to be treated as inseparable. We will engage with Evagrius's views about the growth of the inner self in God as, through praxis and contemplation, it strives to overcome the limitations of the current fallen existence (to Evagrius, existence in "time, worlds, and bodies") and develop it to full maturity in God. Maximus the Confessor adheres to an identical theological ethics, and his progression of the soul from *praxis* to contemplation undeniably relies on Evagrius's.[1] Likewise in his metaphysical and cosmological presuppositions, notably his theology of the *logoi*, Maximus belongs within the Origen-Evagrius tradition. In fact, so much is Maximus a follower and developer of Evagrius that to realize the full extent of the metaphysical underpinnings of Evagrius's theology requires one to look to Maximus. The first part of this chapter will revisit Evagrius's theory of natural sense perception and thought formation in the mind, maintaining that, to Evagrius and those in his milieu, all cognitive activity has ethical value. It will maintain that in Evagrius's view, *praxis* is not primarily bodily striving but a cognitive therapy for thoughts in the mind and even natural sense perception. The second part will engage with Evagrius's theory of contemplation, *theōria*, as the spiritual stage that grows out of *praxis*, the sine qua non of *theōria*. Both form a dynamic circular movement of the mind's spiritual attention: *praxis* building up towards *theōria*, and *theōria* giving rise to more excellent *praxis*. We will demonstrate how the entirety of the practical-contemplative life of the Christian seer, *gnōstikos*, is grounded in a specific essentialist metaphysics, whereby the world and all creatures, prior to being actualized in spatiotemporal, bodily existence, eternally preexist their creation as thoughts (*logoi*) in the mind of God. In virtue of this essentialist concept of creation, according to Evagrius, Maximus, and the contemplative tradition of the *Philokalia*, all rational beings without exception are inherently good and the immortal life of illumination is accessible to all. To actualize the potential for immortality in God, however, one needs to strive to build one's self up through a life of virtuous contemplation, *theōria*, whose focus is God's master plan for us. This chapter will likewise reflect on the communal and societal dimensions of ascetic contemplation that emerge from Evagrius's and other premodern Christian reflections on the building of the spiritual self.

Our intention, therefore, is to show how late antique monastic *praxis* and *theōria* concern the rise of a self that is both authentically true and radically new: the seer-*gnōstikos*. The spiritual vision/knowledge of the *gnōstikos* translates seamlessly into communal and societal dimensions, the new contemplative self bringing its knowledge and wisdom to the service of the entire community. As the *gnōstikos* continues to grow "into the fullness of the measure of Christ" (Eph. 4.13), the community responds by acknowledging him as their *vir dei*. Finally, far from being confined to "premodern" cultural domains, elucidating the subject of late ancient contemplation has value for us today, suggesting the possibility of an interface with contemporary philosophical debate, as represented by Charles Taylor and traditions of postsecularism.

PART I: THE BUILDING OF THE FALLEN SELF THROUGH *PRAXIS* AND TOWARDS *THEŌRIA*

The ancient world was pervaded by concerns about identity, authentic living, and dying. How to live optimally in the face of death's inevitability? If death is the ultimate test for the validity of a life, can a worthy death redeem a seemingly worthless life? Or, what manner of dying would undermine and cast a shadow backward over a life apparently good and virtuous? And how could a life be redeemed through a manner of spiritual "dying" to evil, even prior to the end of one's physical life on earth? Fourth-century Origenist Egyptian ascetics offered their own solution to the problem of dying, viewing both life and death from the perspective of God's creative plan for the universe and the universe's response to it. This perspective was essentially dynamic: it presupposed that all persons and rational beings were called to fulfill a certain goal of existence, to grasp their *telos* in a union with God through a voluntary death to one's old self. A *telos*, fulfillment one achieved already in this life, was the one God had preeternally planned for each and every of his rational creatures.

God's initial plan of immortality for the creation was interrupted at the fall. Then mortality arose as "the wages of sin" (Rom. 6.23) and mankind's original journey towards its *telos* detoured, as a gulf came between God and creation. God's response to this catastrophic rupture was to administer healing and restoration to the creatures by means of successive revelatory theophanies active in time and space, the greatest of which was the Incarnation of the divine Logos. Within the context of this early Christian understanding of creation, Christian ascetics' response to God's acts of love for creation and the fallen human condition was to reject what they perceived as "earthy," unheroic, or downright unvirtuous existence imposed upon the individual by the fallen order, in favor of a life of actively pursuing Christian virtue and contemplation, cultivating the true self through mystical communion with God.

Praxis and *Theōria* Held Together

To Evagrius and Maximus, Christian practical virtue, *praxis*, and contemplation, *theōria*, were the tools for crafting one's personal transformation, molding the self into a new God-oriented personality. This new self, which constitutes a different, higher, order of created existence, is turned towards immortality because, to early Christians, the higher manner of being within the temporal-spatial frame is inseparable from the longing for immortality in eternity. To Evagrius, as to other premodern Christians, this new higher self, which develops through *hesychia*, was God-oriented, manifesting some of the characteristics of goodness proper to God himself: unfailing moral uprightness, freedom from evil inclinations (*apatheia*), spiritual knowledge (*gnōsis*), and the ability to create new realities, in imitation of the very creativity of God.

Early Christian thinkers saw the goal of human life as its conformity to the divine manner of being and variously defined it as partaking of God, *methexis Theou* ("partakers of the divine nature," of 2 Pt. 1.4), uniting oneself with the divine powers and energies in *deification*, *theōsis*,[2] or as configuring oneself to the raison d'être of one's being, one's *logos*,[3] nurturing in oneself what was termed "the new man" (*ho theos anthrōpos*).[4] The distinctiveness of Evagrius's work consists in the way he for the first time defines the rise of the new self through grace out of the pursuit of *praxis* and *theōria*.

His famous definition of Christianity as comprising "*praxis*, natural contemplation, and theology"[5] describes the three stages of the spiritual ascent and might be taken as contrasting practical virtue with the life of mystical contemplation as two distinct spiritual stages to be kept apart, the latter achievable only on condition that the former is surpassed. Evagrius's grammar of spiritual growth might suggest that the distinctiveness of the stages is the key point he wishes to emphasize. Yet, to give the Evagriana a fair reading, it is key to realize that *praxis* and *theōria* go together, as one multitrack dynamic progression of the same life unfolding towards the goal of the Christian *eudaimonia*, whereby *praxis* acts as the building blocks and the stepping stones towards *theōria*. The latter then opens up horizons for a further increase of virtue and improvement of *praxis*, which in turn bring about further contemplative states. It is clear, then, that in this tradition the stages of spiritual progression, which might be distinguished for purposes of pedagogy, are in real life to be kept together, perpetually crossfertilizing.

The Soul and Its Parts

In his psychology Evagrius stands within the long Hellenistic-Roman tradition of moral philosophy,[6] which functioned also as philosophical or cognitive therapy.[7] In Christianity, these psychological theories were of course adapted specifically along the lines of the Christian God-centered cosmology, so that the kind of therapy Christian ethical writings offer is itself emphatically theo- and Christo-centric. Nevertheless the same principle holds for both Christian and Hellenistic philosophizing: proficiency in the philosophy of the self provides therapy for the soul.

Evagrius's rational soul, *psychē logikē*, is Platonic, in that it structures itself into three hierarchically ordered immaterial levels: the rational *nous*, or the *logistikon*, combined with the more irrational and impulsive *thumos*, anger, and *epithumia*, desire, which the *nous* governs.[8] The preeminence of the *nous* is fundamental to all ancient philosophical psychologies. There, the *nous*-intellect constitutes the true self or person, the lower soul and the body comprising something the intellect-person, in its optimal condition, *has* but is not reducible to. At its spiritual best, the mind (*nous*) is the seat of self-determination and freedom, and, in Christianity, the locus of the "image of God."[9] As already suggested, Evagrius's theory of virtue and contemplation is about therapy for the healing of the entire person, but primarily of *nous*. The *nous* being preeminent, the remedies of virtue and contemplation apply in the first place to it and then spread from the mind "down" to treat the entire person, soul and body. This dualistic system might discomfit modern sensibilities, yet its dualism safeguards its potency: the governance of the intellect, prevailing over the afflictions of the lower soul and body, "gathers up," unifies, and uplifts the entire person. Both in his early and later works, Maximus the Confessor maintains an identical schema. Sherwood and Thunberg in fact trace the trichotomy of the soul in Maximus directly to Evagrius.[10] Thus, *Chapters on Love* 4.44 envisions very similar multiple components within the hierarchical structure of the soul: the reasoning, *to logistikon*, as the governing part, with the incensive, *to thumikon*, and the desiring part, *to epithumikon*, as the lower soul the *logistikon* governs. *Thalassius* 16 describes the *thumos, epithumia,* and *logos*-plus-*nous* schema.[11]

Virtue Ethics in Evagrius

The guiding concepts of Evagrius's ethics (which Maximus closely follows) are those of virtues, *aretai*, and vices/passions, *pathē*. Evagrius is a virtue ethicist, yet his is a specific instance of virtue ethics, with virtue and vice seen in the light of the revelation of Christ as the two key principles within the soul's makeup. Both virtues and vices constitute the soul's powers. Vices/passions appear as the inversions and distortions of virtues, and once they too perhaps were virtues. Vices/passions subvert the authentic dynamics of the psyche, often by attacking the lower, irrational parts of the soul in situations when the intellect weakens its vigilance over them.

By contrast, virtues are the primordial true powers of the human nature, unifying and uplifting the self to its proper *telos* in God. As primarily the faculties of the *nous,* virtues are intelligent and dynamic. It is for virtues to resolve the inherent tension in the soul between the multiplicity of its parts and the preordained program for the self to unite around the *nous,* oriented towards the Creator. To Evagrius, the unifying and the uplifting of all the powers of the soul through the cultivation of virtues are what constitutes the new self, the "new man."[12] For this reason, the fostering of Christian virtues and the elimination or sublimation of vices are at the heart of Evagrius's ethics.[13]

Virtues, therefore, are not mere good Christian actions. To be sure, a good Christian person, of course, acts well—humbly, charitably, chastely—yet there is so much more to virtues than that. Equally, vices, which Evagrius prefers to call "passions," are not mere isolated bad actions. Both are seated deep within the constitution of the soul and go "all the way down": they are about the person's entire disposition or character vis-à-vis the world and other persons, created and divine. They subsume entire ranges of concerns and attitudes: perceptions, emotions, reactions, desires, choices, and the contemplative faculty. Since virtues and vices are causal in respect of choices and actions, and in successions of actions that are character-building, virtues and vices can be said to form characters and mindsets. In traditional Christianity, human freedom is part of how humans are defined to be "in God's image."[14] Evagrius sees this freedom fundamentally as one's capacity for self-governance through the cultivation of virtuous dispositions in the soul and the rejection of their opposites. There is a sense, therefore, that one's character and life are what one freely constructs for oneself.[15]

Moral Value to Sense Perception

Reflecting further on the "deep" concept of virtue in Evagrius's ethics, it becomes clear that, to Evagrius, no function of the soul-mind is morally neutral. Evagrius's close preoccupation with natural sense perception and concept formation manifests this.[16] The data received by the senses are constituted by multiple perceptions: shades of colors, shapes, textures, smells and tastes, light and dark. These multiple perceptions are then processed and unified in the mind to produce unified images of objects and concepts, what Evagrius calls "representations" (*noēmata*) and "likenesses" (*homoiōmata*) of the physical objects of perception.[17] The mind's assimilation of its concepts is described as its "stamping," like wax is stamped by the image on a seal. Thus,

> One ought to expound first how the mind by nature receives the representations of all sensory things and is stamped in conformity with them. . . . Whatever the shape of the object, such of necessity will be the image that the mind (*nous*) receives. This is why the representations of objects are called "likenesses," because the representations [in the mind] preserve the same shape as the objects themselves.[18]

All of this is natural and good sense perception, integral to the healthy functioning of the soul and the formation of virtuous dispositions building up towards mystical contemplation. The underlying suggestion here is that there is, as it were, intentionality and rationality within the very process of natural sense perception, so that one needs to pay attention to the manner in which one exercises one's senses to safeguard the normality of perception. Paradoxical as it may sound, Evagrius believes that our very sense perception has moral value attached to it so that it can function in the right way or in the wrong. And yet this is merely Evagrius expanding on some of the gospel precepts, where it is suggested that the moral agent owns all of its cognitive activity, sense perception included.[19] Thus, Evagrius appears simply to emphasize that one can exercise one's natural senses either virtuously or in opposition to virtue. His is a virtue ethics, then, that is inseparable from epistemology and ontology.

"Evil" Sense Perception, "Evil" Concepts, and Passionate Dispositions

Normal sense perception breaks down, however, when the shapes, textures, and sounds that inform the senses become enmeshed with the soul's own irrational movements and inclinations: impulses of greed, deception, and an inflated idea of oneself. Fused together with sensory data, they form harmful persuasions that Evagrius terms "evil thoughts" (*logismoi*). These are misguided, irrational cognitive responses both to the outer and inner realities: to the neutral stimuli from the external world and to the original benign concepts within the mind.[20] It is this kind of mental cogitation that gives rise to the evil inclinations, vices, which Evagrius calls passions (*pathē*).

The term *pathē* suggests anything suffered, and in ethics, a passive acquiescence to an irrational state of things, whereby the self relinquishes mastery over its life and lets anything happen to it. The term might be Stoic, but in early Christian thought it acquires an additional "passive" dimension because evil thoughts and passions are not naturally part of the self's composition but are instigated by external assaults from evil forces, demons,[21] whereby specific demonic types are responsible for specific evil thoughts in the soul under attack.[22] The problem with the *logismoi* is that they tend to attach themselves to the authentic powers of the soul, masking themselves as part of the authentic self. This, of course, is a demonic ruse, inasmuch as demons are cheaters, forgers, and falsifiers of reality, driving their host beyond the boundaries of sanity.[23]

The Healing of the Self through "Cognitive Therapy"

This ethics of virtues and vices closely links with Evagrius's theory of sense perception and concept formation. In a quasi-Dostoevskian fashion,[24] Evagrius saw as causal the thoughts one thought in the innermost recesses of one's mind: the thoughts and choices in the mind shaped individual lives and, by extension, those of communities and the entire collective history of the world unfolding in time. One's life stood or fell by the kind of cognitive life one nurtured. In this respect, cognitive processes in the mind (thoughts, memories,[25] and dreams[26]) were intimately connected with virtue-vice formation and the entire process of self-construction: either towards a personhood integrated through grace, or fragmenting it into nonbeing.[27] Acts of irrational attachment, greed, and hubris, as also those of Christian self-denial, humility, and love, all arise from specific kinds of thought activity. Moreover, if mental dispositions shape individual selves and lives, by extension, they can also transform the life of a community and the entire collective history of the world.

In the world of Evagrius, therefore, virtues were complex multitiered dynamic structures constructed through the soul's consistent and progressive inclinations towards thinking the "good thoughts" (in the Evagriana, *noēmata*),[28] while rejecting the "evil" cogitations (*logismoi*).[29] In his *Chapters on Love*, Maximus manifests identical ethical concerns with the formation of Christian virtues through the purification and sublimation of cognitive processes in the mind: "thinking good thoughts." While he acknowledges his indebtedness to earlier "holy fathers,"[30] it is really to Evagrius that Maximus owes the substance of his ethical teaching. Consequently, even though bodily asceticism might have its value, especially when educating audiences less proficient in hesychia,[31] the essence of the hesychast *praxis*, as Evagrius and Maximus outline and the subsequent Philocalic tradition elaborates, is not primarily about exercises for the body. *Praxis* and ascetic struggle, even at their initial levels, focus on the content of one's thought: nurturing the good dispositions while resisting the bad ones.

When the demonic *logismoi* thus attack the soul, the process has a momentum, since evil thoughts tend to develop into evil actions and then "harden" into passionate dispositions. This is why the soul under the attack of *logismoi* requires immediate spiritual treatment of purification. The mind must purify itself by fostering good cognitive processes (peaceful dispositions of Christian virtue and love and images associated with the Christian commandments) and banish the evil ones—as the shepherd (= the mind) guards his sheep (= good thoughts) by driving away the wolves (= demonically inspired delusions).[32] Evagrius's lasting contribution to early Christian ethics (and perhaps modern psychoanalysis as well) is that he also instructs on how we are to achieve this purification of the mind. Since personhood is fundamentally rational and cognitive, effective psychotherapy ought to be cognitive as well. To Evagrius, evil cogitations and the associated vices are not authentically part of the fabric of the *psychē* but are something alien and added. It follows that they are not robust and are detachable, and it is the task of the wise "shepherd," the mind, to disengage the evil added elements from the good and authentic powers of the soul. Consequently, when assailed by unnatural feelings and emotions that are alien to the true nature of the soul, the mind must proceed, first, by "analyzing" (*diele*) the emotion into its constitutive parts. Thus, the unnatural emotion/*logismos* of avarice subsumes within itself the concept of gold, its reference to the actual gold "out there," plus the unhealthy disturbance (*tarachē*)[33] and pleasure (*hedonē*) of greed that goes with it. Neither gold nor its representation in the mind is evil in itself. Greed alone is. The mind then rejects the pleasure associated with the idea of gold, making the demon of avarice flee and regaining one's mastery of oneself.[34] This cognitive strategy consists of analysis followed by detachment (what Taylor calls "disengaged objectification" and "distance of scrutiny"[35]) and is to be applied to any alien intrusive thought in the mind, so as to prevent passionate impulses and thoughts from growing into habitual passions and wrong actions. The ultimate goal of this therapy is the self's overall well-being, *eudaimonia*, which is brought about in stages. First comes the separating of the soul from the sickness-passion attached to it. The Philocalic tradition, of which Evagrius was the founding father, terms this therapy "the cutting" of the evil thought.[36] As with physical surgical intervention, this initial stage of the self's liberation from its sickness is associated with spiritual pain. On account of this Evagrius calls the process "spiritual warfare" and, among other imagery, employs military metaphors for his analysis of the cutting of the thoughts. This initial stage of purification is then followed by an onset of calm and often unperturbed happiness: *anachōrēsis* is sweet, once passions have been eliminated.[37] A completely identical schema of self-therapy based on the separation of evil thoughts from neutral and beneficial cognitive processes is presented in Maximus Confessor, who was clearly learning from Evagrian writings. Thus, *Chapters on Love* 3.42:

> An object in the world (*pragma*), a conceptual image [in the mind] (*noēma*), and a passion (*pathos*) are all quite different from one another. For example, a man, a woman, gold, and so forth are things. A conceptual image is a passion-free memory (*mnēmē psilē*) of one of these things. A passion is a mindless affection or indiscriminate hatred for one of these same things. The monk's battle, therefore, is against passion.

Chapters on Love 3.43 further elucidates the principle of the analysis followed by detachment from or cutting of the wrong impulse:

> An impassioned conceptual image (*noēma empathes*) is a thought that consists of a passion and a conceptual image [of a thing] (*logismos sunthetos apo pathous kai noēmatos*). If we separate (*chorizōmen*) the passion from the conceptual image, what remains is the passion-free thought (*ho logismos psilos*). We can achieve this separation by means of love and self-control if only we have the will.[38]

Conclusions to Part I

We have seen that practical virtue is closely associated with every aspect of cognition, down to sense perception and concept-formation.

Fourth-century desert (and later ascetical) Christians would thus seem to suggest, outrageously, that there is no such thing as simply neutral breathing, touching, seeing, and hearing: all these natural activities possess a moral dimension and have to be executed with care and virtue. Cognitive activity is never neutral in the sense of being value-free. It is always value-charged because it affects the self's natural orientation, which is meant to be directed towards its ultimate *telos* in God. In this sense, meanings, including those grasped via ordinary sense perception, are not simply received but are constructed. Moreover, they are not *arbitrarily* constructed. Instead, they are fashioned in freedom and virtue and through uncovering the truths that are already there within the fabric of reality, in us and the universe. On this reading, in premodern systems like Evagrius's, virtues are indeed part of the very "furniture of things."[39]

Once purified, the soul-mind is ready for the next formative step, contemplation. At this point it is appropriate to turn to Evagrius's and Maximus's doctrine of the *logoi* and their contemplations. As touched on above, the purified self builds itself up by contemplating the *logoi* as the principles of the unity and diversity of the created order and the presence of God's creative intention in it and in the soul.

Part II: Evagrius and Maximus—The Doctrine of Creation and Contemplation of the *Logoi*

Instances of Christian Exemplarism

In premodern Christian traditions contemplation, *theōria*, is a spiritual formative activity based on the person's awareness of how all things cohere and relate to God's plan about them. In early Christian writers, Evagrius included, this doctrine has both epistemological and metaphysical dimensions. Epistemologically, contemplation concerns the manner of our knowing the essence of creation and the way we (re-)build and (re-)create ourselves on the basis of this knowledge. Contemplation, then, is a spiritual cognitive activity whose purpose is the growth of awareness and attunement in the soul-mind.

Just as virtues in the soul are metaphysically grounded and are for us to build up through "discovery," so also is the contemplation of the world rooted in a certain kind of metaphysics whereby we discover the *logoi* in things as the beauties and graces of the created order hidden within its very fabric. The metaphysics that makes such contemplation possible (and necessary) is called "exemplarist" because it is based on the principle that both the physical and spiritual dimensions of the world were created by God as copies of the spiritual exemplars and paradigms for creation that were preeternally present in the divine mind. All the created beings are therefore actualized copies of God's eternal ideas and contemplation-thoughts about them. The majority of premodern Christian cosmologies are exemplarist along these lines in some sense.[40]

Early Christian cosmological exemplarism is rooted in Plato, who, in the *Timaeus*, endeavoured to grasp the unifying harmony of the cosmos by having recourse to the Pythagorean cosmological myth and the concept of the World Soul. In Plato, the Demiurge fashions the cosmos by imposing order (*taxis*) upon the disorder (*ataxia*) of preexistent matter. The principle of order and coherence that holds all parts of the world together is its Soul. In addition, the Demiurge fashioned the cosmos on the model of the eternal transcendent Ideas, or "thoughts," in the mind of the Demiurge.[41] The World Soul and exemplarism account for the relationships of cause to effect and the eternal to the temporal. Consequently the *Timaeus*'s exemplarist theory is built on the principle of a correspondence between the thoughts in the divine mind and the arrangement of the disparate pieces of the universe. Via a variety of philosophical channels, this exemplarism was imported into the premodern Christian cosmologies, including those of Evagrius and Maximus, even though neither Maximus nor Evagrius make use of the World Soul concept per se. Instead, both have recourse to the concept of the spiritual *logoi* of beings as encapsulating God's preeternal plan for the universe and his creative powers that he used in fashioning it. Unlike Maximus, Evagrius tends to employ the idea of the personified manifold Wisdom of God[42] as a quasi-synonym for God's creative powers-*logoi*.

The *Logoi* as Principles of Multiplicity and Unity within the Cosmos

One often despairs over much of the content of Evagrius's *Kephalaia gnostika*, in particular the obscure material about the similarity between our activity of contemplation as the acquisition of *gnōsis*, and God's and Christ's contemplative activity as the essence of his creative act:

> In the second natural contemplation, we behold "the manifold wisdom"[43] of Christ, which he used in his creation of the worlds. (*KG* 2.2)
>
> The knowledge of the first nature is the spiritual contemplation which the Creator employed in fashioning the minds alone; these are receptacles of His nature. (*KG* 3.24)

What can help in interpreting something of this material is studying the cosmological *logoi*-doctrine in Maximus—that is, what Maximus relates about the *logoi* and their simultaneous location in God and in beings, as well as their triple function: as God's preemptive ideas about the world-to-be, God's creative/contemplative activities in making the world, and the spiritual principles of the existence of the world, located in the world itself—and relating all of it back to Evagrius. Evagrius may not be saying exactly what Maximus does, nor does Maximus envisage a double creation doctrine, which Evagrius adamantly upholds. Nevertheless, when reading him side by side with Maximus, something of Evagrius's meanings begins to clarify.

Maximus's *Ambiguum* 7 and Evagrius's *Kephalaia gnostika* on Creation

Evagrius's passages about contemplation—God's and ours—are nicely elucidated when considered in the light of the material about God's creative act contained in Maximus's seventh *Ambiguum*, where his teaching on the *logoi* is primarily elaborated. I shall ignore Maximus's polemic against the Origenists of North Africa, which provided the occasion for the writing of the *Ambiguum*, and shall rather focus on the cosmology and the *logoi*-doctrine arising out of this polemic. It is my approach that, just as it was the case with his ethics, Maximus's theory of creation and of the *logoi* overlaps and in some sense stems from a corresponding theory in Evagrius. In itself the present outline of Maximus's thoughts on the subject is nothing new on the Confessor's logology, as the subject has been extensively treated in the recent insightful studies by Louth, Törönen, and Tollefsen.[44] I shall nevertheless retraverse some of Maximus's fundamental points. In this text, Maximus focuses upon rational beings—angels, humans, and demons—coming into being "out of nothing" (*ek tou mēdenos*):

> What exists was brought out of nonbeing into being by God. (*Ambiguum* 7, PG 91:1077C)

In his *Chapters on Love*, extensively dependent upon Evagrius, Maximus states that God's creative act was an act of infinite divine love and was accomplished by God in his Wisdom and Logos, specifically at the (nontemporal) moment when God so wished:

> Existing eternally as Creator, God creates when He wishes by His consubstantial Logos and Spirit from His infinite goodness. (*Chapters on Love* 4.3)

Consequently, the world has a definite moment of beginning, when God brings it into existence out of his divine love and according to his divine will. Yet precisely because he in his essence is goodness and love,[45] God is said to exist eternally as Creator, even though the actualized world of created beings itself is not eternal. In *Ambiguum* 7, Maximus further elucidates this particular point more extensively by claiming that God eternally was and is mindful of being the Creator, inasmuch as he "always and in all things" (*aei kai en pasin*) has a desire to become "incarnated" or "embodied," as Maximus puts it, in the created being.[46] God, then, creates with the purpose of becoming in some sense "embodied" and thus remaining present in the world he makes. Here the "embodied" does not primarily mean the Logos's Incarnation as the

God-Man, but the indwelling of God in the entirety of the created order in a variety of ways. And this is how he is omnipresent in the universe, whilst all along remaining transcendent. That God is in truth present in every tiny morsel of his creation, while simultaneously remaining the transcendent God that he is, is emphasized in Evagrius's *Kephalaia gnostika* 1.43:

> God is present in every place, yet He is not in a particular place. He is everywhere, because in all things that He made He is present through "His manifold wisdom."[47]

Something of Evagrius's meaning begins to elucidate itself: while he "does not belong to the category of beings," God desires to be fully present in beings. Since he creates out of his love, that is, "in his goodness," it is for the same reason, that is, love, that he wishes to reside inside the beings that he makes. The Incarnation of the Logos is then a particular instance of God's overall quasi-pantheistic embodiment and presence within the created world for the reason of his goodness and for the purpose of the salvation of the world. Moreover, to Maximus, God's presence within his creation is far from incidental. God's eternal foreknowledge always planned it this way. The various kinds of divine embodiment are all part of God's preeternal plan.[48] Thus, *Ambiguum* 7 stresses that God "always" (*aei*) wished to become embodied in all things created.

Just as human *praxis* and contemplation are free acts of cognition, so also is God's activity of creation. Even though the divine plan to create, or the divine foreknowledge, concerns the making of the created order, which eventually is brought into being, this divine plan, inasmuch as it is *eternal*, is part of God's own, that is, his divine rather than created, contemplative/cognitive sphere.

This principle may not be elaborated in Evagrius, yet the overall logic of the Evagriana calls for a very similar theory. In Maximus, this preeternal divine plan concerning creation constitutes God's eternal contemplative activity. This activity is as eternal and uncreated as God himself and is not necessarily tied up with the actual creative act. Before he fashions and arranges the complex universe in all of its various parts, God has it all planned in his head, so to speak. What is germane to the subject of contemplation in Evagrius is that he—with Maximus following—construes God's engagement with his eternal plan about creation on the analogy of a human mind thinking thoughts through before implementing them in act. When at last he creates, God realizes his plan, or thoughts, about creation by bringing his internal willing and planning to create things outside the sphere of his uncreated being. He thus externalizes, if one might so put it, his thinking about creating the universe, which is thus the product of his cognitive activity.

How are we to bridge the gap between God's "thinking" or "willing" to create—which God does within himself and which is uncreated—and the actual coming into existence of beings, which are created? To Maximus and Evagrius alike, the *logoi* provide this bridge. Maximus's vision of God's making beings and then providentially caring for and redeeming them by residing within them is accounted for in terms of his *logoi*-doctrine. Conversely, Evagrius's theory of our contemplation of the *logoi* of beings is based on precisely this metaphysics.

The *Logoi* as the Thoughts in God's Mind

What, then, are the *logoi* and where are they located? In the first place, the *logoi* are the eternal thoughts-contemplation in God's mind, through which God eternally *thinks* creation. Here, the *logoi* are both God's thoughts and the objects of these thoughts in the divine mind. In *Ambiguum* 10 (PG 91:1177b–c), Maximus specifically identifies God's eternal plan about creatures with the *logoi*. They are God's nontemporal multiple intellections concerning the created order. The multiplicity of the *logoi* accounts for the multiplicity of God's imagined diverse universe and subsequently his *actually created* universe. As divine thoughts of God, the *logoi* inhabit the divine mind and are part of the divine, not created, being. There is thus in Maximus a sense that an aspect of creation is preexistent and coeternal with God. At the same time, it is essential to bear in mind that the *logoi* as the thoughts of God are not the created beings themselves but ontologically precede creation. Maximus stresses the eternity of the *logoi* in God's mind when he refers to them as the "preexistent *logoi* of what came into existence." God also is said to "possess" the *logoi* of what has come into existence "before the ages were established" (*Ambiguum* 7, PG 91:1080a). Thus, Maximus maintains, "the *logoi* of our being are established as preexisting in God" (*Ambiguum* 7, PG 91:1081c).

The *Logoi* at the Moment of Creation

At the moment of creation, however, God changes his cognitive activity from internally engaging the *logoi*-thoughts within his mind to that of reaching outside of himself in the act of creation. He thus externalizes his eternal *logoi*-thoughts about creation, transforming them from his thoughts into his creative activity, which overflows beyond his inner being and extends itself towards the *other*, the being that is not God, granting it existence.

The *Logoi* inside the Beings

Beside being "thoughts" in the mind of God and God's dynamic activities of creation, the *logoi* also reside in beings themselves. There the *logoi* are the principles of harmony and coherence of the universe, making it into a *cosmos* out of *chaos*. They are also the spiritual identities, the raisons d'être and destiny of each individual being. Through the *logoi*, Maximus tells us, the Logos is "incarnated" within his creation and is "present in every place."[49] On account of the multiplicity of the *logoi*, the One Logos, the "hidden God," becomes revealed to his creation as the wise Creator and Redeemer. It is through these *logoi* that "All creation proclaims 'God's manifold wisdom,'"[50] just like the reflection of rays upon the surface of the ocean manifests the sun.[51] Located within the creatures and the soul alike, these *logoi* are the object of human contemplation. Eternally "thoughts" and contemplations in the mind of God, they now exist as created things and in this form are the objects of our own contemplations. By engaging in the *theōria* of the *logoi* of beings, then, we become partakers of the creative life of God himself—a life that assimilates us to him in what early Christians term *deification.*

Contemplation as Infinite (Re-)Creation

Evagrius thinks that we must all contemplate. Here we touch on the heart of his metaphysical exemplarism, which provides the ontological grounding for his theory of *theōria* and *praxis.* Conversely, Evagrius's need to conceptualize ontology in exemplarist terms arises out of the ascetic and ethical desire for the contemplative-virtuous hesychia. His conceptions of the very fabric of reality and of the soul as copies of the divine graces and the beauties of God are robustly experiential, in the sense that both come out of the experiences and exigencies of the hesychastic contemplative life. Put simply, contemplation uncovers to us the *logoi* within the creatures and the human self. Since they are the luminous principles of the eternal divine wisdom within this temporal, contingent, and less-than-optimal world,[52] in their original divine plan, the entire creation, and our lives, are "*logoic*," that is, inherently "wise" and teleological. By (re-)uniting itself through contemplation to the original divine wisdom locked within the creatures, the human person successfully grows into authentic personhood, that of becoming the virtuous contemplative, *gnōstikos.*

This helps elucidate some of the key psychological aspects of contemplation, which, in Evagrius's scheme, are inseparable from metaphysics. Maximus does not dwell on these, and yet the overall logic of Maximus's argument entails that they must underlie his vision of things also. What is it like to be a contemplative? What happens to the life of one who contemplates? In addressing these dilemmas, Evagrius is adamant that, in contemplation, humans participate in the momentous picture of the universe's (re-)making. Based on the traditional premodern Christian tenet of humans made in the divine image (cf. Genesis 1.26), Evagrius establishes a fundamental analogy between the human person engaged in *theōria*, on the one hand, and, on the other, God the Creator fashioning beings through his own contemplation. When the human *nous* contemplates creatures in their unspoiled essences, the *logoi*, it acquires godlike properties of creativity and potency to effect spiritual transformations of reality. These properties are godlike because, Evagrius tells us, when God thought the thoughts (*logoi*) of creation, at some point actualizing them as created beings external to himself, he did so through contemplation.

Consequently, when we contemplate with the purified mind, we too bring about new spiritual realities, in ourselves and the universe, akin to what God did when he first fashioned the world. What are these realities and how does this analogy hold? The similarity must of necessity be partial, because God, of course, creates out of nonexistence while we do not. We make something new out of what already is. Or, perhaps, the new things that we make are also already in existence and need re-creating in the sense of "uncovering" and "perfecting" out of our less-than-optimal temporal state. Thus, Evagrius indicates that when we contemplate beings some kind of pure mind comes to be written or imprinted upon the creation through knowledge. One way of reading this would be that this pure mind is our very own mind-self. In other words, *theōria* is a two-way formative activity: remaking the cosmos by uncovering its capacity to reflect God's glory, while at the same time transforming the contemplating agent because the transfigured universe is internalized within him.

What contemplation ultimately creates is a new fortified self, armed with an array of dynamic powers that makes it the "temple of God"[53] and prepares it for the even higher activity of "pure prayer." The rise of the new contemplative self means that the person's entire life changes and improves. This concerns all aspects of the self's life, both cognitive and social, all its parts, and all the contexts in which it is lived. The new life is unified and "stretches out" to envelop, through repentance, not only the present but the future and even the past, in the sense that the past can change by being redeemed. When not engaged in contemplation, one falls back on the life of sense perception. However, the transformative power of contemplation is such that it swallows up the entire life, including the level of sensory activity. The effect of being a contemplative is that eventually every aspect of life moves closer to becoming ontologically virtuous and ontologically contemplative. And so the gnostic life unfolds towards its completion along the perpetual ascending trajectory of perception > virtue > contemplation > prayer > perception > virtue > contemplation > prayer . . . Yet the drawing nearer to the true being is never ending, because the true being is always living already now the fulfillment that is not yet.

For Evagrius, as for other representatives of the Origenistic and Philocalic traditions, notably Gregory of Nyssa and later Byzantine hesychastic writers (especially Gregory Palamas), existing within "time, worlds and bodies," as Evagrius likes to put it, is the locus and sine qua non of our meeting with God the Creator. It is also the context for the continuing unfolding of his "plan," his Providence and Judgment,[54] for the creation (as in John 5.17: "My Father is still working, and I also am working"). Creation is not yet finished, and it will continue for the entire extension of the "time, worlds, and bodies," that is to say, the entire duration of this *diastemic* existence within the fallen "fashion of this world" (cf. 1 Cor. 7.31). Evagrius's views about human contemplation, therefore, can only be understood within the overall context of his idea of God's original creation and the current state of the world characterized by "time, worlds, and bodies." Consequently, the aim of contemplative vision is, for as long as there is still time (cf. Rev. 10.6), to continue the task of the (re-)creation of oneself and the world, to bring to restorative completion the original work of the Creator.

Final Remarks

To Evagrius, perceiving things through undistorted sense perception and then contemplating them in their *logoi* is a way of growing into one's authentic, sound self—the very knowing person, the *gnōstikos*, God pre-eternally meant one to become. After undistorted sense perception, contemplation is the next "brick" in the building of the spiritual edifice of the soul. Contemplation is ultimate and eschatological, for it attunes the self to authentic nontemporal realities, both within and without, containing and being contained by all things. Contemplation transforms the self into an eternal mind sharing in divine immortality. This is not a collapse of the person through the blurring of the boundaries between the self and the alien *other* (the world or the divine). On the contrary, contemplation unlocks the secret of the ancient Christian personal "living well," *eudaimonia*, through opening the self up to the authentic beings and selves within the universe as God ordained them. To employ Taylor's concept of the "porous" and "buffered" selves[55] in a somewhat heterodox fashion, one becomes at once both "porous" and "buffered," but in a positive and fruitful way: opening oneself up, that is, "being porous," to the beneficial spiritual realities, while establishing firm "buffers" between oneself and the alien demonic influences.

Consequently, in contemplation the contemplating self is in a strong and unshakable position occupying an impregnable vantage point from which it is able to grasp the ultimate realities of being for all things as designed by God, while itself remaining violated by nothing. It is firmly in control of itself and its own contemplations, having become the master of the meanings for itself. In this manner contemplative activity rebuilds and pieces together the self, arming it against what is "alien," that is, "demonic," and not part of the authentic fabric of the universe and the self. The self thus "buffered" through contemplation henceforth itself chooses its own "enchantments" (echoing Weber's "disenchantment of the world," *Entzauberung der Welt*, concept),[56] first and foremost, God the Creator. Evagrius, then, can be characterized in modern terms not only by his instructing about the remaking, through contemplative repentance, of the new fortified personhood in God, but by expecting that the self *can* and must be so remade.[57] Could Evagrius, with the help of Maximus, thus help reread the story of Western secularization?

Notes

1. As Joshua Lollard has recently emphasized in his *Life of Things*, 137–65, esp. 137.

2. See especially Russell, *Doctrine of Deification*. Evagrius may not be using the term, but the idea of salvation as the conformity to the divine life is fundamental in his writings.

3. As elucidated in Maximus, notably in *Ambiguum* 7. For the definition of Maximus's *logoi* of beings as both the creatures' principles and goals of existence (*skopos*) see Larchet, *La divinisation*, 113.

4. Evagrius, *Thoughts* 3. Cf. Gal. 3.28 and Col. 3.10–11.

5. Evagrius, *Praktikos* 1.

6. See especially Gill, *Structured Self.* Plato, Aristotle, Galen, Chrysippus, Seneca, Posidonius, and Plutarch all contributed, in their ways, to the early Christian psychology.

7. On ancient ethics as therapy see Sorabji, *Emotion and Peace of Mind*, parts I and II.

8. For the soul as tripartite see, for instance, Evagrius, *Praktikos* 38, 78, and 89. Evagrius also presents the soul as consisting of two parts, the rational and the irrational, in, e.g., *Praktikos* 66 and 84.

9. Evagrius, *Thoughts* 19.11–12.

10. Maximus, *Ascetic Life*, 84; Thunberg, *Microcosm and Mediator*, 185.

11. See Maximus the Confessor, *Thalassius* 16, PG 90:301C. In Maximus the *logos* or the *logistikon* of the soul seems to signify the reasoning faculty, which is hierarchically below the most supreme level of the psyche, the *nous*, directly associated with the knowledge and love of God. In a similar way, in Evagrius, the *logistikon*, as in *Praktikos* 86, appears to be the rational faculty, below the most sublime part of the rational faculty, *nous*. Whereas the function of the *nous* is to grow in *theologia*, the knowledge of God, that of the *logistikon* is to be engaged in the contemplation of beings, *theōria phusikē*. In many contexts, however, Evagrius does not draw this distinction but assigns all spiritual contemplative functions to the *nous*.

12. Evagrius, *Thoughts* 3.

13. Evagrius elucidates his theory of the ordered chains of impressions and thoughts that feed into the formation of either virtues or vices and thus determine the functionality of the soul especially in *Praktikos* and *Thoughts*. Recent contributions to the discussion of Evagrius's ethics include Konstantinovsky, "Evagrius Ponticus on Being Good," and Stewart, "Evagrius Ponticus and the Eastern Monastic Tradition."

14. As in Gen. 1.28.

15. This point shall be completed below, to demonstrate that the full early Christian anthropological picture was a character and a personhood that was *both* constructed for oneself and discovered in God's plan for the creation.

16. Especially in *Praktikos* and *Thoughts*.

17. As suggested previously, these are neutral and benign concepts in the mind, which arise in accordance with nature and not contrary to it.

18. Evagrius, *Thoughts* 25.8–18.

19. Consider, for example Mat. 5.28: "But I tell you that anyone who looks at a woman with lust has already committed adultery with her in his heart."

20. As in Evagrius, *Thoughts* 25.

21. Evagrius generally categorizes all mental processes in us as initiated either by angels, demons, or, in some situations, ourselves: *Thoughts* 8.

22. As in Evagrius, *Thoughts* 2: "All demonic thoughts introduce into the soul concepts of sensory things. The mind is stamped by them and carries around within itself the shapes of those objects. Thus from this it recognizes the demon that has approached."

23. Similar to Palladius's accounts in *Historia Lausiaca* of insanity and death through wrongful thoughts: chapters 25–26.

24. Notably *Crime and Punishment* and *The Devils*, where persons die and the life of the society descends into chaos as a consequence of the ideas of nihilism and anarchy that some of the characters entertain.

25. Evagrius, *Thoughts* 4.

26. Evagrius, *Thoughts* 4, 27–29.

27. What Gill calls, referring to Stoic thought, "the development of a non-character" and "a failed personality," which "fails to reach its potential" (*Structured Self*, 207).

28. As expounded in Evagrius, *Thoughts* 25.8–18. See Konstantinovsky, *Evagrius Ponticus*, 27.

29. The entire treatise *Thoughts* demonstrates Evagrius's use of the term *logismoi* as negative mental activity.

30. St. Maximus the Confessor, *Chapters on Love*, "Foreword to Elpidios the Presbyter." Cited from the English translation by Palmer, Sherrard, and Ware, 2:52.

31. As, for instance, in Maximus's *Outline Teaching on Asceticism*, in Nicodemus the Hagiorite and Makarios, *Philokalia*, 1:31–36.

32. "The Lord entrusted the concepts of this age to man as a kind of sheep to a good shepherd. For it is said: 'He gave the world to his heart' (Eccl. 3.11) to help him, he joined to him the irascible part and the desirous part, so that with the former he would put to flight the representations that are from the wolves, and with the latter he would cherish the sheep" (Evagrius, *Thoughts* 17.1–7).

33. Evagrius, *Thoughts* 2.16, 32.19.

34. Evagrius, *Thoughts* 19.

35. Taylor, *Sources of the Self*, 45.

36. See chapter 2 in this volume, by Kevin Corrigan.

37. Evagrius, *Praktikos* 36.6–7.

38. Maximus Confessor, *Chapters on Love* 3.43 (PG 90:1029B). This insight is also developed in Törönen, *Union and Distinction*, 186–88.

39. Taylor, *Sources of the Self*, 54, where he counters John L. Mackie's claim that "values are not part of the fabric of the world." See Rawls and Mackie, *Ethics*, 15. For the place of an ontological and teleological conception of virtue in modern ethical discourse see MacIntyre, *After Virtue*.

40. Evagrius's immediate Christian authority with regard to exemplarism is unsurprisingly Origen, whose *First Principles* 2.11.5.176–83 states that the fullness of knowledge that Christ will reveal to us is the knowledge of "the reasons (*rationes*) for all things that happen on earth." The Latin *rationes* evidently translates the Greek *logoi* of the original.

41. Plato, *Timaeus* 30a–c; 39d–40a.

42. See Eph. 3.10: "So that the manifold wisdom of God might now be made known to the principalities and powers in heavenly places through the church." For instances of "wisdom" in Evagrius see his *Kephalaia gnostika* 1.43, 2.2, 2.21, 5.32.

43. Cf. Eph. 3.10.

44. See under Maximus the Confessor in the bibliography, as well as Törönen, *Union and Distinction*, and Tollefsen, *Christocentric Cosmology*.

45. Cf. 1 John 4.8.

46. Maximus the Confessor, *Ambiguum* 7, PG 91:1084c–d.

47. Eph. 3.10.

48. Cf. Maximus the Confessor, *Thalassius* 60, CCSG 22:75.40ff.

49. *KG* 1.43.

50. *KG* 2.21. Cf. Eph. 3.10.

51. The sun and its rays analogy for God's manifestations in creation was standard in premodern Christian literature, notably Gregory of Nazianzus, *Oration* 28.17: "A small ray of the great light."

52. Thus, *KG* 2.1 maintains that God's action of creation was performed "in wisdom" and that this wisdom is reflected, as in a mirror, in the "wise" *logoi* of creation: "Created out of non-existence, [creatures] are the mirror of the goodness of God, of His power and of His wisdom."

53. Evagrius, *S-Ps.* 83.3.

54. Evagrius, *S-Ps.* 138.16, no. 8.

55. The concept is used especially in Taylor, *Secular Age*. See Taylor's explanation of it in his blog post at http://blogs.ssrc.org/tif/2008/09/02/buffered-and-porous-selves/: "Here is the contrast between the modern, bounded, buffered self and the porous self of the earlier enchanted world. As a bounded self I can see the boundary as a buffer, such that the things beyond don't need to 'get to me,' to use the contemporary expression. That's the sense to my use of the term 'buffered' here and in *A Secular Age*. This self can see itself as invul-

nerable, as master of the meanings of things for it." See also the response to Taylor in Warner, VanAntwerpen, and Calhoun, *Varieties of Secularism.*

56. Weber first coined the term in his 1918 lecture on "Science as a Vocation." It was subsequently used in contemporary sociology to designate the state of modern society whereby it has disengaged itself from prior engagement with religion, mysticism, and belief and is orientating itself towards rational and secularized goals.

57. Cf. Warner, VanAntwerpen, and Calhoun, *Varieties of Secularism*, 17.

CHAPTER 6

The Role of Letters in the Works of Evagrius

Robin Darling Young

In the final years of his life,[1] Evagrius of Pontus wrote a letter responding to Abbot Lucius of the Enaton Monastery. He began it with customary courtesy and modesty:

> I have seen the letter of Your Holiness, in which you amply demonstrated your love for us, and commanded us to send you something from our labors. I had not wanted to send anything of my own accord, because of my embarrassment in the face of your temperance. But now, because I have been commanded, I have readily obeyed, and have sent you the treatise of responses, so that you might read it, correct it and complete whatever is lacking, in case we have represented any of the unclean thoughts imprecisely, or we have not properly found the answer that opposes them.[2]

In the pages following his cover letter to the abbot, Evagrius had copied out his own handbook containing scriptural verses useful in repelling eight types of demonic thoughts as a set of prescriptions to restore health to the soul. Many of Evagrius's works are similar: they aim to provide helpful medicine against a common ascetic illness, and personal letters precede some of them. In the letters, though, as with many such collections, readers seem to encounter Evagrius at closer hand than in his other works, and that personal tone holds an undeniable appeal.

The correspondence, though, is also crucial to interpreting his work, because it shows how Evagrius exercised the roles that he himself describes elsewhere, roles of both ascetic teacher and struggling monk. In the letters, he applies portions of his teaching in ways he has judged appropriate to a particular recipient.[3] Evagrius guarded the shape of his own work, and he left, through the letters, a portrait of his leadership in the "fellowship" at Kellia. The entire collection thus allows a view of the intersection between Evagrius's consistent and orderly philosophical program for practice and contemplation, on the one hand, and his give-and-take with those men and women who had sought his advice for their own ascetic lives, on the other.

Yet Evagrius's correspondence remains far less well known than his other works, especially now that many of the latter are available in a reliable, one-volume English translation. The correspondence, however, is hard to use. It is available as a diplomatic edition—a printed work of one surviving Syriac version, with a Greek retroversion. A complete German translation exists, and French and English translations are projected; just a few letters are available in English publications.[4]

Furthermore, at some point during their transmission, portions of the letters seem to have been truncated; at the very least, their salutations and closings have been removed. The state of their Syriac translation makes the letters, therefore, difficult to date and to interpret. Yet there remains an opening for better understanding the letters. Evagrius was a notably consistent, single-minded author and thinker; he repeated his statements across the body of his works. Many portions of his letters preserve portions of other works—works that do survive in Greek. For this reason, interpretation of his letters will become easier when their contents can be compared to his other works. The result of such a comparative effort will very certainly show the close degree of similarity between the content of his letters and various other works. In the present essay, however, I want to make three observations about the letters' contents, based on preliminary work with the letters.

First, although the entire correspondence originates in a monastic setting, it testifies to its rarefied circumstances as a carefully crafted work of the second half of the fourth century, when epistolography flourished. Furthermore, many of these monks, and Evagrius most of all, knew and employed the recent works of pagan philosophers in the Neoplatonic tradition. Like Clement and Origen before him and Gregory of Nyssa and Didymus his contemporaries, Evagrius was highly trained in rhetoric and philosophy, and confident that philosophy elucidated the scriptures and with them taught Christians how to live.[5] Without an understanding of Evagrius's philosophical knowledge, his letters remain somewhat opaque.

Second, Evagrius's letters do not manifest a merely moral or pastoral intention. Where Origen had avoided the term gnosis, Evagrius deliberately revived it, possibly because he encountered and opposed other kinds of gnostics in Egypt.[6] Rather, the correspondence exhibits Evagrius's pedagogic practice of synkatabasis—teaching elementary knowledge to beginners—and also his dedication to gnosis—to that advanced contemplation appropriate only to the advanced. In the examples that follow, Evagrius appears as both a philosopher and a gnostic.[7]

Finally, Evagrius's correspondence contains letters that express the purpose of letter writing itself. They show him teaching his correspondents by example how letters can reinforce ascetic practice and point their recipients toward the difficult goal of contemplation.[8]

The Letter on Faith

One letter stands outside the corpus of letters written from the desert. To the lone surviving letter intact in Greek, the so-called *Letter on Faith*, an important volume of studies has been dedicated.[9] Yet the essays in the volume concern not that letter's relationship to the overall corpus but its connection to the work of Evagrius as Gregory's archdeacon, and they all assume that the letter was written as the author purportedly left Neocaesarea for Constantinople and work with Gregory.

Joel Kalvesmaki has successfully challenged the traditional chronology of the *Letter on Faith* and shown that it was composed, not on the way to Constantinople in approximately 380, but after Evagrius's departure from that city for Jerusalem in 382. Thus this apparently singular letter still can be seen as the first of Evagrius's corpus—but its context is in his anachoresis, not his flight from a monastic community, as earlier scholars supposed.[10]

This letter is of great interest because it is the only letter of Evagrius's directed toward a wide public—now, as Kalvesmaki has argued, to be understood as the supporters of Gregory and the Nicene cause left behind in Constantinople under the leadership of Nectarius, Gregory's somewhat inept successor. The letter itself has little to say about letter writing, but its valedictory sentence indicates Evagrius's literary interests. He wrote: "But giving thanks to the Father and the Son and the Holy Spirit, we have put a limit on the letter, since 'every measure is best' (*pan metron ariston*, or 'everything in moderation') as also the proverb (or, 'maxim') says."

As Gregory's aide-de-camp in Constantinople, possibly assisting in the composition of his "Theological Orations," and participating in discussions of strategy and the literary presentation of theology, Evagrius surely knew a wide circle of highly placed Christians.[11]

The last passage, though, shows already a reflective side of Evagrius, and even his capacity for humor and self-deprecation—a capacity he would deploy when he became a solitary a few years later. For the last line, describing his very long letter, seems to have been written tongue-in-cheek. At fifteen pages of modern printed Greek text, it is by far his longest letter—a parade of technical Trinitarian theology, already marked by his interest in gnosis, and flouts its own advice delivered in the final maxim. It also pays tribute to Gregory Nazianzen's *Letter* 51 on the art of letter writing, which advises concise expression in letters.

This final maxim also shows that Evagrius has learned, not only from the Cappadocians, but also from earlier authors in the Alexandrian tradition, notably Eusebius and Clement. In all his works, the latter wove elements of Greek poetry into the fabric of his thought about gnosis and the gnostic to show how the gnostic finds truth in the *praeparatio evangelica*, the pre-Christian authors in whom the Logos spoke darkly, or secretly, of his own coming. Thus in quoting one of the seven sages by means of a proverb traditionally attributed to Theoboulos of Lindos, and using a word now traditionally (since the LXX) applied to Solomon's proverbs, Evagrius not only fuses biblical and Hellenic wisdom, but also quotes an author whose father's alleged name—Evagoras—echoes his own.

Finally, the substance of the proverb expresses the virtue that Evagrius notoriously lacked—temperance. According to Palladius, Evagrius's life in Constantinople and Jerusalem looked like that of a vain, excessive man in full—one who certainly did not practice "moderation in all things." Ancient humor is notoriously hard to catch, but here Evagrius manages a wry twist at his own expense, right at the end of this long and complicated letter.

Yet in a sense, the proverb, if he meant it seriously, also set Evagrius on the course of *metron*. If he had learned the rhetoric of his teachers Basil and Gregory, and of others who were involved in the discussions and disputes of late-fourth-century Christianity, for the remainder of his writing life he eschewed all but the traces of rhetorical figures that lingered in his letters. Although some of his works take the form of discourses (*To Eulogius*, for example), most employ the customary philosophical genre of the kephalaion, and his commentaries are in the form of scholia—glosses on short biblical texts.[12] Evagrius measured them out carefully, by number, their rhythm contributing to ease of rumination and memorization. Indeed, some of his letters stand as introductions to these works—they have a limited audience, one whose confidence Evagrius had gained and upon whose discretion he came to depend.[13]

A Theory of Letters

The *Letter to Melania*[14] is another lengthy epistle, like the *Letter on Faith*. This one, however, unlike *Letter on Faith*, does not use a mention of a letter to terminate itself. Rather, Evagrius divides the letter into two parts. The first part uses his concept of epistolography to describe the possible relationships between the sender and recipient of a letter, to mark degrees of separation and nearness between human minds and the divine mind. The second part of the letter builds upon the first by showing how the Trinity draws near to the gnostic who has disposed the mind for such an inhabitation and thus overcome the very distance that letters express and bridge.

Ironically, letters are for concealment: they contain "those intentions and hidden secrets that are not for everyone and are not to be revealed to anyone except those who have a kindred mind" (1.1). When Evagrius states this general purpose for the sending of letters, he has not only put himself within the gnostic monastic context; he has also provided the possibility of finding a way to decode his other letters. It seems more than likely that at least some of his letters contain figures—taken from biblical texts or from the natural world—that can be understood only by those who not only possess a key to this symbolic teaching, but who are *gnostikoi* by virtue of their training in the *praktikē* and are in a position to apprehend natural and theological *theōria*.

The *Letter to Melania* takes a highly schematic view of letters based on the idea that the Trinity has written creation—where God the Father, the mind of the epistolographer, has used his "power and his wisdom" to inscribe an ordered creation as an intermediary between the human mind and the mind of God. Strongly implied throughout the first part of the *Letter to Melania* is that not only does the virtuous and knowledgeable human mind decode the writing of creation, but that that mind also can imitate God in writing a secretive interpretive manual—a gloss on the "scripture of creation," so to speak, that points both to the meaning of that scripture and to the power of its interpreter. Evagrius himself exemplifies this, for instance, in his glosses on the books of Ecclesiastes and Proverbs—or, interestingly, in his guide to the attacks of demonically prompted *logismoi* to be found in his *Antirrhetikos.*

Evagrius begins the *Letter to Melania* with a description of the necessity of writing letters; he may be recalling the unfortunate necessity of writing and reading that is found in Plato's *Phaedrus* (275a–d). Letters are the direct result of unfortunate distance:

> My dear sir, You know that when those who are separated far from each other by a great distance (which many different necessities may occasionally bring about) want to know—or to make known

> to one another—those intentions and hidden secrets that are not for everyone and are not to be revealed to anyone except those who have a kindred mind, they do so through letters. (1a)[15]

Evagrius follows this assertion by a description of how letters reduce the distance between correspondents; they also give vision, speech, and hearing. Then the comparison takes a strange turn. Evagrius adds,

> Though they seem to sleep, they keep vigil in that their intended actions are fulfilled; though sick, they flourish; though resting, they are active; I might even say, "though dead, they live"—for a letter is able to relate not only what is, but also what has been and what shall be. (1b)

Thus letters, Evagrius seems to say, are inert signs, yet they contain hidden life, having been inscribed by the members of the body representing the senses corresponding to intellectual intentions. Again, though, Evagrius turns back to subjects that must be concealed: "As for the rest—the many different benefits, significations, differences, and strength that are found in them—now is not the time to speak concerning each and every one of them" (2b).

Letters are occasions, too, of pedagogy—even, it could be said, the form of pedagogy, since they are analogous to the creation by which divine intentions are known. They reach two kinds of readers: the first is illiterate, and this kind of reader is analogous to a person who is still in the process of learning the *praktikē*. It is possible to be illiterate with respect to creation as a letter:

> Just as the matters in letters are hidden from those who do not know how to read, likewise one who fails to understand the visible creation also fails to be aware of the intelligible creation that is deposited and hidden in it, even as he stares at it. (14)

Others, though, can read letters, and the letters of creation: "The one who [can] read these letters rejoices in them—and so, I would say, does one who cannot, when he is helped whenever necessary by one who can" (3). If Evagrius is thinking of the same pedagogy by which he structured the hundred chapters of the *Praktikos* and the fifty of the *Gnostikos*, the "hearers" are beginners, and the "readers" are their teachers: "The former benefits from what he sees, the latter from what he hears. But the benefit of hearing is not as great and stable, as that of seeing: you [Melania] know what a difference there is between them" (3). This second, gnostic, level is admirable by comparison. Attending to creation they read God's letter: "In reading a letter, one becomes aware through its beauty of the power and intelligence of the hand and finger that wrote it, as well as of the intention of the writer; likewise, one who contemplates creation with understanding becomes aware of the Creator's hand and finger as well as of his intention—that is, his love" (5–6).

Yet there is another level, beyond that of hearers and readers who, after all, are still in a state of separation from God:

> All these things done through letters are types for absolutely everything that is undertaken by those who are far from God, who through their contemptible deeds have created a rift between themselves and their Maker. Now God in his love has fashioned creation as an intermediary. It exists like a letter: through his power and his wisdom (that is, by his Son and his Spirit) he made known abroad his love for them so that they might be aware of it and be drawn near. (2)

Beyond them are those who evidently have an angelic status; they are the "pure, rational and intelligible," who do not "read" "letters" of God by means of creatures, but are served by the Word and Spirit (the hand and finger) "directly and not through the mediation of created things." These are the ones who do not need letters, because of their "purity, good deeds, and proximity to God"—to these the Word (hand) and Spirit (finger) of God minister directly. These are "nearby and . . . though creatures, are pure, rational, and intelligible. They give form to their Creator's wisdom and power as clearly as mighty and ancient signs" (10).

In each of these cases, letters beckon to draw close through the understanding, and direct readers so that they "advance by them toward, and come to understand, the things invisible."

> If letters, in service of those far away, can signify what has happened and what will happen, how much more can the Word and Spirit know everything and signify everything to their body, the mind. I can truly say that many pathways (ideas?) full of various distinctions meet me here—but I am unwilling to write them down for you because I am unable to entrust them to ink and paper and because of those who might in the future happen to come upon this letter. Furthermore, this paper is overburdened with presumption and therefore unable to speak directly about everything. My thoughts were drawn to all these things when I was inclined to scrutinize the great gift of letters. And since by this great marvel I was gladdened and roused to the glory and grace of the one who gave it, I was inclined to set down these things for you, my friend, so that you might plait a garland of unending praise for him who makes praise his own. (31)

Finally, Evagrius asks that they may praise God without the mediation of created things, but through the mediation of his Son and Spirit to be worthy "to delight in his unending love and to praise him for all he has done. Amen."

Evagrius then turns to state "what is the reason for this letter to your grace." This reason intends to convey a compact discussion of Evagrius's advanced teaching. This need not detain us now, since the current essay's purpose is not to talk about Evagrius's teaching itself, but to discuss his teaching about letters, and to consider how the latter appears in his collection of letters.

Evagrius's Letters to Friends

In none of his other letters preserved in the collection does Evagrius give such a lengthy theoretical statement of the nature and significance of letters. It can be seen, though, that his understanding of their role carries forward into those letters sent to friends with whom he had the closest personal connection as a scholar and devoted solitary—

Melania, Rufinus, John of Jerusalem, and others. Other correspondents, some of them anonymous, were taught, encouraged, or rebuked—and we may gather Evagrius's estimation of their state from his remarks. If Gabriel Bunge is correct in his identification of the addressees of the letters, there is (in addition to the *Letter to Melania*) only one letter to his guide in which he discusses the character of letters. Yet in *Letter* 1, another to her, Evagrius writes of the very pedagogy that he described in the *Letter to Melania*, indirectly characterizing her as a *gnostikē*:

> Strive therefore, you temperate woman, be a good example not only to women, but also to men, so as to be an archetype of patience. Because it is fitting to a student of Christ to struggle unto blood, showing everyone that Our Lord arms women, too, with manliness against the demons, and that he strengthens weak souls through the gifts of the commandments and of faith. (1.5)

As we shall see, Evagrius often applied to his Jerusalemite friends Melania, Rufinus, and John images drawn from biblical texts having to do with cultivating the land, applying to himself the image of infertile soil. Thus in *Letter* 37, he wrote again to Melania, quoting Proverbs 25.25, "Like cool waters for a thirsty soul, so good tidings to a distant land." "And the letters you sent beautifully quench the fire that comes upon us from toils, as did those [others] you wrote, that your Excellence sent to us before. For everything that is useful to our honor and our refreshment you provide from your whole soul" (37.1).

Letters to Rufinus on the Subject of Letters

Rufinus was Evagrius's guardian and also his physician, a role he assigns to the *gnostikos* in the treatise by that name, as well as in the *On Prayer*. *Letters* 5, 19, 22, and 40 in the Syriac collection are directed toward Rufinus, if Bunge is correct. In these letters, Evagrius repeatedly addresses Rufinus as his superior in the monastic life and as the source of letters that support Evagrius's own work. Thus in *Letter* 19, Evagrius writes, "Sufficiently have the letters of your holiness consoled us, and cooled the multitude of my afflictions." In return for healing letters, Evagrius writes, "may our Lord allow you to gain mercy with the Lord on that day [of judgment], you who remembered us sinners and lowly ones who are lacking anything worthy of your love."

The prologue to *Prayer* is, in some ways, similar to the *Letter to Melania* in that it both reflects on letters and sends a compressed version of a key Evagrian teaching—this time, on the subjects of the dispositions necessary for prayer and the types of occurrences that happen during prayer. If Sinkewicz is correct in his interpretation of the letter-prologue, Evagrius makes a veiled reference to the famed teacher Makarios the Egyptian, "the elder of Sketis," in the opening sentence:

> When I was feverish with the burning of the impure passions, you restored me, as usual, by the touch of your letters filled with love for God; you consoled my mind when it was worn out in the midst of the most shameful things, following the example of (our) great guide and teacher in his blessed manner.

Evagrius goes on to tell Rufinus that "there is no wonder in this, for noteworthy deeds have ever been your lot." Inserting a reference to Genesis 29.20–30, Evagrius compares Rufinus to Jacob working for fourteen years to acquire as wives both Leah and Rachel, where Evagrius creates the original reading of the two women as signs of the practical and gnostic life, respectively.

The matter to note in this particular letter, however, is Evagrius's teaching on the nature of letters. Again, letters offer both a substitute for actual presence; but they also in this instance imitate prayer and recapitulate the relationship between Leah and Rachel as stages of mystagogy. Evagrius writes:

> I hold you in admiration and envy greatly your excellent intention expressed in your desire for the chapters on prayer. For you desire to have them not only in hand and in the ink on the page, but established in your mind through love and freedom from resentment.

Although Sinkewicz does not note the connection, an interpretation of Deuteronomy 11.18 may stand in the background here, possibly connecting Evagrius's interpretation of Rachel and Leah to an equally allegorical, but differently construed, interpretation in Philo.

Evagrius goes on to write: "But since 'all things come in pairs, one opposite the other' (Ecclus. 42.24), according to the wise Jesus (ben Sira), accept them according to the letter and according to the spirit." Here as elsewhere in Evagrius's consideration of letters, it can be pointed out that since the spirit depends, in some sense, upon the material or the flesh, the two aspects of the letter are continually linked, and not opposed, to each other. Nonetheless, "understand," he writes, "that intelligence is prior to any writing, for if this were not so there would be no written work."

The rest of the letter-prologue contains a numerological exegesis of the 153 chapters of the accompanying collection of kephalaia as signifying not only the catch of fish in John 21.11–14, but also the figures of the triangle and the hexagon, geometric figures that correspond to the "knowledge of the Trinity and . . . the ordering of the present world." Ultimately, he writes that there are three additional construals of the number 153, and—once again in what may be an ironic spirit—follows his elaborate, and recondite, interpretation with a plea that "you will not look down on the humble character of the chapters," which he likens both to Philippians 4.12 ("want and plenty") and the widow's mite of Matthew 12.41–44. In the first he evokes the apostle Paul ("I know how to be abased, and I know how to abound; in any and all circumstances I have learned the secret of facing plenty and hunger, abundance and want"); in the second he is a widow, by definition poor. In each case, he gives examples, presents himself as a further example of the same state of poverty—and confirms that it is such a person as himself who is beloved by Jesus, "[who] accepted them over the riches of many others."

Finally, the letter-prologue widens to include not only Rufinus as his addressee, but the Jerusalem community over which Rufinus provides. Evagrius concludes: "Therefore, as you know how to guard the fruit of good will and love for your true brothers, pray for the person who is sick that he may get well and then take up his bed and walk by the grace of Christ (Mark 2.11)." Perhaps by referring to the healing of the paralytic, Evagrius is suggesting here that his "burning of the impure passions" has immobilized him—has made him paralyzed with respect to the *praktikē* and knowledge. In any case, in the letters to Rufinus he consistently presents himself—or at least the "self" on display in letters for others as well to read—as a sick solitary, unable to perform the virtues without the aid of Rufinus.

Again, in *Letter* 22, Evagrius speaks to Rufinus as the healer, now not of his epithumia, but of his sadness (*lupē*). Here, interestingly, Evagrius equates the arrival of a letter from Rufinus with a visit from "chaste brothers" sent by Rufinus. As we shall see below, the prospect of a visit from Severa had anything but a consoling effect, but this may be explained by other factors in Evagrius's self-presentation. It is also of interest that in *Letter* 22, Evagrius refers to Rufinus, and not Melania, as the one who clothed him with the monastic schema and added him to the number of solitaries—by which he perhaps means that he is a numeral "one" added to other "ones":

> Many times have you consoled us, whether by means of letters or by means of the arrival of chaste brothers. And what should I repay to the Lord (Ps. 116.12) for all this grace I have found with you? Only with toil can someone find a genuine father. But now I give praise to our Lord and to the day of his resurrection, on which you gave me the holy schema, and mixed me into the number of the solitaries.[16]

Again, the remainder of *Letter* 22 presents Evagrius as Rufinus's patient—as a sick man, as a sad man, and as someone afflicted by the reasonings that create mental obstacles. Several passages follow:

> Sufficiently has your Holiness's letter cheered us and refreshed the great amount of my afflictions, but "may you find mercy with the Lord's mercy on that day," (cf. 2 Tim. 1:18) since you have remembered us, sinners and humble ones, not possessing anything worthy of your love.

> I am receiving your letters (*epistolai*) with all sweetness, and I am dismissing [my] sadness through rejoicing, and I am causing my mind to enter the "harbor of life" out of the tumult [of the wave-like] thoughts that beat upon it. For as these things that you are writing to us are like something of the love [that] Christ wrote out for you. Because of this I was an obedient child, receiving reproof from a genuine father. And I rejoice that I grow rich through your love, the memory of which encourages me.

> And [how] well your letters sweeten me when, indeed, I make an obstacle for my mind, bringing it close to bodily realities. Ungrudgingly I wait for [my mind] to hasten to you, that it will be similar to your love. Whoever keeps away from you is out of tune with that love. Whoever is discordant to love sins against Christ, who is our Love and who binds the mind of his friend in calm (*apatheia*) through the knowledge of the truth of the holy Trinity.

A final letter to Rufinus, number 40 in the Syriac collection, reflects upon the effects of Evagrius's visit to Rufinus in Jerusalem. Apparently he received a letter from Rufinus that was awaiting him upon his return by ship in 393 from a port in Palestine to, presumably, Alexandria:

> Short was the time of our meeting, and something from the seeds of your virtue were placed in us obscurely—and it is difficult to cultivate them. But the comfort of your letter precedes us. For as something that happens to those who have dream visions, who begin to reap fields, [something similar to] this happened to us in the friendship of your love, for in a little time we multiplied many things.
>
> But we had a cause for this encouragement, this ship that carried us to Egypt and our Lord Jesus Christ, he who drew us to the desert. Now is the time to inspect each of my fields, and to give and to receive the flowers of your letter and to crown it with the fruits of each one, and to renew the love of Christ, which is standing with us, before the chief love which is our Lord. (44.1–2)

Letters to John of Jerusalem, Concerning Letters

John of Jerusalem was himself a monk before he followed Cyril as bishop of Jerusalem in 387. Along with Anatolius, he was another of Evagrius's companions in Jerusalem, and was a monk like Anatolius before his consecration.[17] As bishop of Jerusalem in the 390s, he became involved in the early rumblings of the first Origenist controversy in Palestine, and occupied a more public position generally than did Rufinus or Melania. Evagrius, according to Bunge, sent five letters to John, and these survive in the collection. Of these, three take up the topic of letters and their capacities for conveying healing and knowledge. All three letters also, I believe, speak to John as a public man and a bishop, displaying a kind of respect that might have been expected. The first suggests that John had spoken to Evagrius as one who cultivated the earth, perhaps "the earth of his heart." A short passage, from *Letter* 2, suggests that John has written repeatedly to Evagrius:

> You have continually written to me as if to a farmer, as if I were able to work the spiritual earth. But you have not yet seen my field, which is full of thorns and thistles, nor my vineyard, which is dry, and unfruitful, and lacking in spiritual grapes.

The next two extracts come from two letters to John, and directly describe the effects of the letters upon Evagrius. They do not, however, advance any theory of letters, and thus may adhere to Evagrius's own teaching in the *Gnostikos* to exercise discretion with priests. *Letter* 50 reads:

> You have looked at "the one sitting in darkness and in the shadows" of grace, and have enlightened with the light the eyes that continually looked for consolation. And "what shall I return to the Lord" in the face of the comfort of your letter, in which you have corrected my soul that was wearied in listlessness? And you mentioned the "death dog," which because of the multitude of my evils I am casting out in the desert, up to today. For the bird of prey also does not approach me, as if he would consume the flesh of my evils

and constrain the eyes that many times, as if [they were] a crowd, made sport of the spiritual father.

The third letter to John that describes letters similarly expresses appreciation for encouragement, but without the allegorical interpretation and concealed teachings that were included in his letters to Melania and Rufinus:

> Brother Palladius gave me the letter of your holiness, in which you enumerated the evils of this world that are pressing upon our heart and increasing in our mind. But when I read and was aware of prevailing, I praised our Lord that he condemned me to ignorance and bound me to a mill like an irrational animal to go around in a circle, blindly.
>
> Nonetheless, a letter such as this is useful for solitaries, because demons, by means of [the thought of] vainglory make known a great "calm of the sea" and do not show to us the "drowning" of virtue or knowledge. Write [letters] such as these to me, and awake my drowsiness, I implore you—for I see that the dreams of vainglory are great in me when there presses hard upon me, as well, the cure of the offense from the healing of souls.

Two further letters contain references to the nature and effect of letters. One of them Bunge identifies only as a letter to "an [unknown] friend," but its treatment of the written letter as an image of a moral or spiritual quality is familiar from other letters. Evagrius writes:

> Well has your letter shown your genuine affection toward us, and your guileless love—and I am amazed at how your words resemble an image of the purity of your soul, and the comfort from it is like the soul living in it. (40)

The strong, and continuous, friendship between Evagrius and his teacher Gregory of Nazianzus is well known, and need not be discussed further here. The following extract reflects Evagrius's own regard for Gregory's correspondence, as well as their separation. Gregory died in

390, and as a man who expressed sadness and loneliness in his final years, he may well have sent a letter of rebuke to Evagrius, even though he himself seems not to have written frequently, at least if the following passage is credible:

> A long time have you kept silence from us, oh man of wonder. For you once planted in me the vine, and by means of your letters you have watered its tender growth. But perhaps we have afflicted you to no little degree, because we have not sent you a fruit-basket [i.e., a basket used at the grape harvest] that is full of the grape-clusters of our letters. But I am not the cause of this—rather, it was the one who afterwards planted in me a vine-shoot of evil and has dishonored all my cultivations. But now that you are a herald of grace through our Lord, forgive me because I have delayed, and I promise that I will not do this again. (12)

Two letters of Evagrius may reflect the same kind of reprimand that seems to lie behind the letter just quoted. The first, *Letter* 3, expresses surprise at receiving the news, through a letter, of the whereabouts of a certain solitary—perhaps one of Evagrius's students. Evagrius writes:

> What I had not hoped to receive you have sent us through a letter, but what we longed to learn you have not made known—that is, who has taken you; whether he is blessed; where you live; and with whom you were [staying]. These are the things I very much wish to learn.
>
> But do not be amazed nothing has happened for you according to your will. Remember the one who "had nowhere to lay his head." If they would not receive him who is the head of all things, how much more a man who is small in stature. You indeed know that the earth does not reject the foxes that try to make their dens in it: but how often does it cave in on those who dig wells for themselves, caving in and suffocating them. But we glorify the Lord that you have through love remembered us and demonstrated to all the uprightness of your love.

Another letter, much less mild in its rebuke, forcefully accuses the recipient, who apparently had written an admiring letter to Evagrius, of causing him to entertain one of the "reasonings," *logismoi,* that placed a solitary like Evagrius in danger. The anonymous recipient should not have written such a provocative letter to Evagrius; in fact, no one should write such letters to apotactites. This letter suggests that its recipient was one of the *kosmikoi,* or worldlings, to which Evagrius referred in the *Gnostikos* as members of a group toward whom pedagogical concealment should be exercised.

> We wrote to you no answer [to your letter] but a very great reproof because you sent us a letter and aroused in us a magnitude of the force of vainglory. It annoyed me in the reading of your praises, as in the eye [?] of vainglory. But it is certainly not allowed to write thus to those who have renounced the world, and to weaken the souls of those who are enfeebled with passions and vain desires—but against these words one should not hesitate to write against. (52)

The rest of the letter continues in this vein.

Finally, the series of letters concerning the proposed trip of the deacon Severa is interesting, not only because it shows that Evagrius will no longer be willing to have a personal visit from a female—even a female monastic—but because it seems to have prompted Evagrius to compose a treatise to female solitaries living in community, the *Virgin.* The letter is also interesting because it may reflect Evagrius's judgment about the progress of Severa and her community:

> Your spiritual intention was reported to me—and I am surprised by your love of learning and rejoice at your progress. After you put your hand to the ploughshare, you have not turned back seeking this corrupted world and transitory things. Instead, you "fight the good fight" so as to be "crowned with the crown of righteousness" and behold Christ the bridegroom, whom you seek through good actions. For this is true seeking: when one seeks the Lord through action.

> Now there is no one who works iniquity, yet seeks righteousness; no one who hates her companion, yet seeks love; no one who lies, yet seeks the truth. So now, this is seeking the Lord: to keep the commandments, with true faith and genuine knowledge. The model of these things is the writing we have sent to teach you; it has expanded to you the straight and narrow path that nevertheless leads to the kingdom of heaven.

The above extracts from the letters show that Evagrius presents himself, in conformity with the views of his two best-known treatises, the *Praktikos* and the *Gnostikos*, as a teacher who, though afflicted by the thoughts prompted by demons, and by the vices of anger and sadness, remains a *gnostikos*. In this sense, Antoine Guillaumont was right to call the letters Evagrius's workshop.

If the letters are considered from the point of view of Evagrius's developed theology, then they do indeed seem to be the early sketches for his treatises, reflecting associations and conversations that probably formed the basis for a teaching expressed in the style of proverbs and kephalaia. Yet in this essay, and in considering how best to translate the letters, I have considered the letters as works of ascetic discipline in their own right. Ultimately, it will be necessary to compare them more closely with the letters of other ascetics, and of his teachers Gregory and—more distantly—Basil, as well as with the letters of Gregory of Nyssa, with whom, as Kevin Corrigan has shown, Evagrius has much in common. Yet even a cursory investigation demonstrates that Evagrius, like other late ancient writers, intended his letters to charm their recipients and to teach them at a level appropriate to the recipient and, finally, to maintain the bonds of friendship.

Notes

1. For the dating, see A. Guillaumont, *Un philosophe au désert*, 26.
2. Brakke, *Talking Back*, 45.
3. A brief survey of the letters and their importance is in A. Guillaumont, *Un philosophe au désert*, 140–45. Gabriel Bunge's annotated translation, with extensive introduction, is fundamental: *Briefe aus der Wüste*.

4. Frankenberg, *Euagrius Ponticus*, 564–610. A partial Armenian version exists: Sargisean, *Vark' ew mantenagrut'iwnk'*. The surviving Greek fragments are discussed in C. Guillaumont, "Fragments grecs inédits," and Géhin, "Nouveaux fragments grecs." For English translations, see Luke Dysinger's translation of the corpus along with the *Letter to Melania* and the *Letter on Faith* at http://www.ldysinger.com/Evagrius/11_Letters/00a_start.htm; Augustine Casiday's translation of six letters in his *Evagrius Ponticus*; Joel Kalvesmaki's translation and discussion of *Letter* 57 in "Soul's Cure"; my discussion of *Letter* 55 in Young, "Cannabalism"; and the letters accompanying surviving Greek treatises, most recently in Sinkewicz, *Evagrius of Pontus*. An earlier version of the *Ad Melaniam/Letter to Melania* was made available in Parmentier, "Evagrius of Pontus' *Letter to Melania*," and reprinted in Ferguson, *Forms of Devotion*.

5. Driscoll, *Evagrius Ponticus*, discusses Evagrius's adaptation of ancient philosophical techniques as a "way of life"; see now Kevin Corrigan's correlation of the thought of Evagrius with the Platonic and Aristotelian traditions in his *Evagrius and Gregory*.

6. See Goehring, "Monastic Diversity"; Goehring describes the various pathways for ascetic practice in fourth-century Egypt, including strong evidence for Manichaean asceticism, with its emphasis upon a related form of gnosis.

7. See Young, "Evagrius the Iconographer."

8. Young, "Path to Contemplation."

9. Bettiolo, *L'epistula fidei*. No further bibliography for this much-studied text will be cited here; two works worth mentioning in this connection are, however, Gain, *L'église de Cappadoce*; Gregg, "Form."

10. Kalvesmaki, "*Epistula Fidei*."

11. The relationship between the two is attested not only in Evagrius's letters to Gregory, and in his praise in the *Letter on Faith* and in the *Praktikos*, but also in Gregory's will, published most recently in English translation in Daley, *Gregory of Nazianzus*, 188: "To Evagrius the deacon, who has labored much with me and shared in my thinking, and has shown his kindness in many ways, I confess my gratitude before God and men. God will repay him with greater kindnesses; but that we might not neglect even little signs of friendship, I wish that he should receive a shirt, a colored tunic, two cloaks, and thirty gold pieces."

12. See von Ivánka, "ΚΕΦΑΛΑΙΑ," and an extensive examination of the kephalaion as a philosophical form in Brisson, *Porphyre, Sentences*.

13. For instance, the letter to Anatolius, acting as an introduction to the *Praktikos*, or the letters (7, 8, 19, and more properly 20) that raise the matter of an unwelcome visit to Evagrius proposed by the deacon and *hēgoumenē* Severa, the last one to Severa herself introducing the *To a Virgin*. See Elm, "The

Sententiae Ad Virginem by Evagrius Ponticus and the Problem of Early Monastic Rules," and "Evagrius Ponticus' *Sententiae Ad Virginem.*" Sinkewicz discusses the works of Evagrius possessing dedicatory epistles as prologues and introductions: the treatise *Eulogios*, *Vices*, *Praktikos*, and *Prayer* (see introduction, Sinkewicz, *Evagrius of Ponticus*, 183–84). The same is true of the *Antirrhetikos*, but its dedicatory epistle has been separated from the body of the work and transmitted separately, as *Letter* 4 (to Abba Loukios) in the collection. David Brakke reattached and translated it from the Syriac in *Talking Back*, 45.

14. In addition to the discussions of the *Letter to Melania* in Parmentier, "Evagrius of Pontus' *Letter to Melania*," and in Casiday, *Evagrius Ponticus*, see Niculescu, "Coping."

15. Section numbers for the *Letter to Melania* are taken from Parmentier, "Evagrius of Pontus' *Letter to Melania*."

16. Unless specified otherwise, the translations that follow are taken from my own working—and as yet unrefined—translation of those portions of the Syriac letters that have to do per se with writing letters.

17. For a discussion of Evagrius's relationship with John of Jerusalem, see Clark, *Origenist Controversy*, 190–91.

CHAPTER 7

Philoxenos of Mabbug and the Simplicity of Evagrian Gnosis

Competing Uses of Evagrius in the Early Sixth Century

DAVID A. MICHELSON

> *Write also to him, if it seems proper to you, that he cease from his blasphemies on an ineffable, pure, incomprehensible, and holy doctrine.*
>
> —instructions from Philoxenos of Mabbug regarding the "Evagrian" Stephen Bar Sudayli[1]

The identification and condemnation of Evagrius as an Origenist at the Fifth Ecumenical Council in 553 has long exercised a powerful influence over the interpretation of his works. In antiquity, this condemnation resulted in the suppression of the "speculative" portions of the Evagrian corpus. In the modern era, the recovery of these texts has been a top priority for scholarship on Evagrius. While contemporary scholars have been less interested in making theological condemnations, their efforts to reconstruct the *Kephalaia gnostika* and other texts have nevertheless been guided by the same intellectual question originally set out by the council of 553: Were Evagrianism and Origenism synonymous systems of speculative metaphysics?[2]

The modern scholarly answer to this question has usually concurred with that of the council in 553. One recent survey characterizes Evagrian mystical theology as "desert Origenism, the bold speculative Origenism of Evagrius and his friends."[3] While such scholarly observations may be useful for understanding the historical Evagrius, it is also important to ask what has been obscured by both the ancient and modern rush to associate Evagrianism with speculative Origenism. To either champion or condemn Evagrian speculation were not the only possible interpretations of the Evagrian corpus in the early sixth century.[4] *Pace* the council and its opponents, some fifth- and sixth-century followers of Evagrianism actually downplayed the speculative elements of Evagrianism as peripheral to, or even in tension with, his overall system for the attainment of divine knowledge. Too much scholarly attention to the council's charges of speculative excess may cause us to overlook the full range of Evagrian schools of thought in fifth- and sixth-century theology. In this chapter, I will demonstrate that the Evagrian system of ascesis and contemplation had developed in multiple directions by the sixth century such that it could also be mobilized as a powerful polemical tool *against* theological speculation. Specifically, in the writings of some West Syrian authors, such as Philoxenos of Mabbug, we find a hermeneutic of simplicity that profitably paired the Evagrian emphases on ascetic practice and the ineffability of contemplation with traditional Syriac approaches to denouncing heresy. The result was a decidedly Evagrian path to contemplation that also rejected theological speculation. In the case of Philoxenos, the emphasis on simplicity was motivated by what he perceived to be the speculative excesses of his era, excesses that later came to be synonymous with the intellectual tradition of Evagrius. As such, the writings of Philoxenos offer a window into a dispute and reveal diversity within the reception of Evagrius in the early sixth century. These conflicting interpretations of Evagrius may or may not accurately reflect the intent or design of

Evagrius himself. Nevertheless, understanding their viewpoint is essential for understanding the contested legacy of Evagrius and the varied reception history that his works enjoyed across the Mediterranean and Mesopotamian worlds.

Historical Background

Born to Syriac-speaking parents in Persia in the mid-fifth century and dying under imperial exile in Thrace in 523, Philoxenos lived a life that spanned varied geographic, political, and religious environments.[5] Most likely educated as a dyophysite (i.e., an adherent of a two-nature Christology) in the School of Edessa (now in Nisibis), Philoxenos eventually adopted miaphysite or one-nature Christology and became a monastic organizer and agitator in Antioch during the 470s. During the brief ascendency of the miaphysite party under the emperors Zeno and Anastasius, Philoxenos was elevated to the metropolitan see of Mabbug/Heirapolis in the imperial diocese of Euphratensis. Occupying a see strategically positioned on the Euphrates at the imperial border, Philoxenos involved himself in the ecclesiastical politics of both Persia and Antioch. Philoxenos was a prolific author who developed a reputation as a theologian of asceticism (in the tradition of Syrian monks and Evagrius) and Christology (in the tradition of Ephrem and Cyril). For Philoxenos, these two themes were interrelated. He considered his fight against Christological error to be part of the spiritual contest of asceticism; both were struggles in pursuit of the knowledge of God. Philoxenos's numerous works, primarily written for monastic audiences, reveal a series of monastic networks that were the focus of his pastoral care and polemical energies. These monastic networks were also the locus for Philoxenos's involvement in the struggle over the correct interpretation of Evagrianism.

Philoxenos as Evagrian Theologian

Nearly all of Philoxenos's works show some influence of the Evagrian ascetical and contemplative system.[6] In addition, several works are particularly marked by their direct interaction with themes or texts from the Evagrian corpus. These works can be classified into roughly two categories based on genre and the nature of their participation in the Evagrian tradition.[7] In the first group, we may place Philoxenian works that were intended as constructive theology in an Evagrian mode. These texts emulate the writings of Evagrius himself or elaborate on his themes. A second category of works may be distinguished from this first one based on the occasion for their composition. Works in this second category are reactions to competing schools of Evagrianism. These texts are polemical interventions within the Evagrian tradition and address specific questions concerning the correct interpretation of Evagrius. Texts in the first category include Philoxenus's fragmentary biblical commentaries and his ascetic discourses on the path of perfection.[8] Texts in the second category are fewer, namely, two letters—one to a certain Patrikios of Edessa and another to a certain Abraham and Orestes concerning Stephen Bar Sudayli.[9] Of these two, the lengthy *Letter to Patrikios* (running to sixty-four pages of Syriac text in its *Patrologia Orientalis* edition) offers the most detailed evidence of Philoxenos's involvement in a struggle over the reception and interpretation of Evagrius and will be a major focal point of this study.

Before turning to Philoxenos's intra-Evagrian interventions, however, it is useful to briefly survey Philoxenos's own interpretation and adaptation of Evagrius as found in his constructive works. His most explicit discussions of Evagrian contemplation occur in his biblical commentaries on Matthew, Luke, and the prologue of John. For example, in his commentary on the prologue of John, Philoxenos directly quotes from the prologue of the *Praktikos*:

> For thus have said some of the fathers and the ancient doctors, who thus knew how to understand the meanings of the words of the holy scriptures, that each one who wishes to become a full man in Christ, and a seer of the knowledge of his mysteries, that he must be born again of water and the Spirit, as Our Lord said. And instead of the milk that feeds the natural born, he must suckle and grow through faith and learn by that to fear God and to keep the commandments. And here are the words said by them on this sub-

> ject: "My sons, the fear of God confirms faith, and abstinence from food guards faith, hope and perseverance keep abstinence unwavering, and by these is also acquired impassibility, which begets spiritual love, which is the door to the vision of natural knowledge, from whence one is transported to divine words and another kind of blessedness."[10]

This passage is representative of how Philoxenos adapted the Evagrian path of *praktikē* (ascetic practice) and *theōria* (mystical contemplation) to fit both his own scriptural hermeneutic and the vocabulary of Syrian monasticism. Philoxenos's attachment to Evagrius is pragmatic rather than slavish. For Philoxenos the value of the Evagrian corpus is derived not from the authority of its author but from the fact that it eloquently epitomizes a number of early Christian views concerning the nature of the ascetic life (e.g., themes also found in Origen, Athanasius, the Cappadocians, and the *apophthegmata* of desert fathers). Thus not only did Philoxenos not appeal to Evagrius by name (indeed he is only named once in all of the Philoxenian corpus), but he even attributes Evagrius's words to a plural subject, for example, "some of the fathers and the ancient doctors."[11] A similar observation can be made about Philoxenos's preferred shorthand for the Evagrian ascetic system, that is, "keeping the commandments" and "learning the fear of God." Although these terms were frequently used in the Evagrian corpus, they were also part of a widely shared monastic lexicon.[12] Much of what Philoxenos valued about Evagrianism was not uniquely Evagrian, but was conveniently systematized and consolidated in the Evagrian corpus.

In his biblical commentaries, Philoxenos frequently appealed to "keeping the commandments" and the "fear of God" to explain how the mind ought to approach the meaning of the biblical text or the mystery of the incarnation. This use of the Evagrian path to divine knowledge is perhaps most evident in his commentary on Matthew.[13] For example, Philoxenos explains at several points that divine knowledge is not received through a hyper-literal attention to the words of the biblical text:

> It is necessary for those who desire to become receivers of knowledge about these mysteries [of the incarnation] that instead of

> study with words, and especially of these which engender controversy, they should be steadfast in the labours of life and keep the commandments which were entrusted [to us] by our Saviour, by which they can gain wholeness of soul and a purified mind and become impassible. . . . And from there they will be able to receive inside themselves the knowledge of these things—things which are inward beyond the body and about which we first receive instruction through the obedience of faith.[14]

In this passage the force of Philoxenos's Evagrian epistemology stands out in the phrase "instead of study with words"—a statement that one would not readily expect to find in a biblical commentary. Instead of a focus on the biblical text, Philoxenos argued that divine knowledge (e.g., a knowledge inward and beyond the body) is acquired through a specific Evagrian formula for contemplation based on ascesis.[15]

In addition to Philoxenos's biblical commentaries, his thirteen ascetic discourses offer a broad view of his ascetic theology and some hints about his theological preferences in adapting the Evagrian tradition. The date of these ascetic discourses is uncertain; they perhaps date to a period earlier than the biblical commentaries, which can themselves be securely dated to the first decade of the 500s.[16] Because the Evagrian element is less explicit in the *Discourses* (e.g., the term *theōria* does not appear), some earlier scholarship saw these works as representing a pre-Evagrian period of Philoxenos's ascetic theology.[17] But work by Paul Harb and Paul Géhin among others has now shown that Evagrian themes are constantly present just below the surface of the text.[18] The strongest evidence comes from one direct citation of *Praktikos* 2, which follows the pattern we have seen above, identifying the source of the quotation as "one of the spiritual teachers."[19] Similarly, Philoxenos used Evagrian ascetic terminology throughout the *Discourses*, though not to the exclusion of older Syriac ascetic categories.[20] As Irénée Hausherr has noted about the *Discourses*:

> Through knowledge of the theories of Evagrius . . . Philoxenos occupies a very interesting place in the history of Syrian spiritual theology: the intersection where the ancient spirituality of Aphrahat

> and Saint Ephrem . . . meets philosophy. . . . Firmly attached to the Syrian tradition . . . [Philoxenos] is nevertheless open to receive Alexandrian speculations, on the condition that they do not disrupt [monastic] simplicity, which is itself the mother of all the virtues and of faith itself.[21]

In short, Philoxenos valued the Evagrian system to the extent that it was compatible with or epitomized the broader traditions of asceticism to which he was already committed.

In practice, this use of Evagrian themes proceeded in a manner similar to how Philoxenos employed Evagrius in his biblical commentaries.[22] In one discourse, Philoxenos exhorts his hearers to take up the steps of ascesis toward spiritual love and divine vision:

> . . . let us wake up wholly to keep all His commandments. For the nature of the fear of God is that it urges us [to do] one thing, and one thing only, for it stirs us up to do all the commandments. . . . Now the end of the path of good works is spiritual love, therefore from love divine wisdom is produced, and the blessed David well taught us that the beginning of this way of wisdom is the fear of God.[23]

The monastic way of life presented in the *Discourses* is built on an Evagrian epistemology and vision of spiritual progress from ascetic practice to divine knowledge. Thus in the ninth discourse Philoxenos calls his listeners to aim for "purity of the soul, from which a man enters into spiritual love, from which is born knowledge, the mirror of everything, and from which the understanding rises step by step unto divine conversation."[24]

The steps on the path toward perfection in the *Discourses* are built around seven themes: faith, simplicity, the fear of God, poverty, gluttony, abstinence, and fornication.[25] Of these themes, it is "simplicity of nature" that holds the pride of place, as the key for one to "be able to receive the knowledge of the mysteries that were above nature."[26] Philoxenos puts forward simplicity (a concept closely intertwined with stillness/*shelyā* in his writings) as a defining characteristic for those embarking on the monastic life:

> Now by simplicity is not to be understood the "simplicity" of the world, I mean "stupidity," but the singleness of one thought (or mind) which is simple to hear and judges not, and which accepts and enquires not, after the manner of a child receiving the words from his nurse, and like a child also who receives the instruction of books from his master without criticizing, or asking questions [concerning] those things which are said to him. . . . Simplicity then befits the life and conduct of solitaries . . . and simpleness belongs to poverty.[27]

For Philoxenos, simplicity is not the final stage of the ascetic pursuit of purity and divine knowledge; it is the essential beginning point, a mental stance without which no progress toward perfection would be possible. Philoxenos points out that this ideal monastic state is the same as that of Adam and Eve enjoying God's presence in the innocence and simplicity of paradise:

> For who is there that does not know how simple was that first union of those at the head of the race of men, and how simple they were with respect to the whole way of life of the world . . . because the course of the things of the world had not yet been revealed to them; but they drew near divine visions, and face to face God would speak to them continually. . . . And in the form of a man He would show them everything firsthand, and they never thought in their mind as to where was the dwelling of Him that was showing them [these things]; or from what time He was; or if He had been made, and if He had been made, who made Him; and why He created us; and for what reason He set us in this Paradise and transmitted this law to us. These things were far from their minds because simplicity does not think of such things, but it is wholly and entirely drawn to the hearing of that which is being said to it, and its whole thought is mingled with the word of him that speaks with it . . . just as the child is with the speech of whoever talks to him.[28]

In this passage we catch a glimpse of how Philoxenos envisioned that simplicity of mind served as a check on the temptation to speculation in later stages of the monastic life. True divine vision could occur only if the state of simplicity was maintained. Philoxenos intended simplicity to serve as a powerful test between competing interpretations of Evagrianism. Those that allowed speculation to trump simplicity revealed that they had been corrupted by worldly wisdom and craftiness.

Competing Evagrianisms

The *Discourses* and the biblical commentaries offer a general outline of Philoxenos's constructive adaptation of Evagrius. To glimpse the polemical interventions that Philoxenos made over the proper interpretation of Evagrianism we must turn to his *Letter to Patrikios* and his *Letter to Abraham and Orestes*. Although neither letter can be dated securely, their tenor fits what would be expected from the correspondence of an influential bishop responding to requests for his opinion. Philoxenos perhaps wrote these letters during the first two decades of the sixth century when he was at the height of his influence as a bishop.[29] Regardless of their date, both letters reveal how Philoxenos mobilized his particular adaptation of Evagrianism as an antispeculative resource within the monastic debates of his day.

Philoxenos's letter to Abraham and Orestes offers the most direct criticism of competing interpretations of Evagrius. According to Philoxenos, the immediate occasion for his letter to Abraham and Orestes was that he had learned that Stephen Bar Sudayli (who was then in Jerusalem) had written to them in Edessa as part of a propaganda campaign.[30] Philoxenos was concerned to refute Stephen's promotion of *apokatastasis*, a doctrine of universal restoration in which all creation becomes consubstantial with divinity. Philoxenos's letter was not, however, the opening salvo in this dispute. Apparently Stephen had previously been circulating his writings in Edessa and Antioch and at one point had even been on respectful terms with both Philoxenos and Jacob of Serugh.[31] Once the full extent of Stephen's teaching on *apokatastasis* became known, however, he was sent letters of censure by both Jacob and Philoxenos (the latter, alas, does not survive).[32] Having fled Edessa for Jerusalem, Stephen was now writing to Abraham and

Orestes, perhaps sending them a copy of his teachings. While it is not clear if Philoxenos was worried that Abraham and Orestes were inclined toward Stephen's teaching, Philoxenos's letter does allege that Stephen has been falsely claiming in Jerusalem that he had followers in Edessa (perhaps including Philoxenos himself!).[33] In response, Philoxenos encouraged Abraham and Orestes both to write a rebuttal to Stephen and to take precautions lest Stephen's heresy spread in Edessa.

Little is known about the specific contents or sources of Stephen Bar Sudayli's teachings.[34] In his letter to Abraham and Orestes, Philoxenos mentions two sources by name in an effort to prove Stephen guilty of heresy by association. First, Philoxenos accuses Stephen of having been a follower of John the Egyptian (it remains uncertain to whom Philoxenos is referring): "He [Stephen] desired, being puffed up like a vain and proud man, to originate heresies himself also, like John the Egyptian, whom for a short time he even followed."[35] Next Philoxenos explicitly criticizes Stephen for having misunderstood or misrepesented Evagrius's teaching on motion (*meṣiʿanutā*) and the fall as part of his system of *apokatastasis*:

> Following the Jewish doctrine, he [Stephen] appoints after the resurrection two retributions, one of which he calls rest and the other perfection, one liberty and the other divinity, together with other names which he has contrived and applied to them. . . . But regarding his belief, that rest is one thing and the kingdom another; and the glory before the consummation one thing, and the consummation itself another; we would ask, from what Holy Book, or prophet, or apostle, or teacher, has he received this doctrine of a division into three orders? For he understands, as he says, by the sixth day motion, having taken the term motion from the monk Evagrius; by the Sabbath, that Christ will be all and in all men; and by the first day, that God will be all in all.[36]

This mention of Evagrius as the source for Stephen's heretical ideas reveals a new dimension of Philoxenos's engagement with the broader Evagrian tradition. Although Philoxenos found much to adapt and appropriate from Evagrius, this passage reveals that his commitment to Evagrius was nuanced and specific to one school of Evagrian interpretation. There were certain interpretations of Evagrius that Philoxenos considered inappropriate and perhaps others of which he was not even aware.[37]

The nuance of Philoxenos's position becomes even more apparent when this passage from the *Letter to Abraham and Orestes* is set within the larger context of the Philoxenian corpus. In the first place this passage is notable in that it is the only occurrence in any of his writings in which Philoxenos actually refers to Evagrius by name. Moreover, it is also the only instance in his entire corpus in which Philoxenos portrays Evagrius in a negative light, namely, as the source of heretical ideas. Interestingly, Evagrius and John the Egyptian are the only two theologians named in the whole letter. While Philoxenos's condemnation of John the Egyptian is strongly worded, his mention of Evagrius is ambiguous. Contrary to how some have read this passage, it is important to note that Philoxenos does not directly condemn Evagrius as a heretic nor does he make it clear if Stephen's theological errors arose directly from Evagrius or if they were instead the result of Stephen's mistaken interpretation of Evagrius. Nevertheless, by associating Evagrius with Stephen's heretical speculation Philoxenos makes it clear that he does not consider the wider Evagrian tradition to be beyond criticism. In fact, the strength of Philoxenos's condemnation suggests that Stephen's interpretation of Evagrianism had currency among the monasteries and churches of Syria and Palestine. The letter offers a tantalizing glimpse into this controversy. Philoxenos criticizes Stephen for resorting to theological sloganeering on his cell wall and also for sending pamphlets from Jerusalem to Edessa to spread his views.[38] Philoxenos warns Abraham and Orestes against letting Stephen's writings fall into the hands of "nuns dwelling within church-precincts" and other parties whom he thought might be easily swayed.[39] Finally, Philoxenos concludes by admonishing Abraham and Orestes to take action themselves: "Write also to him, if it seems proper to you, that he cease from his blasphemies on an ineffable, pure, incomprehensible and holy doctrine."[40] Philoxenos's exhortation here is not merely a condemnation of speculative theology:

it draws rhetorically on an "Evagrian" epistemology to make its point. Philoxenos condemns Stephen's speculations as indicative of error, vainglory, and a lack of inward simplicity. In Philoxenos's interpretation of the Evagrian system, speculative biblical interpretation such as Stephen's was futile since pure divine knowledge is ineffable and not attained through human wisdom.

Philoxenos and Patrikios

The *Letter to Abraham and Orestes* offers only a snapshot of Philoxenos's polemical intervention over the proper interpretation of Evagrius. Fortunately a second relevant source, the *Letter to Patrikios*, offers greater detail concerning Philoxenos's engagement in an intra-Evagrian dispute. This letter is arguably Philoxenos's most explicitly Evagrian work. The occasion for the letter was an inquiry sent to Philoxenos concerning the correct way to follow the Evagrian path to divine knowledge. In response, Philoxenos made a spirited defense for his particular interpretation of Evagrianism. Aware that other competing interpretations of Evagrius were attractive to his audience, he went to great lengths to defend his version of the Evagrian system. In this regard, the appeals to Evagrius in the *Letter to Patrikios* diverge from Philoxenos's usual practice of employing Evagrius as representative of the larger monastic tradition. Instead, Philoxenos's objective in this letter is to establish his own Evagrian *bona fides*. To this end we find him appealing directly to the authority of Evagrius in the singular as "one of the blessed," "one of the saints," or "one of the fathers."[41] Moreover, throughout the letter Philoxenos emphasizes strict adherence to the Evagrian path toward divine love as set out in the *Praktikos* and *Gnostikos*. He refers to this gnostic system as a "just canon of spirituality" and "an order and a lawful course."[42] Philoxenos also displays his commitment to the Evagrian system by extensively employing Syriac equivalents of a number of Evagrian technical terms.[43] Indeed, Philoxenos makes more frequent use in this letter of direct quotations from Evagrius than in any of his other works. (In the *Letter to Patrikios*, Philoxenos quotes from *Praktikos* 15, *Gnostikos* 36, *Gnostikos* 25, and *Praktikos* 79.[44] This letter is the only one of Philoxenos's works with more than one direct quotation from Evagrius.) In addition to direct citations, Philoxenos also alludes to a number of additional Evagrian works including *Antirrhetikos, On the [Evil] Thoughts, The Eight Spirits of Wickedness, Treatise to the Monk Eulogius, Counsel to Monks, Chapters to Monks, Kephalaia gnostika,* and the *Letter to Melania.*[45] In short, comparison of the *Letter to Patrikios* with the rest of the Philoxenian corpus makes it clear that in this instance Philoxenos made an extraordinary effort to mobilize the authority of Evagrius behind his arguments in order to persuade his Evagrian audience.

Unfortunately we have very little specific information about the immediate audience for this letter. According to manuscript colophons, the text is a response to an inquiry from an Edessene monk (lit. "solitary") named Patrikios.[46] Patrikios, if that is indeed the name of Philoxenos's correspondent, had asked "whether it is right that the commandments of our Lord must be kept indeed or if it is not possible that one could be saved who had not kept them."[47] For Philoxenos "keeping the commandments" served as a shorthand description for the first half of the Evagrian path leading from ascetic practice to *theōria*. Philoxenos thus interprets Patrikios's question about "keeping the commandments" as a hostile attempt to find a loophole in the Evagrian system that might allow advanced monks to dispense with ascesis in favor of "spiritual contemplation."[48] Philoxenos vehemently opposes such a suggestion. In his view, true Evagrian contemplation is not possible without continuing ascesis. Obedience to the commandments is the first step in defeating vices. This stage of *praktikē* leads to impassibility. In some cases (and this is the point of contention in the letter), the monk who has been restored to the prelapsarian purity of the soul may then be granted to progress to the highest levels of *theōria*. The monk is then a seer of the soul, exercising discernment to perceive the movement of the love of God and to acquire divine gnosis.[49] If the monk ceases his ascetic practice, then he is no longer able to achieve divine vision. Philoxenos strongly warns Patrikios that contemplation without ascesis is actually just unfettered theological speculation posing as *theōria* in order to distract the monk from true ascetic practice.

Patrikios seems to have been asking whether the monk was obligated to fulfill the commands of Christ in Matthew 25 to care for the "least of these" or whether the monk's need for solitude allowed the monk to be free of obligations that might become distractions to contemplation. Over the course of answering this particular question, Philoxenos deepens the topic, turning Patrikios's question into an occasion for a systematic inquiry into the relative value of the two main steps of the Evagrian ascetic system (*praktikē* and *theōria*). Philoxenos firmly insists that the monk must never cease *praktikē* because "fulfilling the commandments" is a requisite part of *theōria*. In other words, the monk must be doing the one to maintain the other. To abandon the commandments would mean an end to contemplation. Philoxenos emphasizes to Patrikios that his strict interpretation of the Evagrian system is the only acceptable path for the monk to reach the ultimate stage of gnosis, that is, divine love and wisdom.[50] It is for this reason that the letter is so marked by Evagrian terminology and content. Philoxenos's objective in writing is not to persuade Patrikios to become an Evagrian (it seems obvious enough that Patrikios already was one) but to remind Patrikios of the norms required by a particular interpretation of the Evagrian theory of spiritual progress. Indeed, this emphasis on "right order" is evident in the way that Philoxenos refers to the path to gnosis as "an order and a *lawful* course."[51] This is such a recurrent theme that René Lavenant's index for the *Letter to Patrikios* cites twenty-five occurrences of the word "order" in the letter.[52] Noting this in the letter, one medieval copyist of the text noted in his colophon that Philoxenos wrote the work to inform Patrikios that his questions were "out of order."[53] Modern readers such as Géhin have noted that Philoxenos situates his Evagrianism within "a framework of strict orthodoxy."[54]

This emphasis on order comes out most strongly when Philoxenos categorically states that the monk should commit himself to *praktikē* and not presume to advance to the stage of *theōria* at his own discretion instead of awaiting the divine gift of *theōria*.[55] Philoxenos's preference for *praktikē* seems initially counterintuitive because the purpose of the Evagrian progression is to lead to *theōria*. Philoxenos does hold a high view of *theōria* in the letter, but the monastic context of this letter has determined Philoxenos's priorities and rhetorical strategy. Specifically, Philoxenos sees disordered *theōria* as one of the most dangerous pitfalls for those on the monastic path. In a lengthy section at end of the letter, which begins with comments on Paul's account of the third heaven in 2 Corinthians 12, Philoxenos warns that "fantasies" posing as spiritual *theōria* threaten to lead astray those on the path to true *theōria*.[56] Philoxenos does not mince words as he condemns such fantasies as the handiwork of heresiarchs and demons in a long list stretching from the opponents of the apostle Paul in ancient Corinth through Valentinus, Bardaisan, Marcion, Mani, and John the Egyptian (the same heresiarch condemned alongside Evagrius in the letter on Stephen Bar Sudayli).[57] Although the list is archaizing, Philoxenos is particularly concerned about speculative theologians among his contemporaries who, in the vein of such "heresiarchs," threaten to lead the monk astray and distract him from the true path of *praktikē* and *theōria*. For this reason Philoxenos supplements the list of heresiarchs with two much longer and more recent narrative examples, both of whom were (like Bar Sudayli and, perhaps, Patrikios) Edessene monks led astray by false contemplation.

The first case is a Messalian named Adelphos, who mistakenly believed in a demonic impersonation of the divine (presented as a reverse image of a saint from the *apophthegmata* whom Philoxenos mentions as successfully resisting such a temptation).[58] The second case is another monk, Asuna, whom Philoxenos claims was deceived by a demon into throwing himself from a cliff.[59] Before and after these examples, Philoxenos makes it clear to Patrikios that he raises the issue because this danger is particularly grave for monks: "indeed this is the monk's battle."[60] In short, Philoxenos fears that the monk will be overly drawn to speculation, neglecting the true path to contemplation, which is *praktikē*.

This contemporary monastic context perhaps explains Philoxenos's use of the four explicit citations from Evagrius in the letter. Based on their rhetorical placement, the citations fall into two categories: those in support of Philoxenos's argument and those that hypothetically call it into question. The first citation in the letter falls in this second category—Philoxenos puts a passage from the *Praktikos* in the mouth of Patrikios as a hypothetical objection.[61] Philoxenos begins by cautioning Patrikios against too much reading of scripture as a possible source of dissipation either through distraction back to the text or worse through enticement to false (human) knowledge:

> Those who seek to learn the knowledge of Christ through words raise questions about it and desire to find it through a multiplicity of readings. By doing this, however, they do not go forward but fall backward. For a multiplicity of readings produces a multiplicity of thoughts in the soul.[62]

He then anticipates that Patrikios will object by citing *Praktikos* 15, where reading scripture is praised by Evagrius as useful toward contemplation:

> And if you say to me that it is written by one of the blessed ones [Evagrius], that readings of the scriptures collect the thoughts, I say that also this is true. It does collect the thoughts of him who answers the world or of him who turns toward the world and of him whose whole self is apart from himself. Thus it is necessary for one to read in the scripture for a short time until he becomes conscious that his thought has been collected and then one should turn from reading to purity of prayer lest in reading one seek the knowledge and interpretation of the words and fall again into the same state of distraction. Instead, one should seek the spiritual *theōria* of the words, for in that alone does the mind take delight.[63]

Philoxenos goes on to justify this advice with an explanation that reflects the concerns of a bishop who knew well the troubles that could arise in monasteries in an age of theological controversy such as the early sixth century.

> For not everyone reads the scriptures well or with knowledge, so there is one who reads the scriptures in order to recite it, and another to memorize it, and another desiring to learn interpretation, and another to learn exercises of the knowledge of the soul, and another disputation with heretics, and another is moved by passion for learning—though to tell the truth it is [all] vainglory. And in any one of these goals or in all of them, the mind reads until it is looking outside [itself]. For what need does a solitary have for what the interpretation of a certain word is or for what the mean-

> ing of such-and-such a phrase is? Walk the path before you and stand in the place of [spiritual] knowledge and you will have no need for questions about it [spiritual knowledge].[64]

Returning to consider the role of the citation of Evagrius at this point, we can make two interesting observations. The first observation concerns the authority accorded Evagrius. It is worth noting again that Philoxenos anticipates that Patrikios will cite Evagrius against him. This context makes it clear that the *Letter to Patrikios* should be interpreted as an intervention in an intra-Evagrian dispute. Second it seems that for Philoxenos the most important concern is not simply to explain the Evagrian system but to curtail illicit intellectual activity or temptation by the monks that threatens to derail that Evagrian system—in this regard Philoxenos will not permit even Evagrius to be used to justify exegetical speculation. It may be that Philoxenos purposefully interjects this hypothetical objection so that he can point out that the "true" Evagrian position is not concerned with "a multiplicity of readings" because that only produces a multiplicity of evil thoughts.[65] Whether or not Philoxenos was familiar with the whole range of competing Syriac interpretations of Evagrius, his strict warning against reading scripture for speculative reasons offers a glimpse of the monastic audience he is writing to, one in which recitation, interpretation, disputation, and passion for learning were prized, perhaps even above monastic stillness.

Evidence to support this interpretation appears when we consider the rhetorical placement of the other three citations from Evagrius in the letter. In each of these three cases, Philoxenos cites Evagrius at a particularly crucial point in his argument.[66] Of these three Evagrian citations, the first two (from *Gnostikos* 36 and 25) occur back-to-back immediately following the examples of false monastic contemplation (that is, Adelphos and Asuna). Rhetorically, the words of Evagrius serve as a bookend and imprimatur to Philoxenos's warning that inappropriately seeking *theōria* is out of line with the Evagrian system of contemplation. Géhin has noted that these passages are construed in such a way as to bring in the authority of Evagrius to support Philoxenos's warnings about the dangers of illicit questions.[67] Thus Philoxenos seems to be using the *Gnostikos* to promote ascetic practice rather than seeking divine knowledge. It also seems likely that Philoxenos has again called upon the authority of Evagrius at this point because he is aware of competing interpretations of the Evagrian system, specifically that of Patrikios, but perhaps also that of Stephen Bar Sudayli, which we have already seen.

Further evidence of Philoxenos's involvement in an intra-Evagrian dispute comes in the final Evagrian quotation used in the *Letter to Patrikios*.[68] This quotation serves as a seal on the whole letter, appearing in the final paragraph of the whole work and further underlining Philoxenos's point that speculation beyond the straight path of the orthodox faith is incompatible not only with attaining *theōria* but even with obedience to the *praktikē*. Thus, as a final argument, Philoxenos draws upon *Praktikos* 79 to remind Patrikios to follow the proper order in his pursuit of divine love: "On its own, the act of obeying the commandments is not able to purify the strength of soul unless the true faith which befits the commandments is found in the soul."[69] In this quotation, a subtle change has been introduced from the Greek version of *Praktikos* 79. Philoxenos or a prior Syriac translator has substituted the phrase "true faith" in place of "*theōria*." One can see how such a translation would appeal to Philoxenos. Rather than speculative false *theōria*, which would lead to heresy, Philoxenos encourages Patrikios to hold to the "true faith." Indeed, he concludes his letter by mentioning that he has appended a treatise on the faith. It is not clear what this document was, but it seems likely to have been one of the many confessions of faith that Philoxenos wrote and circulated, documents designed to quash inappropriate theological speculation.[70]

In short, the *Letter to Patrikios* is profoundly Evagrian in its outlook, yet at the same time Philoxenos is aware that the interpretation of Evagrius was contested. Philoxenos was concerned lest distorted emphases on *theōria* encourage speculative exegesis, spawn heretical doctrines, and divert monks from the obedience and stillness needed to reach true contemplation.[71] Perhaps because this impulse toward speculation and exegesis was coming under an Evagrian authority, Philoxenos relied explicitly on Evagrius to counter such inclinations. In a manner very similar to a passage in Evagrius's *Treatise to Eulogios*, Philoxenos urged Patrikios and all monks to eschew words and undertake *praktikē*: "The commandment [of Christ] is not interpreted in a word but by its keeping! Just as the mysteries of natures and the scriptures are not interpreted in words or discourses but are 'interpreted' by their illuminated *theōria*, so also the commandments are not interpreted by words but actions!"[72] In short, Philoxenos relied on an interpretation of Evagrian gnosis where the rigidity of the path to knowledge and an emphasis on the ineffability of *theōria* could serve as useful antidotes to theological speculation. To play on words, he advocated a "practical" Evagrianism.

Monastic Milieux

The observation that the *Letter to Abraham and Orestes* and the *Letter to Patrikios* reveal an intra-Evagrian dispute should not come as such a great surprise if we put these letters in the context of two contemporary but better known and competing forms of Evagrianism in Syriac intellectual circles, the S1 and S2 versions of the *Kephalaia gnostika*.[73] Indeed, Guillaumont had speculated (but without sufficient evidence) that Philoxenos was perhaps even responsible for the adaptations made in the translation of the S1.[74] One need not go as far as attributing authorship to Philoxenos to see the relevance of the S1 to the theological priorities of the *Letter to Patrikios.* As David Bundy has noted in his sympathetic reading, "The philosophic structures [of the S1] which sustain the spirituality *require little speculation* beyond the boundaries of what an Alexandrian or Cappadocian reading of the Biblical narratives could offer."[75] There is much room for future study of the relationship between S1, S2, and the *Letter to Patrikios*. Already our reading of the *Letter to Patrikios* allows us to begin to revise scholarly appraisal of the S1, a branch of the Evagrian tradition generally neglected in contemporary scholarship. Even a nuanced treatment like that of Bundy (which notes that "the redactor of the S1 so painstakingly crafted the new version to be congruent with Evagrius' text") begins by asserting baldly "S1 does not help us understand Evagrius. That much is certain."[76] Such a judgment may or may not be the case, but we should not allow such assertions to blind us to the fact that for some fifth- and sixth-century authors, the S1 revision was most likely viewed as an important theological corrective needed to preserve the true path to divine gnosis from those who, under the cover of Evagrius, threatened to divert ascetics from that path with speculation and heresy.[77]

Who were these ascetics that composed Philoxenos's intended audience? Who were these Evagrian readers he hoped to sway to the side of anti-speculative Evagrianism? Few historical details are available, but we may at least offer a composite image based on hints found in the text. It seems likely that these readers were almost universally monastic. In the *Letter to Abraham and Orestes*, Philoxenos is concerned about Stephen sending "followers of his with letters and books" and warns the presbyters, "If therefore he has either written unto you, as I have learned, or has sent unto you his blasphemous books, be careful lest they fall into any person's hands, and especially into those of the nuns dwelling within church-precincts."[78] Philoxenos also expresses concern about monks visiting Stephen in his own cell. Similarly Philoxenos warned Patrikios that his pursuit of contemplation should avoid "all the false books called 'revelations' which were put forth by the heresiarchs which contain worldly fantasies and heavenly dwellings and regions, and changed heavens, and distinctive places of judgment, and diverse images of powers from above—all of which are illusions of a mind disturbed by passion and the work of demons."[79] Beyond the works of Philoxenos we may also find parallels elsewhere from the later popularity of such texts as the *Corpus Dionysiacum* or the *Book of the Holy Hierotheos*. Géhin has posited at least three schools of Evagrian interpretation that varied in their receptivity to "Origenism," that of Philoxenos, that of Stephen Bar Sudayli, and that of Sergius of Resh'ayna (which Géhin posits as the same as the S2 tradition).[80] Similarly, Brian Daley has also shown a wide variety of positions among early sixth-century authors to either promote, moderate, or oppose "Evagrian Origenism."[81] In particular Daley notes that opposition to Origenism (such as by Philoxenos or Severus of Antioch) often correlated with efforts to promote a "Christological middle ground."[82] In short, we may place Philoxenos's efforts to promote a moderated S1 Evagrianism within a larger volatile context in which he was seeking to persuade an audience of monastic readers perhaps interested in both speculative cosmologies and speculative Christologies.[83]

Philoxenos's *Letter to Patrikios* lays out a reasoned case against speculation. It is worth noting here, however, that the struggle between competing Evagrianisms was not merely played out in the realm of texts. In the monastic milieux of sixth-century Syria, authority could be earned as much by ascetic performance as by adherence to a theological system. We catch a glimpse of this in the opening of his letter to Patrikios, where Philoxenos rhetorically dismisses his own ability (as a busy and distracted churchman) to give advice to the solitary Patrikios, whom Philoxenos himself describes as "a holy one" even though the letter soon makes it clear that Philoxenos strongly disapproves of the theological tendencies of Patrikios's thought.[84] Even more startling is the opening of the letter by Jacob of Serugh (Philoxenos's contemporary and ally) written directly to Stephen Bar Sudayli in which Jacob seems to praise Stephen's ascetic piety.[85] While in both of these cases a certain literary trope of deference is at work, there also seems to be a real acknowledgment that the reputations of both Patrikios and Stephen were such that, even apart from the appeal of their preference for the speculative extremes of Evagrianism, they might also win followers through their ascetic practice. How late antique monastic audiences perceived the relationship between *praktikē* and *theōria* is a complex question; nevertheless the evidence from Philoxenos suggests that it is a mistake to reduce questions of Evagrianism, or even Origenism, down to debates over specific cosmological or eschatological claims. These controversies were firmly embedded in a context of ascetic practice and monastic community.

Awareness of this context brings us to a standpoint where we may perhaps better understand the diversity of the Evagrian tradition. Augustine Casiday has written much to point out how the long shadow of anathema continues to shape our understanding of Evagrius.[86] Although he perhaps overstates his case, Casiday is right that both ancient and modern views of Evagrius have been too ready to see the Origenist elements as the defining key to Evagrian thought. Setting aside any sort of "quest for the historical Evagrius," it seems clear that a strong case should be made that for some Evagrians in the early sixth century, the "real" Evagrian legacy—at least the one worth defending—was a gnostic system whose attraction was not the depths of its speculative offerings but, in fact, the simplicity of its epistemology, a narrow path to divine knowledge that bishops such as Philoxenos hoped might serve as a ready defense against blasphemous speculation in an age rife with doctrinal controversy.[87] Moreover, as we begin to recognize the diversity of viewpoints that could fall within the bounds of the Evagrian tradition, we are better positioned to understand how and why certain elements were preserved as "orthodox" and others condemned. Istvan Perczel has suggested just such a similar reconsideration for the related specter of sixth-century Origenism: "While the ecumenical condemnations focus on a mythical-metaphysical system labelled 'Origenism' that was apparently in circulation in the sixth century, the 'Origenists' whom we encounter, Sergius and Stephen [bar Sudayli] included, are more concerned with the ascetic life and the inner contemplation of the soul."[88] As we have seen, a similar argument may be made with respect to Philoxenos as an "Evagrian" theologian, in other words, a theologian who sought to safeguard the Evagrian path to *theōria* against the theological distraction of Evagrian speculation.[89]

Notes

I would like to thank the editors and other contributors to this volume, particularly Robin Darling Young and Joel Kalvesmaki, for their roles in the roundtables that made the collaboration in this volume possible. The support of both Notre Dame and Dumbarton Oaks was greatly appreciated by all the participants. I was also pleased that the paper of Maria Doerfler, "Socializing Evagrius: The Case of Philoxenus of Mabbug's *Letter to Patrikios*," at the Sixth Syriac Symposium (Duke University, June 2011) gave me a further chance for an insightful interlocutor on the questions of Philoxenos's use of Evagrius. Finally, I would also like to thank Dan Riches, Christopher Johnson, and Bob Kitchen, who gave comments, and to thank my research assistant at the University of Alabama, Chris Sherrill, who died too soon to see this work completed although he did much to help me research the topic. Finally, I would like to thank Oxford University Press for permission to re-work some translations and arguments from my book, *Practical Christology*, in this present chapter.

1. Philoxenos of Mabbug, *Letter to Abraham and Orestes*, 45 (from Frothingham, "Letter of Mar Xenaias").

2. The leading scholar in the recovery and interpretation of Evagrius has been Antoine Guillaumont. See especially A. Guillaumont, *Les "Képhalaia gnostica,"* 124 ff.

3. Harmless, *Desert Christians*, 363.

4. Augustine Casiday has led the way in drawing attention to what he calls the "multiple trajectories of interpreting Evagrius." Casiday's theological agenda for the rehabilitation of Evagrius as orthodox is outside the aim of the present essay, but his call for a reconsideration of Evagrius apart from the agenda of the second Origenist controversy is a valuable observation for historical approaches to Evagrian reception history. See Casiday, *Evagrius Ponticus*, "Gabriel Bunge," and "On Heresy."

5. For further historical background and recent literature on Philoxenos see Michelson, "Bibliographic Clavis," and *Practical Christology*. The classic work on Philoxenos remains Halleux, *Philoxène de Mabbog*.

6. Philoxenos's Evagrianism has been the subject of some scholarly treatment. For previous scholarship in addition to the monograph of Halleux see Géhin, "En marge"; Géhin, "D'Égypte en Mésopotamie"; Hausherr, "Contemplation et sainteté"; Hausherr, "L'influence"; Hausherr, "Les grands courants"; Hausherr, "Aux origines"; Hausherr, "Le *De Oratione*"; Hausherr, "Spiritualité syrienne"; Hausherr, "Grand auteur"; Hausherr, "Ignorance infinie"; A. Guillaumont, *Les "Képhalaia gnostica"*; Harb, "Vie spirituelle"; Harb and Khouri-Sarkis, "L'Attitude de Philoxène"; Harb, "Conception pneumatique"; Harb, "Rôle exercé par Philoxène"; Watt, "Philoxenus"; Watt, "Syriac Adapter"; Michelson, "It Is Not the Custom"; Young, "Influence of Evagrius." A brief word of explanation about my approach is in order here at the outset. I have approached this topic not as a specialist in Evagrius but as a scholar interested in Philoxenos and in the intellectual grounding of his miaphysitism. In writing my monograph on Philoxenos, I realized that his polemical method in the post-Chalcedonian controversies could not be understood outside the context of his Evagrian epistemology and his commitment to asceticism as the path of divine gnosis. So this essay is part of a larger effort to work out that context. After this present essay was first prepared for publication in 2011, Paul Géhin published "D'Égypte en Mésopotamie," which approaches many of the same questions but from the perspective of a scholar of Evagrius interested in Syriac reception. I am pleased to find myself in substantial agreement with his conclusions, in particular his rejection of the theory that we can trace an "evolution" in Philoxenos's Evagrianism (see the discussion in note 7 below). I have attempted to

engage Géhin's interpretation when relevant, but should note that most of my article took shape before his work was published. In addition to the recent work of Géhin, the reader is also referred to my subsequent reflections on Philoxenos's use of Evagrius in Michelson, *Practical Christology*, 82–112, 178–203.

7. As Géhin notes, earlier interpretations by Guillaumont and Hausherr attempted to divide Philoxenos's works into "three periods" of evolution in Philoxenos's Evagrianism: "une première où il l'ignore presque totalement, une autre où il le découvre avec enthousiasme, et une dernière où il se montre plus critique et reserve à son égard" (Géhin, "D'Égypte en Mésopotamie," 37–38). I concur with Géhin in rejecting this approach, which is largely based on the false assumption that Philoxenos's *Discourses* do not show evidence of Evagrianism (and over-confidence about our ability to date Philoxenos's works). As I have shown in *Practical Christology* and as Géhin has shown in "D'Égypte en Mésopotamie," Philoxenos's discourses are profoundly Evagrian in their theological assumptions and structure. Finally, as will become clear below, I also strongly agree with Géhin that Philoxenos's later criticism of certain types of Evagrianism should not be taken as an indication that his own regard for Evagrius had faded (ibid., 41).

8. See Philoxenos of Mabbug, *Commentary on the Prologue of John* (ed. Halleux, *Commentaire du prologue johannique*); *Commentary on Matthew and Luke* (ed. Watt, *Philoxenos of Mabbug*), and *Discourses* (ed. Budge, *Discourses of Philoxenus*). Robert Kitchen's new translation of Philoxenos's *Discourses* appeared too late for inclusion in this study, but readers are referred to this translation as the new standard English version of the text. In particular, it should be noted that Kitchen corrects some of the errors surrounding Evagrian terminology introduced in the French translation by Lemoine. See Kitchen, *The Discourses of Philoxenos of Mabbug*; Lemoine, *Philoxène de Mabboug, Homélies.*

9. Philoxenos of Mabbug, *Letter to Patrikios* (ed. Lavenant, *La lettre à Patrikios de Philoxène de Mabboug*) and *Letter to Abraham and Orestes* (from Frothingham, "Letter of Mar Xenaias").

10. Philoxenos of Mabbug, *Commentary on the Prologue of John* (text), 173–74; cf. Sinkewicz, *Evagrius of Pontus*, 96.

11. Certainly, the fact that Evagrius's legacy was suspect and embattled may also have led Philoxenos to be reluctant to mention his name, but it is also true that at the points in the commentaries where Philoxenos quotes Evagrius he is almost universally doing so to illustrate a point that could be found in other authors. As discussed in the roundtable that accompanied the essays in this volume, it may be that the value of the Evagrian corpus was the fact that it

could be used as a more systematic and practical application of the same traditions found in the *Apophthegmata Patrum*. In other words, the attraction of Evagrianism to Philoxenos may be what Columba Stewart has described as Evagrius's own fascination, "a unified theory of everything" (Stewart, "Imageless Prayer," 181).

12. J. Leclercq, *Love of Learning*, 76.

13. The most salient fragments are nos. 9, 10, 11, 12, 26, and 28 in the commentary on Matthew and nos. 49 and 51 in the commentary on Luke. Unfortunately, this commentary has survived only in citations and excerpts, with the result that the overall objective or scope of the work is no longer clear. Nevertheless, in the fragments that survive the role of Evagrian *theōria* is particularly pronounced.

14. Philoxenos of Mabbug, *Commentary on Matthew and Luke*, 6–7. Translation adapted from Watt.

15. For further analysis of this position by Philoxenos see Michelson, "It Is Not the Custom."

16. The biblical commentaries can be securely dated to the middle of Philoxenos's ecclesiastical career (sometime between 500 and 510 since the earliest MS bears that latter date). The ascetic discourses may date from earlier, perhaps even before Philoxenos was consecrated in 485. See Philoxenos of Mabbug, *Commentary on Matthew and Luke* (Watt translation), 13*–14*, and Halleux, *Philoxène de Mabbog*, 287–88.

17. See the discussion in Géhin, "D'Égypte en Mésopotamie," 37–38.

18. See Géhin, "D'Égypte en Mésopotamie," 38n47. On this same topic, Géhin glosses over Irénée Hausherr's argument that Philoxenos purposefully conceals his knowledge of Evagrianism in the *Discourses*. See Hausherr, "Spiritualité syrienne," 183.

19. Philoxenos of Mabbug, *Discourses* (Budge), 1:297. English translation adapted from that of Budge.

20. For an overview of some of the unique traditions of Syriac asceticism of which Philoxenos was one of the last heirs, see Griffith, "Asceticism in the Church of Syria."

21. "Par cette connaissance des théories d'Evagre (et sans doute d'Origène) Philoxène occupe dans l'histoire de la théologie spirituelle des Syriens un place tout à fait intéressant: le carreour où l'antique spiritualité d'Aphraate et de Saint Ephraem, qui s'en tenait à la seule tradition evangélique, rencontre la philosophie. . . . Voilà donc la mentalité théologique de Philoxène: fermement attaché à la tradition syrienne qui appuie plus qu'aucune autre sur la foi, il a

cependant l'esprit assez ouvert pour recevoir les spéculations alexandrines, à condition qu'elles ne fassent pas tort à la simplicité, qui est la mère de toutes les vertues et de la foi elle-même" (Hausherr, "Contemplation et sainteté," 175–76). In a later publication Hausherr elaborated, "En spiritualité, Philoxène est au carrefour où, en pays syriens, la mystique vécue sans théorie rencontre l'enseignment de la théorie" (Hausherr, "Spiritualité syrienne," 185).

22. See note 10.

23. Philoxenos of Mabbug, *Discourses* (Budge), 1:212–13. English translation adapted from that of Budge.

24. Ibid., 348–49. English translation adapted from that of Budge.

25. Although these themes are virtues and vices, it does not seem that Philoxenos intended them to adhere closely to the Evagrian scheme of eight *logismoi*. These themes are more likely drawn from the discourses of Aphrahat and from the *Book of Steps*.

26. Philoxenos of Mabbug, *Discourses* (Budge), 1:86. English translation adapted from that of Budge.

27. Ibid., 74 and 153. English translation adapted from that of Budge.

28. Ibid., 83–84. English translation adapted from that of Budge.

29. Hausherr has suggested that the period of 513–16 may be taken as a possible date for Philoxenos's letter to Abraham and Orestes (Hausherr, "L'influence," 196–97).

30. Philoxenos of Mabbug, *Letter to Abraham and Orestes* (Frothingham, "Letter of Mar Xenaias"), 28, 46–48.

31. Philoxenos explains that at first he considered Stephen misguided but not dangerous, "at the time I did not know that he dared to imagine such blasphemies, for I had only met with his commentaries on a few of the Psalms" (ibid., 45–47). Moreover we have preserved from Jacob (who was more irenic than Philoxenos in general) a letter directly addressed to Stephen that reasons with him to abandon his doctrine of *apokatastasis* and goes as far as to address Stephen as a "friend of God" (Jacob of Serugh, *Letter to Stephen Bar Sudaili*, 11 [Frothingham, *Stephen Bar Sudhaili*]).

32. Philoxenos of Mabbug, *Letter to Abraham and Orestes* (Frothingham, "Letter of Mar Xenaias"), 46–48.

33. Ibid., 47.

34. Traditionally Stephen's name has been attached to the *Book of the Holy Hierotheos*, a speculative work of cosmology, which scholars have connected with both Evagrianism and the Pseudo-Dionysian corpus. Some scholars have proposed that this work is a redaction consisting of an initial Evagrian text by Stephen and a later revision that brought the work into conversation

with the Corpus Dionysiacum. For recent scholarship see Arthur, "Sixth-Century Origenist"; Arthur, *Pseudo-Dionysius as Polemicist*; Pinggera, *All-Erlösung und All-Einheit*; Perczel, "Earliest Syriac Reception." See also Van Rompay, "Sṭephanos bar Ṣudayli."

35. Philoxenos of Mabbug, *Letter to Abraham and Orestes* (Frothingham, "Letter of Mar Xenaias"), 32–33. See also Daley, *Hope of the Early Church*, 257n34; A. Guillaumont, *Les "Képhalaia gnostica,"* 316. On the confusion over the multiple figures known in Syriac tradition as John of Apamea or John the Egyptian, see Kitchen, "Yoḥannan Iḥidaya."

36. Philoxenos of Mabbug, *Letter to Abraham and Orestes* (Frothingham, "Letter of Mar Xenaias"), 34–37. For further background see Perczel, "Earliest Syriac Reception," 571. See also *KG* 1.57 and 2.64, and A. Guillaumont, *Les "Képhalaia gnostica,"* 208.

37. Géhin has argued that Philoxenos was not aware of the S2 version of the *Kephalaia gnostika* (Géhin, "D'Égypte en Mésopotamie," 41–42). This argument from silence is necessarily uncertain. While it may be the case, it should also be noted (as Géhin does) that Philoxenos is certainly aware of a number of competing interpretations of Evagrius that were more speculative and in conflict with Philoxenos's own position. It should also be noted that Géhin perhaps too quickly dismisses Philoxenos's access to materials in Greek (32). While it is fairly certain the Philoxenos was neither the translator of the S1 version nor its sponsor, it is also the case that he was the active patron of a scriptorium in Mabbug that was founded to address problems arising from the inaccessibility of Greek texts and the unreliability of existing Syriac translations. Though we have no direct evidence, it is equally possible that he might have been aware of debates or accusations about the reliability of the S1 translations of Evagrius. On the scriptorium see Michelson, *Practical Christology*, 115–19.

38. Philoxenos of Mabbug, *Letter to Abraham and Orestes* (Frothingham, "Letter of Mar Xenaias"), 42.

39. Ibid., 44.

40. Ibid.

41. Philoxenos of Mabbug, *Letter to Patrikios*, 92, 134–36, 152.

42. Ibid., 72, 108, and also 148.

43. Among others these include: *praktikē* (*pulḥana*), impassibility (*la ḥashushuta*), prelapsarian purity of the soul (*dakyuta d'nap̄šā*), *theōria* (transliterated as *te'oriya* in Syriac), seer of the soul (*hazzāyā d'nap̄šā*), discernment (*puršānā*), movement of divine love (*zaw'a d'ḥuḇā 'alahāyā*) and divine gnosis (*yid'ātā d'alāhā*). See ibid., 36, 42, 44, 56, 64, 92, 100, 152, et passim.

44. Ibid., 92, 134–36, 152. The citations from the *Gnostikos* are roughly comparable to—though not identical to—those published by Frankenberg from BL MS. Add. 14,578 (*Euagrius Ponticus*, 548–50).

45. For example compare the concept of *parrhēsia* in *Antirrhetikos* 8.10, 20, 28, with *Letter to Patrikios, 72*. Philoxenos also makes use of Evagrian analogies about contemplation of material objects (namely, gold and female anatomy) found in *Thoughts* and in *Eight Thoughts*; cf. *Letter to Patrikios*, 52–56, and Sinkewicz, *Evagrius of Pontus*, 78, 170. Compare also *Letter to Patrikios*, 44, with Sinkewicz, *Evagrius of Pontus*, 51, 222. Identification of these passages is, of course, provisory due to the ambiguities of the allusions.

46. Philoxenos of Mabbug, *Letter to Patrikios*, 22–23. It is worth noting the possibility that this is not a real letter but rather a set piece by Philoxenos and that "Patrikios" is a rhetorical device created by Philoxenos rather than an actual correspondent. If this is the case then even the name "Patrikios" might itself be intended as a caricature of a certain type of elite intellectual monk who aspires beyond his station. Against this interpretation it should be noted that Philoxenos's ire is sufficiently raised by Patrikios's question that even if it had not actually been sent to him, he must have encountered it as an opinion held by those under his episcopal care. The question and Philoxenos's response are awkwardly matched enough that it seems unlikely that it was invented merely as a heuristic device. Also of note is that the salutation and conclusion of the letter seem to be more particular than one would expect from a mere rhetorical trope.

47. Ibid., 24.

48. Ibid., 128.

49. Ibid.

50. Philoxenos does note that some (e.g., the Apostles and others from the New Testament era) reached this final state through a more direct means: a dispensation of divine grace. Nevertheless, he is firm in saying that for those in Philoxenos's own era this is the only possible path.

51. Syriac: *taksā wyubālā namosāyā* (Philoxenos of Mabbug, *Letter to Patrikios*, 108).

52. S.v. *taksā* (ibid., 158a).

53. Syriac: *law btaksā* (ibid., 22). There is perhaps more than one way that this colophon should be taken.

54. Géhin, "D'Égypte en Mésopotamie," 40.

55. Philoxenos of Mabbug, *Letter to Patrikios*, 112.

56. Syriac: *phantasias* (ibid., 130).

57. Ibid., 128. Notably, Evagrius is *not* included in Philoxenos's list.

58. Ibid., 132 and 80.

59. Philoxenos equates this Asuna with the Syriac hymnographer of the same name (ibid., 134).

60. Ibid., 130.

61. Ibid., 92.

62. Ibid., 90. In this case, Philoxenos has made an argument very similar to that of Evagrius in *Thoughts* 33.

63. Ibid., 92. See also Philoxenos of Mabbug, *Commentary on the Prologue of John* (text), 188.

64. Philoxenos of Mabbug, *Letter to Patrikios,* 92–94.

65. Ibid., 90.

66. It is also worth noting here that the only other extra-biblical authorities that Philoxenos cites directly are the *apophthegmata* and the Cappadocians. Neither, however, are introduced in support of an argument in the same way Evagrius is. Cf. ibid., 163.

67. Géhin notes how this rhetorical placement functions: "Évagre est en quelque sorte invoqué pour un bon usage d'Évagre" (Géhin, "D'Égypte en Mésopotamie," 40).

68. Philoxenos of Mabbug, *Letter to Patrikios,* 152.

69. Ibid. Cf. A. Guillaumont and C. Guillaumont, *Le gnostique,* 667.

70. For the confessions of faith see Michelson, "Bibliographic Clavis," 293–96. Philoxenos was an enthusiastic supporter of the strategy of the *Henoticon,* i.e., that theological controversy was best resolved by discouraging theological statement altogether, a theme compatible with the condemnation of speculation found in the *Letter to Patrikios.*

71. In Philoxenos's running attack on heretics in the letter, his archrival Theodore also makes an appearance as a threat to ascetic practice by allowing his misguided commentaries on the commandments to distract the monks from obeying them (Philoxenos of Mabbug, *Letter to Patrikios,* 144).

72. Ibid. Compare *Eulogios* 23 in Sinkewicz, *Evagrius of Pontus,* 50.

73. A. Guillaumont, *Les six centuries.*

74. On the relationship of Philoxenos and the *KG* see A. Guillaumont, *Les "Képhalaia gnostica"*; Bundy, "Philosophical Structures of Origenism"; Young, "Armenian Adaptation"; Watt, "Syriac Adapter"; Watt, "Philoxenus"; King, *Syriac Versions.* King makes it clear that Greek into Syriac translation work was flourishing well before Philoxenos, from which we may conclude that it is not necessary to assume Philoxenos was responsible for the translation of Evagrius, though he may have been.

75. Bundy, "Philosophical Structures of Origenism," 583. Italics mine.

76. Ibid., 583, 577.

77. What is not yet clear is whether Philoxenos or the redactor of the S1 saw himself as correcting Evagrius or correcting excesses made in his name. Nevertheless, it is clear that what matters for Philoxenos is not that the system he proposes is faithful to Evagrius but that it conforms to the teaching of scripture and to what he considered to be the spiritual and epistemic reality of how divine knowledge occurs. To some degree whether some portions of the Greek works of Evagrius were heretical is a moot point for Philoxenos (though it would be problematic and Philoxenos does seem to tiptoe around mentioning Evagrius by name, perhaps for this reason). Philoxenos's primary concern is making it clear to Patrikios how divine gnosis is achieved. In short, the *Letter to Patrikios* and the S1 should be taken as legitimate strains in the Evagrian tradition in their own right and not viewed as somehow inferior to the "proper Evagrian Origenist lens" (ibid., 578) that scholarship has privileged since the work of Guillaumont.

78. Philoxenos of Mabbug, *Letter to Abraham and Orestes* (Frothingham, "Letter of Mar Xenaias"), 28, 44.

79. Philoxenos of Mabbug, *Letter to Patrikios*, 130.

80. Géhin, "D'Égypte en Mésopotamie," 42.

81. Daley, "What Did 'Origenism' Mean in the Sixth Century?"

82. Ibid., 629.

83. For further on this connection see Michelson, *Practical Christology*, 178–203.

84. Philoxenos of Mabbug, *Letter to Patrikios*, 24.

85. Jacob of Serugh, *Letter to Stephen Bar Sudaili*, 10 (Frothingham, *Stephen Bar Sudhaili*).

86. Casiday, "Gabriel Bunge," and "On Heresy."

87. This position also finds support in Young, "Influence of Evagrius."

88. Perczel, "Earliest Syriac Reception," 566. Perczel also notes, "Be this as it may, the recognition of the Origenism of the CD [*Corpus Dionysiacum*] is a puzzling fact, for here we have a 'heretical' body of literature that has exerted a tremendous influence on 'orthodox' tradition. With the Origenism of the CD, then, we are facing the borderlines of the categories of 'orthodoxy' and 'heresy.' The CD is another instance in a mounting body of evidence that demonstrates how elements from this specific 'heresy' survived—even flourished—in the 'orthodox' fold. Perhaps we need to shift our focus from figures (who was or was not a 'heretic'?) to specific doctrines, and inquire which elements in the system disparagingly called 'Origenism' were rejected and which were incor-

porated into the orthodox tradition. . . . This spiritual element of 'Origenism' was never condemned; instead, it was warmly welcomed and enthusiastically incorporated into orthodox tradition. The CD—in its second edition, to which generations of theologians appended the appropriate commentaries—was one of the main vehicles of this incorporation. 'What God hath cleansed, that call not thou common' (Acts 10:15)" (566).

89. Perczel's portrait of Bar Sudayli being himself more oriented toward ascetic practice than speculation calls into question the reliability of Philoxenos's condemnation of Bar Sudayli, but that is an issue for future study.

CHAPTER 8

Evagrius beyond Byzantium

The Latin and Syriac Receptions

Columba Stewart, OSB

My subject is the reception of Evagrius's writings and thought in the Latin and Syriac traditions. This survey will reveal a range of receptions, from the eventual Latin near-effacement of Evagrius, to the well-known mixed reception in Greek, and finally into the warm and enduring Syriac embrace of Evagrian literature. The Latin Evagrian tradition is weak in surviving texts and little studied, but important for being the first language into which Evagrius's writings were translated. The Syriac tradition features many still-extant translations and is important for launching the translation of Evagrius's works into Armenian, Arabic,[1] and even Sogdian: fragments of Evagrius's *Antirrhetikos*, found among the manuscripts at the Turfan oasis in the Xinjiang province of northwestern China, testify to the ultimate reach of Evagrian literature into Central Asia and even beyond through the Syriac missionary efforts along the Silk Road.[2] Comparing the Evagriana latina and Evagriana syriaca will reveal particular historical circumstances that affected the reception of Evagrius's thought and the transmission of his works, and cast new light on the controversies surrounding Evagrius and his association with Origen. We will also find that many of the distinctive features of these two traditions, as well as the differences between them, will be explained by the century-long interval between the first Latin and the first Syriac translations.

Evagriana latina

The Latin reception of Evagrius's thought and writings in the first millennium can be considered in six phases:

1. Circa 400: translation of major works by Rufinus; one of the extant translations of *Chapters to a Virgin* and *Chapters to Monks* may be his.
2. 410s–420s: indirect transmission by John Cassian of Evagrian thought, terminology, pedagogy, and at least one very close textual parallel.
3. Late fifth century: translations and revision of existing translations by Gennadius of Marseilles, of which none survive.
4. Fifth–sixth centuries: anonymous translations of *Eight Thoughts* (in two versions) and at least one of the extant versions of *Chapters to a Virgin* and *Chapters to Monks* (possibly both versions if neither was translated by Rufinus).
5. Sixth–seventh centuries: Pelagius and John (sixth c.) translate excerpted Evagrian texts found among the Greek *apophthegmata*; Defensor of Ligugé (seventh c.) includes excerpts from the *Chapters to Monks* and *Eight Thoughts* in his *Liber scintillarum*.
6. Ninth–tenth centuries: circulation of *Chapters to Monks* as part of the monastic reform emanating from Reichenau and other centers.

The first Latin translations of Evagrius's writings were the earliest of all the versions, by almost a century.[3] More significantly, they were made by someone who had known Evagrius well, Rufinus of Aquileia.

Jerome witnesses to Rufinus's translations in his *Letter* 133, written to Ctesiphon in 415 at the height of the Pelagian controversy, and closely associated with Jerome's *Dialogue against the Pelagians* (*CPL* 615). Jerome's acquired dislike for Origen, which he then extended to Evagrius and, by more tragic extension, to his own friend Rufinus, need not discredit the accuracy or value of his reference to Rufinus's translation of several Evagrian texts.[4]

Deploying the classic strategy of devising a genealogy for a targeted heresy, Jerome grafts Origen, Evagrius, and Pelagius into a lineage of dangerous personalities reaching as far back as Pythagoras and Zeno.[5] Evagrius's Greek writings, Jerome notes, were read by many in the west thanks to "Rufinus, his translating disciple." Jerome adds that Rufinus was also responsible for a book about monks featuring many Origenists, among them Evagrius. Jerome is referring here to the *Historia monachorum in Aegypto* (*BHL* 6524), Rufinus's translation and redaction of a Greek monastic travelogue written in the mid-390s by a Palestinian monk.[6] Caroline Bammel has suggested that Rufinus's translations of Evagrius date most likely from 403–4, the same period when he was translating and revising the *Historia monachorum*.[7] The fallout from the Origenist Controversy was very much still in the air, which may explain why the *Historia monachorum*, with its praise of "Origenist" leaders such as the Tall Brothers, lacks a translator's preface. Rufinus may have preferred to avoid any unnecessary advertisement of his role in bringing this partisan view of Egyptian monasticism to western readers.

Jerome refers to these works of Evagrius:

> scribit ad virgines,
> scribit ad monachos,
> scribit ad eam, cuius nomen nigredinis testatur perfidiae tenebras [i.e., Melania],
> edidit librum et sententias περὶ ἀπαθείας, quam nos 'inpassibilitatem' vel 'inperturbationem' possumus dicere.[8]

These were most likely the texts we know as the *Chapters to a Virgin* (*CPG* 2436), *Chapters to Monks* (*CPG* 2435), the *Letter to Melania*

(*CPG* 2438),[9] and the *Praktikos* (*CPG* 2430). Presumably, although this is not explicit in the letter, Jerome is claiming that Rufinus had translated all of them.[10]

Jerome also berates Rufinus for translating the collection of Hellenistic (likely Pythagorean) maxims known commonly as the *Sentences of Sextus*, and then trying to pass them off as the dicta of the martyred Pope Sixtus II (or Xystus, d. 258).[11] Rufinus had translated them for Avita, wife of his friend Apronianus. The couple was now living together ascetically as brother and sister rather than husband and wife, and Rufinus was offering Avita guidance for her new path in life.[12] Rufinus's translation would prove to be very popular in the Latin monastic tradition.[13] In his preface, Rufinus notes that he has added to the original collection a few "additional and select [sentences] from a devout father to his son."[14] Scholars have commonly assumed that the additional maxims were by Evagrius even though the appendix containing them has not survived.[15] Other versions of the maxims of Sextus have tangled histories of transmission. In Armenian, the collection attributed to "Sextus" in Greek was combined with "Maxims of the Pythagoreans" to form a collection known as the "Discourse of Xystus." This compendium circulated in the manuscripts alongside the works of Evagrius.[16] Some have suggested, though with little evidence, that Evagrius edited the Greek compilation on which the Armenian version was based.[17] In later Greek florilegia, Evagrius's gnomic sayings sit alongside the Sistine ones, a fact perhaps readily explicable as an affinity of genre rather than as an indication of any direct editorial intervention by Evagrius. Sadly, it is impossible to know anything about Rufinus's additional maxims, but the Armenian and Greek evidence suggests the possibility that they were indeed by Evagrius.

Despite Rufinus's industrious propagation of the works of Evagrius, it is uncertain whether any of the extant Latin translations are his. The older versions of *Monks/Virgin* (see below) are perhaps by Rufinus. The lack of any translator's prefaces for the extant Evagriana latina means that only close philological analysis of these texts could determine a connection with Rufinus. Given that there are no certainly Rufinian translations of Evagrian works to serve as a control, however, such analysis would have to rely on Rufinus's translations of Origen and other authors. Such an undertaking would be challenging, and any conclusion would at best be tentative.[18]

Phase two of the Latin reception of Evagrius is marked by the influence of Evagrian thought and writings on the monastic theology of John Cassian (ca. 365–ca. 435). The definitive role played by Evagrius in shaping Cassian's ascetic agenda of eight *vitia* (as outlined in books 5–12 of the *Institutes* and in *Conference* 5), as well as his teaching on imageless prayer and spiritual interpretation of the Bible (*Conferences* 9–10 and *Conference* 14), has been acknowledged since the rediscovery of the Evagrian corpus in the early twentieth century.[19] Cassian's debt to Evagrius may have originated in personal contact between them in Egypt in the 380s–390s, but it was surely literary as well. The very structure of the *Institutes*, beginning as they do with a discourse on the spiritual understanding of monastic dress, was inspired by Evagrius's *Letter to Anatolios* (prefaced to the *Praktikos*). Much of Cassian's teaching on biblical interpretation and pedagogy in *Conference* 14 parallels the *Gnostikos*.[20] Cassian's description in *Conference* 24 of the tripartite nature of the soul is obviously based directly on chapter 89 of the *Praktikos*.[21] Cassian's silence about his principal, even pervasive, inspiration points to the already-clouded reputation of Evagrius: Cassian began to write his compendium of monastic instruction around the time of Jerome's *Letter* 133 savaging Origen and Evagrius. There is only a story about an unnamed brother from Pontus, "careful about the purity of his intention of heart and divine contemplation," who after fifteen years in Egypt burned all of his letters from home lest they stir up distracting thoughts.[22] Given Cassian's reticence about Evagrius, it is ironic that an extract from the Greek epitome of the *Institutes* would later be attributed to Evagrius.[23]

The evidence from phase three demonstrates less reluctance to name Evagrius or to refer to his writings. Sometime in the late fifth century, the presbyter Gennadius of Marseilles took up Jerome's project of listing famous men and their accomplishments.[24] Gennadius's update to the *De viris inlustribus* (hereafter *Vir. inlustr.*) would surely have shocked Jerome (at least the later Jerome), making room as it did for both Evagrius and Rufinus. Gennadius's tolerance is at least in part to be understood as a tribute to Cassian's inculcation of Evagrian monastic thought in southern Gaul. Gennadius's own possibly Greek origin and obvious familiarity with Greek monastic literature would have given him a context for understanding Evagrius's contribution.[25] In the chapter on Evagrius (*Vir. inlustr.* 11), Gennadius lists the Evagrian texts known to him and describes his own role in translating and emending some of them.[26] Unfortunately, Gennadius's translations do not survive and we cannot know how widely they were read.[27] Presumably they circulated in monastic milieux favorably disposed toward Evagrian thought by figures such as Rufinus and Cassian. Gennadius also mentions that he had read about Evagrius in what he calls the *Vita* [sic] *patrum*, surely a reference to Rufinus's *Historia monachorum in Aegypto*.[28] Gennadius lists the following works by Evagrius:

1. *Adversus octo principalium vitiorum suggestiones*, described as eight books composed of testimonies taken from the "holy Scriptures," obviously the *Antirrhetikos* (*CPG* 2434), which Gennadius himself translated from Greek;
2. *Centum sententiarum* for anchorites, *per capitula digestum*, obviously the *Praktikos* (*CPG* 2430), which he says had already been translated but had suffered in transmission (*per tempus confusum*) and thus required both retranslation and emendation;
3. *Quinquaginta sententiarum* intended for *eruditi ac studiosi viri*, obviously the *Gnostikos* (*CPG* 2431), of which Gennadius made the first translation;
4. teaching for "cenobites or synodites" about the common life, surely the *Chapters to Monks* (*CPG* 2435) since the Latin title parallels the Greek dedication of the text to monks dwelling ἐν κοινοβίοις ἢ συνοδίαις;
5. a small book (*libellus*) for a "consecrated virgin," surely the *Chapters to a Virgin* (*CPG* 2436);
6. "a few very obscure maxims (*sententiolae*), which as he himself says in them, 'are known only by the hearts of monks,'" translated by Gennadius and perhaps, as Guillaumont suggested, to be identified with the *Instructions* (*CPG* 2477), which contain a similar phrase.[29]

Since Gennadius makes no mention of a translator for numbers 4 and 5, one can presume that he received them in Rufinus's version. These must be the *sententiae* of Evagrius he mentions in the entry on Rufinus as examples of Rufinus's work of translation (*Vir. inlustr.* 17).[30] There he notes his translation of "sentences" by both Evagrius and "Sixtus Romanus."[31]

It will be helpful at this point to compare Gennadius's list of Evagrian works in Latin to the list of those known in Greek by the slightly earlier Byzantine historian Socrates Scholasticus. Table 8.1 provides a view of Evagrian textual transmission in the mid to late fifth century, between the first and second Origenist controversies. One sees that there were Latin versions of all of the Greek texts listed by Socrates, with the exception of the *Kephalaia gnostika* (Gennadius's *paucae sententiolae obscurae* would seem to refer to a much shorter work). Nor does any extant Latin source mention the *Kephalaia gnostika*. Did Rufinus—or someone else—ever produce a translation of that final part of Evagrius's fundamental trilogy on monastic theology? Its sheer impenetrability suggests that this was unlikely.

Few of the Latin translations in Gennadius's possession remain. Soon to disappear were the *Praktikos*, *Gnostikos*, and *Antirrhetikos*. Gennadius knew two of the three works that did survive in the west: the *Chapters to Monks* and the *Chapters to a Virgin*. The third, the treatise *Eight Thoughts* (*CPG* 2451), seems to have been unknown to him. Remarkably, all three of these texts are extant in two versions, original and revised (phase four). Although one of the versions of the *Chapters to Monks* and the *Chapters to a Virgin* (presumably the earlier ones) could be by Rufinus, this cannot be proven.[32] For *Eight Thoughts,* the two Latin versions are linked, one of them being a revision of the other by someone well acquainted with Greek monastic literature and its terminology.[33] Uniquely among the Evagriana latina, both translations of the text attribute it to Nilus of Ancyra, as in the Byzantine tradition. The first version is likely from the fifth–sixth centuries (as suggested by Wilmart,[34] Muyldermans, and Marchini), though the manuscripts themselves are from the ninth century and later. The oldest manuscript of the revised version, Paris Lat. 12,205, is from the late sixth–early seventh centuries. The unanimous witness of these manuscripts to the Nilus

Table 8.1 Evagrian textual transmission in the mid to late fifth century

Socrates, *Ecclesiastical History* 4.33.36–38	Gennadius, *De viris inlustribus* 11
Μοναχός/Περὶ πρακτικῆς	Centum sententiarum . . . anachoretis
Γνωστικός	Quinquaginta sententiarum . . . eruditis ac studiosis viris
Ἀντιρρητικός	Adversus octo . . . suggestiones . . . ex Sanctarum Scripturarum testimoniis
ἑξακόσια Γνωστικὰ προβλήματα (= *KG*)	———
Στιχηρὰ ἐν τοῖς κοινοβίοις ἢ συνοδίαις μοναχούς (= *Sentences for Monks*)	Coenobitis ac synoditis doctrina apta vitae communis
[Στιχηρὰ] πρὸς τὴν παρθένον (= *Sentences for a Virgin*)	Libellus ad virginem
———	Paucae sententiolae obscurae (?)

tradition suggests an early date for the reassignment of Evagrian writings to Nilus. If the first Latin version of *Eight Thoughts* was made in the late fifth or early sixth century from a Greek manuscript that already bore the attribution to Nilus, it would indicate an earlier than expected intervention in the transmission of Evagrius's writings in the Byzantine world. The condemnation of Evagrius associated with the events of 553 has usually been seen as the watershed event leading to the disappearance of many Evagrian texts in Greek and the reattribution of the surviving ones to Nilus; on the basis of this Latin evidence, it could well have happened earlier. An Evagrian association does survive in at least one early eleventh-century manuscript containing the older Latin version, Paris Lat. 3784. There, *Eight Thoughts*, attributed to Nilus, is followed by extracts from Palladius's *Lausiac History* about Evagrius and others associated with him, including Ammonius and Melania.[35]

The further diffusion of the Evagriana latina depended, naturally, on monastic authors and advocates (phase five), even if their awareness of the author's identity was doubtful and their knowledge of his works limited. Gregory the Great's spiritual teaching was deeply influenced by Cassian, most obviously so in his adaptation of the Evagrian system of the eight generic thoughts (transmitted by Cassian) to create his schema of seven cardinal vices.[36] Gregory the Great quotes a maxim on anger from *Eight Thoughts* in his *Moralia in Iob*.[37] Though he probably had little sense of its true author, Gregory would have found an Evagrian ascetical text such as *Eight Thoughts* to be congenial.[38] A century later, Defensor of Ligugé included excerpts from both the *Chapters to Monks* and *Eight Thoughts*[39] in the florilegium known as the *Liber scintillarum*. Evagrius is never named; each quotation is introduced with the formula, *In Vitis patrum dixit . . .*, as is the case for Defensor's other citations of Egyptian monastic texts. The fact that neither Gregory nor Defensor refers to any other Evagrian text may indicate that the Evagriana latina had already shrunk to something like its current state.

The Latin *Verba seniorum*, translated by the deacon Pelagius and the subdeacon John in the sixth century, feature extracts from the *Praktikos*, the *Hypotyposis or Principles of the Monastic Life* (*CPG* 2441), and the treatise *For Eulogius* (*CPG* 2447).[40] These are not witnesses to the already existing Latin translations of Evagrius but rather a distinct Latin version made directly from the Greek collection(s) of *apophthegmata*. Here again the Latin version sheds light on the dynamics of the Byzantine legacy of Evagrius. In the Latin, all of these sayings are attributed to Evagrius, as they must have been in the Greek text from which they were translated. The extant Greek manuscripts, however, all of which are considerably later than the period in which the Latin translation was made, have erased Evagrius's name. In them the dicta have become anonymous: "an old man said," "someone said," "again he said." In other cases where the *Verba seniorum* feature Evagrius as a speaker or interlocutor, the later Greek tradition preserves the story without any mention of Evagrius.[41] As with much of the Evagriana graeca, the teacher disappears but the teaching remains.

There is abundant manuscript evidence from the ninth–tenth centuries demonstrating that the *Chapters to Monks*, correctly attributed to Evagrius, was included among the works deemed useful for the post-Carolingian monastic renewal and *ressourcement* (phase six). Many of these manuscripts are traceable to the reforming center of Reichenau on the Bodensee, and the *Sentences* are also abundantly witnessed in later manuscripts from other German and Austrian libraries.[42] Evagrius takes his place among various Egyptian monastic figures; Basil the Great; Isidore and other Iberian monastic authors; and famous monks from Gaul. Two tenth-century Visigothic manuscripts from Spain even include the *Chapters to Monks* as a kind of appendix to Smaragdus's commentary on the *Rule of Benedict*, thereby associating Evagrius with one of the key texts of the early ninth-century Benedictine reform.[43]

Though Evagrius's name is still found in these manuscripts, after so many troubled centuries there was some uncertainty as to who he was. In an important ninth-century manuscript, much copied in later centuries, the *Chapters to Monks* is offered as the *Rule of Saint Evagrius the Bishop.*[44] It is poignant to see the conferral of sainthood on a most controversial figure, and ironic that he is commemorated as a bishop, despite having declined Theophilos of Alexandria's offer of the see of Thmuis.[45]

In the west, knowledge of Evagrius and of his writings continued to dim. The early twelfth-century writer Honorius of Autun wrestled with Gennadius's catalogue entry on Evagrius when compiling his own list of ecclesiastical writers, the *De luminaribus ecclesiae*. He was obviously baffled, misconstruing Gennadius's reference to Evagrius as one of the "most strict and learned men" mentioned in the *Vitae patrum* to mean that Evagrius himself was the author of that work. Faced with the array of Evagrian texts cited by Gennadius, most of them by now long-lost, Honorius dropped the references to the *Praktikos* and *Gnostikos*. He assumed that the "eight books" against the "eight principal vices" meant the familiar treatise *Eight Thoughts,* since the *Antirrhetikos* was unknown to him.[46] The "doctrine suited for *coenobitis ac synoditis*" and the *libellus* for virgins kept their place in the list, for, despite his cognomen, Honorius lived in the southern German monastic milieu that had been so industriously copying the *Chapters to Monks*.

Given this much-reduced corpus, Evagrius's influence on Latin monasticism was primarily mediated through Cassian, or at one remove, through Gregory the Great. Gennadius's catalogue is the high-water mark of the Evagriana latina. The fate of many of the works was probably linked to that of the "Semi-Pelagian" monasticism of southern Gaul with which Cassian was associated. Even though the bulk of the Evagriana latina was lost, two points should be emphasized. First, at least some of the works never lost their correct attribution to Evagrius, whereas in the Greek tradition reattribution to Nilus became normative. Had more survived in Latin, one wonders how this issue of authorship would have been handled in later centuries, given Jerome's vituperative comments and the condemnation of 553 (which explains the disappearance of so much). Second, as noted earlier, the Latin translations were the earliest, and the Latin manuscripts containing the *Chapters to Monks*, *Chapters to a Virgin*, and *Eight Thoughts* are older than any extant Greek copies of those works, being from the seventh, ninth, and sixth/seventh centuries respectively.[47] Like the Syriac manuscripts, those in Latin bring us closer to the time of Evagrius than do any in Greek.

Evagriana syriaca

The Syriac Evagrian corpus is remarkable for three reasons: its breadth, the correct attribution of the works to Evagrius (rather than to Nilus, as in the Greek), and the antiquity of its manuscripts.[48] In Syriac one finds all of the major spiritual and doctrinal writings, excepting the exegetical scholia.[49] More importantly, the Syriac tradition has conserved writings that are lost or fragmentary in the original Greek. Most notable among them are parts two and three of Evagrius's monastic trilogy, the *Gnostikos* and *Kephalaia gnostika* (the *Praktikos* survived in Greek); the *Antirrhetikos*; a collection of Evagrius's letters; and the doctrinal treatise known as the *Letter to Melania*. With a single and easily explicable exception, the Syriac versions of Evagrius are attributed to him.[50] The Syriac manuscript tradition is also unique in being *overly* generous in attributing writings to Evagrius, with several works by other authors bearing his name.[51] Syriac translations of Egyptian monastic texts also contain biographical and other information about Evagrius not found in later Greek manuscripts.[52] In Greek, Evagrius's ascetic writings survived only by reattribution to other authors, and the more speculative works were lost. In Syriac, both the ascetic and more advanced texts were preserved, and under Evagrius's name.

Evagrius's works first came into Syriac in the late fifth or early sixth centuries, a period of intensive translation of philosophical and Christian texts.[53] The Syriac versions were made later than Rufinus's Latin translations, and probably also later than those by Gennadius. The Syriac translations bear no indication of who translated them. In this respect they are like the Evagriana latina. Unlike the Latin tradition, however, Syriac literature offers little information from other sources about translators of Evagrius. Any clues are meager indeed when compared with the data provided by Jerome about Rufinus, or by Gennadius about both Rufinus and himself.

The earliest citation of Evagrius in Syriac literature is found in Philoxenos of Mabbug's *Letter to Patrikios*, citing texts from the *Praktikos* (chap. 89, the same paraphrased by John Cassian in *Conferences* 24) and *Gnostikos* (chaps. 25 and 36).[54] Remarkably, the oldest dated Evagrian manuscript in Syriac (and in any language) was written just a decade after Philoxenos's death in 523. Finished in "the year 845" of the Seleucid Era (AD 534), this is one of several Syriac Evagrian manuscripts from the sixth–seventh centuries that were kept at Deir Al-Suryan, the "Monastery of the Syrians" in Egypt's Wadi Natrun, until being taken to Europe in the nineteenth century.[55] These manuscripts contain the same translations used by Philoxenos, and are several hundred years earlier than any extant in Greek (the oldest Greek manuscripts of the *Praktikos*, for example, are eleventh century).[56] Only the Syriac Evagrian tradition provides such an abundance of very early manuscripts; as we have seen, the oldest Latin Evagrian manuscript (Paris Lat. 12,205) is, exceptionally, from the sixth or seventh century.

We owe to the Evagriana syriaca a comprehensive view of Evagrius's theology and cosmology, for only in Syriac does one find the complete *Kephalaia gnostika* and the *Letter to Melania*, with their echoes of Origen's *On First Principles*. This should not suggest that Syriac readers were oblivious to the doctrinal issues that so damaged Evagrius's reputation in the Byzantine and Latin traditions. As Antoine Guillaumont discovered in the 1950s, the *Kephalaia gnostika* have survived in two different Syriac recensions.[57] The original translator, finding problematic elements in the Greek text, suppressed or corrected them. We do not know how this unknown translator understood the presence of such speculative material in the *Kephalaia gnostika*. Faced with an analogous problem, Rufinus claimed that the Greek manuscripts of Origen's *On First Principles* had been corrupted, though his claim is surely somewhat disingenuous.[58]

In Syriac, this sanitized presentation became the "common" version (Guillaumont's S1).[59] It enjoyed a wide circulation and was the subject of commentaries by two outstanding theologians of, respectively, the East and West Syriac traditions, Babai the Great (d. 628) and Dionysios Bar Salibi (twelfth c.).[60] Not long after the first translation was made, however, someone else who had access to the Greek text of the *Kephalaia gnostika* drafted a new Syriac version (S2). It made abundant use of the first, expurgated effort,[61] while restoring the theologically problematic features of the original text.[62] Both versions are found in the early manuscripts from Egypt preserved in the British Library. S1 is in the manuscript from AD 634 (BL Add. 12,175). The more accurate version S2 survives in a single manuscript of the sixth–seventh centuries (BL Add. 17,167). Even so, both Babai and Bar Salibi knew of its existence. In their view it was not—as commonly accepted today—a restoration of Evagrius's authentic theology, but a subversive distortion of it. A note by Joseph Ḥazzaya (eighth c.) claims that the original text of the *Kephalaia gnostika* had been corrupted by the same person who had translated Dionysius the Areopagite into Syriac.[63] This and other clues—the only evidence for any Syriac translator of Evagrius—were once thought to point to Sergius of Reshaina (d. 536), a prolific translator who had also continued the work of translating Aristotle into Syriac begun in the previous century. Paul Géhin has recently rejected this attribution, as the inconsistent handling of Greek philosophical terminology by the translator of S2 suggests someone much less experienced.[64]

Though the Syriac commentators misunderstood the facts, they were aware of the problem facing those drawn to Evagrius's ascetic and spiritual teaching: how to relate the perceptive monastic psychologist and advocate of imageless prayer to the esoteric theoretician revealed in version S2 of the *Kephalaia gnostika* and the *Letter to Melania*. The debates about "Origenism" in the fifth and sixth centuries, which focused on the speculative themes first proposed by Origen and developed further by Evagrius, created fault lines that ran through the legacies of both Origen and Evagrius, with a profound effect on the transmission of their works in Greek. The Latin and Syriac traditions, however, took different positions on the writings of Origen and Evagrius, and on the linkage between them. In Latin, Origen's works survived, while Evagrius's largely disappeared. In Syriac, Origen was not even translated (apart from two small exceptions discussed below), but Evagrius's writings flourished.

On this key point of differentiation between the Latin and Syriac receptions of the two authors, timing proved to be everything. In the Latin west, the translation of Origen and Evagrius was occurring more or less simultaneously. Both Jerome and Rufinus were at work on Origen's writings in the late fourth and early fifth centuries (and soon fighting on opposing sides of the first Origenist controversy). At the same time, Rufinus was translating Evagrius. Despite Jerome's best efforts to purge the Latin church of Origen's influence and writings, a large corpus of Origen's works continued to be copied in their Latin versions, including many texts destined to disappear in the original Greek. Latin proved to be for Origen what Syriac would be for Evagrius: a medium of preservation. Koetschau's critical edition of Origen's most controversial work, *On First Principles*, for which only some of the Greek survives, was based on dozens of Latin manuscripts with the complete text.[65] Origen's exegetical writings, especially his *Homilies on Exodus* and *Homilies on Leviticus*, were copied throughout the Middle Ages, always with his name attached. In Defensor's *Liber scintillarum* there is no reluctance to cite "Origenes," even as Evagrius disappeared into the mass of monks cited anonymously by Defensor from the *Vitae patrum*. As we have seen, one of Jerome's polemical tactics was to include Evagrius in his attack on Origen. Because of this and because of later criticisms of the monastic traditions of southern Gaul that had proven receptive to Evagrius and Cassian (by, e.g., Prosper of Aquitaine), Evagrius's writings did not fare well in the later Latin tradition, though neither his name nor his works entirely disappeared. Origen did comparatively better, presumably because his work was considered to be more fundamental, and his scope broader, than Evagrius's more narrowly monastic focus.

In the Syriac tradition, Evagrius was never associated with Origen. We owe the substantial Syriac Evagrian corpus, and thus our closest approach to the full range of Evagrius's writings, to this curious fact. By the time Evagrius and other Greek Christian authors were being translated into Syriac in the late fifth century, Origen's reputation had already been so compromised in Greek-language ecclesiastical circles that his writings were not thought to be suitable for translation into Syriac.[66] Origen's contribution to later Syriac Christian theology, though significant, was thus mediated entirely through other writers.[67] Most important among them was Evagrius. But because Evagrius never explicitly cited Origen, it was possible for Syriac theologians, lacking direct knowledge about Origen and his theological system, and consequently ignorant of Origen's pervasive influence on the Cappadocians and on Evagrius, to condemn Origen and "Origenism" even as they embraced Evagrius.[68]

As Antoine Guillaumont and others have pointed out, in the Syriac world Origen was targeted from every direction, even if only in caricature. To the Miaphysites he was suspect because of his alleged subordinationism (which they could interpret as both proto-Arian and proto-Nestorian). For the Dyophysites he was an Alexandrian theologian and the exegetical antithesis of their own beloved "Interpreter," Theodore of Mopsuestia. Caught in the poisonous thickets of the Christological debates, Origen stood no chance in the Syriac world. And though by the mid-sixth century Evagrius's fate had been explicitly tied to Origen's in Byzantine theological discourse, it was too late for such concerns to have much influence farther east. For those Syriac Christians who had broken with the imperial church after the Council of Ephesus in 431, and for those who did so in the decades after the Council of Chalcedon in 451, the anti-Origenist imperial condemnations of 543 (which named Origen and included extracts from *On First Principles*) or 553 (focused more on Christological positions held by Palestinian monastic devotees of Evagrius and based on the *Kephalaia gnostika*), were largely irrelevant.[69] In any case, Syriac observers would have attributed the propositions anathematized in 553 not to Evagrius, whose theology was known to them in the sanitized version S1 of the *Kephalaia gnostika*, but to his corrupters, those who had produced the "distorted" version S2.

In Syriac, Evagrius's works were almost always transmitted in monastic anthologies containing both doctrinal and ascetic texts. Such compilations are a common feature of monastic literary culture, and are found even among the earliest Syriac manuscripts.[70] This same phenomenon applies across the Greek, Latin, and Syriac traditions: one rarely finds manuscripts that consist exclusively of Evagrian texts.[71] In Greek and Latin monastic anthologies one finds relatively stable collections of associated monastic writings, as well as formal anthologies such as Defensor's *Liber scintillarum* (seventh c.), or the Greek *Pandect* by Nikon of the Black Mountain and the *Synagōgē* of Paul Evergetinos (both eleventh c.). The Syriac anthologies are far more varied, and the transmission of the Evagriana syriaca accordingly more random than one finds with the Greek and Latin versions. The work of Herman Teule has revealed that there was a fairly standard list of authorities whose writings appear in such anthologies, a list that expanded over time to include newer authors,[72] even if the choice of particular texts, and their arrangement within the anthology seems to have been left to the individual compiler/scribes.[73]

In Syriac one has the additional complication of manuscripts associated with three different traditions, West Syriac/Miaphysite, East Syriac/Dyophysite, and Melkite/Chalcedonian.[74] There are dozens of West Syriac anthologies that are already known, including many in the British Library trove from Deir Al-Suryan, as well as important manuscripts in the Vatican Library and in Berlin.[75] To these one must add the manuscripts in the major Near Eastern libraries now becoming available for research through digitization and cataloging projects. Collections at the Syriac Orthodox Church of the Forty Martyrs in Mardin, Deyrulzaferan, Mor Gabriel Monastery, the Chaldean collections of Baghdad, Diyarbakir, Mardin, and other sites will complement existing knowledge of the European holdings and considerably enrich our understanding of the transmission of ascetic texts.[76] In Mardin, for example, one can find important fifteenth-century anthologies with

Evagrian texts,[77] and the unusual case of a twentieth-century manuscript consisting entirely of extracts from Evagrius.[78] In the East Syriac tradition such anthologies seem to be less common. Teule has identified only three, which include Evagrius alongside other Syriac and Greek authors.[79] Here, too, as more manuscript evidence becomes available from collections in Iraq and southeast Turkey, the number of identified anthologies may well increase. Finally, examples of Chalcedonian Syriac anthologies can be found in the library of Saint Catherine's Monastery at Sinai. One among them (Sinai Syr. 10) includes Evagrius's *Eight Thoughts* correctly attributed to him as in the non-Melkite Syriac manuscripts, rather than to Nilus, as became customary in Greek.[80] In the same collection, another manuscript (Sinai Syr. 24), probably written at Mar Saba in Palestine, demonstrates a more typically Melkite reaction to Evagrius—every mention of his name in the *Homilies* of Isaac of Nineveh has been altered.[81]

Amidst the abundance of Evagriana syriaca it is important to remember that not all of Evagrius's works were translated into Syriac; not everything that was translated proved to be popular; and not everything that was initially popular remained so. The transmission history of Evagrius's works in Syriac over many centuries will be clear only when the greatest possible number of manuscripts have been surveyed. At this point only general observations are possible.[82] Unsurprisingly, the ascetic and parenetic works were copied more widely, and for a longer time, than the more speculative writings. Thus one finds more manuscripts with the *Praktikos* and *Gnostikos* than with the *Kephalaia gnostika* or *Letter to Melania*. The later transmission of these two texts, if indeed there was any, remains obscure. The treatise *For Eulogios* (or at least excerpts from it) was widely copied through the twentieth century,[83] as were *Eight Thoughts* and *Foundations*, as well as spuria such as *The Just and the Perfect* (*CPG* 2465, actually an excerpt from the *Book of Steps*) and *Masters and Disciples* (*CPG* 2449, probably to be attributed to Nilus of Ancyra, as in the Greek).[84] The collection of maxims known as the *Vices Opposed to the Virtues* (*CPG* 2448) may have been more popular in Syriac than previously thought, as it appears in several of the recently digitized Near Eastern manuscripts, including one written at Mor Gabriel in 1961 by the monk Isa, later the bishop Mor Julius Çiçek, famous for his calligraphy.[85] The anthologizing tendency over the centuries meant that longer works tended to be broken up into smaller pieces or abandoned entirely. The *Antirrhetikos*, despite its ascetic focus, was perhaps just too long to have been widely copied, especially as the anthologies themselves expanded over time with the addition of new authors.

There are other peculiarities of the Evagriana syriaca worth noting. Evagrius's *Letters* are found in many early manuscripts, but the *Letter on Faith* (PG 2439) appears in only one.[86] Despite its importance for the history of spirituality, *On Prayer* does not seem to have been very popular, and the most common version is found in a truncated state corresponding to chapters 1–32, or about 20 percent, of the Greek text.[87] Even in this abbreviated form, the Syriac version provided crucial support for Hausherr's argument in reclaiming the work for Evagrius.[88] The treatise *Thoughts* circulated in three parts that were copied independently; some manuscripts contain all three, others two or only one.[89]

As in the west, Evagrius's importance for Syriac Christianity was also expressed by his influence upon subsequent theologians and spiritual authors. His impact upon Syriac ascetical and mystical thought was much more pervasive than proved to be the case for Latin Christianity. The influence of Evagrius on Philoxenos has already been noted. Sergius of Reshaina integrates elements of Evagrian theology into his own *Mēmrā on the Spiritual Life*. Stephen Bar Sudaili was to take Evagrius's more esoteric speculations even further in the curious synthesis of Evagrian and Dionysian themes found in his *Book of the Holy Hierotheos*.[90] John of Dalyatha would create a rich synthesis of the Evagrian and Macarian traditions akin to those of Diadochus and Maximus in Greek,[91] and of John Cassian in Latin.[92] The Evagrian tradition came to its richest fruition in the writings on prayer and the spiritual life of Isaac of Nineveh, perhaps the greatest of all ascetic writers, east or west.[93] Cassian felt unable to mention Evagrius by name, but Isaac did so freely. The survival of a rich corpus of Evagriana syriaca, and its openly acknowledged importance for subsequent writers, marks the sharpest difference between the Latin and Syriac receptions of Evagrius.

EVAGRIUS WEST AND EAST

At the end of this long review, it may be helpful to summarize the key points (see table 8.2). On the face of it, the Latin reception seems feeble, at least in terms of extant translations. Secondary transmission through other writers was the principal medium for Evagrian influence in the West. The Syriac tradition benefitted from both wide circulation of many translated Evagrian texts and a pervasive secondary influence. But there are always surprises when tracing the fate of texts and ideas through time and across linguistic and cultural frontiers. In the library at Sinai, one finds a tenth-century anthology, Sinai Syr. 14. The manuscript includes works by important monastic figures from Egypt and Sinai itself, as well as by Isaac of Nineveh and various Greek theologians. Evagrius is absent, perhaps not surprisingly for a manuscript of Melkite origin, but in his place one finds a "Mar Abbā Qīsyanōs," who offers "selected words on the eight passions."[94] It seems that a Syriac translator of ascetic texts had come across the Greek epitome of books 5–12 of Cassian's *Institutes*. In that section of the *Institutes*, Cassian presents the ascetic agenda he had learned from Evagrius.[95] Had the translator simply discovered a useful text, and tucked it into the anthology along with so

Table 8.2 A comparison of the Evagriana latina and Evagriana syriaca

	Evagriana latina	*Evagriana syriaca*
Known translated works	8 (and one spurious)	30+ (and spuria)
Surviving translations	3	30+ (and spuria)
Works lost in Greek?	None	Several
Oldest mss	Seventh c.	AD 534 and many sixth c.
Attribution	Non-extant works: Evagrius Extant works: Evagrius, Nilus	Evagrius (with one exception)
Translators known?	Rufinus, Gennadius	None certain
Anthologized?	Occasionally	Frequently

many others? Or had he recognized that this Qīsyanōs was proffering Evagrian ascetic theology and thought that he could be a safe stand-in for his controversial master? Whatever the truth of the matter, it demonstrates how pervasive, and sometimes unexpected, Evagrius's influence has been in both the Latin and Syriac traditions.

Notes

1. Among the Arabic versions are some minor works lost in Greek and unrepresented in other translations; see Géhin, "La tradition arabe d'Évagre le Pontique," amplifying Samir, "Évagre le Pontique dans la tradition arabo-copte." Arabic also preserved a unique instance of a letter written *to* Evagrius, from the monk Lukios, published by Hausherr, "Eulogios—Loukios."

2. Sims-Williams, *The Christian Sogdian Manuscript C2*, 168–82 and plates.

3. On these generally, see A. Guillaumont, *Un philosophe au désert*, 78.

4. The relevant portion of *Letter* 133 is sec. 3.5–6, as in Hilberg, *Sancti Eusebii Hieronymi Epistulae*, 3:246; on the context, see Clark, *Origenist Controversy*, 222–23; Driver, *John Cassian*, 57–58.

5. Jerome makes a similar link between Pythagoreans, Stoics, Origen, Rufinus, Evagrius, and Jovinian in his *Commentary on Jeremiah* 4.1.2 (Reiter, *Sancti Evsebii Hieronymi*, 220–21), written about the same time as *Letter* 133. In the prologue to his *Dialogue against the Pelagians*, he expands the list to include the Messalians, *totius pene haereticos, quos sermone gentili διεστραμμένως Massalianos, Graece εὐχίτας vocant* (PL 23:496A).

6. Hilberg, *Sancti Eusebii Hieronymi Epistulae*, 3:246, lines 9–20. The section on Evagrius in the *Historia Monachorum*, which replaces a much briefer mention in chapter 20 of the Greek text, praises Evagrius for his asceticism and discernment of thoughts, but says nothing about his writings (*Historia Monachorum* 27, as in PL 21:448B–449B; Rufinus, *Historia monachorum*, 363–64).

7. Bammel notes the cross-references between Rufinus's translation of Eusebius's *Ecclesiastical History* (11.4, GCS 9, p. 1007) and the *Historia Monachorum* (29, PL 21:455), thus dating the latter to after 401–2, the firm dates for the former. She then logically places the Evagrian translations in the same period: Hammond-Bammel, "Last Ten Years," 394–97, 428.

8. Hilberg, *Sancti Eusebii Hieronymi Epistulae*, 3:246, lines 2–5.

9. It is possible, though highly doubtful, that Jerome's first three references are to Evagrius's correspondence rather than to these three specific works. The corpus of his letters survives only in Syriac, with only four addressees named. Gabriel Bunge, who has studied them closely, identified several as written to Melania (*Letters* 1, 8, 31, 35–37); one to Severa, a deaconess in Melania's monastery, for whom the *Chapters to a Virgin* may have been written (*Letter* 20; cf. *Letters* 7 and 8); at least three to both Rufinus and Melania (*Letters* 7, 20, 32). Many are written to monks. See Bunge, *Briefe aus der Wüste*, 176–90.

10. In the late fifth century, Gennadius refers to existing translations of all but the *Letter to Melania*, as described below.

11. Hilberg, *Sancti Eusebii Hieronymi Epistulae*, 3:246, lines 20–247, line 6; cf. a similar charge in Jerome's *Commentary on Jeremiah* 4.41.4 (Reiter, *Sancti Evsebii Hieronymi*, 267).

12. Hammond-Bammel, "Last Ten Years," 387.

13. One of the maxims, *sapiens verbis innotescit paucis,* made it into the *Rule of Benedict* via the *Rule of the Master*: *Sentences of Sextus* 145, at *RB* 7.61.

14. Rufinus's prologue is most conveniently found in Chadwick, *Sentences of Sextus*, 10.

15. A suggestion dating back to Bardenhewer; more recently, Catherine Chin has noted it as "generally accepted," but there seems to be no new evidence for this conclusion; see Chin, "Rufinus of Aquileia," 635.

16. Muyldermans, "Le discours de Xystus." Chadwick seems to have been unaware of Muyldermans's study, citing the less incisive article of Hermann, "Die armenische Überlieferung der Sextussentenzen," as the only work on the subject known to him. Hermann equally seems to have been unaware of Muyldermans's analysis.

17. Beginning with Conybeare in his *Ring of Pope Xystus* and repeated thereafter by others. See A. Guillaumont, *Un philosophe au désert*, 154.

18. Leclercq concludes, "il demeure impossible de faire sortir de l'anonymat les traducteurs" of the two versions of the *Chapters to Monks* (J. Leclercq, "L'Ancienne version latine," 201n42). A further note of caution arises for *Virgin* from the rubric in Paris N. Acq. 239, presenting it as *epistola . . . ad virginem*; as we will see, Gennadius mentions Evagrius's composition of a *libellus . . . ad virginem* and notes Rufinus's translation of *sententiae* of Evagrius. Are the *sententiae* to be understood as including the *libellus*? Of course one should not place too much weight on titles found in particular manuscripts.

19. Beginning with Salvatore Marsili's foundational *Giovanni Cassiano ed Evagrio Pontico*, based on Irénée Hausherr's work in recovering the proper

attribution of Evagrius's writings. On Evagrius and Cassian, see Stewart, *Cassian the Monk*, passim; Stewart, "John Cassian's Schema."

20. Stewart, *Cassian the Monk*, 95 and 196nn66–70.

21. John Cassian, *Conferences* 24.15.3: "quam [animam] cum sapientissimi quique tripertitae definiant esse virtutis . . . aut λογικόν id est rationabile, aut θυμικόν id est irascibile, aut ἐπιθυμητικόν id est concupiscibile" (Petschenig, *Iohannis Cassiani Conlationes XXIIII*, 691); cf. Evagrius, *Praktikos* 89: τριμεροῦς δὲ τῆς λογικῆς ψυχῆς οὔσης κατὰ τὸν σοφὸν ἡμῶν διδάσκαλον . . . ἐν τῷ λογιστικῷ . . . ἐν τῷ ἐπιθυμητικῷ . . . ἐν τῷ θυμικῷ (Guillaumont and Guillaumont, *Traité pratique*, 680–82).

22. John Cassian, *Institutes* 5.32.1 (Cassian and Petschenig, *Iohannis Cassiani De institutis coenobiorum*, 105–6).

23. See Vogüé, "Un morceau célèbre." The passage is significant for its outline of ten indices of humility (as in Cassian, *Institutes* 4.39), which was the basis for the famous "Ladder of Humility" in chapter 10 of the *Rule of the Master*, which then passed into the *Rule of Benedict* (*RB* 7).

24. See Contreras, "Evagrio Pontico."

25. See the entry by Charles Munier in *DSp* 6:205 (1967); much of Gennadius's biography remains speculative, particularly with regard to his monastic associations. Gennadius's notice about himself in *Vir. inlustr.* 101 (Gebhardt and Richardson, *Hieronymus*, 97) focuses entirely on his doctrinal writings.

26. *Vir. inlustr.* 11 (Gebhardt and Richardson, *Hieronymus*, 65).

27. Gennadius claims that he also translated an appeal of Timothy Aelurus to the Emperor Leo I, with a cautionary introduction (*Vir. inlustr.* 73 [Gebhardt and Richardson, *Hieronymus*, 86]). This translation does not survive.

28. This text was commonly included in the Latin compilations of Egyptian and Palestinian monastic literature that circulated under the general heading of the (more commonly plural) *Vitae patrum*.

29. A. Guillaumont, *Un philosophe au désert*, 135–36. The Greek text remains unpublished; the Syriac version reads "the hearts of monks understand the words and they will find the deceptions of the demons in them," as in Muyldermans, *Evagriana syriaca*, 138 (Syriac) and 167 (French).

30. A complication arises, however, in that Gennadius observes that Rufinus always accompanied his translations with a preface. If there is no preface, he writes, then it is not Rufinus's work (*Vir. inlustr.* 17 [Gebhardt and Richardson, *Hieronymus*, 68.4–6]). As noted earlier, none of the extant Latin versions is accompanied by a preface. Nor, for that matter, do any of the Syriac translations have a preface.

31. *Vir. inlustr.* 17 (Gebhardt and Richardson, *Hieronymus*, 68).

32. In his new edition of *Monks* and *Virgin*, Joest assumes that the translations published by Holstenius and reprinted in Migne are by Rufinus (Joest, *Ad monachos*, 145 and 152), despite Leclercq's caution noted above. For *Monks*, both Leclercq ("L'ancienne version latine," 199–200) and Mühmelt ("Zu der neuen lateinischen Übersetzung," 103) demonstrate that the text in Holstenius represents a revision of a more primitive text that was published by Leclercq from Paris Lat. 12,634. Joest also mistakenly inverts the relationship between the two versions (145). As for *Virgin*, Joest does not mention the other Latin translation published by Wilmart from Paris N. Acq. 239.

33. The earlier version, still unpublished, was based on the longer recension of the Greek text as published by Muyldermans, "Nouvelle recension"; on the Latin, see 259–61. The later version, published in part by Emeric Bigot in *Palladii episcopi helenopolitani*, 356–82, seems closer to the shorter recension of the Greek found in PG 79:1145–64. On the two Latin versions, see now Marchini, "Tradizione latina." Marchini is preparing an edition of both versions. I thank him for kindly answering my questions about this complex topic.

34. Wilmart, "La fausse lettre latine de Macaire," 413n11.

35. Folios 122–24: *Eight Thoughts*; fols. 124–28: extracts from Palladius (Evagrius, Moses, Macarius the Egyptian, Macarius the Alexandrian, Nathanael, Ammonius, Or, Pambo, Melania, Benjamin). The manuscript is dated to before 1034 and was written at Saint-Martial de Limoges; see Bibliothèque Nationale de France, *Catalogue général des manuscrits latins*, 7:64.

36. See Straw, "Gregory, Cassian, and the Cardinal Vices."

37. Gregory the Great, *Moralia* 5.45 (Adriaen, CCSL 143:278), citing *Eight Thoughts* 10 (cf. PG 79:1156A) in the revised version, as noted by Marchini, "Tradizione latina," 575: *unde bene ante nos quidam sapiens dixit: cogitationes iracundi vipereae sunt generationes, mentem comedunt matrem suam.*

38. Marchini wonders whether Gregory actually knew which *sapiens* he was quoting (Marchini, "Tradizione latina," 575); given that all of the extant manuscripts attribute the text to Nilus, he probably did not—it would have been for him another example of the Egyptian monastic tradition he knew also from Cassian's writings.

39. Defensor, like Gregory, cited the earlier of the two versions.

40. *Praktikos* 91 and 95 (= *Verba seniorum* 1.4–5, as in PL 73:855B/Greek *Systematic Collection* 1.1–5, as in Guy, *Les Apophtegmes des Pères*, 1:102–4), 99 (= 4.14, PL 73:866b/Gk. *Syst.* 4.14, Guy, 1:190); 97 (= 6.5, PL 73:889b/Gk. *Syst.* 6.6, Guy, 1:318); 15 (= 10.20, PL 73:915d–917a/Gk. *Syst.*

10.25, Guy, 2:30); 92, 94, 96 (= 4*.16–19, PL 73:1018cd/not in Gk. *Syst.*); *Principles* 11 (12.4, PL 73:941c/Gk. *Syst.* 12.4, Guy, 2:210); *Eulogius* 9.9 (12.5, PL 73:941cd/Gk. *Syst.* 12.5, Guy, 2:211).

41. The Latin (and the Syriac) also preserve Evagrius's name as the interlocutor with Arsenius in *Verba seniorum* 10.5 (PL 73:912d–913a)/Syr. 2.217, ed. Budge, *Book of Paradise*, 2:676 = Bedjan, *Acta martyrum et sanctorum*, 7:784–85, as no. 228. The Greek has τις (*Syst.* 10.7, ed. Guy, *Les Apophtegmes des Pères*, 2:18). Cf. the similar case of *Verba seniorum* 10.19 (PL 73:415cd/Syr. Budge 1.58 [2.447–48] = Bedjan, 7.464), where the Latin and Syriac both attribute the saying to Evagrius, while the equivalent Greek has "a brother" (*Syst.* 10.24, ed. Guy, 2:28–30).

42. For example, Lambach 31 (ninth–tenth c.); Vienna Pal. 1550 (twelfth c.), 3878 and 3912 (fifteenth c.); Lilienfeld 113 (fifteenth c.); S. Petri Salisburgensis b. IX.20 (fifteenth c.).

43. Silos 1, as in J. Leclercq, "L'ancienne version latine," 197.

44. Lambach 31, fol. 91v. The later copies also feature "Evagrii episcopi proverbia" as in Admont 331, fol. 61r (thirteenth c.), "Proverbi sancti Evagrii episcopi" as in Klosterneuberg 587, fol. 93v (twelfth c.), "proverbia sancti Evagrii" as in Klosterneuberg 570, fol. 104r (fourteenth c.).

45. See the Coptic *Life* in Amélineau, *De Historia lausiaca*, 115.9–11, and Socrates, *CH* 4.23.75 (Hansen, 256.12–14). After Evagrius's death, it was this same Theophilos who suddenly turned against the Origenist monks of Scetis, Nitria, and Kellia.

46. *De luminaribus* 2.11, as in PL 172.212C.

47. The sole Greek manuscript of *Monks* and *Virgin* is thirteenth c. (Vat. Barb. gr. 515); the oldest Greek witnesses of *Eight Thoughts* are tenth–eleventh c. (Paris gr. 913, 1066, 1188; Coislin gr. 109, 123, 283).

48. See the groundbreaking article of Hausherr, "Versions syriaque"; A. Guillaumont, "Le rôle des versions orientales"; A. Guillaumont, "Versions syriaques"; A. Guillaumont and C. Guillaumont, "Les versions orientales"; Géhin, "D'Égypte en Mésopotamie"; and other works by Paul Géhin cited below. I thank Dr. Géhin for his kindness in reading a draft of this essay and offering very helpful suggestions to improve it.

49. This omission is probably attributable to the close adherence of the scholia to the Greek text of the Septuagint version of the Old Testament. Because they key Greek biblical vocabulary to Evagrius's monastic system, translation of them into other languages would have been very challenging.

50. The exception is a version of *Prayer* attributed to Nilus, as found in Leiden Or. 2346 (eighth c.; formerly Hebrew Warner 57 [de Goeje, *Catalogus*

codicum Orientalium Bibliothecae Academiae Lugduno Batavae, 5:67–69]) and in the palimpsest Sin. Syr. M37N (as in Philothea, *Nouveaux manuscrits syriaques du Sinaï*, 405–21). The Leiden manuscript has chapters 1–11, with the attribution to Nilus; the Sinai one contains fragments of chapters 24–119. Both seem to be of Melkite origin, which would explain the attribution to Nilus, echoing the Greek practice. See Teule, "L'Échelle du Paradis dans la tradition syriaque," 283–84 (n.b. that Teule cites it as Or. 3246, which should be corrected to Or. 2346); Géhin, "Fragments patristiques syriaques des Nouvelles découvertes du Sinai," 81. Géhin dates the Sinai manuscript to the late eighth century; the cataloger, Mother Philothea, had dated it a full century earlier, but Géhin sees the style as typical of slavish eighth-century Syriac translations from Greek. This manuscript seems to have been the basis for the Arabic version found in Sin. Ar. 329, 549, 237; see Géhin, "Les versions syriaques et arabes des *Chapitres sur la prière* d'Évagre le Pontique."

51. See A. Guillaumont, *Un philosophe au désert*, 150–52. These texts were published in Muyldermans, *Evagriana syriaca*.

52. The chapter on Evagrius in the Syriac version of the *Lausiac History* contains distinctive elements (Syr. text: Draguet, *Formes syriaques*, CSCO 398, pp. 266–83; French translation in CSCO 399, pp. 178–88). Similarly, among the mass of Syriac "Palladiana" in the *Paradise of the Fathers* compiled by "Enanisho" in the seventh century is material about Evagrius, included in chapters about Stephen and Eukarpios (bk. 2.24–25, Syr. text: Bedjan, *Acta martyrum et sanctorum*, 7.292–99; English translation only in Budge, *Book of Paradise*, 1.401–6). They are merely named in the common Greek text of Palladius's *Lausiac History*, without mention of Evagrius (*Lausiac History* 47 [C. Butler, *Lausiac History* 2.137 = Syr. ch. 42, as in Budge, *Book of Paradise*, 1.218]). See also the material in *Paradise* App. 22–24 (Syr. ed. Bedjan, *Acta martyrum et sanctorum*, 7.911–919; English translation only, Budge, *Book of Paradise*, 2.1016–23).

53. See Brock, "Towards a History of Syriac Translation Technique," and "L'apport des pères grecs à la littérature syriaque."

54. As already observed by Irénée Hausherr in his "Contemplation et sainteté"; on Philoxenos and Evagrius, see also Guillaumont, *Les "Képhalaia gnostica,"* 207–11; Géhin, "D'Égypte en Mésopotamie," 37–40. See also the discussion above by Michelson.

55. The manuscript dated to 845/534 is BL Add. 12,175 (= Wright, *Catalogue*, 727 and 736, at 2:633–38 and 2:657–58). Also from the sixth century, reckoned on paleographical grounds rather than explicit dating in the manuscripts themselves: BL Add. 14,635 (Wright 568, 2:449–450), possibly older than BL

Add. 12,175; BL Add. 14,581 (Wright 734, 2:655), BL Add. 14,635 (Wright 568, vol. 2:449–450). Slightly later (from the late sixth or seventh centuries) are BL Add. 17,167 (Wright 743, 2:676–78); BL Add. 14,578 (Wright 567, 2:445–58); BL Add. 14,616 (Wright 744, 2:678–80); BL Add. 14,650 (Wright 949, 3:1103–7). Of these, perhaps the most important is BL Add. 14,578, which provides an almost complete Evagrian corpus; see Géhin, "En marge." I thank Dr. Géhin for sharing his paper with me before its publication.

56. See, for example, the superb analysis of the manuscripts of the *Praktikos* by Claire Guillaumont in C. Guillaumont and A. Guillaumont, *Traité pratique*, 1:129–86.

57. As described in A. Guillaumont, *Les "Képhalaia gnostica"*; both recensions were published in A. Guillaumont, *Les six centuries.*

58. As suggested in Rufinus's letter *On the Adulteration of the Books of Origen*, offered as an epilogue to his translation of Pamphilus's *Apology for Origen.*

59. Note that Guillaumont's suggestion that Philoxenos was responsible for S1 (*Les "Képhalaia gnostica,"* 211–13) was based in large part on a mistaken attribution to Philoxenos of a text actually by Joseph Ḥazzaya.

60. Babai's commentary can be found in Frankenberg, *Euagrius Ponticus*, 8–423 (based on Vat. Syr. 178, fourteenth–sixteenth c.); see A. Guillaumont, *Les "Képhalaia gnostica,"* 259–90; Géhin, "D'Égypte en Mésopotamie," 43–46. Bar Salibi's commentary was published by Mar Julius Çiçek in 1991: Çiçek, *Commentary*; see A. Guillaumont, *Les "Képhalaia gnostica,"* 290–97.

61. A. Guillaumont, *Les "Képhalaia gnostica,"* 227–58.

62. A similar strategy was alleged of Rufinus's translation of Origen's *Peri archōn*, prompting Jerome to make his own supposedly more literal translation. See the judicious discussion by Henri Crouzel in his introduction to Origen, *Traité des principes*, 1:26–29. The major difference between Origen and Evagrius, however, is that Origen presents alternative positions as part of what Crouzel has elsewhere termed his *théologie de recherche*, leaving the questions open, while Evagrius presents a definitive view, which was all the more daring (or foolish) in the very different theological situation of the late fourth century.

63. See A. Guillaumont, *Les "Képhalaia gnostica,"* 215–27, citing a manuscript originally in the Chaldean library at Diyarbakir (Diyarb. Chald. 100 as in Scher, "Notice [pt. 2]," 403–4). The manuscript was later taken to the Patriarchate in Mosul, and then to Baghdad when the Patriarchate moved there in 1950. Guillaumont was able to consult a microfilm copy. The

manuscript has recently been recovered and digitized as shelfmark CPB 131. Another manuscript containing the same text by Joseph was destroyed with the rest of Addai Scher's library at Siirt in 1915, when Scher himself was killed. Fortunately, Scher had published a few extracts from it, including a French translation of the critical passage, in Scher, "Joseph Hazzâyâ écrivain syriaque du VIIIe siècle," 60–61.

64. Géhin, "D'Égypte en Mésopotamie," 32–36.

65. As described in his introduction in Koetschau, *Origenes Werke*, 5:xv–xlvi.

66. I am aware of only two brief snippets transmitted in commentaries on the Psalms. The first translates a text published by Pitra, *Analecta sacra*, 2:428.20–432.37, found in BL Add. 14,434, ff. 5r–6r (early eighth c.?; Wright, *Catalogue*, 54, 1:35–37), as being from Origen's "discourse (*šarbā*) on the Psalms." This text is one of several excerpted patristic commentaries used to create a preface for the Greek *catena* on the Psalms (see, e.g., Bodleian Barocci 235, ff. 6rb–8rb). The prefatory material was translated into Syriac, and in most extant manuscripts used as a preface for the Syro-Hexapla Psalter (as in BL Add. 14,434, and also Milan Ambros. C313, ff. 5va–6rb), though it may originally have circulated independently (as in Vat. Syr. 135, ff. 4v–5r). It is also in Diyarbakir Chald. 36, one of the manuscripts taken to the Patriarchate in Mosul and then to Baghdad, the fate of which remains uncertain; in this case it was not the Syro-Hexapla to which the set of texts was prefaced, but the Peshitta version (see Baumstark, *Geschichte*, 164; cf. Scher, "Notice [pt. 1]," 346–47; a microfilm of this manuscript is kept at the Peshitta Institute, now located at the Vrije Universiteit in Amsterdam). The second is BL Add. 12,154 (Wright, *Catalogue*, 860, 2:980), f. 33v, a scholion of Origen on why there are 150 psalms.

67. See Dominique Gonnet's helpful "Liste des oeuvres patristiques traduites du grec en syriaque."

68. A. Guillaumont, *Les "Képhalaia gnostica,"* 166–70.

69. The formal acts of the Second Council of Constantinople do not include the anathemas of "Origenist" propositions, but both contemporary reports (e.g., Cyril of Scythopolis's account in the *Life of Sabas*) and later Byzantine accounts refer to condemnations of Origen, Didymus, and Evagrius. The evidence suggests that the anathemas from 553 should be associated with the council. See the admirable summary and translation of relevant texts by Price, *Acts of the Council of Constantinople of 553*, 2:270–86.

70. Thus BL Add. 12,175, the earliest dated Evagrian manuscript, consists of two parts, perhaps by the same scribe (Wright, *Catalogue*, 736+727,

2:657–58+633–38). The first part contains Syriac Palladiana and related Egyptian monastic texts, as well as some Evagrian texts; the second part contains writings of Evagrius, Mark the Monk, the Palladiana, "Macarius" [= Ps. Macarius], Ammonius, the biblical prophet Isaiah, and Basil.

71. One important exception in Syriac is BL Add. 14,578, noted earlier; BL Add. 17,165 (sixth c.; Wright, *Catalogue*, 733, 2:654–55) is another example, identified in the colophon as the "*asqetīqōn* of blessed Mar Evagrius, monk of Egypt" (fol. 110v). Given the greatly diminished state of the Evagriana latina, it is no surprise that no *Codex Evagrianum* is to be found among the extant Latin manuscripts.

72. Teule notes that from the seventh century one finds Isaiah of Scetis, Philoxenos, Isaac of Antioch, Jacob of Serugh, John Chrysostom; from the eighth century onwards the East Syrian ascetics Abraham of Nathpar, Gregory the Solitary/of Cyprus are added; from the twelfth century onwards one finds Isaac of Nineveh and John Dalyatha. Both become very important and prominent in later anthologies. See Teule, "Les compilations monastiques syriaques."

73. Ibid., 259. One does find some more or less standard "packets" of excerpta in the manuscripts alongside complete works.

74. Grigory Kessel is currently undertaking a comprehensive study of all known Syriac monastic anthologies.

75. See the list in Teule, "Les compilations monastiques syriaques," 263–64. To these one can add the twelfth-century manuscript now at St. Ephrem the Syrian Monastery in Holland, analyzed in Brock, "A Monastic Anthology from Twelfth-Century Edessa," which contains excerpts from *Eulogius*, *Principles*, and an unidentified work.

76. See Géhin, "En marge," on the importance of exploring these collections. Fortunately most of the important libraries in these regions have worked with the Hill Museum and Manuscript Library to digitize and catalog their manuscripts.

77. CFMM (= Mardin Orth.) 420, with *Vices* among works of standard Greek and Syriac authors (including East Syrian writers such as Abraham of Nathpar and Isaac of Nineveh), and concluding with the *Book of the Holy Hierotheos*; CFMM 422 with extracts from *Eulogius*, *Eight Thoughts*, and *Counsel to Monks*.

78. CFMM 438, with selections from many texts, including *Eulogius*, *Eight Thoughts*, *Vices*, *Thoughts*, *Foundations*, as well as spuria attributed to Evagrius. It came from the library of Elias Qoro, former abbot of Deyrulzafaran and later Patriarchal Delegate to the Malankara Church in India, and may have been written by him.

79. Teule, "Les compilations monastiques syriaques," 253–57. The most important is Baghdad Chaldean Monastery 680 (formerly Notre Dame des Sémences 237, dated 1289), which contains among other sentences the text of *Reflections* 1–39 with a commentary (apparently not that of Babai). The manuscript was described by Vosté, "Recueil d'auteurs ascétiques nestoriens." Teule notes copies at the Vatican, Birmingham, and Alqosh (Teule, "Les compilations monastiques syriaques," 254).

80. Géhin, "Reconstitution et datation."

81. Kessel, Briquel-Chatonnet, and Debié, "Sinai Syr. 24," 213–15.

82. For the earlier manuscripts, I rely on the work of Joseph Muyldermans, Antoine and Claire Guillaumont, and Paul Géhin.

83. Following the version found in BL Add. 14,616, which omits the prologue and first chapter.

84. These are all, for example, in CFMM 438, the twentieth-century manuscript from Mardin.

85. MGMT 132, which opens with the Evagrian text (ff. 1–11).

86. BL Add. 17,167, the seventh-century manuscript that also contains the only known copy of version S2 of the *KG*. In Greek this text circulated most commonly as a letter of Basil the Great; the Syriac attribution to Evagrius is unique. See Géhin, "La place de la *Lettre*."

87. What appears to have once been a complete version survives only in the two partial copies mentioned above, Leiden Or. 2346 (chs. 1–11) and Sinai Syr. M37N (with fragments of chs. 24–119). As noted, the Leiden manuscript follows the Greek custom of attributing the work to Nilus, reflecting the Melkite origin of the translation/manuscript.

88. Hausherr, "Le *De Oratione.*"

89. See the summary by Claire Guillaumont and Paul Géhin in the introduction to Géhin, Guillaumont, and Guillaumont, *Sur les pensées*, 73–79, and the table on 307–10.

90. Géhin, "D'Égypte en Mésopotamie," 40–42.

91. See Muravjev, "Macarian or Evagrian."

92. Stewart, *Cassian the Monk*, 114–30.

93. See Brock, "Discerning the Evagrian"; Chialà, "Evagrio il Pontico."

94. The extract from Cassian begins on f. 54v, line 6, and concludes at f. 58v, line 6. See the description by John F. Stenning in the appendix to Lewis, *Catalogue of the Syriac Mss. in the Convent of S. Catharine on Mount Sinai*, 137. The manuscript was among those microfilmed by the Library of Congress expedition in 1950.

95. The Greek text, itself a selection from the *Institutes*, can be found in PG 28:849C–905B; the relevant section begins at col. 872C. On Cassian in Greek, see Stewart, *Cassian the Monk*, 25, with bibliography. I do not agree with the recent argument by P. Tzamalikos that the Greek is original and the Latin a later expansion of it; see Stewart, "Another Cassian?" The Greek version of Cassian also served as the basis for various Arabic translations: see Graf, *Geschichte*, 401. As Graf notes, Cassian is a unique example of a Latin author being translated into Arabic in the early period (299). I thank Thomas Burman for this reference.

CHAPTER 9

Evagrius

East of the Euphrates

ANTHONY J. WATSON

Although his influence in the Mediterranean and Syriac worlds is broadly familiar to scholars, the contributions of Evagrius of Pontus specifically to the development of thought on virtue and the ascetic life among Christians east of the Euphrates River remains largely unexplored. This essay will begin to map the reception of his works and thought farther east, by reviewing how they were transmitted through the Church of the East to Persia, Central Asia, and beyond (herein also referred to as Eastern Christianity). It will introduce ways in which concepts central to Evagrian theology also came to guide ideas of virtue and spiritual life within the medieval Church of the East, whose history will be briefly described. It will then review references to Evagrius by writers of the Church of the East and the Syriac Orthodox Church. Finally, it will examine some concepts and terms found in the theology of Evagrius Ponticus, and describe the application of those terms and concepts in the early-fourteenth-century hagiographical text *The History of Mar Yaballaha III* (the *History*).[1] The essay will demonstrate that Evagrius's thought on the monastic life remained pervasive within Eastern Christianity through the end of the thirteenth century.

Pertinent Aspects of Evagrian Theology

Although the intricacies of Evagrian theology have been well explored elsewhere, it is worth highlighting aspects relevant to this essay.[2] Evagrian theology emphasizes the cultivation of virtue and purity through an ongoing struggle with evil thoughts, such as pride or gluttony, represented as demons (*daemones,* or air spirits). In works of Evagrius demons play a central role in seducing the ascetic from the pure path and toward sin. As he states in the *Praktikos*: "demons fight openly against the solitaries . . . or those who practice virtue in the company of others. . . . [T]here is not to be found on earth any men more fierce than the demons, none who support at the same time all their evil deeds."[3] In fact, this battle with demons—the personification of evil thoughts—was central to Evagrius's theological view, and the arming of the ascetic with words and passages by which he might resist evil is a significant aim of his *Antirrhetikos*. As David Brakke describes it,

> Intense conflict with demons . . . lay at the heart of the early Egyptian monk's struggle for virtue, purity of heart, and thus for salvation. . . . Evagrius of Pontus crafted the most sophisticated demonology to emerge from early Christian monasticism and perhaps from ancient Christianity as a whole.[4]

While the original Greek of the *Antirrhetikos* is lost, its full text, like so many of Evagrius's other works, is nonetheless available in Syriac, Armenian, and even Sogdian (see below).[5] The *Antirrhetikos*—as well as many of Evagrius's other works on the evil thoughts—follows a basic schema centered on eight thoughts. This concept of thoughts personified by demons is different from the tradition of the Latin West, which associated the thoughts with sins, not demons, and placed them in opposition to virtues. Observing this, Brakke has noted:

> Use of the term *vices* reflects the inward turn in how Evagrius's teachings were appropriated in the West. John Cassian had initiated this trajectory by speaking more frequently of vices than of demons and by situating the monk's conflict with temptation more within the interior division between the fallen human being's spirit and flesh than within Evagrius's cosmic division between humans and demons.[6]

The association of evil thoughts with demons found in Eastern writings is consistent with Evagrius's cosmology. As Evagrius writes: "Among the demons, some are opposed to the practice of the commandments, others are opposed to the mental representations of nature, and others are opposed to the *logikoi* which concern the Divinity, because the gnosis of our salvation also is composed of these things."[7] According to the *Kephalaia gnostika*, lost in the original Greek but fully extant in the Syriac in two different translations, demons oppose humans in their quest for virtue and salvific gnosis.[8] By living a virtuous, ascetic life, one attains purity (*dakyuthā*) and combats passions, leading to the transformation of the earthly body into a spiritual one, like that of the angels, who are the opposite of demons and are made of fire, light, and knowledge of God.[9]

Because demons govern darkness and impurity, light and purity are also important spiritual themes in Evagrius's works. In each Syriac version of the *Kephalaia gnostika* Evagrius expands on the purity-impurity antinomy by distinguishing between the knowledge granted to the pure and the lack of knowledge among the impure.[10] He states, "Among the *logikoi,* some possess spiritual contemplation."[11] As described in *Prayer,* the soul achieves purity through virtue and obedience to the commandments of God in order to achieve the desired state of receptiveness to pure prayer and mental communion with God.[12] This can lead to revealed knowledge. Julia Konstantinovsky, describing this connection between light, purity, contemplation, and revelation, says, "The contemplative knowledge of 'God's essence' replaces the contemplation of beings and banishes from the mind all preoccupation with creation. It is the 'direct' knowledge/vision of the Creator Himself."[13] Writers in the Syriac tradition, such as Isaac of Nineveh, a bishop in the Syriac Church of the East, make this link between purity and revelation even more explicit.

An Alternate Trajectory: Evagrius and the Church of the East

The works of Evagrius reached Persia and Central Asia primarily by means of the expansion of the Church of the East, a church community that over a span of centuries became increasingly independent of Byzantine and Latin Christendom, in both geography and culture. It is an ancient community with many antecedents and reliably traceable from as early as the third century to Syriac-speaking Christians living in Sassanian territory.[14] By the second half of the third century, an independent ecclesiastical structure outside the Roman Empire had developed, with the bishop of Seleucia-Ctesiphon holding primacy over other bishops within the Sassanian Empire.[15] During this period, Sassanid Christian communities played a significant diplomatic role in relations with the Byzantine Empire, and synods in 410, 420, and 424 established formalized structures within the Church of the East, promoting unity under its catholicos, the bishop of Seleucia-Ctesiphon.[16] A separate theological and philosophical tradition began to take root, and the Western repudiation of the beliefs of Nestorius and his followers at the Council of Ephesus in 431 only served to push the Church of the East toward greater independence from the rest of Christianity. Soon after Ephesus, the Church of the East affirmed its diophysite beliefs at the Council of Seleucia-Ctesiphon in 486, and by the time of the Patriarchate of Babai (497–502) it had consolidated its influence across Mesopotamia.

With greater autonomy, and less connection to Byzantine affairs, the Church of the East began to look increasingly eastward. Missionaries fanned out along the trade routes of Asia into Sogdia and beyond. In 635, one missionary known to history as Alopen reached China, and Christianity received official sanction from the Tang emperor, with an East Syrian monastery being established in Xi'an in 638. By the early eighth century bishoprics had been established in Herat, Samarkand, and China. Meanwhile, the Islamic conquest of Seleucia-Ctesiphon in

632 and the death of the last Sassanian emperor in 651 began the gradual expansion of Muslim control within Persia, introducing a new political situation for the Church of the East.[17] With the movement of the Islamic capital to Baghdad under the Abbasids in the mid-eighth century, the catholicos became vital to the success of the Church of the East, and close relations between the caliph and the catholicos led to East Syrian access at court.[18] With the ascension of Catholicos Timothy I (780–823), the Church of the East moved the Patriarchate to Baghdad and enjoyed both strong relations with the caliph and a significant period of expansion.[19] Under Timothy, missionary activity continued into China, India, Turkestan, Yemen, and around the Caspian Sea: at his death, the Church of the East had swelled to tens of millions of members located in 230 dioceses across Asia.[20]

As a consequence of the church's expansion into Persia, Central Asia, and China, a unique form of theological and spiritual literature also began to develop. By the beginning of the fifth century, a separate East Syriac literature tradition from Edessa and Nisibis took form. Within this East Syriac tradition, Greek Christian works—including controversial ones—were translated into Syriac as early as the fourth century. Up through the seventh century, the translation of these texts evolved from paraphrastic to literal.[21] Equally important during this period was the flourishing of monastic literature composed in Syriac, such as that of Isaac of Nineveh, often using translations of Greek texts as inspiration, and greatly influenced by the works of Evagrius. Eventually, that influence became an independent, native force. By the thirteenth century, Syriac writers such as Bar Hebraeus were incorporating without distinction both Greek thinkers such as Evagrius and John Climacus and Syriac thinkers such as Isaac.

Despite the condemnation of the writings of Evagrius in Constantinople in 553, the Syrian Church embraced Evagrian teachings as part of its ascetic and mystical tradition.[22] In the East, his works were widely copied and commented on in Syriac; the extant Syriac manuscripts are earlier than the surviving Greek ones.[23] This Syriac transmission preserved his literary corpus, for after his teachings were condemned, many of his works that were not destroyed outright were attributed to other writers. For example, his *On Prayer*, attributed to

Nilus of Ancyra in the Greek tradition, is preserved intact in Syriac as well as Armenian, Georgian, and Arabic translations, all rightly attributed to Evagrius.[24] In short, the prominence of Evagrius as a mystical writer was undiminished in the lands beyond the Euphrates.

Meanwhile, as the Church of the East continued to extend across the steppes of Asia, it took the works of Evagrius with it, and by the eleventh century several of the nomadic tribes of Central Asia had been converted to Christianity. Many of these tribes were unified under Genghis Khan (d. 1227) to form the core ruling structure of the Mongol Empire; indeed, several prominent queens in Genghis's line were Christian.[25] Christian tribesmen rode at the head of the army that sacked Baghdad in 1258 under the Il-Khan Hulegu, and Baghdad's Christian community was spared the massacre that befell the Muslims of that city.[26] With the rise of the Mongol Empire, travel between the expanse of Asia and the rest of the world became possible, and with the support of the Mongol Il-Khans a renaissance of Syriac literature occurred within the Persian homelands of the Church of the East. In 1281 a Turkic monk from China, Mar Yaballaha III, gained the favor of the Mongols and was elected Patriarch of the Church of the East. An acquaintance of Bar Hebraeus (see below), Mar Yaballaha is the subject of the *History of Mar Yaballaha III,* a hagiography that echoes Evagrius regarding purity and demonic warfare. Indeed, these themes had become common tropes in East Syriac literature by the thirteenth century.

Persian and Central Asian Examples of the Use of Evagrius Ponticus within the Eastern Churches

The Christian C2 Manuscript at Bulayïq

A treatise of Evagrius on combating the eight demonic thoughts, his *Antirrhetikos*, was translated into Sogdian. This treatise consists of eight books, about two-thirds of which are direct quotations from the Bible, selected according to their effectiveness in combating one of the eight evil thoughts. A manuscript partially preserving the Sogdian translation of the *Antirrhetikos* was discovered in the twentieth century at the monastery site of Bulayïq north of Turfan.[27] When the *Antirrhetikos* was translated, Sogdian was the *lingua franca* of the Silk Route throughout medieval Central Asia and was the language spoken by Alopen, the missionary to China.[28] The Christian Sogdian C2 manuscript, in which the version of the *Antirrhetikos* was found, is presumed to date from the ninth or tenth centuries, and was intended for use by monks at the monastery.[29] The presence of Evagrian writings at this monastery, an outpost of a church whose dioceses stretched from the Euphrates to the Tang imperial capital at Chang'an, is indicative of the widespread use of Evagrius within the Church of the East in Central Asia. The passing of the writings of Evagrius into Sogdian, the vernacular of sizeable communities that had settled at Turfan and in China, bespeaks the spread of his teachings along the Central Asian trade routes. The *Antirrhetikos* of the C2 manuscript also bears evidence of textual manipulation to place it into dialogue with other religious texts, such as the *Peshitta*, the Syriac Vulgate. In analyzing the biblical quotations within the *Antirrhetikos,* Nicholas Sims-Williams notes that the Sogdian translation "occasionally seems to agree with the *Peshitta* rather than with the Syriac text of Evagrius."[30] As further evidence of the circulation of Evagrius as part of a larger corpus of Eastern monastic texts, Sims-Williams also notes that the Sogdian *Antirrhetikos* also bears some similarity to the Armenian version.[31] Thus the influence of Evagrius is not limited to the mere transmission of texts. Readers were much more concerned with what Evagrius had to say and how he used biblical quotes to explain virtue than they were about preserving his original biblical passages. Over time, concepts described by Evagrius permeated later works concerning proper ascetic practice and virtue. Mary Hansbury claims that "Evagrius shaped the basic concepts of ascetic vocabulary for all East Syrian writers, including [Isaac of Nineveh]."[32]

Bar Hebraeus

Bar Hebraeus was a leader of the West-Syrian Church who lived in the thirteenth century. He died in Maragha in 1286, and is a noted author of several histories, theological treatises, commentaries, and other works.[33] Among his several notable texts are two books meant to serve as spiritual guides, the *Ethicon* and *The Book of the Dove*. The *Ethicon* was conceived of as a guide for lay people, while *The Book of the Dove* was intended for monks, specifically those "without or far from a director."[34]

The writings of Evagrius exercised great influence on Bar Hebraeus, who freely quotes Evagrius.[35] Herman Teule has listed no less than twelve different works by Evagrius quoted by Bar Hebraeus.[36] Within the *Ethicon*, Bar Hebraeus cites Evagrius by name no less than thirty times, using various honorifics, such as Master Evagrius (approximately seven times), Father of the Initiated (three times), Master of the Initiated (two times), and Father Evagrius (twenty-one times).[37] Even the title of Bar Hebraeus's work—*Ethicon*—is found in the writings of Evagrius.[38]

In both *The Book of the Dove* and in its lay companion, the *Ethicon*, Bar Hebraeus provides a description of the "Evil Passions" (*ḥašē bišē*). These Evil Passions are aligned with the evil thoughts described by Evagrius in the *Antirrhetikos*.[39] Bar Hebraeus juxtaposes, in both the *Dove* and the *Ethicon*, the "Evil Passions" with virtues that might be employed to combat them. While this approach is found in the *Antirrhetikos*, it also corresponds with the Latin tradition of placing the sins in opposition to the virtues, particularly with regard to setting specific types of sins against specific virtues.[40]

Mar ʿAbdisho bar Brika

ʿAbdisho bar Brika was a bishop of the Church of the East who lived in the thirteenth and early fourteenth centuries, dying in 1318. During his life he was bishop of a number of dioceses within the Church of the East, including Sinjar, Bet ʿArbaye, Nisibis, and Armenia.[41] Mar ʿAbdisho was also a contemporary of the Patriarch Mar Yaballaha III and his successor, Timothy II.[42] ʿAbdisho bar Brika wrote several important works, including the *Metrical Catalogue of Syriac Writers*, the *Nomocanon* (subsequently authorized by Timothy II for use in the Church of the East), *The Pearl*, and *The Paradise of Eden*. Of particular interest is the *Metrical Catalogue*. This work provides an excellent view of the works available to Syriac writers within the territories of the Church of the East and lists a number of works that are no longer extant. Several significant libraries within the thirteenth-century Il-Khanate provided source material for the catalogue. Histories of the sacking of Baghdad in 1258 and the destruction of the *Bayt al-Hikma* often fail to mention the enthusiastic patronage the Mongol Il-Khans demonstrated for institutions of learning. The observatory in the new capital of Maragha built by the first Il-Khan, Hulegu, for the astronomer Nasir al-Din Tusi contained a significant library. This library attracted Bar Hebraeus, who praised it, saying that within its walls he found "many volumes of the Syrians, the Saracens, and the Persians."[43] The *Metrical Catalogue* of Mar 'Abdisho also tersely suggests the works of Evagrius were held by these thirteenth-century libraries—"Evagrius wrote three books"—yet it indicates that Evagrius's works, as well as works possibly attributed to others, were read in the Christian intellectual circles of the Il-Khanate.[44] The *Praktikos* was used by Bar Hebraeus, thus one might speculate this was one of the works within the Il-Khanate. If so, then Evagrius's *Gnostikos* and the *Kephalaia gnostika,* his major speculative philosophical treatise, may have been the second and third books mentioned.[45] Mar 'Abdisho also describes "two wonderful volumes" written by Nilus the Monk, whose name was attributed to a number of works written by Evagrius after his condemnation.[46] Many of these thirteenth-century Eastern Christian figures were familiar with one another. Mar Yaballaha presided at the funeral of Bar Hebraeus, and recent scholarship has suggested that Timothy II, who knew both Mar Yaballaha and Mar 'Abdisho, is the author of the *History of Mar Yaballaha III*.[47]

All these examples show that texts of Evagrius were present within the medieval Eastern churches. Equally important to the presence of the texts are the underlying concepts that undergird them, especially in the thirteenth century.

Evagrian Concepts in Medieval East Syriac Writing: *The History of Mar Yaballaha III*

The *History of Mar Yaballaha III* (the *History*) provides the account of two Turkic monks, Rabban Marcos and his mentor, Rabban Sauma, who set out from their cells near Mongol Khan Baliq on a pilgrimage to Jerusalem.[48] They travel along the southern Silk Route to the Il-Khanate, where Marcos is elected catholicos of the Church of the East and Rabban Sauma is sent to the capitals of Europe in an effort to gain Latin allies for the Il-Khan.

The *History* is not an explicitly theological text. Rather it applies the theology and thought of its time to describe Mar Yaballaha as the *exemplum* of a virtuous life in which the grace of God is evident.[49] The *History* states nearly from the outset that in Mar Yaballaha "there is the concern of an exalted life," an elect life in which the author of the *History* "must tell the method of his election and confirm this as complimentary to his will."[50] The *History* describes Yaballaha's virtuous actions and so remains consistent with the trajectory of Evagrian thought. We read that Mar Yaballaha is pure, is in union with God and has revelations, and is opposed by Satan and demons. These terms and the concepts they represent can be traced through the intellectual tradition of the Church of the East, from Evagrius to the *History*, in three specific concepts and terms used in the *History*: purity (*dakyuthā*), revelatory vision (*gelyānā*), and adversarial demons (*šidē*, or *daywā*) or Satan (*bʿeldarā*, *bišō*, *saṭānā*).

Mar Yaballaha and Purity

The *History* introduces Mar Yaballaha (Marcos) as coming from a pure lineage: his father, Archdeacon Baniel, is described as being "pure" (*dakythā*) and of no blemish.[51] Rabban Sauma's lack of blemish is also quickly established, for when Marcos enters into his novitiate with Rabban Sauma, the *History* states: "And the monks (Rabban Sauma and Marcos) were labouring on that mountain in the cultivation of purity (*dakyuthā*) and holiness (*qaddišuthā*), and they were comforted by God into whom they had committed their souls."[52] Clearly Rabban Sauma at this point had also attained a reputation for piety, this being the reason Marcos had sought him out as a teacher.

The term for purity has a long tradition of use in the Syriac corpus and can be traced back to Evagrian terminology. This term is used by Bar Hebraeus in *The Book of the Dove* to describe the search for knowledge by the "pure soul" (*napšā dakyuthā*);[53] elsewhere Bar Hebraeus uses the same root, *dki*, to explain the purity of the mind required for contemplation.[54] The term is again used in the *Ethicon.*[55] In a letter about the solitary life and avoidance of contact with the outside world, John of Dalyatha (d. 780?) establishes the protective nature of purity in describing God as the "protector of the Pure (*nātrā d'dakyē*) who guards solitaries who love him against 'opposers.'"[56] He describes such monks as loving the stench and poverty of their cell and clothing, and who through such poverty "in their sleep" know holiness and "separate out (*praš*) the opposers (*lqbaliyē*)."[57] Dalyatha also frequently quotes Matthew 5.8: "Blessed are the pure for they shall see God in their heart."[58]

While Dalyatha hints at it, in the East Syriac tradition Isaac of Nineveh (d. 700) directly explores the link between purity and revelation: "the things of God come of their own accord . . . if your heart is pure and undefiled."[59] In his *Perfectione Religiosa*, Isaac sums up the role of purity and virtue as a path that enables the captivation of revelation: "the pure of mind (*dakyē d're'yānē*) is not one who does not know evil, such a person would be an animal. . . . [P]urity of mind (same term) is the capture of divine things which comes about after the practice of many virtues."[60]

Revelation from Purity: Mar Yaballaha and Visions

Yaballaha's "exalted life" is one of ascetic virtue,[61] and results in an elect relationship with God. Immediate signs of this relationship are divine favor and the gift of prophecy and vision.[62] As such, the *History* presents multiple passages in which Yaballaha has dreams and visions with Sauma acting as interpreter. Yaballaha is described as being terrified by these visions, declaring to Sauma in one instance, "I have seen a dream, and it terrified me."[63] Sauma interprets each dream, once telling Yaballaha, "you will attain to the great stature of the Fathers" and that "by the heavenly gift which has fallen on you . . . you will delight many peoples."[64]

In another dream, Yaballaha is teaching a large crowd while seated on a lofty throne. While he speaks, his tongue lengthens and divides "into three forks, on each fork appearing something like fire. And the people there were marveling and praising God."[65] Sauma again interprets the dream, saying, "This is not a dream but a revelation, and resembles a revelation."[66] The dream foretells Yaballaha's elevation: Yaballaha is elected patriarch in the next passage.

These visions link Yaballaha to a larger Christian motif of received visions by those with a special relationship with God. Visions and dreams are discussed throughout the range of Christian tradition—from the Gospels to Origen and onward—as a sign of election.[67] The term for revelation used by Rabban Sauma to describe Mar Yaballaha's dream in the *History* is *gelyānā*, which is identical to that used by Bar Hebraeus in the *Ethicon*.[68] Bar Hebraeus also uses the term (*d'gelyānā*) in the *Dove*, where he discusses the nature "of dazzling revelations."[69] The term is again used in the *Ethicon* in describing "revelations and visions."[70] John of Dalyatha links revelation and purity, writing that the kingdom of God is "revealed to the pure."[71] John Climacus (ca. 579–649) uses the Greek equivalent term (ἀποκάλυψις = *apokalypsis*) for revelation in his ladder.[72]

Isaac of Nineveh developed Evagrian concepts in his writing and directly associated contemplation, or *theoria*, with revelation. To Isaac, virtue is the bodily path that tames the body, allowing grace and illumination: "Think of virtue as being the body, but contemplation as being the soul; and the two as being one complete spiritual person."[73] Contemplation (*ṭēoriyā*), Isaac writes, is "the spirit of revelation (*ruḥā d'gelyānā*).... Contemplation is the perception of the divine mysteries hidden in the things which are spoken [in the scriptures]."[74] Thus Yaballaha's visions are demonstrative of an inner vision with the power of revelation and foresight.

The terrifying nature of Yaballaha's dreams is explained in the Greek tradition by John Climacus, who states that terrifying revelations stand in contrast to the comforting lies told by demons.[75] Equally significant is the role Rabban Sauma plays in interpreting these visions, carefully guiding Yaballaha along the razor-thin line between vainglory and humility. This is necessary, for as John Climacus states in the *Scala*:

> The devils (*daemones fumos vanae gloriae* = δαίμονες κενοδοξίας) of the smoke of vainglory do their prophecies in dreams. . . . [T]hey appear to us in sleep and talk to us so that they can push us into unholy joy and conceit when we wake up. . . . [W]hat angels actually reveal are torments, judgments, and separation, with the result that on waking up we tremble and are miserable.[76]

Thus, through Rabban Sauma's intervention, the reader of the *History* is assured both that the dreams are authentic and that Yaballaha is their humble recipient. As Yaballaha is terrified by his dreams, they are revelations; as he requires Sauma to interpret their meaning, Yaballaha's humility is preserved and his purity verified.

Satan and Demons Thwarting the Virtuous

The hagiographical nature of the *History* highlights the virtue and purity of Yaballaha through showing Satanic and demonic opposition to his work. This is particularly demonstrated in the *History* where "two envious clergy . . . slandered Yaballaha the Catholicus and Rabban Sauma and accused them . . . by the counsel of the Devil."[77] The Syriac term used in the *History* here for Devil is *bʿeldarā*, commonly used for Adversary or Enemy, thereby bringing the theme of opposition into play. The theme of the Devil as the Adversary against whom all Christians must struggle is found in early Christian theology, and such struggle was even conceived of as a salvific necessity.

This sense of demonic ensnarement is also echoed in writings contemporaneous to the *History*. Bar Hebraeus describes in the *Dove* the manner of the fall of the Perfect: "if the perfect is not cautious against the snares laid by the Evil one, he will quickly fall from that height of elevation."[78] Bar Hebraeus then uses a number of terms in rapid succession to illustrate his concept (using *bišā*, "Evil One" and *sāṭānā*, "Satan" in the same passage). This combination of terms is not exceptional, since it appears to reflect authorial preference across the corpus. Some writers prefer certain terms for Devil over others, and writers use terms interchangeably. The important aspect is the concept of Satanic or demonic opposition that is being developed. Bar

Hebraeus, for example, specifically relates that pride in one's own piety can lead the unguarded to envy and hate those "colleagues whose speeches are in better favor . . . and whose teaching is more beloved," thereby falling into a trap of Satan (the Adversary). On a conceptual level, this recalls the trap into which the two conspirators in the *History* fall prey.[79]

The work of John of Dalyatha and Isaac of Nineveh provides both a conceptual and linguistic link between Evagrian theology and the terms used in the *History*. In both writers, demons—in league with the Devil—are seen to physically act against the virtues of the ascetic. John of Dalyatha uses the term for Devil used later in the *History*: "This is the state of which holy Evagrius spoke when he distinguishes those with spiritual knowledge from those who do not possess understanding. . . . [T]he demon of fornication begins thus to produce heat in [them and] . . . the Enemy migrates toward the lower members and begins kindling his heat in them."[80] Dalyatha portrays demons as spirits in opposition to the pure, using the term *šādā* multiple times: "everything which appears [tempting to the solitary] is a deception of the demons."[81] John of Dalyatha additionally uses the terms *bišā* (Evil One) and *sāṭanā* (Satan) in his eighteenth letter, specifically placing Satan in opposition to the novice solitary: "Let him not keep company with anyone who is held by possessions, or by worldly people, lest he become a slave of Satan."[82]

Isaac of Nineveh views the Devil and demons as working against the pure, and warns against pride specifically. Among the terms used, Isaac refers to the Devil as the Adversary (*bʿildarā*): "When you are defeated, depressed and slothful; bound and ensnared before your Adversary by terrible misery and weariness from the practice of sin . . . in the heated struggle against Satan and sin . . . [r]emember the fall of the strong that you may be humble in your virtues."[83] Isaac continues, "Persecute yourself and your Adversary will be driven away from you."[84] Isaac cautions against the sin of pride through arrogance: "Pray that through your mind's self esteem you do not enter into temptation with the demon of blasphemy and pride . . . [or] enter into the manifest temptations of the sense which Satan knows how to bring upon you, when God permits him."[85] Thus, while variable terms are used for

Devil and demon in these works, the conception of demonic opposition remains, and both Isaac of Nineveh and John of Dalyatha use the term used in the *History* (*b'ildarā*) in their writings. The Evagrian conception of the "Devil" or "Demons"—regardless of actual terms used—is consistently employed to describe the opponent of those seeking the path of purity and sight of God.

Conclusion

The legacy of Evagrius Ponticus in Persia and Central Asia can be documented from texts dating from the seventh to thirteenth centuries, which show that his writings were relevant across linguistic, cultural, and even historical boundaries. There is also evidence of a progression in the conceptual framework introduced by Evagrius over several centuries. Evagrian concepts came to pervade the Church of the East, informing views on monastic life, demonology, revelation, and virtue. Such conceptions are recognizable within the narrative of the *History*.

While intellectual exchange occurred between the Latin West and the culture of the East at various points after Evagrius, it is fair to say that the influence Evagrius had on the Eastern Churches was different from that in the Western and Orthodox Churches.[86] For a start, many texts lost in Latin and Greek circles circulated freely east of the Euphrates. In the East, Evagrius remained a strong part of the tradition. Eastern Churches did not have to "recover" Evagrius, and his influence worked its way into the basic fabric of Eastern theology and ascetic practice. This is a very different approach from the Latin reception of Evagrius, which addressed only certain aspects of Evagrius's thinking and focused more internally upon individual sin, the fallen human being, and the division between body and soul.[87]

There remains much work to do in exploring the influence of the writings of Evagrius in other texts within Syriac literature, such as on his doctrines of creation and anthropology, but at least this much is clear. In the East, Evagrian theology remained strongly rooted in and developed through a tradition of asceticism, and organically permeated thinking within the Church of the East on virtue. Purity is attained by taming the body, a process which in turn leads to grace and illumination. Through this grace and illumination certain exceptionally pure individuals gain revelations.[88] The process is fraught with challenge, for the Devil and his demons will seek to discourage, entice, and defeat the ascetic on the path to purity. Hope springs from grace and from the understanding that God will not test one beyond the capacity to resist. These are all themes found in the Eastern corpus and played upon within the *History,* which is imbued with the ideas of Evagrius.

Notes

Some of the material in this essay is drawn from my doctoral thesis and was presented at the Third International Conference on Research on the Church of the East in China and Central Asia, Salzburg, Austria, June 4–9, 2009.

1. Murre-van den Berg, "Church of the East"; Borbone, *Storia di Mar Yahballaha*. It is worth also noting A. Guillaumont, "Versions syriaques."

2. For a more detailed explanation of Evagrian theology, see Konstantinovsky, *Evagrius Ponticus*, and the introduction to Sinkewicz, *Evagrius of Pontus*.

3. See Evagrius, *Praktikos* 5 (Bamberger, 16).

4. Brakke, *Talking Back*, 1–2.

5. Ibid., 1; see Sims-Williams, *The Christian Sogdian Manuscript C2*, discussed below.

6. Brakke, *Talking Back*, 6.

7. A. Guillaumont, *Les six centuries*, 20–21.

8. Ibid., 24–25; Payne Smith and Payne Smith, *Compendious Syriac Dictionary*, 89.

9. A. Guillaumont, *Les six centuries*, 24 (I.22); A. Guillaumont, *Les "Képhalaia gnostica"*; Bamberger, *Praktikos*, lxxvi. In this explicit encompassing of pre-Christian Stoic ideals, Evagrius associates the sin and physicality of humans with their muddled, earthy form, their "bodies thickened, above all by passion," with demons—representing sins—in the lowest position, their bodies "the darkest, most immersed in matter, most thickened by hatred, anger and resentment, most devoid of light." Angels, by contrast, are described as light, with bodies made of fire. *KG* 1.22, 1.68, 3.68.

10. A. Guillaumont, *Les six centuries*, 138–39 (IV.5–6).

11. Payne Smith and Payne Smith, *Compendious Syriac Dictionary*, 602; *ṭēoriyā*, from the Greek *theōria*. This term *theōria* recurs in the *KG*; see A. Guillaumont, *Les six centuries*, 22–23 (I.13), 174–75 (IV.87), 178–79 (V.6), 182–83 (V.15–16), 216–17 (VI.1–2).

12. Sinkewicz, *Evagrius of Pontus*, 193, 275. The Greek terms used are *theōria* (θεωρία) and *apokalypsis* (αποκάλυψις); the Syriac terms used are *ṭēoriyā* and *gelyārā*.

13. Konstantinovsky, *Evagrius Ponticus*, 77; Sinkewicz, *Evagrius of Pontus*, xvii: Evagrius reputedly experienced visions himself.

14. Baum and Winkler, *The Church of the East*, 7–11.

15. Ibid., 9; Klimkeit and Gillman, *Christians in Asia before 1500*, 116–27.

16. Baum and Winkler, *The Church of the East*, 14–21; Klimkeit and Gillman, *Christians in Asia before 1500*, 116–27.

17. See Baum and Winkler, *The Church of the East*, 22–58, for a more complete account of the above.

18. Hunter, "Interfaith Dialogues"; Baum and Winkler, *The Church of the East*, 58–61.

19. Klimkeit and Gillman, *Christians in Asia before 1500*, 131–36.

20. Baum and Winkler, *The Church of the East*, 60–61; Klimkeit and Gillman, *Christians in Asia before 1500*, 148–51.

21. Baum and Winkler, *The Church of the East*, 160–62.

22. Bamberger, *Praktikos*, li; Brock, "Isaac of Nineveh"; Brock, "Towards a History of Syriac Translation Technique."

23. Bamberger, *Praktikos*, li; Muyldermans, *Evagriana syriaca*, 6, 31.

24. Sinkewicz, *Evagrius of Pontus*, 183; A. Guillaumont, *Un philosophe au désert*, 125–29.

25. Boyle and Juvaynī, *Genghis Khan*, 549–52; Rashīd al-Dīn Ṭabīb, *The Successors of Genghis Khan*, 168–71, 184–86; Moffett, *History of Christianity in Asia*, 1:400–405; Klimkeit and Gillman, *Christians in Asia before 1500*, 139–40.

26. Bar Hebraeus, *Chronography*, 1:429–431; Moffett, *History of Christianity in Asia*, 1:422–28.

27. Sims-Williams, *The Christian Sogdian Manuscript C2*, 168–82.

28. Baum and Winkler, *The Church of the East*, 73–76.

29. Personal communication with Nicholas Sims-Williams, June 2011, and Erica C. D. Hunter, April–May 2009. The dating is speculative, and may be as early as eighth century. Although recent work on the Syriac Christian manuscripts at Turfan indicate a wider historical period, ranging up to the Mongol period, certainly the C2 manuscript is no later than tenth century.

30. Sims-Williams, *The Christian Sogdian Manuscript C2*, 168.

31. Ibid., 168–82.

32. Isaac, *On Ascetical Life*, 17.

33. Hage, *Syriac Christianity in the East*, 80–93.

34. Bar Hebraeus and Teule, *Ethicon*, xxx; Bar Hebraeus, *Liber columbae*, 521; Wensinck, *Bar Hebraeus's Book of the Dove*, 3.

35. Bar Hebraeus, *Liber columbae*, 557.

36. Bar Hebraeus and Teule, *Ethicon*, xviii n. 52.

37. Wensinck, *Bar Hebraeus's Book of the Dove*, xx; the terms used are *rbā āwgris, ābā didútanā, rbā didútana, ābā āwgris*, with the first term, Master Evagrius, corresponding closest to Greek appellation.

38. Bar Hebraeus and Teule, *Ethicon*, xviii.

39. Brakke, *Talking Back*, vii–viii; Bar Hebraeus, *Liber columbae*, 550–557. The Evil Passions described by Bar Hebraeus and their corresponding definition in relation to both the *Antirrhetikos* and later sin lists found in the Latin tradition are: *qúṭʿ* (Despair, Sloth), *lʿbútā* (Gluttony), *šrihúthā* (Lust/Lechery), *rúgzā* (Wrath), *āktā* (Wrath), *hsmā* (Envy), *rgigthā* (Desire), *iʿnútā* (Avarice), *šúbhā skiqā* (Vainglory), *āskma dglā* (Vainglory), *dmútā* (Pride), *šúbhrā* (Pride). An interesting aspect of Bar Hebraeus's use of the Evagrian thoughts is his juxtaposition to and compatibility with Latin schema. This suggests further work might be usefully undertaken on the Latin influences of Bar Hebraeus.

40. Bloomfield, *Seven Deadly Sins*, 69–80.

41. Assemani, *Bibliotheca orientalis Clementino-vaticana*, 3:325–362, 667.

42. Ibid., 3:325.

43. Rossabi, *Voyager from Xanadu*, 63; Aydin, "The Observatory in Islam"; Hage, *Syriac Christianity in the East*, 80–93; Bar Hebraeus and Teule, *Ethicon*, x–xi.

44. ʿAbdisho Bar Brika, *Metrical Catalogue of Syriac Writers,* in Badger, *Nestorians and Their Rituals*, 2:361–79.

45. Bamberger, *Praktikos*, lx. Evagrius describes in his introductory letter to Anatolius, "We shall make a concise distribution of the material into one hundred chapters on the ascetic life and fifty plus another six hundred on contemplative matters" (15).

46. Badger, *Nestorians and Their Rituals*, 2:367.

47. Murre-van den Berg, "Church of the East"; Hage, *Syriac Christianity in the East*, 80–93; Abbeloos, Lamy, and Bar Hebraeus, *Gregorii Barhebraei Chronicon ecclesiasticum*, 3:471–76; Takahashi, *Barhebraeus*, 1–55.

48. This is the focus of the first half of the *History*, and is drawn from a now lost Persian account written by Rabban Sauma. The second half of the text is concerned primarily with the reign of Mar Yaballaha after the death of Rabban Sauma. Bedjan, *Histoire de Mar-Jabalaha*, 85–86; Murre-van den Berg, "Church of the East," 381.

49. Murre-van den Berg, "Church of the East," 381.

50. Bedjan, *Histoire de Mar-Jabalaha*, 8–9; Montgomery, *History of Yaballaha*, 30.

51. Bedjan, *Histoire de Mar-Jabalaha*, 10.

52. Ibid., 11–12.

53. Bar Hebraeus, *Liber columbae*, 579; Wensinck, *Bar Hebraeus's Book of the Dove*, 62.

54. Bar Hebraeus, *Liber columbae*, 586; Wensinck, *Bar Hebraeus's Book of the Dove*, 138, also notes its usage in sentences 25, 58, 62, and 74, among others.

55. Bar Hebraeus, *Ethicon*, 484.

56. Hansbury, *The Letters of John of Dalyatha*, 65.

57. Ibid.

58. Ibid., 69, 103. Hansbury notes the use of the root *dki* in 19:6–7; 40:1; and 43:1.

59. Bedjan, *De perfectione religiosa*, 16; Isaac, *On Ascetical Life*, 38.

60. Bedjan, *De perfectione religiosa*, 27; Isaac, *On Ascetical Life*, 48–49.

61. Bedjan, *Histoire de Mar-Jabalaha*, 8–9; Montgomery, *History of Yaballaha*, 30.

62. Luibheid and Russell, *The Ladder of Divine Ascent*, 289: "Love grants prophecy, miracles. It is an abyss of illumination, a mountain of fire . . . it is the condition of angels, and the progress of eternity."

63. Bedjan, *Histoire de Mar-Jabalaha*, 29–30; Montgomery, *History of Yaballaha*, 42.

64. Bedjan, *Histoire de Mar-Jabalaha*, 30; Montgomery, *History of Yaballaha*, 42.

65. Bedjan, *Histoire de Mar-Jabalaha*, 31; Montgomery, *History of Yaballaha*, 42.

66. Bedjan, *Histoire de Mar-Jabalaha*, 30–31; Montgomery, *History of Yaballaha*, 42.

67. Origen, *De principiis* 1.3.8 (Butterworth). Wensinck, *Bar Hebraeus's Book of the Dove*, 19, 54–55: Bar Hebraeus describes "the elect . . . have been chosen by God before to be the vocated and the saints, to know the creatures from the Creator . . . the Initiated know His divinity by essential knowledge

and the foundation of their love is placed as upon a rock." Bar Hebraeus notes that the purpose of the solitary life is to aid in the attainment of illumination: "The habitation of the cell . . . consists in expecting from the Lord the gift of the illumination of the mind and the aptitude to behold the spiritual things in their nature and to have communion with them."

68. Wensinck, *Bar Hebraeus's Book of the Dove*, 137. Wensinck notes its use in Bedjan's text on pp. 488, 491, 497.

69. Bar Hebraeus, *Liber columbae*, 575; Wensinck, *Bar Hebraeus's Book of the Dove*, 58, 137.

70. Bar Hebraeus, *Ethicon*, 488; Wensinck, *Bar Hebraeus's Book of the Dove*, 99.

71. Hansbury, *The Letters of John of Dalyatha*, 163.

72. Wensinck, *Bar Hebraeus's Book of the Dove*, 137. Wensinck notes John Climacus, *Opera Omnia*, 218. The Latin here is side by side with the Greek: "*divina illustratione*" "prophetic revelation." The passage is from the *Scala* XV (On Chastity): "One wrestles, one is humble, another through divine revelation keeps this worthy tyrant in fetters." Note that the word for tyrant in Greek is τύραννος = *tyrannos*. Luibheid and Russell, *The Ladder of Divine Ascent*, 172. See PG 88:881–882.

73. Isaac, *On Ascetical Life*, 39.

74. Ibid.

75. John Climacus, *Scala* III (Exile and Dreams), in John Climacus, *Opera Omnia*, 36; Luibheid and Russell, *The Ladder of Divine Ascent*, 89.

76. John Climacus, *Scala* III, in John Climacus, *Opera Omnia*, 36; Luibheid and Russell, *The Ladder of Divine Ascent*, 89–90.

77. Bedjan, *Histoire de Mar-Jabalaha*, 39–43; Montgomery, *History of Yaballaha*, 47.

78. Bar Hebraeus, *Liber columbae*, 575; Wensinck, *Bar Hebraeus's Book of the Dove*, 58.

79. Bar Hebraeus, *Liber columbae*, 575–576; Wensinck, *Bar Hebraeus's Book of the Dove*, 58–59.

80. John of Dalyatha, *Letter* 49:21, in Hansbury, *The Letters of John of Dalyatha*, 300–305. This concept of heat is an implicit demonic trait in Evagrius: see *Eight Thoughts* 1.5–6, 27, 31, 33; *Monks* 11; *Eulogios* 13.12, 21.22.

81. John of Dalyatha, *Letter* 49.22, 24, 25, in Hansbury, *The Letters of John of Dalyatha*, 305.

82. John of Dalyatha, *Letter* 18.21, 28, 30, in Hansbury, *The Letters of John of Dalyatha*, 91–93.

83. Bedjan, *De perfectione religiosa*, 11–12; Isaac, *On Ascetical Life*, 33–34.

84. Bedjan, *De perfectione religiosa*, 12; Isaac, *On Ascetical Life*, 34.

85. Bedjan, *De perfectione religiosa*, 36; Isaac, *On Ascetical Life*, 57.

86. Brock, "From Antagonism to Assimilation"; Zonta, "Syriac, Hebrew and Latin Encyclopedias"; Takahashi, *Barhebraeus*, 35–37.

87. Brakke, *Talking Back*, 6.

88. Bedjan, *De perfectione religiosa*, 17; Isaac, *On Ascetical Life*, 39.

CHAPTER 10

Evagrius in the Byzantine Genre of Chapters

Joel Kalvesmaki

Byzantine authors explicitly express, in general, two attitudes toward Evagrius and his work. On the one hand, he is frequently castigated as one of the three chief Origenist heretics. The names Origen, Didymus, and Evagrius co-occur as a catch-all label for speculative heresy, usually absent discussion of specific theological error. On the other hand, some authors commend him to their readers, especially for his diagnostic tools, albeit with caution.[1] The prevalence of the former attitude and the seeming hesitancy of the latter may lead one to regard the Byzantine tradition as being overall dismissive of Evagrius. In this chapter I argue that this perspective should be tempered by evidence not so explicit, but equally telling. The proliferation of the Byzantine literary form of chapters (*kephalaia*) reveals a special kind of admiration for Evagrius, sometimes only for his literary technique but oftentimes for much more. The genre, catalyzed by Evagrius, was a vehicle for authors who were comfortable with, even if not beholden to, Evagrius's writings and legacy. Later authors, even those outside the religious sphere, tacitly acknowledged Evagrius's model, experimented with the genre's form and content, applied its core literary principles to new social settings, and wrote texts as strikingly original in their time as Evagrius's were in his. The contours of the tradition, in fact, provide insight on the pedagogical function of the genre, and so shed indirect light on Evagrius and what he intended readers to do with his chapters.

The Creation of a Literary Form

Evagrius's dense and rich prose is especially fitting for the textual form that he called "chapters."[2] The chapter treatises that survive have a number of defining features.[3]

First, Evagrius normally chose a symbolic number of chapters to frame the composition. *On Prayer*, for example, assembles in its literary "net" 153 fish conveyed "through an equal number of chapters." That is, the 153 chapters on prayer point the reader to the quantity of fish Simon Peter caught (John 21.3–11), a number that Evagrius creatively interprets in the preface as a theological symbol, an arrangement of triangles, squares, hexagons, and circles.[4] In the preface to *On Prayer*, Evagrius prompts his readers to connect scripture to geometry to contemplation of the Trinity (symbolized by the triangular number) and the natural world (symbolized by the hexagon, representing the six days of creation). These symbols, and hence the very organization of the composition, set the stage for the main subject, prayer.

A similar interest in the number of chapters appears in other works, such as his two alphabetical treatises of chapters, the *Parenetikos* and the *Spiritual Chapters Alphabetized*, and his famous trilogy, the *Praktikos*, the *Gnostikos*, and the *Kephalaia gnostika* (*Gnostic Chapters*), composed of one hundred, fifty, and five-hundred-forty (six short centuries) chapters respectively. The reason for the number chosen for the alphabetical treatises is patent but not interpreted. The numbers of chapters in the trilogy are also not explained, and they could point to any number of meanings. Drawing from number symbolism that circulated in late antiquity, one could reasonably say the one hundred points to a square number based on ten (itself considered a number of perfection); the fifty, to Pentecost; and the six hundred less sixty, to creation. But unlocking the symbolism continues to be an exercise in speculation, particularly concerning the *Kephalaia gnostika*[5] and the *Praktikos,* which in its first version had only ninety chapters.[6]

Evagrius employs other formal devices in his chapters. There is no division other than the chapters themselves. They are sequentially numbered or lettered, although one should probably not attribute theological significance to the numbering. Evagrius himself does not; the only time he uses the numbering system is by way of cross-reference.[7] The chapters are relatively short, typically from eight to fifty words per chapter (although *On the Thoughts,* whose divisions Evagrius calls chapters, has more than two hundred words per chapter; see fig. 10.1). Columba Stewart has argued that the length of the chapters was an important part of Evagrius's pedagogy and indicative of his theology.[8] The *Praktikos,* which describes the most elementary stage of spiritual development, is about forty-nine words per chapter; the *Gnostikos,* the next level up and the second part of the trilogy, decreases to about forty per chapter; the highest, the *Kephalaia gnostika,* is about twenty-five. It is as if the reader was being invited to ascend into wordless contemplation.[9] Perhaps this trend explains, or at least makes fitting, the ten chapters missing from each of the six centuries of the *Kephalaia gnostika*—a tapering into silence. As if to punctuate this *telos,* most of Evagrius's chapter treatises end on a chapter shorter than average (fig. 10.1).

Evagrius seems to have insisted upon a formally encoded silence in the presentation of his works. A marginal note attached to several manuscripts of the *Praktikos* admonishes the scribe always to begin a chapter on a new line. This note, generally agreed to originate with Evagrius, would have had the scribes produce pages with numerous long blank spaces, a departure from the stichometric approach to the codex, whose pages tended to be filled maximally, and much closer to the colometric form that was sometimes used for the Bible.[10] This convention, plus the relative brevity of the chapters, has led scholars to infer that Evagrius meant the chapters to be read slowly and repeatedly, even

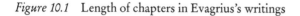

Figure 10.1 Length of chapters in Evagrius's writings

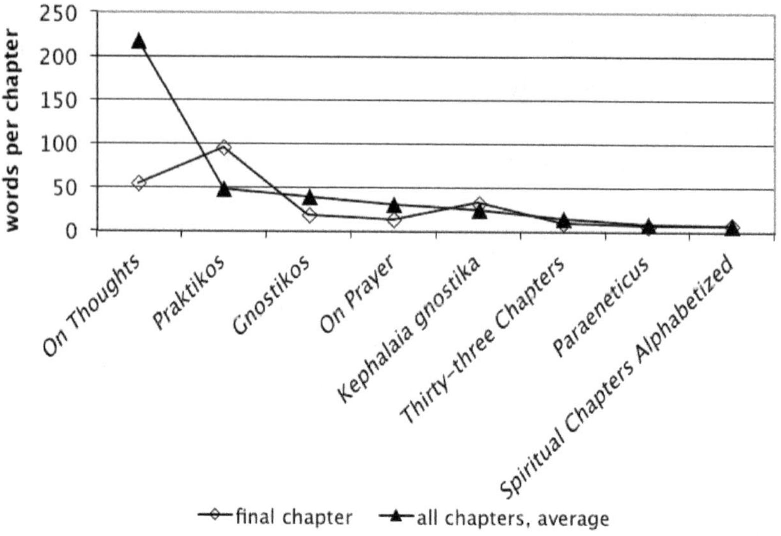

memorized, much like the Bible, particularly the Psalms, which were also memorized in fourth-century monasticism.[11] Evagrius, who taught that reading should be used to bring a wandering mind to a standstill, seems to have wanted his chapters to assist in this training.[12]

Several other defining features of Evagrius's chapters pertain to their content. All the chapters are gnomic, or resemble gnomic literature. His treatises have no overarching narrative. One chapter may or may not relate to the previous one. The treatises are difficult to confuse with any of the other genres then in use, such as letters, sermons, histories, or even miscellanies (*stromateis*), which only superficially resemble chapter treatises.[13] Some of Evagrius's opening chapters take the form of definitions. In the closing chapters of some treatises he reflects upon the teaching of his masters. Although all the chapters draw from philosophical, biblical, and religious traditions, they are presented in the single voice of the master. Even the chapters that reflect upon the teachings of Evagrius's forebears are not merely sayings of the desert fathers; any quotations attributed to them are ultimately his own words.

Roots

Every new literary form has roots that, when exposed, tempt scholars to greatly reduce or altogether eliminate any claims to originality. The temptation is moderated when one steps back and observes the conjunction of a genre's roots and trunk and the different trajectories taken by each. This holds for Evagrius's chapters as well, which seem at first glance to be the genre's point of origin. That first impression turns out to be correct, but it is properly adjusted only after understanding Evagrius's various literary models.

Biblical books of poetry, aphorisms, and wisdom, specifically the Psalms, Proverbs, and Ecclesiastes, were highly influential. It is no coincidence that Evagrius focused on these books in his scholia, and they inspired the form and content of many of his other writings.[14] His preferred term, *kephalaia*, may derive from early Christian and Jewish habits of calling pericopes of scripture "chapters."[15] These biblical precedents provided Evagrius an ample source for key aspects of his literary form, such as brevity, voice, and sequence. But the Bible explains only some of the defining features of Evagrius's chapters. For example, these scriptural books invest no symbolism in the number of "chapters," shown in part by their lack of any numbering system. Very general devices, such as the twenty-two alphabetic sections of Psalm 118 (119), provide a pattern and framework, but one whose symbolism is elusive and not explicitly connected to the mode of reading expected by the author.

Furthermore, Psalms, Proverbs, and Ecclesiastes do not explain the content of Evagrius's chapters, particularly their proclivity for philosophical definitions and terse rumination. Those are found in the second class of influential texts, a genre of teaching literature used in late antique Stoicism, represented by texts such as the *Handbook of Epictetus* (Arrian's second-century distillation of his master's discourses), Marcus Aurelius's *Meditations* (also second century), and Porphyry's *Aphormai* (late third century).[16] Like Evagrius's chapters, these texts consist of short paragraphs of original advice or philosophical insight that require careful, deliberate reading, richly endowed as they are with philosophical vocabulary. The treatises occasionally quote and use the sayings of previous luminaries, much like the ones Evagrius provided at the end of some chapter treatises; but they are primarily original compositions.

These philosophical texts did not have the pedagogical function Evagrius's had. The length of the paragraphs is most informative here. Marcus Aurelius's sections are about sixty words each; Epictetus's, nearly one hundred; Porphyry's, more than one hundred seventy. Although one may safely assume that the texts were meant for rumination, there is no evidence that they were to be memorized, to be read as one would read oracles, or to be used to enter a world of wordlessness.[17]

Further, the quantity of chapters and their numbering has no precedent in Stoic aphoristic literature (just as it is missing in scripture). Precedents for this feature are to be found in a trend among late antique authors to build their compositions in harmonic patterns evocative of number symbolism. One of the best examples is Plotinus's *Enneads,* which were arranged by their editor, Porphyry, in an ascending metaphysical sequence of six sets of nine discourses. Porphyry even split up some long but unified lectures into multiple discourses to keep the numerical pattern of the *Enneads*. The six sets follow a thematic hierarchy, recreating the cosmological architecture of Plotinus's metaphysical system.[18] Iamblichus structured his magnum opus, the ten-book work *On Pythagoreanism,* to adumbrate in its sequence the contours of the *tetraktys*—a Pythagorean number symbol based on the shape achieved by arranging ten objects in an isosceles triangle.[19] Even the Psalter was invested with a numerically symbolic framework starting in the third or fourth century, when Psalm numbers played a factor in patristic interpretation, most notably in the commentaries by Jerome and Didymus the Blind.[20]

In sum, the defining characteristics of Evagrius's chapters are found in a variety of precedents, but in no single one. Evagrius was the first to synthesize these elements. None of his literary models call their component parts *kephalaia,* a term that, when applied to literature, traditionally meant "epitome" or "extract."[21] He remained true to the term's original meaning, since, as noted by Robin Darling Young (chapter 6, this volume), he extracted from his epistolary corpus to build his chapter treatises; yet, as if to signal an original literary form, Evagrius defined "chapter" anew by fitting these extracts into biblical and philosophical literary models.

A Literary Form Becomes a Genre

In late antiquity there were a number of experiments with literary form.[22] There is no evidence that Evagrius intended to create a genre. But that is what happened. Numerous treatises organized into *kephalaia* were written throughout Byzantine times, both in the empire and beyond it.[23] Many of these treatises were collected and combined in anthologies, itself a creative activity that had significant cultural impact, most notably the famous eighteenth-century *Philokalia* of Nicodemos the Hagiorite.[24]

The historical contours of the composition and reception of Greek chapters, like so many topics from Byzantine culture, are poorly understood.[25] By identifying a few of those contours and comparing them to Evagrius's corpus, I hope to provide insights reciprocally helpful, refining our understanding of both Evagrius's pedagogy and a Byzantine literary genre. It seems to me that whatever managed to survive in Byzantium of Evagrius's legacy, after his sixth-century *damnatio memoriae*, was preserved, cultivated, and even enriched by authors of chapter treatises. Writing and using chapters, especially centuries of chapters, was how a spiritual writer and reader set himself within the Evagrian tradition as it was known in Byzantine culture.

To argue for these claims, I analyze two different aspects of the Byzantine tradition of chapters. First, I assess in very broad terms how the defining literary traits of Evagrius's chapters fared across the centuries. Much of this analysis is assisted by the accompanying table 10.1 (at the end of this chapter), which lists in chronological order, as far as can be determined, about fifty surviving examples of κεφάλαια treatises (a list that is extensive, but not exhaustive, and excludes chapter anthologies).[26] I reserve explanations or interpretations of these changes for my second approach, where I consider metanarrative in Byzantine chapter treatises. There I explore what instructions, explicit or implicit, the writers of these compilations gave on how to use the chapters. In my conclusion I synthesize these two different approaches to discern how and where Evagrius continued to exercise influence on Byzantine thought and culture, noting questions that still need to be explored.

Changes and Constants in Byzantine Chapters

A few of the characteristic features of Evagrius's chapters never took hold in the genre. Although the use of the alphabet as an organizing device was popular in other Byzantine genres, it is found rarely within chapters.[27] Evagrius's acknowledgment of his spiritual fathers becomes, in later Byzantine *kephalaia*, a tendency to cite not from the masters one has personally known but from great ecclesiastical luminaries who lived centuries before.[28] Evagrius's use of chapters as a vehicle for defining terms is not reflected later, except for Diadochos, or rather a scribal addendum.[29] (But that may be to say merely that no chapter authors had philosophical systems that required Evagrius's sort of taxonomical definitions.) Most chapter treatises, from all periods, end on a chapter longer than the average, frequently noticeably longer (see fig. 10.2).[30] Given the general aesthetic preference in Greek literature to end a series of items with one longer than average, à la the *tricolon crescens* (e.g., "life, liberty, and the pursuit of happiness"), this should not be a surprise. It rather highlights Evagrius's distinctive approach in eschewing the technique (fig. 10.1).

One important aspect of Evagrius's model was maintained throughout most of the history of the genre: the length of chapters. Up to the eighth century, chapters averaged fewer than sixty words each. This most closely resembles Evagrius's *Praktikos*, which has about fifty words per chapter. It also resembles the word length of the smallest divisions of the Gospels, which were sometimes also called *kephalaia*.[31] Some writers in the ninth to eleventh centuries began to employ longer chapters, but even then most kept to an average of fifty to one hundred words per chapter. In texts from the late Byzantine period, word counts spike, with averages hovering between one hundred and two hundred fifty words per chapter. When graphed (fig. 10.2), the change in word count suggests, by and large, stability through the early Byzan-

Figure 10.2 Changes in the length of Byzantine Greek chapters across time

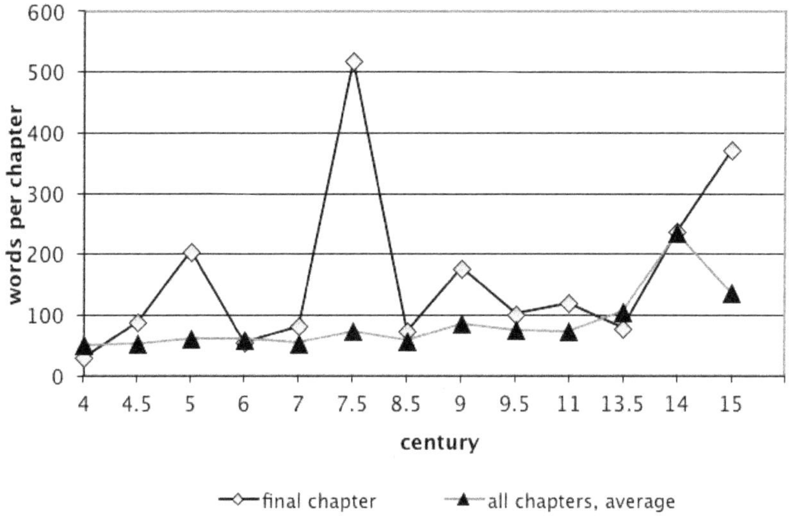

Note: texts that are difficult to date have been assigned a median century.

tine period, with a significant increase noticeable only in the late Byzantine period.

With increased word length come other late Byzantine innovations. Some chapters begin to be divided into subchapters (e.g., the Xanthopouloi; see table 10.1). Some lengthy chapters begin to resemble in miniature other genres, such as sermons or short treatises.[32] The finely tuned rhetorical devices that make earlier chapter treatises laconic, such as brachyology, are not found as often. Thus, late Byzantine authors did not expect their chapters to be memorized, perhaps not even lingered over slowly, deliberately, and repeatedly, as Evagrius's chapters were.

A new feature that creeps into a handful of chapter treatises is the acrostic.[33] Where the initial letters in Evagrius's chapters spell out the alphabet, those of later authors spell out entire sentences. The earliest example is found in Agapetus the Deacon (a sixth-century tutor to the emperor Justinian), and the device appears in six other works. The convention appears in most of the secular or political chapter treatises (those written by or to an emperor). Like Evagrius's use of number symbolism to regulate the number of chapters, the acrostic was an important framing device, stating who authored the work, explaining how to approach it, or praising the author. Leo VI wrote the acrostic governing his *On Different Gnomic Chapters* to honor by name both himself and his brother Alexander. This particular acrostic later fell victim to a *damnatio memoriae*. After Alexander attempted to have Leo's son Constantine VII castrated, the latter ordered that ten chapters forming the letters of his uncle's name (and his name alone) be altered to turn that particular part of the acrostic into gibberish.[34]

So much for changes in the genre. Several aspects remain constant over the centuries. There continues to be no overarching narrative in any of the treatises structured on chapters. A given chapter may or may not have anything to do with the subject matter of the preceding one. All chapter treatises, even if not written as tersely as Evagrius's, are parenetic in tone and content. The number of texts chosen for each treatise frequently follows number symbolism. Most often they come in sets of one hundred, the so-called century. Sensitivity to symbolic numbers and structure is evident in several compilations. Maximus the Confessor likens his four centuries on love to the four Gospels. Simeon of Thessalonike uses number symbolism to explain the structure behind his chapters on the twelve divisions of the creed. Leo VI orders his *Steering Outline for Souls* (*Oiakistikē psychōn hypotypōsis*) into three books of thirty, sixty, and one hundred chapters—an allusion to Jesus's parable of the crops (Mark 4.8) and an imitation of Evagrius's approach to organizing texts.

True to Evagrius's example, the great majority of Byzantine chapter treatises are not bricolages. They tend to be original compositions written by a single author, directed to a specific audience. On the few occasions when a previous author is cited, the quotation is put to creative use, in much the same spirit as Evagrius, who devoted the last ten percent of his *Praktikos* and *Gnostikos* to the sayings of previous luminaries.[35] This is all the more striking when one considers the attraction of the Byzantine habit of sylloge, and in how many ways florilegia and centuries might have resembled each other but do not.[36] The handful of chapter treatises that rely extensively on extracts from previous authors tend to be connected not with the religious sphere but with the political.[37]

Perhaps of the greatest significance, most of the chapter treatises deal with spiritual, particularly ascetic, topics. The asceticism is frequently accompanied by philosophical terms and concepts. Authors are not as speculative as the Evagrius of, say, the *Kephalaia gnostika*, but, like the Evagrius of the *Praktikos* or the Evagrius-cum-Nilus of the *On Prayer*, they frequently point the reader to (or assume the reader knows) philosophically informed asceticism.

Metanarrative

Most chapter treatises do not explain to their readers how to use them. But there are occasional exceptions, most often in a prefatory note or in an acrostic. Some of those comments are not informative about pedagogy because they amount merely to an acknowledgment of who the writer and recipients are (so Basil I) or to a request for prayers (so Thalassios and John of Karpathos). But a few others more amply describe their intended use.

Readers and users of the chapters were expected to make significant changes in their lives, to convert theory to reality. Mark the Monk, in the opening to his longer chapter treatise, *On Those Who Think Themselves Justified by Their Works,* says, "In the texts which follow, the beliefs of those in error will be refuted by those whose faith is well founded and who know the truth."[38] Although Mark's chapters occasionally argue against the Messalian sect, his best-known opponents, the primary object of his promised refutation is those who have theoretical knowledge of God but no obedience to his commandments. Diadochos of Photikē has the same message: "Explaining what kind of spiritual knowledge we need in order to reach, under the Lord's guidance, the perfection which He has revealed, so that each of us may apply to himself the parable of deliverance and bring to fruition the seed which is the Logos."[39]

The hows and whys for both reading and writing the chapters are presented by Maximus the Confessor in the prologue to his *Chapters on Love*, sent to a certain monk Elpidius. Maximus says that his chapters were meant to be memorized: "Your Grace should know that these are not the fruit of my own meditation. Instead I went through the writings of the holy Fathers and selected from them whatever had reference to my subject, summarizing many things in few words so that they can be seen at a glance to be easily memorized."[40] This seemingly benign sentiment provides several other cues to the reader. His claim that his chapters are an act of compilation, not writing, is a nod to the culture of compilation literature, and it provides him with a cloak of humility. The modesty is a pretense, since most of the chapters are his own words, even if they turn frequently to scripture and from time to time reuse the texts of Evagrius, Gregory of Nazianzus, and Dionysius the Areopagite. But closer examination shows that Maximus was actually claiming to be neither original nor derivative. He says in the quote above that he has traversed the fathers' *logoi* (implying rationality, ideas, and even divine principles—much more than just treatises) and selected a *nous* converging onto a *hypothesis*, and collected together many things in a few words.[41] The specialized vocabulary I have italicized directs the reader not to simple text reuse but to a path into the mind of the fathers. Such a journey requires the unmediated voice of originality—not the originality of an individualistic author but that of spiritual master. Maximus humbly claims that he has absorbed the corporate intellect of the fathers and invites his readers to do the same.

Maximus goes on to tell Elpidius how to read the chapters:

> [R]ead them with indulgence and look for only what is of profit in them, overlooking a style that lacks charm, and to pray for my modest ability which is bereft of any spiritual profit. I further request that you not be annoyed by anything that is said; I have simply fulfilled an obligation. I say this because there are many of us who give annoyance today by words while those who instruct or receive instruction by deeds are very few.
>
> . . . [P]lease pay careful attention to each chapter. For not all, I believe, are easily understandable by everyone, but the majority will require much scrutiny by many people even though they appear to be very simply expressed. Perhaps it might happen that

> something useful to the soul will be revealed out of them. This will happen completely from God's grace to the one who reads with an uncomplicated mind, with the fear of God, and with love. But if someone reads this or any other book whatever not for the sake of spiritual profit but to hunt for phrases to reproach the author so that he might then set himself up in his own opinion as wiser than he, such a person will never receive any profit of any kind.[42]

Thus, Maximus reaffirms pedagogical techniques that have been inferred from Evagrius's chapters: the need to move from empty words to deeds and action (in Evagrius's scheme, *praktikos*); the importance of careful, laborious attention to single, individual chapters (ἐμπόνως προσέχειν ἑκάστῳ τῶν κεφαλαίων); the necessity of reading in the grace and power of the Holy Spirit, without striving for one-upmanship.

One other chapter treatise has a lengthy, substantial preface, but its meaning is rather cryptic. This is the *Steering Outline for Souls*, a little-known text by the Macedonian emperor, Leo VI (866–912).[43] Each of the 190 chapters consists of two parts: a relatively brief, gnomic saying and a lengthier explanatory version. The topics pertain largely to insights on how to lead well, particularly in a monastic setting. It is an unusual text on several counts. First, the chapters, particularly the gnomic halves, are littered with rare words, including several hapax legomena.[44] The vocabulary, the difficult grammar, and the explanatory halves indicate that they were meant to be difficult to read. Second, it is rare for imperial texts to provide religious parenetic advice. Emperors (or members of their staff) wrote frequently on ecclesiastical matters, but these tended to revolve around theology, canon law, and so forth, not on pastoral guidance. Third, it is to my knowledge the only Byzantine Greek text where a single author is responsible for both a set of sayings and interpretations of them. This is all the more unusual when one considers that Leo is famous for texts that merely reproduce with modest revisions the work of previous authors (e.g., the *Taktika*). In the preface to the *Steering Outline*, Leo explains that he wrote some of the chapters when they came to his memory out of "anticipatory care for certain sayings"[45]—in other words, his personal reflection on earlier literature—but that most of them underwent no such preparation.

He insists that the texts came to him only by the internal rumination of his mind and by investigating "with an upper light." This claim to literary inspiration is confirmed insofar as the *Steering Outline* quotes from no previous texts, aside from a few Bible verses.[46] This provides some insight, and confirmation, into how writing in the genre of chapters was regarded. Chapters provided an opportunity for an author to think intensely and distill into a few words their loftiest ideas.

Leo addresses the prologue to an unnamed clergyman. The modern editor of the text, Papadopoulos-Kerameus, reasonably surmised the recipient to be Euthymios, an abbot who would later became patriarch of Constantinople (907–912). Leo instructs him briefly in how to use the *Steering Outline* and how to treat chapters that, he notes, are difficult to understand, and explains why each chapter has two versions: "For those who have a greater love of labor, the withdrawal of the intellect toward that which is hard to find is not completely unobtainable. For, either with more careful investigation they who seek find on their own that which is hidden, or else, shirking the labor, they so consider the thing sought to be impossible to flush out. So the explanation in the accompanying scholia grants understanding without much labor."[47] That is, the reader was intended to work hard and long on the first, terser version of each chapter, thinking about it, working within the recesses of his own mind. But Leo offered the longer, easier version for those who were not prepared to work so hard.

In the *Steering Outline* Leo adopts the persona of a teacher of teachers, instructing his reader, a master of a community, to exercise pastoral moderation over those under him, tempering discipline according to the disposition of each person. He adopts Evagrian ascetic terminology, discussing the *logismoi,* defining monks and monasticism, and commenting on the role of demons and bodily inflammations.[48] He offers an interpretation of Paul's admonition to take on the full armor of God (Ephesians 6.13–17) that parallels Evagrius's discourse on the schema of the monk (*Letter to Anatolius*, the preface to the *Praktikos*). Despite the ascetic associations of the genre, Leo's social world shines through. He interprets the symbolic meaning of upper-class garments such as the *loros*, and sprinkles martial vocabulary throughout the chapters.[49]

Evagrius within the Chapters: Observations and Questions

The posthumous condemnation of Evagrius wrought great changes in what was preserved of his corpus in Greek. But the alteration was not, nor could it be, total. The ancient ecclesiastical historians had left summary lists of works Evagrius had written, which meant that those listed texts, if they remained in circulation, could not convincingly be passed off as the writings of someone else. When we look at the numerous texts restored by modern scholars to Evagrius, we should distinguish in the Byzantine Greek tradition between three groups: those writings that were universally known to be by Evagrius (whether or not they survived in Greek), those that survived in Greek but were credited to other authors, and those that survive only outside the Greek tradition.[50]

Of the eight chapter treatises in the table (see p. 274), one was widely read in the Greek and almost always associated by Byzantine readers with Evagrius: the *Praktikos*. The vast majority of manuscripts that preserve most of the treatise credit Evagrius.[51] It is not only the first literary century of chapters, it is the only century Evagrius wrote. It is therefore reasonable to presume that those who imitated the form of the *Praktikos*—that is, those who wrote centuries or variations on the century—were knowingly imitating Evagrius, or drawing from a tradition shaped by Evagrius.

Significantly, nearly half of all chapter treatises written after Evagrius adhere to the century form. The two centuries by Mark the Monk and the century by Diadochos show that this dependence began quite early, before Evagrius's condemnation. That centuries are frequently used in sets of three (Leo VI, Symeon, Niketas, Gregory Palamas), parallel to Evagrius's tripartite ascetic scheme, shows that this early influence persisted.[52]

It would be hasty to conclude that all authors of chapters were imitating Evagrius or responding to him directly. To understand the precise contours of development over time one would need to look carefully at every literary century and compare them, topic by topic, to the *Praktikos*. But the structural pattern suggests that Evagrius continued to exercise an active and, to some, welcome influence throughout Byzantium.

What I have called the imperial chapters shows a different kind of influence. I am inclined to interpret the five texts by Agapetus, Basil I, Leo VI, and Manuel II as cases where the monastic genre shaped and influenced, but did not altogether swallow, imperial paraenesis.[53] In the earliest example, Agapetus quotes frequently from Evagrius's *Parenetikos*, and adopts the acrostic.[54] But no number symbolism governs its structure, and it makes no pretense of being a master's instruction to his student, which would have been an inappropriate way for Agapetus to address the emperor. All five texts are focused on spheres of rulership, virtue, and social polity, not ascetic struggle or monastic *theōria*. This is true even for the most religious in this group, the *Steering Outline*. The novelty of Leo's numerically symbolic structure draws from and points to the monastic genre of chapters. Exactly what this meant, and what advantages such a literary development was presumed to convey, would be excellent topics for further research.

The most perplexing parts of Evagrius's legacy in the genre fall in late Byzantium. Why did the length of chapters increase so markedly in the later centuries? Why does it coincide with the rise of hesychasm? Is this trend a sign of the changing pedagogical function of the genre? Perhaps as more research is invested in understanding the shifts in culture brought by late Byzantine hesychasm such questions can be answered with greater confidence. Some preliminary observations might prepare the way.

What if the increase in chapter length corresponds to a change in reading milieu? In antiquity reading was conducted in a variety of settings, ranging from private to public. Habits of public reading, particularly surrounding the scriptures, are attested with some frequency in antiquity, albeit allusively.[55] When the reading of Christian, nonscriptural texts is attested, it is in connection with private settings. The faithful were to read the writings of the spiritual fathers at home.[56] So it is reasonable to place Evagrius's chapters on the private side of the spectrum, with monks individually reading and rereading his chapters in solitude. This is how Evagrius envisioned private reading within the monastic cell, before a meal:

> When he reads, the one afflicted with acedia yawns a lot and readily drifts off into sleep; he rubs his eyes and stretches his arms; turning

> his eyes away from the book, he stares at the wall and again goes back to reading for awhile; leafing through the pages, he looks curiously for the end of texts, he counts the folios and calculates the number of gatherings. Later he closes the book and puts it under his head and falls asleep, but not a very deep sleep, for hunger then rouses his soul and has him show concern for its needs.[57]

At the monastery of Stoudios (ninth century) monks were instructed to check out from the library for a few hours after a day's work a book for personal study. Just as Evagrius describes, those afternoon reading sessions were oftentimes used instead for napping. Likewise, this reading period preceded the evening meal.[58]

We have no evidence for changes in private reading habits. But there is some evidence that one form of public reading, namely, lections at the monastery's refectory, went through some alterations in the fourteenth or fifteenth centuries. Reading in the monastery's refectory at mealtime is widely attested, even in the fourth century.[59] The typika of Byzantine monasteries indicate that scripture was the bulk of what was read during the meal. Occasionally the founders' typikas were also read (attested in middle Byzantium). But starting sometime in late Byzantium, other writings—the fathers, gerontika, and treatises recently written by spiritual elders—were included in mealtime readings.[60] Those mealtime readings continue in Greek Orthodox monasteries today; they are unhurried and take up the entire mealtime. The older chapter treatises, for their tersely written content, are eminently unsuited to a venue with few pauses. Perhaps the late Byzantine chapter treatises were written to bring the genre into this new reading environment. And perhaps this explains the emergence in late Byzantium of new compilations of spiritual literature, the *philokaliai* that provided the model for the more famous eighteenth-century *Philokalia* of Nicodemos the Hagiorite. This style of compilation has been associated with the hesychastic movement, but the details are murky.[61] To understand better the causal connections between hesychasm, changes in daily monastic life, and literary trends would require extensive manuscript study.[62] In the course of that investigation, future researchers should not be surprised to find Evagrius, imitated and critically admired.

Table 10.1 Examples of *kephalaia* in Byzantine Literature

				Word count			
Cent.	*Author*	*Title*	*No. of chaps.*	*Total*[1]	*Avg*[2]	*Final chap.*	*Comments*
4	Evagrius of Pontus	*Praktikos*	100	5462	48.58	95	Explicitly called κεφαλαῖα: prol., line 56. Text includes both prologue and epilogue.
		Gnostikos	50	*1990*	*39.80*	18	
		Kephalaia	540	*13500*	*25.00*	32	Six centuries (ninety per "century")
		Thirty-Three Chapters	33	469	14.21	9	
		On Prayer	153	5113	30.39	13	Nicodemus the Hagiorite and Makarios, *Φιλοκαλία*, 1:176–89, attr. to Nilus. Fundamentally important for the genre because in the introduction E plays with the term *kephalaia* and number symbolism. E specifically calls this work *The Chapters on Prayer* in *Thoughts* 22.
		On Thoughts	43	9372	217.95	54	
		Parenetikos	24	191	7.96	6	Alphabetized
		Spiritual Chapters Alphabetized	24	172	7.17	7	Alphabetized
4?	[Anthony the Great]	*Counsel on the Custom and Useful Polity of Humans*	170	*8730*	*51.35*	87	Nicodemus the Hagiorite and Makarios, *Φιλοκαλία*, 1:4–27; Latin extracts in PG 40:957–62. By a Stoic writer, perhaps not Christian.

Table 10.1 Examples of *kephalaia* in Byzantine Literature (*cont.*)

				Word count			
Cent.	*Author*	*Title*	*No. of chaps.*	*Total*[1]	*Avg*[2]	*Final chap.*	*Comments*
4–6	Mark the Monk	*On the Spiritual Law*	200/ 201	3931	19.39	31	Durand, *Traités*, 1:74–128; Nicodemus the Hagiorite and Makarios, *Φιλοκαλία*, 1:96–108.
		On Those Who Think Themselves Justified by Their Works	221/ 226	5893	26.64	313	Durand, *Traités*, 1:130–200; Nicodemus the Hagiorite and Makarios, *Φιλοκαλία*, 1:109–26.
5	Diadochos of Photikē	*One Hundred Chapters on Spiritual Perfection*	100	15892	157.28	372	Rutherford, *One Hundred Practical Texts*; Nicodemus the Hagiorite and Makarios, *Φιλοκαλία*, 1:235–73. Very similar to Evagrius in style.
5?	Isaiah the Anchorite	*Chapters on Ascesis and Hesychia*	19	1275	67.11	99	PG 40:1205–12. Some chapters drawn from other texts. Isaiah's *Discourses* were also culled into chapters in Nicodemus the Hagiorite and Makarios, *Φιλοκαλία*, 1:30–35.
5?	[Nilus of Ancyra]	*Gnomai*	135	*3870*	*28.67*	—	PG 79:1239–49. Incomplete. Some chapters are found in, or extracted from, other monastic corpora (e.g., Ephraem Syrus, other works by Nilus). Content, terse phrasing is akin to Evagrius's.

Table 10.1 Examples of *kephalaia* in Byzantine Literature (*cont.*)

				Word count			
Cent.	*Author*	*Title*	*No. of chaps.*	*Total*[1]	*Avg*[2]	*Final chap.*	*Comments*
5–10?	Ephraem Syrus (Graecus)	*On Humility*	100	11241	112.36	704	Phrantzolas, *Ὁσίου Ἐφραίμ τοῦ Σύρου ἔργα*, 2:280–362.
		On the Spiritual Life	96	6296	65.48	92	Phrantzolas, *Ὁσίου Ἐφραίμ τοῦ Σύρου ἔργα*, 2:209–51.
		Beatitudes in 55 Chapters	55	2150	39.04	150	Phrantzolas, *Ὁσίου Ἐφραίμ τοῦ Σύρου ἔργα*, 2:252–66.
		Beatitudes in 20 Chapters	20	2055	102.55	1602	Phrantzolas, *Ὁσίου Ἐφραίμ τοῦ Σύρου ἔργα*, 2:267–79.
		90 Chapters on the Straight Life	90	3592	39.87	35	Phrantzolas, *Ὁσίου Ἐφραίμ τοῦ Σύρου ἔργα*, 3:11–35.
6	Agapetus	*Ekthesis [. . . parainetikon kephalaion]*	72	3422	47.38	57	Riedinger, *Der Fürstenspiegel für Kaiser Iustinianus* (PG 86.1:1163–85). Addressed to the emperor. Forms an acrostic. An ancestor to the medieval genre known as the "mirror of princes," it draws from Isocrates, Eusebius, Nilus (Frohne [*Agapetus Diaconus*, 188–90] counts 52 citations of [Nilus], *Gnomai* = Evagrius, *Maxims 1*), Isidore of Pelusium.
6?	John of Karpathos	*Consolations to the Monks of India*	100	*7540*	*75.40*	75	PG 85:791–826 (Lat. trans.), 1837–56 (Grk.); Nicodemus the Hagiorite and Makarios, *Φιλοκαλία*, 1:276–96. The brief preface and the lengthy hundredth chapter—a letter of consolation—provide context.

Table 10.1 Examples of *kephalaia* in Byzantine Literature (*cont.*)

Cent.	*Author*	*Title*	*No. of chaps.*	*Word count* *Total*[1]	*Avg*[2]	*Final chap.*	*Comments*
		Theological and Ascetic Chapters	117	*6150*	*52.56*	27	Balfour and Cunningham, *Supplement to the Philokalia*; Nicodemus the Hagiorite and Makarios, *Φιλοκαλία*, 1:297–303. Earliest manuscripts have 116 chapters. Synthesis of various levels of Evagrius-inspired thought. The last chapter, imitating in reverse Evagrius's *Praktikos* 1, offers a definition of Χριστιανισμός.
7	Maximus the Confessor	*Centuries on Theology and Economy*	200	*14250*	*71.25*	51	PG 90:1083–1173; Nicodemus the Hagiorite and Makarios, *Φιλοκαλία*, 2:52–90.
		Centuries on Love	400	20094	49.64	68	Ceresa-Gastaldo, *Capitoli sulla carità*; Nicodemus the Hagiorite and Makarios, *Φιλοκαλία*, 2:4–51; PG 90:959–1176. Prologue comparable to Evagrius, *Prayer*. End of century 1 cites luminaries (à la Evagrius).
		Different Centuries Regarding Theology and Economy: On Virtue and Vice	500	*35910*	*71.82*	85	Nicodemus the Hagiorite and Makarios, *Φιλοκαλία*, 2:91–186; PG 90:1178–1392.
7	Thalassios (the Libyan?)	*On Love and Continence and the Life of the Mind*	400	*6525*	*16.31*	122	Nicodemus the Hagiorite and Makarios, *Φιλοκαλία*, 2:205–29; PG 91:1428–69. Author a friend of Maximus. The acrostic constitutes a kind of preface. Last decade of the third century is a prayer.

Table 10.1 Examples of *kephalaia* in Byzantine Literature (*cont.*)

Cent.	*Author*	*Title*	*No. of chaps.*	*Word count*			*Comments*
				Total[1]	*Avg*[2]	*Final chap.*	
8/9?	Hesychios the Sinaite	*On Temperance and Virtue*	200	*11270*	*56.35*	73	Nicodemus the Hagiorite and Makarios, *Φιλοκαλία*, 1:141–73; PG 93:1480–1544.
9	Basil I	*Βασιλείου κεφάλαια παραινετικά*	66	*6730*	*101.97*	117	Emminger, *Studien zu den griechischen Fürstenspiegeln*; PG 107:xxi–lvi. Chapters of political advice, in acrostic (Βασίλειος ἐν Χριστῷ βασιλεὺς Ρωμαίων Λέοντι τῷ πεποθημένῳ υἱῷ καὶ συμβασιλεῖ). About half the text draws from numerous earlier gnomic sources. No prefatory material.
9?	Theodore of Edessa	*One Hundred Chapters Useful for the Soul*	100	*7400*	*74.00*	259	Nicodemus the Hagiorite and Makarios, *Φιλοκαλία*, 1:304–24.
9?	Theognostos	*On Action and Theōria and On Holiness*	75	*5800*	*77.33*	152	Nicodemus the Hagiorite and Makarios, *Φιλοκαλία*, 2:255–71. Ascribed by Nicodemos to the Theognostos mentioned by Photios, *Biblioteca* 106. Argued by Gouillard, "L'acrostiche spirituel" to be fourteenth c. Chapters in acrostic.

Table 10.1 Examples of *kephalaia* in Byzantine Literature (*cont.*)

Cent.	*Author*	*Title*	*No. of chaps.*	*Word count* *Total*[1]	*Avg*[2]	*Final chap.*	*Comments*
9/10	Leo VI	*Οἰακιστικὴ ψυχῶν ὑποτύπωσις*	190	*10020*	*52.74*	131	Papadopoulos-Kerameus, *Varia Graeca sacra*, 213–53. Grouped in 30, 60, and 100 chapters. Each is a gnomic saying followed by an explanation.
		On Different Gnomic Chapters [= *Taktika* book 20]	221	11510	52.08	122	Dennis, *The Taktika of Leo VI*, 536–619. An acrostic of chapters intended as advice for military leaders. Acrostic indicates that it was composed by Leo and his brother Alexander (who suffered *damnatio memoriae* in the form of the text that survives).
9/10?	Philotheos of Sinai	*Chapters of Sobriety*	40	*4750*	*118.75*	49	Nicodemus the Hagiorite and Makarios, *Φιλοκαλία*, 2:274–86.
11	Leo of Ohrid	*Chapters on Temptation and Subsequent Tribulation and the Ensuing Help*	50	3100	62.00	126	Munitiz, "Leo of Ohrid," improving on Büttner, *Erzbischof Leon von Ohrid*.

Table 10.1 Examples of *kephalaia* in Byzantine Literature (*cont.*)

				Word count			
Cent.	*Author*	*Title*	*No. of chaps.*	*Total*[1]	*Avg*[2]	*Final chap.*	*Comments*
11	Symeon the New Theologian	*One Hundred Theological and Practical Chapters*	100	*7960*	79.40	80	Simeon the New Theologian, *Chapitres théologiques, gnostiques et pratiques*, 40–100 (part. Nicodemus the Hagiorite and Makarios, *Φιλοκαλία*, 3:237–70).
		Twenty-Five Gnostic and Theological Chapters	25	*1990*	79.24	99	Simeon the New Theologian, *Chapitres théologiques*, 102–18 (published partially in Nicodemus the Hagiorite and Makarios, *Φιλοκαλία*, 3:237–70).
		One Hundred More Theological and Practical Chapters	100	*7960*	79.52	188	Simeon the New Theologian, *Chapitres théologiques*, 120–86 (part. Nicodemus the Hagiorite and Makarios, *Φιλοκαλία*, 3:237–70).
11	Niketas Stethatos	*Centuries of Practical, Physical, and Theological Chapters*	300	*31185*	*103.95*	106	Nicodemus the Hagiorite and Makarios, *Φιλοκαλία*, 3:273–355 (= PG 120:851–1010). Three centuries structured as *praktika*, *physika*, and *gnostika*. Some chapters are quite long.
11?	Elias Ekdikos	*Other Chapters*	280	*8470*	*30.25*	115	Nicodemus the Hagiorite and Makarios, *Φιλοκαλία*, 2:289–314 (= PG 90:1401–61 = 127:1129–76). Collections of chapters (one run of 243 chaps. in PG 90, ascribed to Maximus; two runs of 109 and 140 chaps. in PG 127; in the *Philokalia* there are three γνωμικά, in 109, 32, and 139 chaps.).

Table 10.1 Examples of *kephalaia* in Byzantine Literature (*cont.*)

Cent.	*Author*	*Title*	*No. of chaps.*	*Word count: Total*[1]	*Word count: Avg*[2]	*Word count: Final chap.*	*Comments*
12/13	Neophytos the Recluse	*Ascetical Chapters*	400	—	—	—	400 chapters, now lost; attested in Neophytos's *Testamentary Rule*, Thomas and Constantinides Hero, *Byzantine Monastic Foundation Documents*, 4:1355.
13/14	Gregory Sinaites	*Most Beneficial Chapters in Acrostic*	137	*12100*	*88.32*	83	Nicodemus the Hagiorite and Makarios, *Φιλοκαλία*, 4:31–62 (PG 150:1240–1300). In acrostic (description of contents).
		Other Chapters	7	856	122.29	73	Nicodemus the Hagiorite and Makarios, *Φιλοκαλία*, 4:63–65 (PG 150:1300–1304).
14	Kallistos I of Constantinople	*Chapters on Prayer*	14	*690*	*49.29*	48	Nicodemus the Hagiorite and Makarios, *Φιλοκαλία*, 4:296–98 (PG 147:813–17).
		Remaining Chapters	69	*26350*	*381.88*	221	Nicodemus the Hagiorite and Makarios, *Φιλοκαλία*, 4:299–367. Sometimes combined with the *Chapters on Prayer.*
14	Gregory Palamas	*One Hundred Fifty Physical, Theological, Ethical, and Practical Chapters*	150	*23344*	*155.49*	116	Nicodemus the Hagiorite and Makarios, *Φιλοκαλία*, 4:134–87 (PG 150:1121–1225).
		Three Chapters on Prayer and Purity of Heart	3	*710*	*236.67*	286	Nicodemus the Hagiorite and Makarios, *Φιλοκαλία*, 4:132–33.

Table 10.1 Examples of *kephalaia* in Byzantine Literature (*cont.*)

				Word count			
Cent.	*Author*	*Title*	*No. of chaps.*	*Total*[1]	*Avg*[2]	*Final chap.*	*Comments*
14?	Kallistos and Ignatios Xanthopouloi	*A Method and Rule That Is, with God, Exact*	100	*34340*	*343.40*	510	Nicodemus the Hagiorite and Makarios, *Φιλοκαλία*, 4:197–295 (PG 147:636–812). Some chapters are so long they are subdivided (e.g., no. 66). Chapters have heads/titles, sometimes lengthy.
15	Manuel II Palaeologos	*Treasury of Imperial Guidance in One Hundred Chapters*	100	*12280*	*122.8*	122	Nicodemus the Hagiorite and Makarios, *Φιλοκαλία*, 156:320–84 (prefatory letter at 313–20), in acrostic (Βασιλεὺς βασιλεῖ Μανουὴλ Ἰωάννῃ, πατὴρ υἱῷ ψυχῆς ψυχῇ, καρπὸν τροφῆν, ἐμῆς τῇ σῇ ὁποιασοῦν ἀκμαζούσῃ ἧ ὁ Θεὸς εἴη κοσμήτωρ)
15	Kallistos Kataphygiotes	*On the Unity with God and on Contemplative Life*	92	*22230*	*241.63*	unkn	Nicodemus the Hagiorite and Makarios, *Φιλοκαλία*, 5:4–59 (PG 147:835–942). Manuscript breaks off, so it may have originally been a century of texts.
15	Symeon of Thessalonike	*Twelve Chapters*	24	1899	42.38	618	Nicodemus the Hagiorite and Makarios, *Φιλοκαλία*, 155:820–29. Two sets of chapters synoptically discussing the articles of the creed, structured by number symbolism. Has preface, interlude, and postscript.

[1] Values in italics represent only approximate word counts.
[2] The words-per-chapter value excludes any prefatory material.

Notes

Revising this essay was helped by comments made by participants at the Dumbarton Oaks roundtable, particularly Margaret Mullett, Dirk Krausmüller, and Julia Konstantinovsky. Research on this chapter occurred before the appearance of the masterly study by Géhin, "Collections." Any undocumented overlap is accidental.

1. A marginal note in a fifteenth-century manuscript of the *Praktikos* cautions the reader that the author was a godly Evagrius different from the eponymous heretic. See C. Guillaumont and A. Guillaumont, *Traité pratique*, 1:239. For a more complete account of Evagrius's reputation in Byzantine literature, see the introduction to this volume.

2. Evagrius calls *Prayer* "the *Chapters on Prayer*" (*On the Evil Thoughts* 22). Also see *On the Evil Thoughts* 24; *Prayer*, prologue; and *Praktikos* pref.9.

3. For an expanded study of Evagrius's chapters, see Stewart, "Evagrius Ponticus on Monastic Pedagogy," 267. For treatments of the genre, see, among other studies cited in this article, Hausherr, "Centuries"; Guillaumont, *Un philosophe au désert*, 92–94, 104–5; Kazhdan, *ODB*, 1:410–11; von Ivánka, "ΚΕΦΑΛΑΙΑ."

4. The number symbolism in the preface to *On Prayer* widely attracts comments in modern scholarship. See, e.g., Harmless, *Desert Christians*, 339–41.

5. A. Guillaumont, *Les "Képhalaia gnostica,"* 19–22, offers an Evagrian interpretation of the short century (according to the number of days in the seasons of Lent and Pentecost). He is more reticent in his posthumously published *Un philosophe au désert*, 102–5.

6. C. Guillaumont and A. Guillaumont, *Traité pratique*, 1:118–20.

7. See Evagrius, *On the Thoughts* 24.4–5, referring to "the seventeenth chapter."

8. Stewart, "Evagrius Ponticus on Monastic Pedagogy," 260.

9. This resembles the habit of Clement of Alexandria, to be prolix in simpler points and terse at the more obscure, gnostic ones.

10. C. Guillaumont and A. Guillaumont, *Traité pratique*, 1:384–85; Gamble, *Books and Readers*, 229.

11. Stewart, "Evagrius Ponticus on Monastic Pedagogy," 258; Dysinger, *Psalmody*, 48–61.

12. Evagrius, *Praktikos* 15; *Exhortation to Monks* 1.3.

13. Clement says in the preface of his miscellanies, the *Stromateis,* that he is offering a "systematic exposition of chapters" (*kephalaiōn systēmatikēn ekthesin*; *Stromateis* 1.1.1.14.2). But this is not a treatise organized into chapters. Clement understands *kephalaion* as functional equivalent to "extract," from which the *Stromateis* have been composed (and whose subdivisions he prefers to call *logoi* or *epidromai*). See Méhat, *Étude sur les "Stromates,"* 119–24.

14. For example, the two works that make up *The Mirrors* (that is, *To the Monks in Community* and *Instruction to a Virgin*) consist of distychs styled much like the Psalms or Proverbs.

15. See Méhat, *Étude sur les "Stromates,"* 121–22.

16. von Ivánka, "ΚΕΦΑΛΑΙΑ"; A. Guillaumont, *Un philosophe au désert,* 114n5.

17. A trend that resonates with the larger pattern of discourse from Greek antiquity through Christian. See Mortley, *From Word to Silence.*

18. See Slaveva-Griffin, *Plotinus on Number*, chap. 6.

19. O'Meara, *Pythagoras Revived.* The shape is: ∴∵.

20. On exegesis of the Psalm numbers see, e.g., Jerome, *Homilies* 3 (on Psalm 6), 5 (Ps. 14), 13 (Ps. 80), 17 (Ps. 84), 60 (Ps. 10); Didymus the Blind, *Commentary on the Psalms* 106.18–109.4 (Ps. 50), 156.20–157.6 (Pss. 30, 31), 186.31 (Ps. 33), 303.23–304.1 (Ps. 42). See also Kalvesmaki, "Canonical References in Electronic Texts."

21. See above, n. 13, and Méhat, *Étude sur les "Stromates,"* 121–22. Clement's use of κεφάλαια to describe his *Stromateis* points to this older definition. Marcus Aurelius, *Meditations* 11.18, gives ten sayings in honor of the nine muses and their leader, and he calls them "chapters." But these apply only to this section of the *Meditations.*

22. Some literary experiments from Evagrius's time, such as the question–answer (*eratapokriseis*), blossomed; others, such as the hexameter biblical epic (e.g., the paraphrases by Apollinarius of Laodicea and Nonnus of Panopolis) did not.

23. Bettiolo, "Povertà e conoscenza." I thank Gregory Kessel for this reference.

24. See the various manuscript descriptions, esp. of Par. gr. 362 and Lavra M 54 (Ath. 1745), in C. Guillaumont and A. Guillaumont, *Traité pratique,* 1:127–271. Some of these chapter-collection manuscripts include Epictetus's *Handbook*, occasionally Christianized, e.g., Vat. Reg. gr. 23 and Par. gr. 39. For discussion of the *Philokalia* tradition see Géhin, "Le Filocalie che hanno prece-

duto la 'Filocalia'"; Konstantinovsky, "Evagrius in the Philocalia of Sts Macarius and Nicodemus"; Géhin, "Collections."

25. In addition to the studies cited in n. 3 and the editions cited in table 10.1, see Krausmüller, "Dating John of Carpathus."

26. The list excludes what one might call dogmatic chapters, such as Leontius of Byzantium, *Thirty Chapters against Severus* (PG 86:1901–1916); Ephrem of Antioch, *Twelve Chapters of the Orthodox* and *Twenty-Two Dogmatic Chapters to Akakios* (Helmer, 262–65, 271–72, respectively); and Zacharias of Mytilene, *Seven Chapters against the Manichaeans* (Richard ed., xxxiii–xxxix). Apophthegmatic literature (e.g., Ammonas's *Nineteen Chapters* [*CPG* 2390]) are excluded. The anthologizing habit that I exclude is exemplified by Maximus the Confessor, *Theological Chapters* (PG 91:721–1017); John of Damascus, *Philosophical Chapters* (Kotter ed.); and Evagrius's *Skemmata* and *The Disciples of Evagrius,* both of which were later compilations from Evagrius's corpus. For a study that treats chapter treatises and chapter collections/anthologies holistically, see Géhin, "Collections." Table 10.1 includes texts classified by others as gnomological: Odorico, "Miroirs des princes," 227. The relation of gnomology to chapter treatises, chapter collections, and related genres (e.g., sylloge) is important, but cannot be addressed here. For my purposes, I include those gnomologies or syllogeis that I regard as having a striking affinity to other chapter treatises.

27. For example, the alphabetical *gnomai.* For examples see Ephrem Graecus, *Alphabetical Paraenesis to Ascetics* (Phrantzolas, 3:338–56, and PG 79:1471–90); Mosqu. Synod. 436, fols. 247–49 (unpublished; see Roueché, "The Place of Kekaumenos in the Admonitory Tradition," 135); Kazhdan, *ODB*, 2:856; H. Leclercq and Cabrol, *DACL*, 1:356–72. Larger alphabetical chapter-like collections also exist: John of Damascus, *Sacra Parallela;* and Makarios Chrysokephalos, *Rhodonia* (a fourteenth-century text also known as *Paroemiae*; Leutsch and Schneidewin, *Corpus Paroemiographorum Graecorum*, 2:135–227).

28. See, e.g., Maximus the Confessor, *Centuries on Love* 2.29 (citing Gregory of Nazianzus), 3.5 (citing Dionysius the Areopagite).

29. Rutherford, *One Hundred Practical Texts.*

30. About three-fourths of all treatises end on a longer chapter. In half of those the final chapter is at least twice as long as the average. Note, especially, most of Ephrem Graecus's texts (hence the anomalous spike around the eighth century in fig. 10.2); Mark the Monk, *On Those Who Think Themselves Justified by Their Works*; Thalassios the Libyan; Elias Ekdikos; and Theodore of Edessa.

31. In the *Suda* the term *kephalaion* (kappa 1441) is contrasted to *titlos* (title). Matthew is divided into 68 titles and 355 chapters; Mark into 48 titles and 36 chapters (an error for 236); Luke into 83 titles and 348 chapters; John into 18 titles and 232 chapters. Based on modern critical editions of the New Testament this yields 51.7, 47.8, 56.0, and 67.3 words per chapter for the four Gospels. Martin Wallraff has noted (personal correspondence, May 19, 2010) that the *Suda*'s use of *kephalaion* and *titlos* is idiosyncratic, the former term corresponding to Eusebius's sections and the latter to what was normally called *kephalaia*.

32. This can be seen especially in Michael Glykas, *Chapters on Difficulties in the Holy Scriptures* (twelfth c.), whose chapters are in reality short treatises. See Eustratiades, *Michael tou Glyka*.

33. On the origins and development of the acrostic see *DACL*, 1:356–72.

34. Grosdidier de Matons, "Trois études sur Léon VI."

35. That treatises of chapters are frequently seen by scholars as derivative and therefore unimportant—see, e.g., Costache, "Queen of the Sciences?"—contributes to scarcity of attention and studies on the majority of texts presented in the table.

36. On the culture of Byzantine compilation literature, see Roueché, "The Literary Background of Kekaumenos"; Roueché, "The Place of Kekaumenos in the Admonitory Tradition"; Holmes, "Byzantine Political Culture."

37. The most extensive use of quotations or compilation is found in each of the treatises by Agapetus and Basil I, and one of Leo VI. On Basil I, see Markopoulos, "Autour des chapitres parénétiques de Basil 1er."

38. Nicodemus the Hagiorite and Saint Makarios, *Philokalia*, 125.

39. Ibid., 253.

40. Berthold, *Maximus Confessor*, 18

41. *alla tous tōn hagiōn paterōn dielthōn logous kakeithen ton eis tēn hypothesin synteinonta noun analexamenos kai en oligois polla kephalaiōdesteron synagagōn.*

42. Berthold, *Selected Writings*, 35.

43. In addition to the edition (see table 10.1), see Ehrhard, "Review of Papadopoulos-Kerameus," where other known manuscripts are briefly discussed.

44. As determined by searches in the Thesaurus Linguae Graecae (accessed February 2011).

45. Papadopoulos-Kerameus, *Varia Graeca sacra*, 214, lines 8–9.

46. The exception to this rule is that Ephrem Graecus, *Interpretatio* 4–8, 10–22, (Phrantzolas, 5:385–91, reliant on one manuscript, Vat. gr. 375 [14th

c.]), corresponds exactly to *Steering Outline* 1.8, 1.9, 1.13, 1.15, 1.22, 1.27, 1.28, 1.29, 2.2, 2.3, 2.4, 2.5, 2.15, 2.17, 2.18, 2.20, 2.35, 2.42, respectively. Rather than shedding light on the date and circumstances of Leo's composition, this commonality merely highlights just how poorly studied is the Ephrem Graecus corpus, which is heterogeneous and chronologically amorphous.

47. Papadopoulos-Kerameus, *Varia Graeca sacra*, 214, lines 22–28.

48. *Logismoi*: 1.29, 2.25. Monks defined: 2.46–50. Bodily inflammations: 2.58.

49. Costume: 3.38–44. Martial vocabulary: 2.21, 2.54, 3.4, 3.35.

50. These three categories are adopted also in the organization of part 2 of A. Guillaumont, *Un philosophe au désert.*

51. Ten of eleven manuscripts, described in C. Guillaumont and A. Guillaumont, *Traité pratique*, vol. 1. In manuscripts where the *Praktikos* is excerpted and preserved only in smaller sections, the attribution tends to be to Nilus, an attribution that had more plausibility because the excerpt did not look like the original composition.

52. Even in middle Byzantium, authors of chapters were responding directly to Evagrius's known writings. Compare Evagrius, *Sentences to the Monks* 3, to Niketas Stethatos, *Century* 2.1. On Niketas's various sources see Nicodemus the Hagiorite and Makarios, *Philokalia*, 4:76–77.

53. On this genre, mistakenly named "mirrors of princes," see, among others, Emminger, *Studien zu den griechischen Fürstenspiegeln*; Frohne, *Agapetus Diaconus*; Odorico, "Miroirs des princes."

54. Frohne, *Agapetus Diaconus*, 188–91.

55. Gamble, *Books and Readers*, 203–41.

56. Ibid., 231–37.

57. Evagrius, *Eight Thoughts* 15 (Sinkewicz); Evagrius, *Thoughts* 33.

58. Thomas and Constantinides Hero, *Byzantine Monastic Foundation Documents*, 1:93, 108. Neilos Damilos (fifteenth century) also commended constant and insatiable reading of Maximus the Confessor's *Chapters on Love*; Thomas and Constantinides Hero, *Byzantine Monastic Foundation Documents*, 4:1468.

59. Cassian, *Institutes* 4.17, Basil of Caesarea, *Shorter Rules* 180, which suggest the earliest readings involved scripture. Further references: Thomas and Constantinides Hero, *Byzantine Monastic Foundation Documents*, 1:27.

60. First attested in the fifteenth century, Charsianeites: ibid., 4:1658.

61. See n. 24.

62. To date the only study is Géhin, "Le Filocalie che hanno preceduto la 'Filocalia.'"

CHAPTER 11

Origenism and Anti-Origenism in the Late Sixth and Seventh Centuries

Dirk Krausmüller

When Evagrius Ponticus died in the year 399 he left behind a corpus of texts that continued to find avid readers in monastic circles. There can be no doubt that many of these readers were attracted to Evagrian spirituality because it grounded their personal endeavors in an overarching providential framework that was based on the teachings of the great Alexandrian theologian Origen. However, this framework also proved to be the most controversial part of Evagrius's legacy. Accusations of heresy began almost immediately after his death and culminated in the year 553, when the Fifth Ecumenical Council condemned both him and Origen as enemies of the church. The following centuries saw a further hardening of attitudes within the Chalcedonian church. Now even authors who were influenced by Origen but did not openly subscribe to his controversial views came under suspicion. In the first half of the seventh century Maximus the Confessor felt the need to offer orthodox interpretations of "ambiguous" passages in the works of

Gregory of Nazianzus, and a few decades later Patriarch Germanus set out to cleanse the treatises of Gregory of Nyssa from supposed Origenist interpolations.[1] Thus it is not surprising that the much more openly Origenist writings of Evagrius have not survived in the Greek original. This does not mean, however, that all interest in Origenism ended at a stroke with its official condemnation.

This chapter has two objectives: to present evidence for the survival of Origenist ideas in the late sixth and early seventh centuries, and to discuss the development of anti-Origenist polemic in the same period. It will first make the case that two authors of Chalcedonian Christological treatises, Pamphilus and Leontius of Jerusalem, asserted the legitimacy of speculation about the soul and affirmed the belief in its preexistence. Through careful analysis of their arguments it will be shown that Pamphilus and Leontius developed elaborate strategies of concealment, which allowed them to signal their beliefs to sympathetic readers without having to make explicit statements that would have laid them open to attacks by their enemies. In a second step, it will then be argued that anti-Origenist polemic was not only directed against genuinely Origenist teachings but also against beliefs that had until then been considered perfectly acceptable, such as the notion that the soul is a self-sufficient being and therefore aware and active after its separation from the body. The impact of this polemic will be assessed through analysis of the writings of Maximus the Confessor, where overt criticism of preexistence is complemented with a subtle attack against the notion of a "sleep of the soul" that was being presented by extreme anti-Origenists as a touchstone of orthodoxy.

After his death in 399, Evagrius's spiritual legacy was kept alive in Palestine, where many of his original followers had lived and where monks continued to study his works and to shape their lives according to his teachings. In the middle of the sixth century, however, a violent attack by their enemies shattered the peace that the Palestinian Origenists had enjoyed for so long.[2] In 543 they were denounced as heretics to Emperor Justinian, who reacted by promulgating an edict "against the impious Origen and his sacrilegious doctrines."[3] And although they subsequently attempted to have this legislation repealed, they could not prevent the condemnation of Evagrius and Origen at the Council of Constantinople in 553.[4] The strident anti-Origenism of part of the Palestinian monastic establishment is reflected in the contemporary saints' *Lives* of Cyril of Scythopolis, which contain vitriolic attacks against the leaders of the Origenist faction, the abbot Nonnus and the hermit Leontius of Byzantium.[5]

Leontius's known writings are not contributions to the spiritual discourse but theological treatises that defend the Chalcedonian interpretation of the incarnation against the attacks of Nestorians and Monophysites. In his treatise *Contra Nestorianos et Eutychianos* Leontius signals his approval of Evagrius in a brief excursus about the spiritual life where he quotes a passage from the *Kephalaia gnostika*, albeit without identification of the author.[6] However, no specifically Evagrian influence can be detected in the Christological arguments that are the main focus of the text. This is not surprising because in the sixth century the Christological debate was conducted within an Aristotelian framework that differed radically from the Evagrian way of thinking.[7] Of course, this does not mean that Leontius could not have expressed his Origenist convictions in a different manner. He devoted a large part of his treatise to the defence of the analogy between the incarnated Christ and the human compound of soul and body, which gave him scope to set out his anthropological views. However, when we analyze these passages we realize that Leontius studiously avoids any overt statements about controversial Origenist teachings.[8] At one point, he is confronted with the Nestorian argument that the human being cannot serve as an analogy for the incarnated Christ because the Word already exists before the incarnation as a complete being, whereas the soul comes into existence together with the body and is therefore by necessity always related to it and to the human being as a whole.[9] It is evident that this argument could be countered most effectively through the claim that the soul, too, exists as a complete, self-sufficient being before its composition with the body. As is well known, such an alternative anthropology had indeed been proposed by Origen and Evagrius, who spoke of a monad of preexisting minds, which then fell away from God and were joined with bodies. However, we wait in vain for Leontius to proclaim his Origenist beliefs. Instead, he declares that he will employ the anthropological paradigm "neither because of the preexistence or simultaneous existence nor because of the incompleteness of the parts" (οὔτε διὰ τὸ προϋπάρχειν ἢ συνυπάρχειν οὔτε διὰ τὸ ἀτελὲς τῶν μερῶν) but only because the human being is an example of an unconfused union of two natures with diametrically opposite sets of qualities such as visible and invisible or mortal and immortal.[10] This, he claims, is entirely justifiable because philosophers define substances exclusively through such qualities and do not consider "relations" (σχέσεις), "times" (χρόνοι) and "places" (τόποι).[11] By taking this approach Leontius neatly sidesteps the issue and thus avoids the need to declare his personal beliefs about the origin of the soul.[12]

It is evident that after 553 the remaining Origenists would have to have been even more circumspect, and only careful analysis can reveal whether texts from the late sixth or early seventh century contain allusions to outlawed notions such as the preexistence of the soul. I will start the discussion with the Christological handbook of Pamphilus, which was written at the behest of a group of people who wished to have an arsenal of ready-made answers that could be employed in defence of the Councils of Chalcedon and Constantinople.[13] Internal evidence permits us to establish the year 567 as a *terminus post quem* for the composition of the text, but it has proved impossible to identify the author: it has been suggested that he was a Palestinian cleric, but this is little more than a guess.[14] Further study of the text reveals that Pamphilus extensively uses the writings of Leontius of Byzantium, although he never mentions him by name.[15] Moreover, he employs the Evagrian concepts of "natural contemplation" and "theology,"[16] and he quotes from Evagrius's *Praktikos*, again without acknowledging the provenance of the borrowing.[17] Even more significant, however, is the fact that he reproduces a passage from Gregory of Nazianzus's first theological oration (*Oration* 27):

> Φιλοσόφει μοι περὶ κόσμου, περὶ ὕλης, περὶ ψυχῆς, περὶ λογικῶν φύσεων, περὶ ἀναστάσεως, κρίσεως, ἀνταποδόσεως, Χριστοῦ παθημάτων. Ἐν τούτοις γὰρ καὶ τὸ ἐπιτυγχάνειν οὐκ ἄχρηστον, καὶ τὸ διαμαρτάνειν ἀκίνδυνον. Θεῷ δὲ ἐντευξόμεθα, νῦν μὲν ὀλίγον, μικρὸν δὲ ὕστερον ἴσως τελεώτερον, ἐν αὐτῷ Χριστῷ Ἰησοῦ τῷ κυρίῳ ἡμῶν, ᾧ ἡ δόξα εἰς τοὺς αἰῶνας ἀμήν.[18]

> Speculate about the world, about matter, about the soul, about rational natures, about resurrection, judgment, retribution, the sufferings of Christ, for in these matters it is not unprofitable to hit the mark and it is without danger to shoot wide! We will encounter God, now a little, but soon afterwards perhaps more fully, in our Lord Jesus Christ himself, to whom be glory forever, amen.

That Pamphilus inserted this exhortation into his text is highly significant because we know from Cyril of Scythopolis's *Life* of Cyriacus that Origenist monks had used it as justification for their cosmological and anthropological speculation.[19] This raises the question: how could Pamphilus quote such an explosive statement more than ten years after the official condemnation of Origenism? An answer presents itself when we consider the context in which it appears. It is found in *Quaestio* 17, where Pamphilus attacks a Nestorian misinterpretation of the formula of Chalcedon, namely, that the "Son" mentioned in the Trinitarian part of the creed is to be distinguished from the "Lord" mentioned in the Christological part and that Christ is therefore not one of the Trinity but rather a fourth entity, the human being that has been assumed by the Son.[20] Pamphilus first denies that one can interpret the terminological discrepancy in this manner because "Lord" and "Christ" are names of the divine Son and not merely of the human being Jesus, and then supports his claim with a short *florilegium* where the passage from Gregory's *Oration* 27 is preceded by a quotation from Athanasius and followed by a further passage from Gregory and a passage from Cyril.[21] The three other quotations contain explicit statements about the identification of the Son and Christ. By contrast, the passage from *Oration* 27 is a much less obvious choice. While Gregory mentions "God" and "Lord Jesus Christ" side by side he gives no indication that God and Christ should be identical. Indeed the reader can draw this conclusion only because the preceding quotations make the case that the name Lord identifies its bearer as true God.[22] This suggests that Pamphilus deliberately constructed this context so that he could reveal his Origenist sympathies without fear of repercussions: by quoting him alongside Athanasius and Cyril he emphasizes the fact that Gregory of Nazianzus was a universally recognized authority in proper theological discourse, and thus insinuates that Gregory's views about anthropological and cosmological speculation should be accorded the same authoritative status.

This raises the question: does Pamphilus in his treatise ever make reference to specifically Origenist ideas? As I have pointed out the primary purpose of the text is the defence of the Chalcedonian doctrine that the incarnation of the Word is to be understood as a composition of a divine and a human nature. However, this does not mean that other themes are absent. Like Leontius of Byzantium before him, Pamphilus bases his arguments on analogies with the created world and in particular with the human being. A typical example of such an argument is found in *Quaestio* 5 where Pamphilus defends the Chalcedonian position that the flesh was created only at the moment of the incarnation against the contention of the Nestorians that the flesh existed already before its union with the Word. He avers that "in the case of compounds it is not necessary that all parts from which the composition (sc. is effected) exist by themselves before the composition of the result" (οὐκ ἀνάγκη δὲ ἐπὶ τῶν συνθέτων πάντα τὰ μέρη ἐξ ὧν ἡ σύνθεσις προϋφεστηκέναι καθ' ἑαυτὰ τῆς συνθέσεως τοῦ ἀποτελέσματος);[23] and then adduces the human being as evidence for the correctness of his view:

> Καὶ ὁ ἄνθρωπος σύνθετόν ἐστι πρᾶγμα, ἐκ ψυχῆς νοερᾶς καὶ σώματος συνεστώς, καὶ τούτου οὐχ ὅλα τὰ μέρη εὑρίσκομεν ἰδιοϋποστάτως καὶ καθ' ἑαυτὰ προϋπάρχοντα τῆς τῶν μερῶν τούτου συνθέσεως. Οὔτε γὰρ τὸ σῶμα προϋπάρχει καθ' ἑαυτὸ καὶ κατ' ἐνέργειαν, εἰ μήτοιγε δυνάμει· τὸ γὰρ σπέρμα καὶ καταμήνιον προϋφέστηκε, δυνάμει ὂν σῶμα ἀνθρώπινον, οὐ μέντοιγε καὶ κατ' ἐνέργειαν· δύναται δὲ ἀχθῆναι εἰς ἐνέργειαν ὑπό τινος.[24]

> The human being, too, is a composite thing, consisting of an intellectual soul and a body, and we do not find that all its parts preexist the composition of its parts with their own hypostasis and by themselves. For neither does the body preexist by itself and in actuality but only potentially: for semen and the menstrual blood

> preexist, which is potentially a human body, but indeed not also in actuality. However, it can be brought into actuality by something.

Here Pamphilus makes the general statement that *not all parts* need to exist before the composition and then applies this statement both to the incarnated Word and to the human being. It is evident that this wording implies an alternative where only one part is preexistent, and this is indeed what we find in the case of the incarnation because there one part, the Word, preexists the composition. A strict analogy would then require that in the case of the human being, too, one part, namely the soul, exists before it is joined with the body.

It needs to be admitted, however, that the evidence is not as clear as one might wish because the phrase οὔτε . . . τὸ σῶμα προϋπάρχει seems to imply a corresponding statement οὔτε ἡ ψυχή, which would mean that both soul and body came into existence at the moment of conception. This view was widely held among Chalcedonians and Monophysites; it is already found in Gregory of Nyssa's treatise *De opificio hominis* and is later reiterated in a letter of Severus of Antioch and in the *Ambigua* of Maximus the Confessor.[25] In their writings these authors contend that they present the orthodox alternative to the misguided Origenist notion of a preexistent soul. At the same time, however, they reject the claim of more extreme anti-Origenists that the human body comes into existence before the soul. Significantly, this claim was made by Antiochene and Nestorian authors who supported their position through recourse to scripture and from the sixth century onwards also to Aristotelian philosophy.[26] As we have seen, Pamphilus rejects not only the preexistence of the flesh but also the preexistence of the human body. Moreover, he makes reference to the Aristotelian concepts of potentiality and actuality, which the Nestorians employed in their arguments. Thus one might dismiss the apparent implications of the phrase *not all parts* and conclude that Pamphilus presents himself as a moderate anti-Origenist in the tradition of Gregory of Nyssa who opposes the Nestorians not only in Christological debate but also in anthropological discourse.

The alternative interpretation, however, should not be completely ruled out because it is noticeable that Pamphilus refrains from making any explicit statements about the soul. Thus it can be argued that he used the adverb οὔτε instead of a simple οὐ in order to conceal his Origenist beliefs that he signalled through the strict parallelism between οὐ . . . πάντα τὰ μέρη in the case of Christ and οὐχ ὅλα τὰ μέρη in the case of the soul. According to this interpretation the focus on the body would be a part of a strategy of concealment. By emphasizing his opposition against the Nestorian belief in the preexistence of the body, which he shared with mainstream Chalcedonians, Pamphilus would then have sought to distract his readers from the Origenist implications of his argument.

That such complex strategies of concealment were indeed being employed at the time is apparent from another Chalcedonian Christological text, the treatise *Contra Nestorianos* of the Palestinian monk Leontius of Jerusalem, which was most likely composed in the early seventh century.[27] Unfortunately, this text, which still awaits a critical edition, has not been systematically studied. Therefore it is as yet unknown whether Leontius of Jerusalem signalled his familiarity with Evagrian spirituality through borrowings from Evagrius's texts in the way that Leontius of Byzantium and Pamphilus had done before him. There can be no doubt, however, that he accepted the conceptual framework on which Evagrian spirituality was based. In a recent article I have made the case that Leontius repeatedly signals his belief in the preexistence of human souls.[28] Again it is the analogy between Christ and the human being that provides him with an opportunity to set out his anthropological views. In the twenty-seventh chapter of the first book of *Contra Nestorianos,* Leontius sees himself confronted with the Nestorian contention that Word and flesh cannot be united in one hypostasis because one part is uncreated and another created.[29] In order to refute this argument he asks whether the stumbling block is the preexistence of one part and then states that in this case "the divine breath, too, would not have been united in a hypostasis with the body of Adam, which had been fashioned first" (οὐδὲ τῷ πλασθέντι πρῶτον σώματι Ἀδὰμ τὸ θεῖον ἐμφύσημα καθ' ὑπόστασιν ἡνώθη).[30] This statement, which is based on Genesis 2.7, creates a parallel between the preexisting Word and the human body. As we have already seen, it was the Nestorians who claimed that the body exists already before it is joined with the soul. Moreover, Genesis 2.7 was their main scriptural proof text. Thus it appears that Leontius appeals to Nestorian anthropology in order to support his Chalcedonian Christology.

This does not mean, however, that he also accepted the further Nestorian claim that the soul is created in the preexisting body. When we look more closely at the wording of Leontius's statement we find that he has rephrased the biblical verse "he breathed into his face a breath of life" (ἐνεφύσησεν εἰς τὸ πρόσωπον αὐτοῦ πνοὴν ζωῆς) in such a way that it now corresponds to traditional definitions of the human being as "the soul . . . that has been united in a hypostasis with the body" (ἡ ψυχή . . . καθ' ὑπόστασιν ἡνωμένη τῷ σώματι).[31] The obvious consequence of this reformulation is the replacement of "the soul" (ἡ ψυχή) with "the divine breath" (τὸ θεῖον ἐμφύσημα), which leaves no doubt that for Leontius these two terms refer to one and the same reality. In order to understand the full significance of this identification we need to turn to the first chapter of book 1, where Leontius characterizes the soul as "breath of the glory of the almighty" (ἐμφύσημα τῆς δόξης τοῦ παντοκράτορος).[32] This phrase is a conflation of Genesis 2.7 and the formula "outflow of the glory of the almighty" (ἀπόρροια τῆς τοῦ παντοκράτορος δόξης) in Wisdom 7.25 and thus signals to the attentive reader that the souls had originally been with God and had then been infused into the bodies from the outside.[33] It is evident that this notion would have been rejected by Leontius's Nestorian adversary. Indeed, Antiochene and later Nestorian authors emphasized the difference between the divine breath and the soul and declared that the former created the latter in order to rule out just such an interpretation of Genesis 2.7.[34] Thus we can conclude that Leontius of Jerusalem adopts the Nestorian view that the body is created before it is joined with the soul in order to hide his own Origenist convictions.

At first one might think that Leontius was merely using a rhetorical ploy in order to unsettle his Nestorian adversary. Yet a look at the contemporary debate suggests that such an interpretation is insufficient. As we have already seen, Gregory of Nyssa, Severus of Antioch, and Leontius's contemporary Maximus claimed that soul and body came into existence at the same time and argued that the Nestorian theory was just as misguided as the Origenist notion of a preexistent soul.[35] Moreover, these authors were at pains to prove that Genesis 2.7 did not suggest the preexistence of the body.[36] I would therefore propose a different explanation for Leontius's decision to deviate from the Chalcedonian and Monophysite consensus and to accept the Nestorian view of a preexisting body instead. When he was writing his treatise the Nestorians were launching fierce attacks against those who believed that body and soul were united from the moment of conception. The Nestorian theologian Babai, for example, stated in his treatise *De unione* that such people secretly followed the teachings of Origen that the souls preexisted and were then forced to enter bodies as a punishment.[37] At that time the Nestorians were, of course, only a small minority within the Roman Empire. However, one can make a case that similar views were also voiced outside Nestorian circles. In the ninth century, the Byzantine archbishop Arethas of Caesarea defended the notion of a simultaneous creation against opponents who used Aristotelian arguments in order to prove that the rational soul only appears in the fully formed embryo. This text bears the telling title: "To those who say that if the rational soul is complete when it is dispatched to the conception, one must necessarily subscribe to the preexistence of souls" (πρὸς τοὺς λέγοντας, εἰ τελεία ἡ λογικὴ τῇ κυήσει καταπέμπεται, ἀνάγκη προΰπαρξιν ψυχῶν πρεσβεύειν).[38] There can be no doubt that Arethas's adversaries were Chalcedonians, and it is highly likely that the debate in which he engaged had late antique precedent. This likelihood in turn suggests that the anti-Origenist trend had gained such momentum that at least some Chalcedonians were prepared to jeopardize the traditional position of their church because they considered it too close to the heretical teachings of Origen and Evagrius. Thus one can argue that Leontius of Jerusalem's argument is a response to the shifting faultlines between orthodoxy and "Origenism" within anthropological discourse. By accepting that the body comes into existence before it is joined with the soul he could present himself as a "hardliner" and thus effectively conceal his belief that the soul, too, already exists by itself before it is united with the body.

From the discussion so far it has become evident that even after the official condemnation of Origen and Evagrius the specifically Origenist doctrine of the preexistence of the soul continued to find adherents. The evidence comes from Christological treatises where authors could express their views when they drew analogies between the incarnated Christ and the human being. Two major Chalcedonian contributions to the Christological debate were written by authors with Origenist leanings. The continuing prominence of Origenists in this debate could be explained by a genuine interest in speculation, but one must also consider the possibility that the writing of Christological treatises served Origenist authors as a means to emphasize their orthodoxy. In order to achieve this aim these authors created arguments of astounding complexity, which allowed them to signal their Origenist convictions to sympathetic readers without having to make explicit statements, which would have laid them open to attacks by their enemies.

The development of effective strategies of concealment was crucial at a time when anti-Origenist polemic was becoming ever more extreme. In the late sixth and early seventh centuries, it targeted not only genuinely Origenist notions such as the preexistence of the soul but also beliefs that had until then been considered perfectly acceptable. This meant that even authors with impeccable orthodox credentials could be branded Origenists if they held such beliefs. I have already mentioned the simultaneous coming-to-be of body and soul. Even more contentious, however, was the notion that the soul is a self-sufficient being and therefore continues to be active and aware after its separation from the body. The controversy surrounding this topic appears in the writings of Maximus the Confessor where criticism of genuine Origenist ideas is complemented with a defence of an active afterlife against extreme anti-Origenists who claimed that the disembodied soul is in a comatose state.

Maximus rose to fame as a fierce opponent to official religious policy during the Monothelite controversy: he died on August 13, 662, in exile after he had been tortured by the emperor's henchmen.[39] His origins are rather murky because the two extant biographies give conflicting accounts. A tenth-century Greek *Life* avers that he was a native of Constantinople and that he served as a government official before he became a monk in Western Asia Minor.[40] By contrast, a Syriac *Life*, which dates to the seventh century, claims that he was born in Palestine and that he entered the Old Lavra near Jerusalem where the abbot Pantoleon became his teacher.[41] Although this second text is highly tendentious—it was written by a Monothelite author in order to blacken Maximus's refutation—its account is much more likely to be correct.[42] Accordingly Maximus would have received his formation as a monk in a milieu that was known for its Origenist and Evagrian sympathies. Indeed, the author of the Syriac *Life* characterizes Maximus's teacher Pantoleon as a "wicked Origenist."[43]

Unsurprisingly, Maximus's spiritual writings are strongly influenced by Origen and Evagrius. Yet this does not make him an Origenist in the strict sense of the word because he repeatedly rejects the notion of a preexistent soul.[44] The most elaborate treatment of this topic is found in his treatise *Ambigua,* where he takes issue with the Origenist interpretation of another passage from Gregory of Nazianzus's writings, the famous dictum that "we are a part of God and have flowed from above."[45] Maximus denies that this dictum is an expression of the view that "the souls have gone from a previous form of life into the bodies as a punishment for previous evil deeds" because such a view would be nonsensical and could therefore not have been held by Gregory.[46] In order to make his case he contends, first, that as parts of a human being, soul and body are linked to the whole and consequently also to each other; and, second, that entities that are connected in this way are always "simultaneous . . . according to their coming-to-be" (ἅμα . . . κατὰ τὴν γένεσιν).[47] This argument, which is based on Aristotle's *Categories,*[48] permits him to draw the conclusion that soul and body cannot preexist one another since otherwise "the category . . . of relation" (ὁ τοῦ πρός τι . . . λόγος) would be destroyed.[49]

Having established this conceptual framework, Maximus then proceeds to offer another reason why the Origenist notion of a preexisting soul must be rejected. He argues that if the soul and the body were originally "a species on its own" (καθ' ἑαυτὸ εἶδος) and would later become parts of the species human being, "they would suffer through transformation into what they had not been, and would be destroyed" (πεπόνθασιν εἰς ὅπερ οὐκ ἦν ἐξιστάμενα, καὶ φθείρεται).[50] Such a scenario, however, could not be reconciled with the common notion that each creature has received from God perfect being, a point that Maximus supports with the general axiom that "it is not possible for any species to change from species to species without corruption" (οὐκ ἔστιν οὖν δυνατὸν ἄνευ φθορᾶς ἐξ εἴδους εἰς εἶδος μεταβάλλειν τὸ οἱονοῦν εἶδος).[51]

Maximus then addresses an Origenist counterargument, namely, that after death the soul has a self-sufficient existence without the body and that the same should then be true for the time before it acquired a body. Maximus accepts that the soul remains fully functioning but argues that it nevertheless retains its relation to the body "because after the death of the body the soul is not just called a soul but rather the soul of a human being and the soul of a particular human being."[52] In this context he makes a clear distinction between the "definition of substance" (οὐσίας λόγος) and the "definition of coming-to-be" (γενέσεως λόγος): the former refers to being and the qualities that constitute this being, whereas the latter refers to the extra-substantial categories of "where" (ποῦ), "when" (πότε), and "towards what" (πρός τι).[53] This distinction allows Maximus to claim that there is a "relation" (σχέσις) between body and soul, which is established at a certain point in time and in a certain place, but that this relation does not affect "the definitions . . . that are innate in them according to substance" (τοὺς κατ' οὐσίαν αὐτοῖς ἐμπεφυκότας . . . λόγους).[54]

Maximus's complex argument is based on a particular anthropological model, which he sets out elsewhere in his writings. According to this model the human compound is made up of two natures, body and soul, which remain unconfused, and can therefore not be called a "nature" (φύσις) in the sense of a unified organism but only insofar as it is a member of a species: since there is more than one human being it is possible to identify common traits and to subsume them into a general definition, which in turn can then be predicated of each specimen.[55] As von Balthasar already observed, Maximus adopted this anthropological model from Leontius of Byzantium.[56] And there can be no doubt that Leontius also provided the inspiration for the specific features of Maximus's anti-Origenist argument because the set of relations that links body and soul to each other and to the human compound has a close counterpart in the earlier author's treatise *Contra Nestorianos et Eutychianos*.[57]

This does not mean, however, that Maximus merely reproduces an already-existing conceptual framework. As we have seen, Leontius claims that the extra-substantial categories of time, relation, and place are irrelevant to his argument. Moreover, he tends to play down the link between soul and body. In *Contra Nestorianos et Eutychianos,* he declares that the soul is complete in itself and incomplete only insofar as it is not the whole human being, just as the divine Word is complete in itself but is not the whole Christ.[58] This straightforward parallel implies that he saw no categorical difference between the two scenarios: just as the divine Word was in no way affected by the composition with the flesh, so does the relation with the body appear to be of no consequence for the soul. Indeed, Leontius seems to have regarded the souls as a separate species. In *Contra Nestorianos et Eutychianos* he states that "beings of the same nature" (τὰ ὁμοειδῆ) are united with each other through a common building plan but distinguished from one another by number and then applies this general axiom not only to the divine Word but also to the soul.[59] And in his later treatise *Epilyseis* he accords souls hypostases of their own during the period between death and resurrection.[60] This evidence suggests that Maximus's anti-Origenist argument was at least in part directed against Leontius's anthropology. That this is so should not surprise us: as I have already mentioned, Leontius had been accused by his contemporaries of Origenist leanings, and while he never states in his writings that the soul preexists the body, he never rules out explicitly that this might be the case.

Thus a new emphasis on species and the category of relation allowed Maximus to establish his anti-Origenist credentials.[61] As we have seen, his proof that the soul was created together with the body was based on the Aristotelian notion that one part of a relation presupposes the existence of the other.[62] However, it is evident that Maximus has not abandoned Leontius's conceptual framework altogether because he still insists that the soul is a self-sufficient substance. This view suggests that he had previously jettisoned some aspects of this framework—either because he considered them unacceptable himself or because he yielded to external pressures—in order to salvage others that were dearer to him. Maximus's strategy must be seen within the context of the contemporary anthropological discourse where some authors held much more extreme views of the interrelatedness of soul and body. These views are set out most comprehensively in a Nestorian text that is quoted in Leontius of Jerusalem's treatise *Contra Nestorianos*.[63] Unfortunately, we know very little about the circumstances that produced this text. All that can be said is that it seems to have been written within the Roman Empire in the late sixth or early seventh century and that it circulated in Palestine.[64] The Nestorian's principal aim is to disprove the Chalcedonian claim that the incarnation of the divine Word can be understood as a composition of two parts. In order to make his case he repeatedly refers to the anthropological paradigm.[65] One of his arguments starts from the axiomatic statement that in a compound the whole is always greater than the parts, which is then applied to the human being:

> Κατὰ μὲν τοὺς Χριστινανοὺς κρείττων ὁ ἄνθρωπος—αὐτὸ τοῦτο τὸ ὅλον ζῷον—καὶ τῆς ψυχῆς καὶ τοῦ σώματος, ἐπεὶ μετὰ τὴν ἔξοδον τῆς ψυχῆς ἐκ τοῦ σώματος καὶ ἡ ψυχὴ πρὸς ἐνέργειαν αὐτοκίνητον ἀδυνάτως ἔχει ὡς ἐν ὕπνῳ βαθυτάτῳ καὶ μηδὲ ἑαυτὴν ἐπισταμένη διάγουσα καὶ τῶν μετὰ τοῦ σώματος πράξεων κατὰ τὴν θείαν γραφὴν ἐκδεχομένη τὴν ἀμοιβήν· ἅστινας οὐκ ἐκφεύξεται τῷ χωρισμῷ τοῦ σώματος οὐδὲ ἐπὶ τὸ κρεῖττον προβαίνουσα οὐδὲ ἐπὶ τὸ χεῖρον τρεπομένη ἵνα μὴ τὰ τῆς γραφῆς διαψευσθῇ. . . . Κατὰ δὲ τοὺς Ἕλληνας καὶ τοὺς Μανιχαίους τοῦ μὲν σώματος κρείττων ὁ ἄνθρωπος τῆς δὲ ψυχῆς ἥττων τούτῳ τῷ λόγῳ· τὴν μὲν γὰρ ψυχὴν καὶ προϋπάρχειν οἴδασι τοῦ σώματος ἀνενδεῆ τε τῶν τοῦ σώματος αἰσθήσεων καὶ πρὸ τῆς εἰς τὸ σῶμα καταπτώσεως, ὥς φασι, μηδὲν ἀγνοοῦσαν, ἀλλὰ καὶ μετὰ τὴν ἐκ τούτου ἔξοδον ὡσαύτως· ὅθεν καὶ ἥττονα οἴδασιν αὐτῆς τὸν ἄνθρωπον, ἐπεὶ καὶ αὐτὴν ἑαυτῆς χείρονα λέγουσι γενέσθαι διὰ τῆς ἐν τῷ σώματι φυλακῆς, ὥς φασι.[66]

> According to the Christians, the human being, this whole living being, is greater than both the soul and the body; because after the departure of the soul from the body the soul, too, is incapable of self-moved activity, persevering as if in a very deep sleep and not even knowing itself, and waiting to be rewarded for the deeds (sc.

> that it performed) together with the body according to Divine Scripture: which it will not escape through the separation from the body, neither progressing to the better nor being changed for the worse lest the content of Scripture be given the lie. . . . According to the pagans and the Manicheans, on the other hand, the human being is greater than the body but lesser than the soul for the following reason: they know that the soul preexists, not needing the body and the senses of the body and that it is not, as they say, ignorant of anything before its downfall into the body, but likewise (sc. the soul is all this) also after the departure from it. Therefore they also know man to be lesser than it, because they also say that it becomes worse than itself through the imprisonment in the body, as they say.

In this passage the author juxtaposes two opinions about the relationship between body and soul, which he attributes to the "Christians" and to the "pagans and Manicheans." According to the "Christians" the soul on its own is "as if in a very deep sleep" and without self-awareness because it can no longer make use of the organs of the body, whereas according to the "pagans and Manicheans" the soul on its own has self-awareness and innate powers of perception. At first sight there seems to be a curious mismatch between these two positions because in the first case the focus is on the time following the separation from the body whereas in the second case the focus is on the time before the composition with it. However, a closer look reveals that the author has created a direct link between the two scenarios through addition of the remark, "but likewise also after the departure from it." This remark, which first appears to be little more than an afterthought, is the pivot of the argument because it hints that the belief in the posthumous activity of souls is held by pagans and Manicheans. The purpose of the sleight of hand is obvious. Only those Christians who accept the "sleep of the soul" deserve this name because those who think that the soul is fully functioning after death are not truly Christians but rather pagans and Manicheans in disguise. Moreover, these same people also believe in a preexistent soul since this is the necessary corollary of the belief in an active afterlife. The focus on the specific theme of preexistence leaves no doubt that the Nestorian author wished to tar his adversaries with the Origenist brush. Indeed, one can make a case that his argument is an elaboration of earlier polemic against the preexistence of the soul where accusations of paganism and Manicheism had played an important role.[67] Thus one can conclude that the author uses the same strategy to brand the belief in an active afterlife as equally heretical, and that he presents his attack on this belief as the logical next step in an ongoing cleansing of Christianity from pagan influences.

It is obvious that Maximus would have been one of the targets of the Nestorian author because he insisted on the self-sufficiency of the disembodied soul.[68] Accordingly one might think that these writers have nothing in common. However, analysis of the Nestorian argument reveals a more nuanced picture. The Nestorian author supports his position with scriptural evidence, but his principal strategy is to disqualify the rival anthropology as irrational and absurd or, in his own words, as a "myth." He claims that on entering the composition the preexistent soul would become "worse than itself" (ἑαυτῆς χείρονα) because it would now be reliant on the body and its senses, and thus implies that the same must hold true for the time after death when the soul would revert to its original state and thus become "better than itself," that is, better than it had been as a part of the human compound. Again the significance of this unstated consequence becomes obvious through comparison with the author's treatment of the "Christian" view of a "sleep of the soul" because here he concludes that in death the soul is "neither progressing to the better nor being changed for the worse" (οὐδὲ ἐπὶ τὸ κρεῖττον προβαίνουσα οὐδὲ ἐπὶ τὸ χεῖρον τρεπομένη). Such denial of a change for the better is evidently the exact counterpart to the position that results from the pagan and Manichean anthropology. This permits the Nestorian to establish the "natural" character of his own views and at the same time to denigrate the concept of a sentient afterlife as irreconcilable with a well-ordered universe.

Comparison of this reasoning with Maximus's argument against the preexistence of the soul reveals clear similarities. As we have seen, Maximus starts with a characterization of the soul as part of the human compound and then contends that if the soul preexisted as an independent entity it would suffer a change when compounded with the body. Moreover, he implies that a similar change would occur if after the separation from the body the soul again became independent. And finally, he avers that such a scenario is entirely hypothetical because it would militate against the notion of a perfect creation. The affinity between the two authors becomes even more pronounced when we consider how Leontius of Byzantium interpreted the relationship between soul and body. In his treatise *Epilyseis* Leontius insists that there are compositions such as the human being,[69] which happen "through a divine . . . reason and one that is stronger than nature" (λόγῳ . . . θείῳ καὶ τῆς φύσεως κρείττονι).[70] The advantages of such a model are obvious: by attributing the composition to a "supernatural" divine intervention into created order, which can by definition only be beneficial, Leontius can counter effectively the argument that a being, which is not by nature part of a compound, would suffer catastrophic "structural" damage if it were joined with another being, and thus rebut the accusation that the Origenist myth of a fall and subsequent embodiment of precosmic intellects was absurd. Significantly, this solution was not even considered by Maximus and by the anonymous Nestorian, who clearly regarded it as unacceptable because they considered the created order to be sacrosanct.

This does not mean, however, that there are no differences between the two authors. As we have seen, Maximus insists that the link with the body is strictly limited to the "coming-to-be" of the soul and the category of relation and that it does not affect its "substance," which he considers to be self-sufficient in very much the same way as his Origenist adversaries do. By contrast, the Nestorian author takes a much more extreme position when he argues that the soul is intimately linked to the body and that without the body it is only potentially active. In-depth analysis of the anti-Origenist argument set out in the *Ambigua* reveals not only that Maximus was aware of the alternative anthropology but also that he sought to counter attacks on his own position by turning the tables and branding his opponents as heretics:

> Εἰ γὰρ καθ' αὑτὸ εἶδος πρὸ τοῦ σώματός ἐστιν ἡ ψυχὴ ἢ τὸ σῶμα, εἶδος δὲ ἄλλο τούτων ἑκάτερον κατὰ τὴν ψυχῆς πρὸς τὸ σῶμα σύνθεσιν, ἢ σώματος πρὸς ψυχήν, ἀποτελεῖ, ἢ πάσχοντα πάντως τοῦτο ποιεῖ, ἢ πεφυκότα. καὶ εἰ μὲν πάσχοντα, πεπόνθασιν εἰς ὅπερ οὐκ ἦν ἐξιστάμενα, καὶ φθείρεται, εἰ δὲ πεφυκότα, ἀεὶ τοῦτο διὰ τὸ πεφυκὸς

ἐργάσεται δηλονότι, καὶ οὐδέποτε παύσεται ἡ ψυχὴ τοῦ μετενσωματοῦσθαι, οὐδὲ τοῦ μετεμψυχοῦσθαι τὸ σῶμα. ἀλλ' οὐκ ἔστιν, ὡς οἶμαι, τοῦ πάθους ἢ τῆς τῶν μερῶν φυσικῆς δυνάμεως κατὰ τὴν πρὸς θάτερον θατέρου σύνοδον ἡ τοῦ ὅλου κατ' εἶδος ἐκπλήρωσις, ἀλλὰ τῆς ἐπ' αὐτοῖς ἅμα κατ' εἶδος ὅλον γενέσεως.[71]

For if before the body the soul or the body is a species on its own, and both of them effect another species through composition of the soul with the body, or of the body with the soul, they effect this evidently either by suffering or by naturally being this way. And if by suffering, they suffer being turned into what they had not been, and are corrupted, but if by naturally being this way, they will do this evidently always because they are naturally this way, and neither will the soul ever cease to become embodied nor will the body ever cease to be ensouled. But, as I believe, the fulfilling of the whole as a species is neither a matter of suffering nor a matter of the natural power of the parts in the coming together of one with the other, but is a matter of their simultaneous coming-to-be as a whole species.

This passage is already known to us because it contains the argument that the embodiment of the preexistent soul would result in change and corruption, which we have discussed before. However, as we can now see, this argument does not stand on its own but is complemented with an alternative scenario according to which the soul has a natural potential for composition with a body. Here Maximus draws the conclusion that the soul would then always strive to realize this natural potential and would therefore go from one body to the next. This can be understood as an oblique reference to the outlawed belief in the "transmigration" (μετεμψύχωσις) of souls, but it is immediately evident that the underlying conceptual framework is utterly alien to Origenist thinking.

Yet this does not mean that this scenario is entirely hypothetical because it conforms exactly to the "Christian" anthropology set out in the Nestorian treatise where the soul is by its very nature conditioned to be part of a body. When the Nestorian author describes this anthropology he does not consider the aspect of preexistence, which is hardly surprising as it would have considerably weakened his argument.

However, it is evident that it is not conclusively disproved. After all, if the soul can exist in a comatose state after death the same should be possible for the time before the composition with the body. Indeed, the Nestorian makes this aspect explicit in a Christological context where he attempts to prove that the preexisting Word cannot be compounded with the flesh. Here we encounter the already familiar argument that the complete and perfect nature of the preexisting Word would "become worse than itself and be shown changeable" (χείρων τε ἑαυτῆς γέγονε καὶ τρεπτὴ δέδεικται) if it were compounded with a human nature.[72] However, this composition "against nature" (παρὰ φύσιν) is now complemented with a scenario where the composition is "according to nature" (κατὰ φύσιν): in this case the composition "did not happen of old, but has now been effected, as if the nature had then been incomplete and had now been brought from potentiality to actuality."[73]

It is immediately evident that this is the same bipartite argument of either change or completion of nature that we have found in Maximus's *Ambigua* where it is applied not to the preexistent Word but to the preexistent soul of the Origenists.[74] However, there is also a noticeable difference. In the Nestorian treatise both cases result in the same scenario: when the complete divine nature is joined to the flesh it suffers a change in its natural make-up, with the result that it, too, becomes an incomplete part of a greater whole. By contrast, Maximus's argument is asymmetrical because here the originally independent soul does not suffer a change of substance at the moment of its composition with the body, which would reduce it to the alternative model, but only a change of species, which is limited to the extrinsic category of relation. It is obvious that Maximus could have restored the symmetry if he had made a similar change in the alternative model and located the potential for eventual composition not in the nature of the soul but in its relationality.

One reason for not taking this step was that it would have had a detrimental effect on Maximus's own position, since it would have implied that preexistence was a possibility here, too. However, a further agenda is revealed in the last part of the passage where Maximus juxtaposes the two absurd scenarios with his own conceptual framework. Here the explanations of the composition as "a matter of the natural power of the parts" (τῆς τῶν μερῶν φυσικῆς δυνάμεως) or as "a matter of their simultaneous coming-to-be as a whole species" (τῆς ἐπ' αὐτοῖς ἅμα κατ' εἶδος ὅλον γενέσεως) create a false opposition for it is evident that the former is no more linked to the Origenist notion of preexistence than the latter. Indeed, as I have just pointed out, one could easily supply such a dimension in Maximus's model, too. What Maximus juxtaposes here is therefore rather two different ways of conceptualizing the relationship between body and soul *within* the human compound. I would argue that this is the real reason why he introduces the notion that the soul might have a natural proclivity for composition. Confronted with an alternative understanding of the human compound, which went much further than he was prepared to admit, he integrated it into an account of the Origenist belief in the preexistence of the soul, which was possible because its proponents could not conclusively exclude such a dimension, and in this way insinuated to his readers that it was also heretical.

This complex strategy is then further developed when Maximus deals with the Origenist claim that after death the soul has a self-sufficient existence without the body and that the same should then be true for the time before it acquired a body. As I have shown at the beginning of this chapter, Maximus accepts that after death the soul is fully functioning but argues that it nevertheless retains its relation to the human compound, and then makes a careful distinction between the substance of the soul, which is self-sufficient, and its coming-to-be, which is related to the body. At first sight the alternative scenario of the soul as an incomplete nature seems to be absent from this further argument. A closer look, however, reveals that it is still in the background. In the previous discussion we have seen that Maximus concluded from the notion of a natural potential of the soul for composition that the soul would then always realize this potential and become embodied again and again. It is evident that this argument is oddly unrelated to the overarching theme of preexistence because it seems to rule out a disembodied state.[75] However, it has clear implications for the fate of the soul after the separation from the body because the incomplete soul would then not remain on its own but would immediately enter another body in order to be completed by it. This suggests that Maximus wished to present the view that body and soul are incomplete parts as intimately linked to the Origenist belief in the transmigration of souls and thus to characterize it as unacceptable for Christians.

At this point we need to ask: why did Maximus expend such effort to discredit the alternative position? Since we have found this position in a Nestorian text one might conclude that he is attacking a Nestorian doctrine. However, in his *Ambigua* Maximus gives no sign that his adversaries are heretics, which suggests that he is engaging in a debate with fellow Chalcedonians. In the previous discussion we have already seen that the Nestorian notion of a preexisting body was finding acceptance in Chalcedonian circles that were opposed to Origenism. That the debate about the "sleep of the soul" followed a similar trajectory is confirmed by Maximus's seventh letter, which bears the title "about the fact that the soul has its intellectual operation also after death and that it does not lose any natural faculty."[76] In this letter, which is addressed to the same John of Cyzicus to whom he also dedicated his *Ambigua*, Maximus states that if one strips the soul of its constitutive qualities rationality and intellectuality it will be either nothing or will have suffered a change.[77] Then he considers an alternative, namely, that the soul is intellectual and rational not because of its own being but because of the body: in this case, he argues, the soul would not be a "self-subsistent" (αὐθυπόστατος) substance but would merely be an accident of the body and therefore disappear with it.[78] In this context he accuses his adversaries of holding an Aristotelian or Epicurean point of view, thus employing the same strategy that the Nestorian had used when he accused his opponents of being pagan Platonists.[79]

At the beginning of the letter Maximus explains why he felt the need for such a thorough refutation. He confesses to his addressee that he was greatly worried "about the doctrine concerning the soul that as you have written is freely proclaimed there, considering how great a force and an outspokenness such an evil has here, too."[80] This complaint leaves no doubt that by the middle of the seventh century the "sleep of the soul" had gained ground among Chalcedonians as well and that it was threatening to eclipse the alternative view of a self-sufficient soul. Indeed, in the then-popular literary genre of *Questions and Answers* the soul is regularly presented as being comatose after death. Anastasius of Sinai, for example, claims that it loses all its functions and "cannot speak, remember, be angry or see, but is in a stupor by itself" until it is reunited with the body at the resurrection;[81] and a similar argument is developed in the *Questions and Answers* of Pseudo-Athanasius.[82] Such statements must be seen against the backdrop of hardening attitudes against dualistic interpretations of the Christian faith.[83] In his letters Maximus not only struggles to disprove the notion of a "sleep of the soul" but also the related ideas that the soul is material and that the resurrection body is not categorically different from this present body. In the latter case he complains that this new-fangled doctrine "is championed by almost everybody, and in particular by the supposedly famous monks,"[84] and it comes as no surprise that such views are also expressed in contemporary collections of *Questions and Answers*.[85] It is evident that in a world where even moderates such as Maximus struggled there was no room for genuine Origenists, and so it is not surprising that after Leontius of Jerusalem we have no further evidence for engagement with Origenist and Evagrian speculation in Greek-speaking Christian communities.

To conclude: In this chapter I have argued that even after the official condemnation of Origen and Evagrius the doctrine of the preexistence of the soul continued to find adherents among Chalcedonian Christians. Analysis of the Christological treatises of Pamphilus and Leontius of Jerusalem reveals that these authors developed elaborate strategies of concealment, which allowed them to signal their Origenist convictions to sympathetic readers without having to make explicit statements that would have laid them open to attacks by their enemies. They invariably set out their views in the context of Christological arguments where the human compound serves as an analogy for the incarnated Word. Thus they could emphasize their role as defenders of Chalcedon against Nestorian heretics while at the same time giving the impression that their anthropological statements were only a means to an end and therefore not in need of further scrutiny. The development of such strategies was crucial at a time when anti-Origenist polemic was becoming ever more extreme. In the late sixth and early seventh centuries it targeted not only genuinely Origenist notions such as the preexistence of the soul but also the belief in an active afterlife of the soul, which had until then been considered perfectly acceptable. The controversy surrounding this topic can be reconstructed through detailed analysis of arguments put forward in the *Ambigua* of Maximus the Confessor and in an anonymous Nestorian treatise of the late sixth or early seventh century. The Nestorian attempts to establish the "sleep of the soul" as the only acceptable belief for Christians by emphasizing the fact that the alternative view of an active afterlife was shared by non-Christians and by linking this view to the outlawed notion of preexistence, which permitted him to label his opponents as crypto-pagans and crypto-Manicheans and by implication also as crypto-Origenists. In contrast, Maximus presents an interpretation of preexistence that is based on the Nestorian's conceptual framework and insinuates that those who believe that the soul on its own is an incomplete substance must subscribe to the outlawed Origenist view that souls are repeatedly embodied. The discussion of the evidence shows clearly that in the late sixth and early seventh centuries the controversy about the correct Christian anthropology had reached unprecedented levels of complexity. All participants, whether Origenists like Pamphilus and Leontius of Jerusalem, moderates like Maximus, or hardliners like the Nestorian author, constructed multilayered arguments, which need to be carefully decoded if we wish to understand their true convictions.

Notes

1. Maximus the Confessor, *Ambigua*, PG 91:1061–1417, esp. col. 1089C6–D3, Patriarch Germanus, *Antapodotikos-Anotheutos*, cf. the summary in Patriarch Photius's *Bibliotheca*, Codex 233, 291b40–292b42, in Henry, *Bibliothèque*, 5:80–83 (*CPG* 8022).

2. For a general discussion of the "Second Origenist Controversy" see most recently Hombergen, *The Second Origenist Controversy*, with an extensive discussion of earlier secondary literature.

3. Justinian, *Edictum contra Origenem*, in Schwartz, *Collectio Sabbaitica*, 189, line 20: κατὰ Ὠριγένους τοῦ δυσσεβοῦς καὶ τῶν ἀνοσίων δογμάτων αὐτοῦ.

4. Hombergen, *The Second Origenist Controversy*, 57–130.

5. Ibid., 255–368.

6. Ibid., 206–22; Daley, "The Origenism of Leontius of Byzantium," 334–35. Cf. Leontius, *Contra Nestorianos et Eutychianos*, PG 86:1285A6–B1

(Daley, 13.17–24). The passage quoted by Leontius is the first part of *KG* 4.50 (Guillaumont, 158–59). Cf. *KG* 4.51 (Guillamont, 158–59): "tous seront dieux."

7. Krausmüller, "Aristotelianism."

8. Hombergen, *The Second Origenist Controversy*, 157–64; see also Daley, "The Origenism of Leontius of Byzantium," 369.

9. Leontius of Byzantium, *Contra Nestorianos et Eutychianos*, PG 86:1280B11–C6 (Daley, 9.21–10.2).

10. Leontius of Byzantium, *Contra Nestorianos et Eutychianos*, PG 86:1280D3–4 (Daley, 10.12). For a detailed discussion of this passage see Krausmüller, "Origenism in the Sixth Century." There I make the case that Leontius is indeed an Origenist in the strict sense of the word.

11. Leontius of Byzantium, *Contra Nestorianos et Eutychianos*, PG 86:1280D3–1281A4, and col. 1281D4–8 (Daley, 10.11–17 and 11.17–19).

12. Loofs, *Leontius von Byzanz*, 295, who points out that the preexistence of the soul is "zum mindesten nicht ausgeschlossen."

13. Pamphilus's treatise is edited in Declerck and Allen, *Diversorum postchalcedonensium auctorum collectanea*, 127–261.

14. Pamphilus is only known to us from the title of his treatise; Grillmeier, *Jesus der Christus*, 2.3: 134–58. Pamphilus responds to John Philoponus's *De trinitate*, which was published in 567; see Krausmüller, "Divine Genus"; Roey, Wickham, and Ebied, *Peter of Callinicum*, 20–23.

15. For a list of these borrowings and a possible identification of Pamphilus with a seventh-century Palestinian cleric of that name, see Declerck, "Encore." See also Declerck and Allen, *Diversorum postchalcedonensium auctorum collectanea*, 81–83.

16. Pamphilus, *Quaestio* 2 (Declerck and Allen, 134.4–23).

17. Pamphilus, *Quaestio* 2 (Declerck and Allen, 140.142–44); cf. Evagrius, *Praktikos* 24. Cf. Declerck and Allen, *Diversorum postchalcedonensium auctorum collectanea*, 61–62.

18. Pamphilus, *Quaestio* 16 (Declerck and Allen, 250.92–99); cf. Gregory of Nazianzus, *Or.* 27.10 (Gallay, *Discours*, 96–98).

19. Cyril of Scythopolis, *Life of Cyriacus* 12, in Cyril of Scythopolis, *Kyrillos von Skythopolis*, 229.24–31. Cf. the discussion of this passage in Hombergen, *The Second Origenist Controversy*, 157–64.

20. Pamphilus, *Quaestio* 16 (Declerck and Allen, 246.1–12).

21. Pamphilus, *Quaestio* 16 (Declerck and Allen, 246.13–250.112).

22. Cf. Pamphilus, *Quaestio* 16 (Declerck and Allen, 248.61–249.90), where the quotation from Athanasius is combined with an interpretation of Psalm 61 in order to make it dovetail with the quotation from Gregory.

23. Pamphilus, *Quaestio* 5 (Declerck and Allen, 154.18–20).

24. Pamphilus, *Quaestio* 5 (Declerck and Allen, 154.38–45).

25. Gregory of Nyssa, *De opificio hominis*, PG 44:229; Maximus, *Ambigua*, PG 90:1324. For Severus, see Braun, *Moses bar Kepha*, 87–88, with a German translation of his letter to the *scriniarius* Simos.

26. Gregory, Severus, and Maximus present their point of view as the "golden mean" between two equally reprehensible extremes. For the Antiochene and Nestorian position, see Braun, *Moses bar Kepha*, 139–40.

27. Krausmüller, "Leontius of Jerusalem."

28. Krausmüller, "Human Souls," which discusses all relevant passages. Leontius's indebtedness to Origenism is most obvious in chapter 12 of book 1 of his treatise *Contra Nestorianos* where he contends that Christ came into this world in order to return the fallen souls to their primeval God-like state (Leontius of Jerusalem, *Contra Nestorianos*, 1.12, PG 86:1449A13–B6). For a full discussion, see Krausmüller, "Human Souls," 63–65.

29. Leontius of Jerusalem, *Contra Nestorianos*, 1.27, PG 86:1493A9–10. For a full discussion of the argument, see Krausmüller, "Human Souls," 45–47.

30. Leontius of Jerusalem, *Contra Nestorianos*, 1.27, PG 86:1493B4–12.

31. Anastasius of Sinai, *Capita vi adversus monotheletas*, 9.1 (Uthemann).

32. Leontius of Jerusalem, *Contra Nestorianos*, 1.1, PG 86:1405D–1408A. Cf. below, note 46.

33. Krausmüller, "Human Souls," 49.

34. Ibid., 47.

35. See n. 22.

36. This aspect is particularly evident in Severus, who devotes a large part of his letter to a reinterpretation of Genesis 2.7; Braun, *Moses bar Kepha*, 87–88.

37. Vaschalde, *Mar Babai*, 88, lines 18–23: "Hi enim miseri etiam hic delirant et blasphemant dicentes in errore suo: Ab initio conceptionis anima et corpus fuerunt simul in unione hypostatica. Quod non [?] antecedunt partes aliae alias, est sententia impiorum horum, et si secreto dicant, ipsi et Origenes impius, 'animas prius exsistere, et deinde coacte in corpora venire ut crucientur.'" This is, of course, a deliberate misrepresentation of Origen's position.

38. Westerink, *Arethae*, 1:343, lines 21–23; cf. lines 26–27.

39. Also see Allen and Neil, *Maximus the Confessor*.

40. Michael Exaboulites, *Life of Maximus Confessor*, PG 90:69–109. For a discussion of the text and its date, see Neil, "Lives of Pope Martin I."

41. Anonymous *Life of Maximus Confessor* 4, trans. in Brock, "Early Syriac Life"; see esp. 315.

42. See the discussion of the manuscripts of the Syriac text, the earliest of which date to the seventh and eighth centuries, and of its provenance and date in Brock, "Early Syriac Life," 332–40. The broad outline of the narrative is most likely correct because otherwise the slander would not have been effective. By contrast, the Byzantine text is much later and its sources for the early career of the saint are unknown; see Lackner, "Zu Quellen."

43. Anonymous *Life of Maximus Confessor* 4, trans. in Brock, "Early Syriac Life," 315.

44. Thunberg, *Microcosm and Mediator*, 52–99.

45. Gregory of Nazianzus, *Oratio* 14, PG 35:865B12: μοῖραν ἡμᾶς ὄντας θεοῦ καὶ ἄνωθεν ῥεύσαντας.

46. Maximus, *Ambigua*, PG 91:1089C10–12: ἐκ προτέρου εἴδους ζωῆς τῆς ψυχῆς εἰς σώματα ἐλθεῖν ἐπὶ τιμωρίᾳ τῶν προγεγονότων κακῶν.

47. Maximus, *Ambigua*, PG 91:1100C9–13.

48. See Porphyry, *Commentary on the Categories* (Busse, 118, lines 1–16); see esp. Maximus, *Ambigua*, PG 91:1101B6–8.

49. Maximus, *Ambigua*, PG 91:1100C13–D1.

50. Maximus, *Ambigua*, PG 91:1100D1–7.

51. Maximus, *Ambigua*, PG 91:1101A4–6.

52. Maximus, *Ambigua*, PG 91:1101B1–4: οὐχ ἁπλῶς γὰρ λέγεται ψυχὴ μετὰ τὸν τοῦ σώματος θάνατον ἡ ψυχή, ἀλλὰ ἀνθρώπου ψυχή, καὶ τοῦ τινος ἀνθρώπου ψυχή.

53. Maximus, *Ambigua*, PG 91:1101A10–14.

54. Maximus, *Ambigua*, PG 91:1101C1–5.

55. See, e.g., Maximus, *Letter* 12 (*ad Joannem Cubicularium*), PG 91:488A3–C4.

56. Leontius of Byzantium, *Contra Nestorianos et Eutychianos*, PG 86:1289D4–1292C1 (Daley, 18.11–19.9). Cf. Balthasar, *Kosmische Liturgie*, 234–43.

57. Cf. Leontius of Byzantium, *Contra Nestorianos et Eutychianos*, PG 86:1288A10–1289B1 (Daley, 15.5–17.9).

58. Cf. Leontius of Byzantium, *Contra Nestorianos et Eutychianos*, PG 86:1289C12–D4 (Daley, 11.12–17).

59. Cf. Leontius of Byzantium, *Contra Nestorianos et Eutychianos*, PG 86:1285D7–1289B1 (Daley, 14.23–17.9).

60. Cf. Leontius of Byzantium, *Solutiones*, PG 86:1244A1–3 (Daley, 94.32–34): ἐκ προϋφεστώτων πραγμάτων . . . ἐξ ὑποστάσεων.

61. See Balthasar, *Kosmische Liturgie*, 239: "Für Leontius was das Gattungshafte wenig mehr als eine logische Aussage auf Grund einer Ähnlichkeit

der Individuen. Für Maximus . . . ist sie ein ontologische Tatbestand. . . . Der Mensch . . . [ist] als arthaftes Wesen in einen kosmischen Zusammenhang eingeordnet."

62. Whether Maximus's contemporaries were convinced by this argument is another matter. After all, both John Philoponus and Pamphilus pointed out that parts do not preexist one another as parts but that they may well do so as beings: for example, a father is only a father when there is also a son, but he is, of course, already a human being before he begets a son; see Pamphilus, *Quaestio* 5 (Declerck and Allen, 154.46–52); and John Philoponus, *Arbiter* 42, trans. in Lang, *John Philoponus*, 211–12.

63. Abramowski, "Ein nestorianischer Traktat."

64. See Krausmüller, "Leontius of Jerusalem."

65. For a discussion of the Christological implications of the following passage, see Krausmüller, "Conflicting Anthropologies."

66. Leontius of Jerusalem, *Contra Nestorianos*, 1.51, PG 86:1513C6–1516A7.

67. See, e.g., Evagrius Scholasticus, *CH* (Bidez and Parmentier, 189, lines 2–5): ἐσπουδάσθη τῷ Ὠριγένει Ἑλληνικῶν καὶ Μανιχαϊκῶν ζιζανίων ἐμπλῆσαι τῶν ἀποστολικῶν δογμάτων τὸ λιτόν. For a discussion, see Grillmeier, *Jesus der Christus*, vol. 2.2, 411–14.

68. As we will see further down, in one of his letters Maximus responded directly to the concept of a "sleep of the soul."

69. Leontius of Byzantium, *Solutiones*, PG 86:1940B1–7 (Daley, 92.13–16).

70. Leontius of Byzantium, *Solutiones*, PG 86:1940B10–11 (Daley, 92.18–19).

71. Maximus, *Ambigua*, PG 91:1100D2–1101A4.

72. Leontius of Jerusalem, *Contra Nestorianos*, 1.23, PG 86:1489B13–14.

73. Leontius of Jerusalem, *Contra Nestorianos*, 1.23, PG 86:1489C3–6: πάλαι μὲν οὐκ ἐγένετο, νῦν δὲ ἐπράχθη, ὡς ἀτελοῦς τότε οὔσης τῆς φύσεως, καὶ ἐκ τοῦ δυνάμει εἰς τὸ ἐνεργείᾳ νῦν προαχθείσης.

74. The only difference is that in the case of the Word composition is rejected whereas in the case of the soul it is preexistence. Interestingly, in the Christological context the Nestorian does consider a third option: a composition of a preexisting being with another being that is "beyond (sc. its) nature" (ὑπὲρ φύσιν). In this case, we are told, "a higher . . . power would have acted on it" (μείζονος . . . δυνάμεως ἔργον εἰς αὐτὴν γέγονε); Leontius of Jerusalem, *Contra Nestorianos*, 1.23, PG 86:1489B10–11. It is evident that this reflects the position of Leontius of Byzantium that compositions do not need to be either "natural" or "unnatural."

75. This is particularly evident when we compare Maximus's argument with its counterpart in the Nestorian treatise. There the focus is on the extended period of potentiality before the eventual composition, which it is implied is irreconcilable with a rationally organized order. Cf. Leontius of Jerusalem, *Contra Nestorianos*, 1.23, PG 86:1489C3–6.

76. Maximus, *Letter* 7, PG 91:433A4–6: περὶ τοῦ καὶ μετὰ θάνατον ἔχειν τὴν ψυχὴν τὴν νοερὰν ἐνέργειαν, καὶ μηδεμιᾶς ἐξίστασθαι φυσικῆς δυνάμεως. Interestingly, here Maximus speaks of a substantial change and not just of a change that is limited to the species. For an in-depth discussion of this text, see Benevich, "Maximus the Confessor's Polemics."

77. Maximus, *Letter* 7, PG 91:436A2–12.

78. Maximus, *Letter* 7, PG 91:437A6–B11.

79. Maximus, *Letter* 7, PG 91:437B9. This accusation may be less farfetched than it first seems because the Nestorian author does indeed use the Aristotelian concepts of potentiality and actuality, and some of his coreligionists had recourse to the Aristotelian definition of the soul as entelechy; see Braun, *Moses bar Kepha*, 143.

80. Maximus, *Letter* 7, PG 91:433B5–8: ἐπὶ τῷ περὶ ψυχῆς δόγματι τῷ ὑπό τινων, ὡς γεγράφατε, ἀδεῶς ἐκεῖσε κηρυττομένῳ, ὅσην κἀνταῦθα τὸ τοιοῦτο κακὸν ἔχειν ἰσχὺν καὶ παρρησίαν ἐννοῶν.

81. Anastasius of Sinai, *Quaestio* 19.6 (Richard and Munitiz, 4–165, esp. 32, lines 53–56): οὐ λαλεῖν, οὐ μιμνήσκεσθαι, οὐ θυμοῦσθαι, οὐ καθορᾶν· ἀλλ' ἐν συννοίᾳ τινὶ καθ' ἑαυτὴν ὑπάρχει.

82. Pseudo-Athanasius, *Quaestiones ad Antiochum ducem* 33, PG 28:617A10–12.

83. Benevich, "Maximus the Confessor's Polemics."

84. Maximus, *Letter* 7, PG 91:433B10–12: ὑπὸ πάντων σχεδόν, καὶ μάλιστα τῶν δῆθεν ἐπιφανῶν μοναχῶν πρεσβευόμενον.

85. See Munitiz, "Anastasios of Sinai's Teaching"; also Haldon, "Works of Anastasius."

CHAPTER 12

The Evagrian Heritage in Late Byzantine Monasticism

GREGORY COLLINS, OSB

Nearly a full millennium separates the work of Gregory Palamas (1296–1359) from Evagrius's in the late fourth century. Yet the later monastic teacher and bishop could still use the thought of his predecessor for purposes quite different from its original context and aims. Like the revival of Augustinian thought in late-medieval and Reformation Europe, or the continuous consultation of Gregory the Great, the puzzling works of Evagrius—preserved in Greek monastic libraries—allowed and perhaps even compelled Byzantine thinkers to rethink their own views against the background of the topics he was the first to articulate for the then-new monastic form of life.

After a brief review of Evagrius's theories as received in Byzantine thought, this essay will focus on the specific issue of his influence on St. Gregory Palamas, fourteenth-century Athonite monk, Metropolitan of Thessalonica, and foremost defender of Athonite Neo-Hesychasm.

THE EVAGRIAN LEGACY

Evagrius's systematic exposition of the dynamics between God and the soul in monastic life and prayer marked forever the entire heritage of Christian monasticism. The Byzantine and Syrian forms of monastic spirituality everywhere reveal the impact of his thought, while on account of the transmission of his work to the West accomplished by St. John Cassian (for the Byzantines, "the Roman"), he exercised a deep and abiding influence on medieval Latin monasticism as well, an influence extending far beyond the Benedictine and Cistercian worlds. Evagrius effectively shaped an entire language of inner experience to describe the anthropological and theological dynamics of the spiritual life in the monastic context.

He did not, of course, invent the language, since his achievement consisted for the most part in using the work of Origen, itself a synthesis of Middle-Platonic thought and scriptural exegesis, to categorize the experiences undergone by the monks of the Egyptian desert. His peculiar genius and distinctive contribution was to have systematized that language so as to attain clarity in matters of monastic experience, making it thereby the *lingua franca* of all later monks and nuns in Byzantium. Thanks to him Eastern Christian monastics speak a language that one may legitimately call "Evagrian," or to be more precise "Evagro-Macarian."

Despite Evagrius's formal condemnation by the Fifth Ecumenical Council and the subsequent blackening of his reputation, "Evagrianism" as a system of ascetical and mystical concepts entered Orthodox monastic tradition so successfully that its presence is diffused throughout it at every point. His conceptualization of monastic life and prayer became so omnipresent in Byzantine monasticism that it is impossible to understand that tradition without knowledge of his work and its reappropriation by Byzantine monks throughout the long history of the Eastern Roman Empire.

Everywhere in Byzantine monastic literature one encounters the Evagrian grammar and vocabulary of the spiritual life, including such typical elements as the following:

- the fundamental division of the spiritual life between *praktikē* and *theōria*;

- the rigorous analysis of the dynamics of demonic temptation and spiritual struggle;
- the listing of eight *logismoi* (or variants that derive from his list);
- the delicate art of *diakrisis*: discriminating spiritually between thoughts (*noēmata*) coming from God, the angelic sphere, or the earthly order and how to distinguish them from the *logismoi*;
- the differentiation of various dimensions of contemplation, with *theōria physikē* as enlightened insight into Holy Scripture, providence, and judgment and God's underlying presence in the *logoi* of creation;
- the notion of a direct contemplation of the Holy Trinity (*theōria theologikē*) whose light begins to shine in and through a mind (*nous*) purified not only of sinful thoughts but of discursive thinking and indeed of conceptuality itself;
- the insistence that prayer entails "the shedding (or laying aside) of thoughts" (*noēmata*);
- the assertion that theology (i.e., the contemplative vision of the Trinity) is the summit of prayer and the fruit of personal purification and contemplative illumination, and that the true theologian is one who prays.

All this became, and remains to this day, the common doctrine of Byzantine monastic theology: without Evagrius's concepts that theology would be literally unthinkable. The Greek monastic tradition quickly joined those ideas and practices to the work of other monastic authors: the *Spiritual Homilies* ascribed to Macarius, the works of Diadochos of Photikē, John Climacus, and Maximus the Confessor, in addition to the Greek translation of the work of Isaac the Syrian. In eleventh- and twelfth-century Byzantium, Peter of Damascus, Symeon the New Theologian, and Theoleptus of Philadelphia also engaged Evagrius's teachings.

Gregory's Evagrian Advice to the Nun Xenia

One treatise in particular serves to show how Gregory adapted Evagrius's teachings. An examination of the treatise on monastic life written by Palamas for the nun Xenia demonstrates an interesting application of Evagrius's theories to a situation very different from their original context. In the years between 1342 and 1346, Xenia was acting as matron and schoolmistress to the children of the recently deceased Emperor Andronikos III. It is possible to see the work as an encouragement addressed to one who may have been distracted by the demands of her work. This text was included in the eighteenth-century Greek *Philokalia* of Sts. Nicodemus the Hagiorite and Macarius of Corinth because it is one of Palamas's most instructive writings.[1] It is a useful source for charting the influence of Evagrius on him.

Written at the beginning of the hesychastic controversy, the treatise shows that Palamas was under fire. He begins his advice to Xenia by lamenting the need to write at all, a conventional enough *topos* but, in this context at least, surely more than a mere literary device.[2] Contrasting spiritual death with the spiritual life that comes from obedience to Christ's commandments, he presents a strongly Christocentric vision of the Christian path based on the incarnation of the Word, his resurrection, and ascension.[3] Human beings, he teaches, are called to participate in these Christ-realities, and time is given us precisely so that through repentance we may begin to do so: but their perfection will come only in heaven.[4]

As is usual with Palamas, this eschatological note is strongly sounded. The Christian life is about becoming one spirit with Christ so as to be united with him forever in heaven. The one who issues the invitation is God the Father, who raises the mind through the power of the Holy Spirit.[5] This Trinitarian account of the path of *theōsis,* grounded in the mysteries of Christ, is what inspires the first stage of spiritual reformation of life, the way of *praktikē*.

Palamas describes it in conventional monastic terms as the pruning away of wealth, soft living, worldly honors, and the passions of body and soul.[6] Virginity is understood as a nuptial relationship with God, though he is careful only to relativize marriage rather than denigrate it.[7] He then launches into an extended encomium on poverty, discusses purification of the tripartite soul, and explains the practical life as a process of interior healing.[8] The passions are seen, in accordance with the teaching of St. Maximus the Confessor, not merely as inherently negative tendencies but as natural propensities of the soul, which acquire an evil orientation only later through the "passion-charged *nous*."[9] Self-control gained through the usual means of fasting, humility, rejection of evil thoughts, and above all poverty of spirit enables the whole person to achieve integration under the guidance of the purified mind.[10] Thus far this is common doctrine: the influence of both Evagrius and St. Maximus is evident.

Interestingly, Palamas also speaks of a kind of negative eschatological experience in which grief, fear, and self-accusation generate a foretaste of hell in this life. Yet they are also a blessing in that they draw Christ down to us in compassion and invoke the consolation of the Paraclete. Thus *penthos* and compunction lead to joy.[11] Throughout this section of the work he draws largely on the common doctrine of Byzantine asceticism—the Evagro-Macarian patrimony and St. John Climacus, from whom he also quotes.[12]

However, another current appears to be flowing in the river. It is hard to say if Palamas is directly echoing Symeon the New Theologian (whom he had read), but he does lay considerable emphasis here and elsewhere on the activity of the Holy Spirit, both in the economy of salvation and in the inner life of the *nous*.[13] Vladimir Lossky perceptively identified an intensified pneumatological tendency as a characteristic trait of middle and late Byzantine theology, something that is certainly true of Symeon the New Theologian and of Gregory Palamas.[14] The latter also recalls Symeon in the distinctly experiential way in which he describes the sudden transition from sadness to joy.[15] This may perhaps reveal something of his personal spiritual experience in addition to the more emotionally charged orientation of later Byzantine spirituality.

Palamas also employs bridal imagery in his exposition, thus emphasizing even more the affective and experiential dimensions of the spiritual life.[16] Although it would be an exaggeration to deny this element in Evagrius's thought, it would not seem to have been central to his understanding. While therefore typically Evagrian themes and terminology drawn from the tradition certainly provide the underlying structure for Palamas's exposition of the monastic path, they are by no means exclusive and are used within the context of other strands of tradition and experience.

Having sketched the fundamental ascetic ground rules at the start, Palamas indicates that the thrust of his exhortation is about to accelerate: "Listen attentively so as to learn!"[17] Joy, light, and consolation, he asserts, will begin to break through in the darkness of self-abasement as, "Prayer changes from entreaty to thanksgiving and meditation on the divine truths of faith fills the heart with a sense of jubilation and unimpeachable hope."[18]

Yet this is by no means all—much more is to come. The Bridegroom (Christ) desires to manifest himself more clearly in the souls of those who have been purified and "arrayed for the bridal chamber."[19] Shameful passions having been expelled and the *nous* having returned on itself—a characteristic emphasis in Palamas and Athonite hesychasm—the mind, purified of evil thoughts, then goes further still, purging away all imprints and accretions of whatever kind, good as well as bad.[20] The requisite purification is not simply a moral one, however, but a cleansing from fragmentation and multiplicity as such: Evagrius (and perhaps Theoleptos) is very much in evidence at this point.

Having become deaf and dumb in God's presence and having transcended all intelligible images and ideas, the process of ascent continues under the transporting guidance of illuminating grace. It is not accomplished by human power alone, however, for the soul is borne aloft on the wings of the Holy Spirit. Transported into an angelic mode of existence, it becomes a participant in the liturgy of heaven. Yet this is no mere abandonment of the earth, no simple matter of a solitary flight towards the Absolute. Palamas insists on the mediating, transforming character of the soul's ascent, for as it goes ahead it does not relinquish the earth but rather brings the lower orders of creation along with it.[21] Palamas was well grounded in the traditional doctrine of man as mediator: "Through itself *it brings every created thing* closer to God, for it itself also participates in all things and even in Him who transcends all, inasmuch as it has faithfully conformed itself to the divine image."[22]

It is at this point that Evagrius (disguised of course as "St. Nilus of Sinai") emerges from the background and takes up a guiding role at the heart of Palamas's exposition. Describing what occurs on the mountain top of *theōria,* he quotes directly from Evagrius's work *Reflections* (*Skemmata*):

> "The *nous*'s proper state (*katastasis*) is a noetic height (*hupsos noēton*), somewhat resembling the sky's hue, which is filled with the light (*phōs*) of the Holy Trinity during the time of prayer (*kairon tēs proseuchēs*)." If you wish to see the proper state of the *nous*, rid yourself of all concepts (*pantōn tōn nōematōn*), and then you will see it like sapphire or the sky's hue. But you cannot do this unless you have obtained a state of dispassion (*apatheias*), for God has to cooperate with you and to imbue you with his co-natural light.[23]

Recent scholarship has alerted us to the centrality of these highly charged images in the thought of Evagrius. Alexander Golitzin rightly insists that the references to the theopanies accorded to Moses in the book of Exodus should encourage us to acknowledge the solidly scriptural substrate of Evagrian "mysticism" (for want of a better word) and alerts us to the prevailing influence of themes and motifs derived from Second Temple "mysticism," such as the holy mountain and mystical ascent to the place of divine revelation—themes not exactly unheard of in the Cappadocian and Syrian traditions either![24] By citing these Evagrian texts, Palamas not only confirms the significance accorded them in contemporary scholarship: he also reveals his own finesse in articulating what transpired at the summit of Byzantine mystical experience and in putting his finger on the pulse of the tradition's heartbeat. These are the very texts that express with such clarity the center of Evagrian mystical theology.

But what is most interesting about Palamas's citation of these particular Evagrian texts is the context in which he places them. He immediately invokes two other leading authorities, first citing Diadochos in a passage emphasizing the essential place of baptism in the spiritual life and the activity of the Holy Spirit whom the purified *nous* begins to perceive in full consciousness, an experience without which it cannot be fulfilled in perfect love.[25] This is about as "Macarian" a theme as one could find anywhere in the tradition and a mainstay of Symeon the New Theologian's teaching.

The second authority Palamas cites is Isaac of Syria, who in this context reads like Evagrius *redivivus*. Palamas quotes him (quoting Evagrius): "And likewise St. Isaac writes that during the time of prayer the *nous* that has received grace sees its own purity (*tēn eautou katharoteta*) to be 'like heaven's hue,' which was also called 'the place of God' (*topos theou*) by the council of the elders of Israel, when it was seen by them in the mountain [cf. Ex. 24.9–10]. Again, he says that 'prayer is purity of the *nous*, and it is consummated when we are illumined in utter amazement by the light of the Holy Trinity.' He also speaks of 'the purity of the *nous* upon and through which the light of the Holy Trinity (*phōs tēs Hagias Triados*) shines at the time of prayer' (*en tō kairō tēs proseuchēs*)."[26]

Commenting on these Evagrian texts in their original context, William Harmless has unpacked the implicit resonances and connections they contain: "Here Evagrius reads the biblical text allegorically. First he transposes outer realities into inner ones. Mount Sinai, the 'place of God,' is not only a place on the map of the Holy Land; it is an inner landmark, a centre on the geography of the soul. The encounter with God is not limited to some past theophany. . . . [S]econd he uses the Bible to interpret the Bible. He notes that the phrase, 'place of God' appears in both Exodus 24 and Psalm 75. He reads Psalm 75 as a cipher for Exodus 24. This leads him to insist that the Mount Sinai of the mind is also a Mount Zion, that the inner mountain is an inner temple. The human person is thus a sacred precinct, a holy of holies."[27]

Likewise, Columba Stewart has commented on Evagrius's spiritualizing of biblical images in providing an interior topography for prayer: "Evagrius universalizes the place of God by shifting it from geographical Sinai to the human mind (*nous*). The relocation of biblical topography to an inner landscape, the reinscription of the biblical text on the heart, is a move typical of Alexandrian exegesis."[28]

Even more significantly, Stewart underlines the importance of this spiritualizing topography in the whole of Evagrius's work: "The internalization of the place of God presents *one of the central paradoxes* of Evagrius's theology. The place of God is to be found *within the human person*, more specifically *within the human mind*, but 'seeing' it requires that one transcend all ordinary mental operation. Although potentially accessible to all, *the place of God is hard to reach*. Its sudden and ephemeral discovery is the *culmination of monastic prayer*."[29]

Palamas had already used his citations from Evagrius and Isaac in the first of his treatises against Barlaam of Calabria in defense of hesychastic monastic experience (*Triads* 1.1). In that work, defending the hesychastic method of prayer, he had upheld the doctrine that the *nous* can be "returned" to the body, which has the capacity to "contain" it, since scripture speaks of the body as a temple in which the divine presence can dwell. Palamas had asked rhetorically, "that which becomes a dwelling place for God—for a person granted intelligence—how could it not be held worthy of accomodating one's own *nous*? And even God, how would he have been able, in the beginning to make the *nous* be in the body?"[30]

The hesychasts waged war against Barlaam specifically on this point, insisting that it is indeed possible for the *nous*, in bringing itself back from dispersion in external activities and focusing on its proper place (the heart whose "eye" it is meant to be), to return into itself *and remain within* the body.

Palamas's rereading of Evagrius allows us to see that a significant development had occurred in Byzantine monastic theology during the hesychastic controversy. Palamas showed, regarding Evagrius's doctrine of the experience of divine light in the inner sanctum of the purified *nous*—the culmination of all that Israel had experienced as it encountered God in the luminous darkness of Sinai and the resplendent glory of Zion—that as in the teaching of Evagrius/Nilus, this culminating experience occurs in the *nous* when it has recovered its proper state through *apatheia* and the abandonment of concepts. By invoking Diadochos, however, he took pains to establish that it is also due to the illuminating work of the Holy Spirit. In traditional Evagrian terms, Palamas saw the *nous* purified from *logismoi* and from multiplicity as identical with the "place of God" (*topos theou*). The purified interiority of the self is the privileged disclosure zone for the manifestation of the divine light.

But by insisting that the *nous* is located not only at the center of the heart (*kardia*) but that its proper place is actually "within" the body—"into" which it can be made to return through prayer—Palamas insisted on the body's significance as a constituent aspect of human existence that can in no way be excluded from salvation or deification.

Far from being merely some external container temporarily housing a soul destined to pass on to higher things, the body for Palamas was a shrine prepared through baptism, communion in the mysteries, and the transforming light of grace, for the eschatological goal of resurrection and deification. His defense of hesychastic prayer and its corporeal concomitants was part and parcel of an anthropological vision that refused to exalt the soul over the body, because both are created, but insisted on its ministerial and mediating capacity in relation to the flesh. Soul, and its deepest (or highest) intensity (the *nous*) as the place of the divine, luminous self-manifestation, is also the link to what lies beneath.

Diadochos had already written: "Sometimes the soul is kindled into love for God and, free from all fantasy and image, moves untroubled by doubt towards him; *and it draws, as it were, the body with it* into the depths of that ineffable love."[31] In his instruction for Xenia, just as in his polemic against the hyper-intellectualism of Barlaam in the *Triads*, Palamas also insisted on this positive evaluation of the body and on the *nous* as agent, mediating the transforming grace of the Holy Spirit. Just as mystical ascension through deification entails a cosmic drawing up of all things to God, so spiritual consummation does not mean that the body is simply to be abandoned. Through the deified *nous* God confers his gifts also on the flesh. As Palamas wrote: "The *nous* that has been accounted worthy of this light also transmits to the body that is united with it many clear tokens of the divine beauty, acting as an intermediary between divine grace and the grossness of the flesh and conferring on the flesh the power to do what lies beyond its power."[32]

By defending the importance of the body, Palamas completed the long process through which it had been granted full acceptance within Byzantine theology. But he also gave fuller significance to the temple symbolism deriving from St. Paul and the third- and fourth-century matrix that had produced Evagrius, inserting the latter's insights about the reception of the divine presence as light into a more somatically affirmative anthropological vision in which the divine light is received—*pace* Evagrius within the purified *nous* and *pace* Diadochos within the heart—but with the fullest assent to biblical revelation, *within* the body of flesh itself. The flesh is the forecourt of the temple-shrine that houses the inner man but also the medium through which the divine light, manifesting itself in that "place," is filtered so as to appear in the world.

Hence the ferocity of Palamas's response to the hyper-intellectualism of Barlaam is understandable. It had threatened man's unifying vocation as mediator and risked losing the essential somatic dimension of Jewish-Christian revelation. Yet at the same time Palamas both preserved Evagrius's fundamental insight into contact with God in the soul's proper place and integrated it more effectively with revelation's emphasis on the dignity of the deified body.

I would like to return tentatively to one of the most difficult aspects of the teaching of Evagrius/Nilus and Isaac re-presented by Palamas: that in the process of prayer the highest experience is that of seeing the light of one's own *nous,* a "state" (*katastasis*) identical with the "place" (*topos*) where God reveals his presence and is experienced as light. The evocative imagery employed, the sapphire blue pavement bright like the sky, is biblical (Ex. 24.10 and Ez. 10.1) and beautiful, but also arcane and impenetrable.

Columba Stewart has perhaps given the clearest explanation of what it means in Evagrius: "To see the place of God, to speak to God in the place of prayer, means climbing above all impassioned thoughts and all depictions, including nonsensory ones. . . . The place of God is, by definition, 'unimaged' (*aneideos, Reflections* 20, cf. 22), meaning that the mind itself, when it becomes the place of God, is free of self-created imagery."[33]

Obscure as it is, this imagery is central to Evagrian spirituality and therefore, as we see clearly in Palamas, to later Byzantine monastic doctrine. Under the influence of Macarius and Diadochos, however, hesychasm and the development of the Jesus Prayer provide us with pointers as to how Byzantine monks aimed to attain this experience of the purified *nous* as the place where, filtered in and through one's own light, the divine light appears.

In his fifty-eighth and fifty-ninth chapters Diadochos had spoken of confining the *nous* within very narrow limits so that one may devote oneself solely to remembering God. He went on to say: "When we have blocked all its outlets by means of the remembrance of God, the *nous* requires of us imperatively some task which will satisfy its need for activity. For the complete fulfillment of its purpose we should give it nothing but the prayer 'Lord Jesus.' 'No one,' it is written, 'can say "Lord Jesus" except in the Holy Spirit' [1 Cor. 12.3]."[34]

It must surely have been the experience of those who practiced prayer according to Evagrius's instructions that it is extraordinarily difficult and demanding to keep the mind free of thoughts and particular forms and focused on what appears to be in effect (at least at the outset but perhaps for a considerable period of time) attention to a void, a kind of interiorized expanse of sky. As Stewart observed, the place of God is hard to reach! Yet, gradually, through the practice of monologistic prayer, Byzantine monks discovered that the in-drawing of the soul's powers and the return of the *nous* on itself are greatly facilitated by focusing on the name of Jesus, which according to Diadochos has the nature of a quasi-sacramental divine self-disclosure: "Let the *nous* continually concentrate on these words within its inner shrine with such intensity that it is not turned aside to any mental images."[35]

We should note here the deliberate use of temple imagery and the claim that in repelling the *logismoi* the invocation of the name is of vital significance, thanks to the intensity of the divine presence mediated through focusing intensely on it. But what Diadochos went on to say was even more illuminating: "Those who meditate unceasingly upon this glorious and holy name in the depths of their heart *can sometimes see the light of their own nous.*"[36]

This is because, as he explains, the concentration of the *nous* on this name purifies the soul like a divine fire, awakens fervent love for God's glory in the heart, and implants therein a love for God's goodness. By perfecting the inner purgation of the *nous*, the invocation of the name allows it to see its own clarity and luminosity, thus opening it up to the manifestation of the uncreated Trinitarian light, the vision of which Evagrius had postulated as the culminating moment of interior prayer.

Evagrius's vision of divine light in and through the light of the purified *nous* (compare to Ps 35[36].9: "In your light we see light"), facilitated by Diadochos's invocation of the name in the heart as the instrumental cause of purification, achieved in Palamas their fullest integration into Byzantine theology through his strong articulation of hesychastic theory with its insistence on psychosomatic methods of prayer and the experience of the light of Thabor, the foretaste of the world to come. It was the last great theological synthesis achieved in Byzantium, and Evagrius supplied one of its most fundamental constituent elements.

Conclusion

In this chapter, I have stressed that the Byzantine reception of Evagrius entailed a long and complex process of interpretation within a tradition in which he was certainly a major player but by no means the only one. There was the direct but veiled influence of his surviving ascetic works. There was his creative reappropriation by other significant figures in the course of the empire's life. There was also his reentry on to the Byzantine scene via the works of Issac of Nineveh. Evagrian ideas and images—though always in a creative synthesis with those of Macarius—effectively provided the standard terminology in Byzantium for describing and categorizing monastic experience.

Recognizing—as the Byzantines did—the harmony between these two great monastic traditions, the Evagrian and the Macarian, is not just a matter of smoothing out differences in the interests of orthodoxy but of accepting that later categories imposed by scholars do not always do justice to the evidence. Hence, just as von Balthasar's negative judgment on Evagrius's thought needs to be revised in the light of recent research, so does his sweeping generalization about the extent of his influence.

Balthasar claimed that Evagrius was "the almost absolute ruler of the entire Syriac and Byzantine mystical theology."[37] That judgment requires qualification at least regarding the Byzantine tradition. It is almost correct yet it says too much. Instead of visualizing him as an almost absolute ruler it might be more helpful to imagine his voice as providing a kind of *cantus firmus* in the rich polyphony of Byzantine ascetical and mystical theology. Other voices were (almost) equally important, as St. Gregory Palamas showed when in the same place he cited "Nilus"/Evagrius, the thoroughly "Macarian" Diadachos of Photikē, and Isaac of Nineveh, an out-and-out "Evagrian." This mixing of authorities is a good indication of the place of the synthetic nature of tradition and the role of the Evagrian heritage in forming Byzantine monastic theory.

NOTES

1. Gregory Palamas, *To the Most Reverend Nun Xenia*, in Nicodemus the Hagiorite and Makarios, *Philokalia*, 4:293–322. This text will hereafter be cited as Gregory, *Xenia*, followed by section numbers.
2. Gregory, *Xenia*, 1–6.
3. Gregory, *Xenia*, 8–15.
4. Gregory, *Xenia*, 16.
5. Gregory, *Xenia*, 15.
6. Gregory, *Xenia*, 20.
7. Gregory, *Xenia*, 20–23.
8. Gregory, *Xenia*, 27–30.
9. Gregory, *Xenia*, 42.
10. Gregory, *Xenia*, 42.
11. Gregory, *Xenia*, 51–55.
12. For John Climacus, see Gregory, *Xenia*, 50.
13. For example, Gregory, *Xenia*, 54.
14. Lossky, *Mystical Theology*.
15. Gregory, *Xenia*, 55–56.
16. For example, Gregory, *Xenia*, 57.
17. Gregory, *Xenia*, 53.
18. Gregory, *Xenia*, 56.
19. Gregory, *Xenia*, 57, modified by author.
20. Gregory, *Xenia*, 58–59.
21. Gregory, *Xenia*, 59.
22. Gregory, *Xenia*, 59.
23. Gregory, *Xenia*, 60.
24. See Golitzin, "Earthly Angels," esp. 148–49, "Hierarchy versus Anarchy," esp. 152–57, and "Vision of God."
25. Gregory, *Xenia*, 60.
26. Gregory, *Xenia*, 61.
27. Harmless, *Mystics*, 153.
28. Stewart, "Imageless Prayer," 196.

29. Ibid., 196–97, emphasis added.
30. Gregory Palamas, *Triads* 1.2.1
31. Diadochos of Photikē, *Gnostic Centuries on Spiritual Knowledge and Discoveries* 33.
32. Gregory, *Xenia,* 62.
33. Stewart, "Imageless Prayer," 197.
34. Diadochos, *Kephalaia praktika* 59.
35. Ibid.
36. Ibid.
37. Balthasar, "Metaphysics," 183, cited in Harmless, *Mystics*, 141.

BIBLIOGRAPHY

Select Works of Evagrius

Listed below are select editions and translations of the works of Evagrius that are cited in this book. Entries are alphabetized by abbreviation, followed by the fuller English title and in parentheses the number assigned by the *Clavis Patrum Graecorum*. Editions cited may contain the work only in part or only in a particular edition.

Readers interested in a detailed account of all of Evagrius's known works (including spuria) and all the editions of those works are encouraged to consult Joel Kalvesmaki, ed., *The Guide to Evagrius Ponticus*, available at http://evagriusponticus.net/corpus.htm.

Antirrhetikos (*CPG* 2434)

Brakke, David. *Talking Back: A Monastic Handbook for Combating Demons*. Cistercian Studies 229. Collegeville, MN: Cistercian Publications, 2009.

Frankenberg, W., ed. *Euagrius Ponticus*, 472–545. Abhandlungen der Königlichen Gesellschaft der Wissenschaften zu Göttingen. Philologisch-Historische Klasse, n. F., 13, no. 2. Berlin: Weidmannsche Buchhandlung, 1912.

O'Laughlin, Michael. "Antirrheticus (Selections)." In *Ascetic Behavior in Greco-Roman Antiquity: A Sourcebook*, edited by Vincent L. Wimbush, 243–62. Studies in Antiquity and Christianity. Minneapolis: Fortress Press, 1990.

Sims-Williams, Nicholas. *The Christian Sogdian Manuscript C2*. Schriften zur Geschichte und Kultur des alten orients. Berliner Turfantexte 12. Berlin: Akademie-Verlag, 1985.

Chapters 33 / Thirty-Three Chapters (*CPG* 2442)

PG 40:1264d–68b.

Sinkewicz, Robert E., ed. *Evagrius of Pontus: The Greek Ascetic Corpus*, 224–27. Oxford: Oxford University Press, 2003.

Chapters to Monks

See *Monks*.

Chapters to a Virgin

See *Virgin*.

Cherubim / On the Cherubim (*CPG* 2459)

Muyldermans, Joseph. "*Sur les séraphins* et *Sur les chérubins* d'Évagre le Pontique dans les versions syriaque et arménienne." *Le Muséon: Revue d'Études Orientales* 59 (1946): 367–79.

Disciples / The Disciples of Evagrius (*CPG* 2483)

Géhin, Paul, ed. *Chapitres des disciples d'Évagre*. Sources Chrétiennes 514. Paris: Éditions du Cerf, 2007.

Eight Thoughts / The Eight Spirits of Wickedness (*CPG* 2451)

Bigot, Émery, ed. *Palladii episcopi helenopolitani De vita s. Johannis Chrysostomi dialogus: Accedunt homilia Sancti Johannis chrysostomi in laudem Diodori, Tarsensis episcopi, Acta Tarachi, Probi et Andronici, Passio Banifatii Romani, Evagrius de octo cogitationibus, Nilus de octo vitiis*. Lutetiae Parisiorum: Apud viduam Edmundi Martini, 1680.

Muyldermans, Joseph, ed. *Evagriana syriaca: Textes inedits du British Museum et de la Vaticane*, 55–59. Bibliothèque du Muséon 31. Louvain: Publications universitaires, 1952.

PG 79:1145–64.

Sinkewicz, Robert E., ed. *Evagrius of Pontus: The Greek Ascetic Corpus*, 66–90. Oxford: Oxford University Press, 2003.

Epistula Fidei

See *Letter on Faith*.

Eulogios / Treatise to the Monk Eulogius or *To Eulogius on the Confession of Thoughts and Counsel in Their Regard* (*CPG* 2447)

PG 79:1093d–1140a.

Sinkewicz, Robert E., ed. *Evagrius of Pontus: The Greek Ascetic Corpus*, 12–59. Oxford: Oxford University Press, 2003.

Exhortations to Monks / Counsel to Monks (*CPG* 2454)

Joest, Christoph, ed. *Ad monachos; Ad virginem; Institutio ad monachos = Der Mönchsspiegel; Der Nonnenspiegel; Ermahnungen an Mönche*. Fontes Christiani 51. Freiburg im Breisgau: Herder, 2012.

PG 79:1235–40.

Sinkewicz, Robert E., ed. *Evagrius of Pontus: The Greek Ascetic Corpus*, 217–23. Oxford: Oxford University Press, 2003.

Foundations / Hypotyposis or *Principles of the Monastic Life* (*CPG* 2441)

Casiday, Augustine, ed. *Evagrius Ponticus*, 81–88. New York: Routledge, 2006.

Muyldermans, Joseph, ed. *Evagriana syriaca: Textes inedits du British Museum et de la Vaticane*, 31–33. Bibliothèque du Muséon 31. Louvain: Publications universitaires, 1952.

Nicodemus the Hagiorite and Saint Makarios, eds. *Φιλοκαλία τῶν νηπτικῶν συνερανισθεῖσα παρὰ τῶν ἁγίων καὶ θεοφόρων πατέρων ἡμῶν ἐν ᾗ διὰ τῆς κατὰ τὴν Πρᾶξιν καὶ Θεωρίαν Ἠθικῆς Φιλοσοφίας ὁ νοῦς καθαίρεται, φωτίζεται, καὶ τελετοῦται*, 1:38–43. 3rd ed. 5 vols. Athens: Ἀστήρ, 1957.

PG 40:1252d–64c.

Sinkewicz, Robert E., ed. *Evagrius of Pontus: The Greek Ascetic Corpus*, 1–11. Oxford: Oxford University Press, 2003.

Gnostikos (*CPG* 2431)

Frankenberg, W., ed. *Euagrius Ponticus*, 546–53. Abhandlungen der Königlichen Gesellschaft der Wissenschaften zu Göttingen. Philologisch-

Historische Klasse, n. F., 13, no. 2. Berlin: Weidmannsche Buchhandlung, 1912.
Guillaumont, Antoine, and Claire Guillaumont, eds. *Le gnostique, ou, A celui qui est devenu digne de la science*. Sources Chrétiennes 356. Paris: Éditions du Cerf, 1989.

Instructions (Prov.) / Proverbs and Their Interpretation (*CPG* 2477)

Muyldermans, Joseph. "Evagriana." *Le Muséon: Revue d'Études Orientales* 44 (1931): 37–68.
———, ed. *Evagriana syriaca: Textes inedits du British Museum et de la Vaticane*, 135–38, 165–67. Bibliothèque du Muséon 31. Louvain: Publications universitaires, 1952.

Just and the Perfect / The Just and the Perfect (*CPG* 2465)

Muyldermans, Joseph, ed. *Evagriana syriaca: Textes inedits du British Museum et de la Vaticane*, 105–9, 142–46. Bibliothèque du Muséon 31. Louvain: Publications universitaires, 1952.

KG / Kephalaia gnostika (*CPG* 2432)

Frankenberg, W., ed. *Euagrius Ponticus*, 422–71. Abhandlungen der Königlichen Gesellschaft der Wissenschaften zu Göttingen. Philologisch-Historische Klasse, n. F., 13, no. 2. Berlin: Weidmannsche Buchhandlung, 1912.
Guillaumont, Antoine, ed. *Les six centuries des "Kephalaia gnostica": Édition critique de la version syriaque commune et édition d'une nouvelle version syriaque, intégrale, avec une double traduction française*. Patrologia Orientalis 28. Paris: Firmin-Didot, 1958.
O'Laughlin, Michael. "Origenism in the Desert: Anthropology and Integration in Evagrius Ponticus." PhD dissertation, Harvard Divinity School, 1987.

Letter on Faith / Dogmatic Letter (*CPG* 2439)

Bunge, Gabriel, ed. *Briefe aus der Wüste*, 284–302. Sophia 24. Trier: Paulinus-Verlag, 1986.
Casiday, Augustine, ed. *Evagrius Ponticus*, 45–58. London; New York: Routledge, 2006.

Frankenberg, W., ed. *Euagrius Ponticus*, 620–35. Abhandlungen der Königlichen Gesellschaft der Wissenschaften zu Göttingen. Philologisch-Historische Klasse, n. F., 13, no. 2. Berlin: Weidmannsche Buchhandlung, 1912.

Gribomont, Jean. "Ps.-Basil, Epistula 8." In *Le lettere*, edited by Marcella Forlin Patrucco, 84–112. Corona Patrum 11. Torino: Società editrice internazionale, 1983.

PG 32:245–68.

Letter to Melania (*CPG* 2438)

Bunge, Gabriel, ed. *Briefe aus der Wüste*, 303–28. Sophia 24. Trier: Paulinus-Verlag, 1986.

Casiday, Augustine, ed. *Evagrius Ponticus*, 63–77. New York: Routledge, 2006.

Ferguson, Everett. *Forms of Devotion: Conversion, Worship, Spirituality, and Asceticism*, 272–310. Recent Studies in Early Christianity 5. New York: Garland, 1999.

Frankenberg, W., ed. *Euagrius Ponticus*, 612–19. Abhandlungen der Königlichen Gesellschaft der Wissenschaften zu Göttingen. Philologisch-Historische Klasse, n. F., 13, no. 2. Berlin: Weidmannsche Buchhandlung, 1912.

Parmentier, M. "Evagrius of Pontus' *Letter to Melania*." *Bijdragen* 46 (1985): 2–38.

Vitestam, Gösta. *Seconde partie du traité, qui passe sous le nom de "La grande lettre d'Évagre le Pontique à Mélanie l'Ancienne."* Scripta minora Regiae Societatis Humaniorum Litterarum Lundensis 3. Lund: Gleerup, 1964.

Letters / 62 Letters (*CPG* 2437)

Bunge, Gabriel, ed. *Briefe aus der Wüste*. Sophia 24. Trier: Paulinus-Verlag, 1986.

Casiday, Augustine, ed. *Evagrius Ponticus*, 59–62. New York: Routledge, 2006.

Frankenberg, W., ed. *Euagrius Ponticus*, 564–611. Abhandlungen der Königlichen Gesellschaft der Wissenschaften zu Göttingen. Philologisch-Historische Klasse, n. F., 13, no. 2. Berlin: Weidmannsche Buchhandlung, 1912.

Géhin, Paul. "Nouveaux fragments grecs des lettres d'Évagre." *Revue d'Histoire des Textes* 24 (1994): 117–47.

Guillaumont, Claire. "Fragments grecs inédits d'Évagre le Pontique." In *Texte und Textkritik: Eine Aufsatzsammlung*, edited by Johannes Irmscher, Franz Paschke, Kurt Treu, and Jürgen Dummer, 209–21. Texte und Untersuchungen zur Geschichte der altchristlichen Literatur 133. Berlin: Akademie-Verlag, 1987.

Young, Robin Darling. "Cannibalism and Other Family Woes in Letter 55 of Evagrius of Pontus." In *The World of Early Egyptian Christianity: Language, Literature, and Social Context; Essays in Honor of David W. Johnson*, edited by James E. Goehring and Janet Timbie, 130–39. CUA Studies in Early Christianity. Washington, DC: Catholic University of America Press, 2007.

Masters and Disciples / On Masters and Disciples (*CPG* 2449)

Unpublished.

Maxims 1 / Parenetikos (*CPG* 2443)

PG 79:1235–40.

Sinkewicz, Robert E., ed. *Evagrius of Pontus: The Greek Ascetic Corpus*, 228–30. Oxford: Oxford University Press, 2003.

Maxims 2 / Spiritual Chapters Alphabetized (*CPG* 2444)

Muyldermans, Joseph, ed. *Evagriana syriaca: Textes inedits du British Museum et de la Vaticane*, 33. Bibliothèque du Muséon 31. Louvain: Publications universitaires, 1952.

PG 40:1268c–69b.

Sinkewicz, Robert E., ed. *Evagrius of Pontus: The Greek Ascetic Corpus*, 230–31. Oxford: Oxford University Press, 2003.

Monks / Chapters to Monks (*CPG* 2435)

Driscoll, Jeremy, ed. *Evagrius Ponticus: Ad Monachos*. Ancient Christian Writers 59. New York: Newman Press, 2003.

Joest, Christoph, ed. *Ad monachos; Ad virginem; Institutio ad monachos = Der Mönchsspiegel; Der Nonnenspiegel; Ermahnungen an Mönche*. Fontes Christiani 51. Freiburg im Breisgau: Herder, 2012.

Leclercq, Jean. "L'ancienne version latine des Sentences d'Évagre pour les Moines." *Scriptorium* 5 (1951): 195–213.
Mühmelt, Martin. "Zu der neuen lateinischen Übersetzung des Mönchsspiegels des Euagrius." *Vigiliae Christianae* 8 (1954): 101–3.
PG 40:1277–82.
Sinkewicz, Robert E., ed. *Evagrius of Pontus: The Greek Ascetic Corpus*, 115–31. Oxford: Oxford University Press, 2003.

Praktikos (*CPG* 2430)

Bamberger, John Eudes, ed. *The Praktikos: Chapters on Prayer*. Cistercian Studies Series 4. Spencer, MA: Cistercian Publications, 1970.
Guillaumont, Claire, and Antoine Guillaumont, eds. *Traité pratique, ou, Le moine*. 2 vols. Sources Chrétiennes 170–71. Paris: Éditions du Cerf, 1971.
Nicodemus the Hagiorite and Saint Makarios, eds. *Φιλοκαλία τῶν νηπτικῶν συνερανισθεῖσα παρὰ τῶν ἁγίων καὶ θεοφόρων πατέρων ἡμῶν ἐν ᾗ διὰ τῆς κατὰ τὴν Πρᾶξιν καὶ Θεωρίαν Ἠθικῆς Φιλοσοφίας ὁ νοῦς καθαίρεται, φωτίζεται, καὶ τελετοῦται*, 1:58. 3rd ed. 5 vols. Athens: Ἀστήρ, 1957.
PG 40:1220c–1236c.
Sinkewicz, Robert E., ed. *Evagrius of Pontus: The Greek Ascetic Corpus*, 91–114. Oxford: Oxford University Press, 2003.
Tugwell, Simon, ed. *Praktikos and On Prayer*. Oxford: Faculty of Theology, 1987.

Prayer / On Prayer (*CPG* 2452)

Bamberger, John Eudes, ed. *The Praktikos: Chapters on Prayer*. Cistercian Studies Series 4. Spencer, MA: Cistercian Publications, 1970.
Casiday, Augustine, ed. *Evagrius Ponticus*, 185–201. New York: Routledge, 2006.
Hausherr, Irénée. "Le *De Oratione* d'Évagre le Pontique en Syriaque et en Arabe." *Orientalia Christiana Periodica* 5 (1939): 7–71.
Muyldermans, Joseph, ed. *Evagriana syriaca: Textes inedits du British Museum et de la Vaticane*, 41–43. Bibliothèque du Muséon 31. Louvain: Publications universitaires, 1952.
Nicodemus the Hagiorite and Saint Makarios, eds. *Φιλοκαλία τῶν νηπτικῶν συνερανισθεῖσα παρὰ τῶν ἁγίων καὶ θεοφόρων πατέρων ἡμῶν ἐν ᾗ διὰ τῆς κατὰ τὴν Πρᾶξιν καὶ Θεωρίαν Ἠθικῆς Φιλοσοφίας ὁ νοῦς καθαίρεται, φωτίζεται, καὶ τελετοῦται*, 1:176–89. 3rd ed. 5 vols. Athens: Ἀστήρ, 1957.
PG 79:1165a–1200c.

Sinkewicz, Robert E., ed. *Evagrius of Pontus: The Greek Ascetic Corpus*, 183–209. Oxford: Oxford University Press, 2003.

Tugwell, Simon, ed. *Praktikos and On Prayer*. Oxford: Faculty of Theology, 1987.

Reflections / *Skemmata* or *Reflections* (*CPG* 2433)

Frankenberg, W., ed. *Euagrius Ponticus*, 452–67. Abhandlungen der Königlichen Gesellschaft der Wissenschaften zu Göttingen. Philologisch-Historische Klasse, n. F., 13, no. 2. Berlin: Weidmannsche Buchhandlung, 1912.

Muyldermans, Joseph. "Evagriana." *Le Muséon: Revue d'Études Orientales* 44 (1931): 37–68.

———. "*Sur les séraphins* et *Sur les chérubins* d'Évagre le Pontique dans les versions syriaque et arménienne." *Le Muséon: Revue d'Études Orientales* 59 (1946): 367–79.

Sinkewicz, Robert E., ed. *Evagrius of Pontus: The Greek Ascetic Corpus*, 210–16. Oxford: Oxford University Press, 2003.

Scholia on Ecclesiastes (*CPG* 2458.5)

Géhin, Paul, ed. *Scholies à l'Ecclésiaste*. Sources Chrétiennes 397. Paris: Éditions du Cerf, 1993.

S-Prov. / *Scholia on the Proverbs* (*CPG* 2456)

Géhin, Paul, ed. *Scholies aux Proverbes*. Sources Chrétiennes 340. Paris: Éditions du Cerf, 1987.

S-Ps. / *Scholia on the Psalms* (*CPG* 2455)

PG 12:1054–1686, passim; 27:60–545, passim.

Pitra, J. B. *Analecta sacra spicilegio Solesmensi parata*, 2:444–83; 3:1–364. Paris: A. Jouby et Roger, 1876.

Thoughts / *On the Thoughts* (*CPG* 2450)

Casiday, Augustine, ed. *Evagrius Ponticus*, 89–116. New York: Routledge, 2006.

Géhin, Paul, Claire Guillaumont, and Antoine Guillaumont, eds. *Sur les pensées*. Sources Chrétiennes 438. Paris: Éditions du Cerf, 1998.

Nicodemus the Hagiorite and Saint Makarios, eds. *Φιλοκαλία τῶν νηπτικῶν συνερανισθεῖσα παρὰ τῶν ἁγίων καὶ θεοφόρων πατέρων ἡμῶν ἐν ᾗ διὰ τῆς κατὰ τὴν Πρᾶξιν καὶ Θεωρίαν Ἠθικῆς Φιλοσοφίας ὁ νοῦς καθαίρεται, φωτίζεται, καὶ τελετοῦται*, 1:44–57. 3rd ed. 5 vols. Athens: Ἀστήρ, 1957.

Sinkewicz, Robert E., ed. *Evagrius of Pontus: The Greek Ascetic Corpus*, 136–82. Oxford: Oxford University Press, 2003.

Vices / On the Vices Opposed to the Virtues (*CPG* 2448)

PG 79:1140b–44d.

Sinkewicz, Robert E., ed. *Evagrius of Pontus: The Greek Ascetic Corpus*, 60–65. Oxford: Oxford University Press, 2003.

Virgin / Chapters to a Virgin (*CPG* 2436)

Casiday, Augustine, ed. *Evagrius Ponticus*, 165–71. New York: Routledge, 2006.

Frankenberg, W., ed. *Euagrius Ponticus*, 562–65. Abhandlungen der Königlichen Gesellschaft der Wissenschaften zu Göttingen. Philologisch-Historische Klasse, n. F., 13, no. 2. Berlin: Weidmannsche Buchhandlung, 1912.

Joest, Christoph, ed. *Ad monachos; Ad virginem; Institutio ad monachos = Der Mönchsspiegel; Der Nonnenspiegel; Ermahnungen an Mönche*. Fontes Christiani 51. Freiburg im Breisgau: Herder, 2012.

Mühmelt, Martin. “Zu der neuen lateinischen Übersetzung des Mönchsspiegels des Euagrius.” *Vigiliae Christianae* 8 (1954): 101–3.

PG 40:1185–88.

Sinkewicz, Robert E., ed. *Evagrius of Pontus: The Greek Ascetic Corpus*, 131–36. Oxford: Oxford University Press, 2003.

Select Editions and Translations of Ancient and Medieval Works

Listed below are editions and translations of ancient and medieval works that have been quoted in this book, ordered alphabetically by author (where known) or title. For other ancient sources, mentioned but not quoted, readers are directed to general reference works such as *The Oxford Classical Dictionary*, *The Oxford Dictionary of Late Antiquity*, and *The Oxford Dictionary of Byzantium*.

Ammonius

Ammonius and Derwas J. Chitty. *The Letters*. Fairacres Publication 72. Oxford: SLG Press, 1979.

Anastasius of Sinai

Richard, Marcel, and Joseph A. Munitiz. *Anastasii Sinaitae Quaestiones et responsiones*. CCSG 59. Turnhout: Brepols, 2006.

Uthemann, Karl-Heinz. *Anastasii Sinaitae Sermones duo in constitutionem hominis secundum imaginem Dei: Necnon, Opuscula adversus monotheletas*. CCSG 12. Turnhout: Brepols, 1985.

Apophthegmata patrum (Sayings of the Desert Fathers)

Guy, Jean-Claude, ed. *Les Apophtegmes des Pères: Collection systématique*. 2 vols. Sources Chrétiennes 387 and 474. Paris: Éditions du Cerf, 1993 and 2003.

Aristotle

Bekker, Immanuel, Christian August Brandis, and Hermann Bonitz, eds. *Aristotelis opera*. 5 vols. Berlin: G. Reimerum, 1831.

Mure, G. R. G., trans. *Analytica posteriora*. In *The Works of Aristotle*, ed. W. D. Ross. 12 vols. Oxford: Oxford University Press, 1910–31.

Babai, Mar

Frankenberg, W., ed. *Euagrius Ponticus*, 8–471. Abhandlungen der Königlichen Gesellschaft der Wissenschaften zu Göttingen. Philologisch-Historische Klasse, n. F., 13, no. 2. Berlin: Weidmannsche Buchhandlung, 1912.

Vaschalde, Arthur Adolphe, ed. *Mar Babai: Liber de unione*. CSCO, Scriptores Syri 34–35. Rome: K. de Luigi, 1915.

Bar Hebraeus

Abbeloos, Jean Baptiste, Thomas Joseph Lamy, and Bar Hebraeus. *Gregorii Barhebraei Chronicon ecclesiasticum: Quod e codice Musei britannici descriptum conjuncta opera ediderunt, Latinitate donarunt annotationibusque. . . .* 3 vols. Louvain: C. Peeters, 1872.

Bar Hebraeus. *The Chronography of Gregory Abû'l Faraj, the Son of Aaron, the Hebrew Physician, Commonly Known as Bar Hebraeus: Being the First Part of His Political History of the World.* 2 vols. Translated by E. A. Wallis Budge. London: Oxford Univ. Press, H. Milford, 1932.

———. *Ktaba d-'itiqon 'al myatrut dubare = Ethicon, seu moralia Gregorii Barhebraei.* Edited by Paul Bedjan. Piscataway, NJ: Gorgias Press, 2007.

———. *Ktaba d-yawna meṭul dubara d-iḥidaye = Liber columbae: Seu directorium monachorum.* Edited by Paul Bedjan. Piscataway, NJ: Gorgias Press, 2007.

Bar Hebraeus, and Herman Teule. *Ethicon (Mēmrā I).* CSCO, Scriptores Syri 218–19. Louvain: E. Peeters, 1993.

Wensinck, A. J. *Bar Hebraeus's Book of the Dove: Together with Some Chapters from His Ethikon.* Leiden: Brill, 1919.

Chaldean Oracles

Julianus the Theurgist and Ruth Dorothy Majercik. *The Chaldean Oracles: Text, Translation, and Commentary.* Studies in Greek and Roman Religion 5. Leiden: Brill, 1989.

Clement of Alexandria

Stählin, Otto, ed. *Clemens Alexandrinus.* 3., durchgesehene Aufl. Die Griechischen christlichen Schriftsteller der ersten Jahrunderte 12, 15, 17, 39. Berlin: Akademie-Verlag, 1936.

Cyril of Skythopolis

Cyril of Scythopolis. *Kyrillos von Skythopolis.* Texte und Untersuchungen zur Geschichte der altchristlichen Literatur 49.4. Leipzig: J. C. Hinrichs, 1939.

Diadochos of Photike

Rutherford, Janet Elaine, ed. *One Hundred Practical Texts of Perception and Spiritual Discernment from Diadochos of Photike.* Belfast Byzantine Texts and Translations 8. Belfast: Belfast Byzantine Enterprises, Institute of Byzantine Studies, the Queen's University of Belfast, 2000.

Dorotheus of Gaza

Dorotheus of Gaza. *Discourses and Sayings.* Cistercian Studies Series 33. Kalamazoo, MI: Cistercian Publications, 1977.

———. *Oeuvres spirituelles.* Edited by Lucien Regnault and J. de Préville. 2nd ed. Sources Chrétiennes 92. Paris: Éditions du Cerf, 2001.

Ephrem of Antioch

Helmer, Siegfried. *Der Neuchalkedonismus: Geschichte, Berechtigung und Bedeutung eines dogmengeschichtlichen Begriffes.* Bonn: [s.n.], 1962.

Ephrem Graecus

Assemani, J. S., ed. *Sancti patris nostri Ephraem Syri Opera omnia quae exstant Graece, Syriace, Latine ad mss. codices Vaticanos. . . .* Rome: ex Typographia Vaticana, 1732.

Phrantzolas, Konstantinos G. *Ὁσίου Ἐφραίμ τοῦ Σύρου ἔργα.* 6 vols. Thessalonica: To Perivoli tis Panagias, 1988.

Evagrius Scholasticus

Bidez, Joseph, and Léon Parmentier. *The Ecclesiastical History of Evagrius with the Scholia.* London: Methuen, 1898.

Galen

Kühn, Karl Gottlob, ed. *Galen: Opera omnia.* 20 vols. Medicorum Graecorum opera quae exstant. Leipzig: C. Cnobloch, 1821.

Gregory of Nazianzus

Daley, Brian. *Gregory of Nazianzus.* The Early Church Fathers. New York: Routledge, 2006.

Gallay, Paul, ed. *Discours.* Sources Chrétiennes 250. Paris: Éditions du Cerf, 1978.

———, ed. *Grégoire de Nazianze: Lettres.* 2 vols. Collection des universités de France. Paris: Les Belles lettres, 1964.

Gregory of Nyssa, all works

Langerbeck, Hermann, ed. *Gregorii Nysseni opera.* Leiden: Brill, 1960.

Gregory the Great, Pope

Adriaen, Marcus, ed. *S. Gregorii Magni Moralia in Job*. CCSL 143, 143A, 143B. Turnhout: Brepols, 1979.

Iamblichus of Chalcis

Dillon, John M., and Wolfgang Polleichtner. *Iamblichus of Chalcis: The Letters*. Writings from the Greco-Roman World 19. Atlanta: Society of Biblical Literature, 2009.

Iamblichus. *Iamblichus on the Mysteries*. Edited by Emma C. Clarke, John M. Dillon, and Jackson P. Hershbell. Writings from the Greco-Roman World 4. Atlanta: Society of Biblical Literature, 2003.

Sodano, Angelo Raffaele. *Lettera ad Anebo*. Napoli: L'Arte tipografica, 1958.

Isaac of Nineveh

Bedjan, Paul, ed. *Mamllā mawtrānā d-'al 'urḥa d-dayrayutā = Mar Isaacus Ninivita, De perfectione religiosa*. Paris: O. Harrossowitz, 1909.

Isaac, Bishop of Nineveh. *On Ascetical Life*. Translated by Mary Hansbury. Crestwood, NY: St. Vladimir's Seminary Press, 1989.

Jacob of Serugh

Frothingham, Arthur L. "Letter of Jacob of Sarub to Stephen Bar Sudaili." In *Stephen Bar Sudhaili, the Syrian Mystic, and the Book of Hierotheos*, 11–28. Leiden: Brill, 1886.

Jerome

Budge, E. A. Wallis. *The Book of Paradise, Being the Histories and Sayings of the Monks and Ascetics of the Egyptian Desert by Palladius, Hieronymus and Others: The Syriac Texts, According to the Recension of 'Ânân-Îshô of Bêth-'Âbhê*. London, 1904.

Gebhardt, Oscar von, and Ernest Cushing Richardson, eds. *Hieronymus liber* De viris inlustribus; *Gennadius liber* De viris inlustribus. Texte und Untersuchungen zur Geschichte der altchristlichen Literatur 14.1. Leipzig: J. C. Hinrichs, 1896.

Hilberg, Isidorus, ed. *Sancti Eusebii Hieronymi Epistulae*. Editio altera supplementis aucta. Vol. 3. Corpus scriptorum ecclesiasticorum latinorum 56. Vienna: Verlag der Österreichischen Akademie der Wissenschaften, 1996.

Reiter, Siegfried, ed. *Sancti Evsebii Hieronymi In Hieremiam prophetam libri sex*. Corpus scriptorum ecclesiasticorum latinorum 59. Vienna: F. Tempsky, 1913.

John Cassian

Cassian, John, and Michael Petschenig. *Iohannis Cassiani De institutis coenobiorum et de octo principalium vitiorum remediis libri XII*. Corpus scriptorum ecclesiasticorum latinorum 17. Vienna: F. Tempsky, 1888.

Petschenig, Michael, ed. *Iohannis Cassiani Conlationes XXIIII*. Corpus scriptorum ecclesiasticorum latinorum 13. Vienna: C. Geroldi filium, 1886.

Petschenig, Michael, and Gottfried Kreuz, eds. *De institutis coenobiorum; De incarnatione contra Nestorium*. Editio altera supplementis aucta. Corpus scriptorum ecclesiasticorum Latinorum 17. Vienna: Verlag der Österreichischen Akademie der Wissenschaften, 2004.

John Climacus

John Climacus. *Opera omnia*. Edited by Matthäus Rader. Lutetiae Parisiorum: Sumptibus Sebastiani Cramoisy, 1633.

Luibheid, Colum, and Norman Russell, trans. *The Ladder of Divine Ascent*. Classics of Western Spirituality. New York: Paulist Press, 1982.

John of Dalyatha

Hansbury, Mary, ed. *The Letters of John of Dalyatha*. Texts from Christian Late Antiquity 2. Piscataway, NJ: Gorgias Press, 2006.

John of Damascus

Kotter, P. Bonifatius. *Die Schriften des Johannes von Damaskos*. Patristische Texte und Studien 7. Berlin: Walter de Gruyter, 1969.

Julian the Theurgist

Julianus the Theurgist and Ruth Dorothy Majercik. *The Chaldean Oracles: Text, Translation, and Commentary*. Studies in Greek and Roman Religion 5. Leiden: Brill, 1989.

Leo of Ohrid

Büttner, Elmar. *Erzbischof Leon von Ohrid (1037–1056): Leben und Werk; Mit den Texten seiner bisher unedierten asketischen Schrift und seiner drei Briefe an den Papst*. Bamberg: [s.n.], 2007.

Munitiz, Joseph A. "Leo of Ohrid: The New *Kephalaia*." *Orientalia Christiana Periodica* 76, no. 1 (2010): 121–44.

Leo VI, emperor

Dennis, George T., ed. *The Taktika of Leo VI*. Corpus Fontium Historiae Byzantinae, Series Washingtonensis 49. Washington, DC: Dumbarton Oaks Research Library and Collection, 2010.

Leontius of Byzantium

Daley, Brian E. "Leontius of Byzantium: A Critical Edition of His Works, with Prolegomena." PhD dissertation, Oxford University, 1978.

Macarius

Nicodemus the Hagiorite and Saint Makarios, eds. *The Philokalia: The Complete Text*. Translated by G. E. H. Palmer, Philip Sherrard, and Kallistos Ware. London: Faber and Faber, 1979.

———, eds. *Φιλοκαλία τῶν νηπτικῶν συνερανισθεῖσα παρὰ τῶν ἁγίων καὶ θεοφόρων πατέρων ἡμῶν ἐν ᾗ διὰ τῆς κατὰ τὴν Πρᾶξιν καὶ Θεωρίαν Ἠθικῆς Φιλοσοφίας ὁ νοῦς καθαίρεται, φωτίζεται, καὶ τελετοῦται*. 3rd ed. 5 vols. Athens: Ἀστήρ, 1957.

Wilmart, André. "La fausse lettre latine de Macaire." *Revue d'ascetique et de mystique* 3 (1922): 411–19.

Mark the Monk

Durand, Georges-Matthieu de, ed. *Traités*. 2 vols. Sources Chrétiennes 445, 455. Paris: Cerf, 1999.

Maximus the Confessor

Berthold, George C., trans. *Maximus Confessor, Selected Writings*. The Classics of Western Spirituality. New York: Paulist Press, 1985.

Blowers, Paul M., and Robert Louis Wilken. *On the Cosmic Mystery of Jesus Christ: Selected Writings from St. Maximus the Confessor*. Popular Patristics. Crestwood, NY: St. Vladimir's Seminary Press, 2003.

Brock, Sebastian P. "An Early Syriac Life of Maximus the Confessor." *Analecta Bollandiana* 91 (1973): 299–346.

Constas, Nicholas, ed. and trans. *On Difficulties in the Church Fathers*. 2 vols. Dumbarton Oaks Medieval Library. Cambridge, MA: Harvard University Press, 2014.

Louth, Andrew. *Maximus the Confessor*. The Early Church Fathers. London: Routledge, 1996.

Maximus, Confessor. *The Ascetic Life: The Four Centuries on Charity*. Translated by Polycarp Sherwood. Ancient Christian Writers 21. Westminster, MD: Newman Press, 1955.

Nicodemus the Hagiorite and Saint Makarios, eds. *The Philokalia: The Complete Text*. Translated by G. E. H. Palmer, Philip Sherrard, and Kallistos Ware. London: Faber and Faber, 1979.

Nicodemus the Hagiorite

Nicodemus the Hagiorite and Saint Makarios, eds. *The Philokalia: The Complete Text*. Translated by G. E. H. Palmer, Philip Sherrard, and Kallistos Ware. London: Faber and Faber, 1979.

———, eds. *Φιλοκαλία τῶν νηπτικῶν συνερανισθεῖσα παρὰ τῶν ἁγίων καὶ θεοφόρων πατέρων ἡμῶν ἐν ᾗ διὰ τῆς κατὰ τὴν Πρᾶξιν καὶ Θεωρίαν Ἠθικῆς Φιλοσοφίας ὁ νοῦς καθαίρεται, φωτίζεται, καὶ τελετοῦται*. 3rd ed. 5 vols. Athens: Ἀστήρ, 1957.

Origen

Butterworth, G. W., ed. *Origen on First Principles, Being Koetschau's Text of the De Principiis Translated into English, Together with an Introduction and Notes*. London: Society for Promoting Christian Knowledge, 1936.

Heine, Ronald E., and Origen. *Homilies on Genesis and Exodus*. Fathers of the Church 71. Washington, DC: Catholic University of America Press, 1982.

Koetschau, Paul, ed. *Origenes Werke*, vol. 5, *De principiis*. Die griechischen christlichen Schriftsteller der ersten drei Jahrhunderte 22. Leipzig: J. C. Hinrichs, 1913.

Origen. *Commentaire sur le Cantique des cantiques*. Edited by Luc Brésard, Henri Crouzel, and Marcel Borret. From the translation of Aquileia Rufinus. Sources Chrétiennes 375–76. Paris: Éditions du Cerf, 1991.

———. *Traité des principes*. Edited by Henri Crouzel. 5 vols. Sources Chrétiennes 252–53, 268–69, 312. Paris: Éditions du Cerf, 1978.

———. *Vier Bücher von den Prinzipien*. Edited by Herwig Görgemanns and Heinrich Karpp. 1. Aufl. Texte zur Forschung 24. Darmstadt: Wissenschaftliche Buchgesellschaft, 1976.

Palladius of Helenopolis

Amélineau, Émile. *De "Historia lausiaca" quaenam sit hujus ad monachorum Aegyptiorum historiam scribendam utilitas: Adjecta sunt quaedam hujus historiae Coptica fragmenta inedita*. Paris: E. Leroux, 1887.

Bigot, Émery, ed. *Palladii episcopi helenopolitani De vita s. Johannis Chrysostomi dialogus: Accedunt homilia Sancti Johannis chrysostomi in laudem Diodori, Tarsensis episcopi, Acta Tarachi, Probi et andronici, Passio Banifatii Romani, Evagrius de octo cogitationibus, Nilus de octo vitiis*. Lutetiae Parisiorum: Apud viduam Edmundi Martini, 1680.

Budge, E. A. Wallis. *The Book of Paradise, Being the Histories and Sayings of the Monks and Ascetics of the Egyptian Desert by Palladius, Hieronymus and Others: The Syriac Texts, According to the Recension of ʾÂnân-Îshô of Bêth-ʿÂbhê*. London, 1904.

Vivian, Tim. *Four Desert Fathers: Pambo, Evagrius, Macarius of Egypt, and Macarius of Alexandria: Coptic Texts Relating to the Lausiac History of Palladius*. Popular Patristics. Crestwood, NY: St. Vladimir's Seminary Press, 2004.

Pamphilus

Declerck, José H., and Pauline Allen. *Diversorum postchalcedonensium auctorum collectanea*, vol. 1, *Pamphili Theologi opus; Eustathii Monachi opus*. CCSG 19. Turnhout: Brepols, 1989.

Philoxenus of Mabbug

Budge, E. A. Wallis, ed. *The Discourses of Philoxenus, Bishop of Mabbôgh, A.D. 485–519*. London: Asher, 1893.

Frothingham, Arthur L. "Letter of Mar Xenaias of Mabûg to Abraham and Orestes, Presbyters of Edessa, Concerning Stephen Bar Sudaili the Edessene." In *Stephen Bar Sudhaili, the Syrian Mystic, and the Book of Hierotheos*, 28–48. Leiden: Brill, 1886.

———. *Stephen Bar Sudhaili, the Syrian Mystic, and the Book of Hierotheos.* Leiden: Brill, 1886.

Halleux, André de. *Commentaire du prologue johannique (ms. Br. Mus. Add. 14, 534).* CSCO 380–81, Scriptores Syri 165 (text), 166 (trans.). Louvain: Secrétariat du CorpusSCO, 1977.

Kitchen, Robert A. *The Discourses of Philoxenos of Mabbug: A New Translation and Introduction.* Collegeville, MN: Liturgical Press, 2013.

Lavenant, René. *La lettre à Patrikios de Philoxène de Mabboug.* Patrologia Orientalis 30.5. Paris: Firmin-Didot, 1963.

Lemoine, Eugène. *Philoxène de Mabboug, Homélies.* Nouv. éd. revue / par René Lavenant. Sources Chrétiennes 44. Paris: Éditions du Cerf, 2007.

Watt, John W. "Philoxenus and the Old Syriac Version of Evagrius' *Centuries.*" *Oriens Christianus* 64 (1980): 65–81.

———. *Philoxenus of Mabbug: Fragments of the Commentary on Matthew and Luke.* CSCO 392–93, Scriptores Syri 171 (text), 172 (translation). Louvain: Secrétariat du CorpusSCO, 1978.

Plato

Burnet, J., ed. *Platonis opera.* 5 vols. Oxford: Clarendon Press, 1900–1907.

Plotinus

Henry, P., and H.-R. Schwyzer, eds. *Plotini opera.* 3 vols. Leiden: Brill, 1951–73.

Porphyry

Brisson, Luc. *Porphyre, Sentences.* 2 vols. Histoire des doctrines de l'Antiquité classique 33. Paris: Vrin, 2005.

Busse, Adolf, ed. *In Porphyrii Isagogen et Aristotelis Categorias commentaria.* Commentaria in Aristotelem graeca 18.1. Berlin: typ. et impensis G. Reimeri, 1900.

Zimmern, Alice. *Porphyry's Letter to His Wife Marcella: Concerning the Life of Philosophy and the Ascent to the Gods.* Grand Rapids, MI: Phanes Press, 1986.

Rabban Sauma

See Yaballaha III.

Rufinus of Aquileia

Rufinus of Aquileia. *Historia monachorum, sive, De vita sanctorum patrum*. Edited by Eva Schulz-Flügel. Patristische Texte und Studien 34. Berlin: W. De Gruyter, 1990.

Sayings of the Desert Fathers

See Apophthegmata Patrum.

Severus of Antioch

Braun, Oskar. *Moses bar Kepha und sein buch von der seele*. Freiburg im Breisgau: Herder, 1891.

Sextus (Xystus)

Chadwick, Henry. *The Sentences of Sextus: A Contribution to the History of Early Christian Ethics*. Texts and Studies 5. Cambridge: Cambridge University Press, 1959.

Conybeare, F. C. *The Ring of Pope Xystus: Together with the Prologue of Rufinus*. London: Williams and Norgate, 1910.

Simeon the New Theologian

Simeon the New Theologian. *Chapitres théologiques, gnostiques et pratiques*. Edited by Jean Darrouzès and Louis Neyrand. 2nd ed. Sources Chrétiennes 51bis. Paris: Éditions du Cerf, 1980.

Socrates

Hansen, Günther Christian, ed. *Kirchengeschichte*. Die griechischen christlichen Schriftsteller der ersten Jahrhunderte, n. F. 1. Berlin: Akademie Verlag, 1995.

Stephen Bar Sudhaili

Frothingham, Arthur L. *Stephen Bar Sudhaili, the Syrian Mystic, and the Book of Hierotheos*. Leiden: Brill, 1886.

Stephen of Thebes

Des Places, Édouard. "Le 'Discours ascétique' d'Étienne de Thèbes: Texte grec inédit et traduction." In *Études platoniciennes, 1929–1979*, 389–413. Études préliminaires aux religions orientales dans l'Empire romain 90. Leiden: Brill, 1981.

Xystus

See Sextus

Yaballaha III

Bedjan, Paul, ed. *Histoire de Mar-Jabalaha: De trois autres Patriarches, d'un prêtre et de deux laïques, Nestoriens*. Paris: Otto Harrassowitz, 1893.

Borbone, Giorgio. *Storia di Mar Yahballaha e di Rabban Sauma: Un orientale in Occidente ai tempi di Marco Polo*. Torino: S. Zamorani, 2000.

Chabot, Jean Baptiste, and Patriarch of the Nestorians Yabhalāhā III. *Histoire de Mar Jabalaha III, Patriarche Des Nestoriens (1281–1317)*. Paris: Ernest Leoux, 1895.

Montgomery, James A. *The History of Yaballaha III, Nestorian Patriarch, and of His Vicar, Bar Sauma, Mongol Ambassador to the Frankish Courts at the End of the Thirteenth Century*. Records of Civilization, Sources and Studies 8. New York: Columbia University Press, 1927.

Zacharias of Mytilene

Richard, Marcel, ed. *Iohannis Caesariensis presbyteri et grammatici Opera quae supersunt*. CCSG 1. Turnhout: Brepols, 1977.

Other Primary and Secondary Studies

Abbeloos, Jean Baptiste, Thomas Joseph Lamy, and Bar Hebraeus. *Gregorii Barhebraei Chronicon ecclesiasticum: Quod e codice Musei britannici descriptum conjuncta opera ediderunt, Latinitate donarunt annotationibusque. . . .* 3 vols. Louvain: C. Peeters, 1872.

Abramowski, Luise. "Ein nestorianischer Traktat bei Leontius von Jerusalem." In *III° Symposium Syriacum, 1980: Les contacts du monde syriaque avec les autres cultures; Goslar 7–11 Septembre 1980*, edited by René Lavenant,

43–55. Orientalia Christiana Analecta 221. Rome: Pont. Institutum Studiorum Orientalium, 1983.

Allen, Pauline, and Bronwen Neil. *Maximus the Confessor and His Companions: Documents from Exile*. Oxford Early Christian Texts. Oxford: Oxford University Press, 2002.

Amélineau, Émile. *De "Historia lausiaca" quaenam sit hujus ad monachorum Aegyptiorum historiam scribendam utilitas: Adjecta sunt quaedam hujus historiae Coptica fragmenta inedita*. Paris: E. Leroux, 1887. http://www.archive.org/details/MN41886ucmf_5.

Arthur, Rosemary A. *Pseudo-Dionysius as Polemicist: The Development and Purpose of the Angelic Hierarchy in Sixth Century Syria*. Burlington, VT: Ashgate, 2008.

———"A Sixth-Century Origenist: Stephen Bar Sudhaili and His Relationship with Ps-Dionysius." *Studia Patristica* 35 (2001): 368–73.

Assemani, Giuseppe Simone. *Bibliotheca orientalis Clementino-vaticana*. 3 vols. Rome: Typis Sacrae Congregationis de Propaganda Fide, 1719.

Ast, Friedrich. *Lexicon Platonicum; sive, Vocum Platonicarum index*. Leipzig: in libraria Weidmaniana, 1835.

Aydin, Sayili. "The Observatory in Islam." *Ankara: Publications of the Turkish Historical Society* 33 (1960): 189–92.

Badger, George Percy. *The Nestorians and Their Rituals with the Narrative of a Mission to Mesopotamia and Coordistan in 1842–1844, and of a Late Visit to Those Countries in 1850*. 2 vols. London: Joseph Masters, 1852.

Balfour, David, and Mary Cunningham, eds. *A Supplement to the Philokalia: The Second Century of Saint John of Karpathos*. 1st critical ed. The Archbishop Iakovos Library of Ecclesiastical and Historical Sources 16. Brookline, MA: Hellenic College Press, 1994.

Balthasar, Hans Urs von. *Kosmische Liturgie: Das Weltbild Maximus' des Bekenners*. Einsiedeln: Johannes-Verlag, 1988.

———. "The Metaphysics and Mystical Theology of Evagrius." *Monastic Studies* 3 (1965): 183–95.

Bamberger, John Eudes, ed. *The Praktikos: Chapters on Prayer*. Cistercian Studies Series 4. Spencer, MA: Cistercian Publications, 1970.

Bar Hebraeus. *The Chronography of Gregory Abû'l Faraj, the Son of Aaron, the Hebrew Physician, Commonly Known as Bar Hebraeus: Being the First Part of His Political History of the World*. 2 vols. Translated by E. A. Wallis Budge. London: Oxford University Press and H. Milford, 1932.

———. *Ktaba d-'itiqon 'al myatrut dubare = Ethicon, seu moralia Gregorii Barhebraei*. Edited by Paul Bedjan. Piscataway, NJ: Gorgias Press, 2007.

———. *Ktaba d-yawna meṭul dubara d-iḥidaye = Liber columbae: Seu directorium monachorum*. Edited by Paul Bedjan. Piscataway, NJ: Gorgias Press, 2007.

Bar Hebraeus, and Herman Teule. *Ethicon (Mēmrā I)*. CSCO, Scriptores Syri 218–19. Louvain: E. Peeters, 1993.

Barnes, Jonathan, and Porphyry. *Porphyry: Introduction*. Clarendon Later Ancient Philosophers. Oxford: Oxford University Press, 2003.

Baumstark, Anton. *Geschichte der syrischen Literatur, mit Ausschluss der christlich-palästinensischen Texte*. Bonn: A. Marcus und E. Weber, 1922.

Bedjan, Paul. *Acta martyrum et sanctorum*. 7 vols. Paris: Harrasssowitz, 1890.

———, ed. *Histoire de Mar-Jabalaha: De trois autres Patriarches, d'un prêtre et de deux laïques, Nestoriens*. Paris: Otto Harrassowitz, 1893.

———, ed. *Mamlla mawtrana d-ʿal ʾurḥa d-dayrayuta = Mar Isaacus Ninivita, De perfectione religiosa*. Paris: Otto Harrassowitz, 1909.

Beeley, Christopher A. *Gregory of Nazianzus on the Trinity and the Knowledge of God: In Your Light We Shall See Light*. Oxford Studies in Historical Theology. Oxford: Oxford University Press, 2008.

Bekker, Immanuel, Christian August Brandis, and Hermann Bonitz, eds. *Aristotelis opera*. 5 vols. Berlin: G. Reimerum, 1831.

Benevich, G. "Maximus the Confessor's Polemics against Anti-Origenism: *Epistulae* 6 and 7 as a Context for the *Ambigua ad Iohannem*." *Revue d'Histoire Ecclésiastique* 104 (2009): 5–15.

Berthold, George C., trans. *Maximus Confessor, Selected Writings*. The Classics of Western Spirituality. New York: Paulist Press, 1985.

Bettiolo, Paolo. *L'epistula fidei di Evagrio Pontico: Temi, contesti, sviluppi; Atti del III convegno del gruppo italiano di ricerca su "Origene e la tradizione alessandrina."* Studia Ephemeridis Augustinianum 72. Rome: Institutum Patristicum Augustinianum, 2000.

———. "Povertà e conoscenza: Appunti sulle 'Centurie gnostiche' della tradizione evagriana in Siria." *Parole de l'Orient* 15 (1989): 107–25.

Bibliothèque Nationale de France. *Catalogue général des manuscrits latins*. Vol. 7. Paris: Bibliothèque nationale de France, 1988.

Bidez, Joseph, and Léon Parmentier. *The Ecclesiastical History of Evagrius with the Scholia*. London: Methuen, 1898.

Bigot, Émery, ed. *Palladii episcopi helenopolitani De vita s. Johannis Chrysostomi dialogus: Accedunt homilia Sancti Johannis chrysostomi in laudem Diodori, Tarsensis episcopi, Acta Tarachi, Probi et andronici, Passio Banifatii Romani, Evagrius de octo cogitationibus, Nilus de octo vitiis*. Lutetiae Parisiorum: Apud viduam Edmundi Martini, 1680.

Bloomfield, Morton W. *The Seven Deadly Sins: An Introduction to the History of a Religious Concept, with Special Reference to Medieval English Literature*. East Lansing: Michigan State College Press, 1952.

Borbone, Giorgio. *Storia di Mar Yahballaha e di Rabban Sauma: Un orientale in Occidente ai tempi di Marco Polo*. Torino: S. Zamorani, 2000.

Boyle, John Andrew, and ʿAlāʾ al-Dīn ʿAṭā Malik Juvaynī. *Genghis Khan: The History of the World Conqueror*. 2 vols. Manchester Medieval Sources Series. Manchester: Manchester University Press, 1997.

Brakke, David. *Demons and the Making of the Monk: Spiritual Combat in Early Christianity*. Cambridge, MA: Harvard University Press, 2006.

———. *Talking Back: A Monastic Handbook for Combating Demons*. Cistercian Studies Series 229. Collegeville, MN: Cistercian Publications, 2009.

Braun, Oskar. *Moses bar Kepha und sein buch von der seele*. Freiburg im Breisgau: Herder, 1891.

Brisson, Luc. *Porphyre, Sentences*. 2 vols. Histoire des doctrines de l'Antiquité classique 33. Paris: Vrin, 2005.

Brock, Sebastian P. "A Monastic Anthology from Twelfth-Century Edessa." In *Symposium Syriacum VII: Uppsala University, Department of Asian and African Languages, 11–14 August 1996*, edited by René Lavenant, 221–31. Orientalia Christiana Analecta 256. Rome: Pontificio Istituto Orientale, 1998.

———. "An Early Syriac Life of Maximus the Confessor." *Analecta Bollandiana* 91 (1973): 299–346.

———. "Discerning the Evagrian in the Writings of Isaac of Nineveh." *Adamantius* 15 (2009): 60–72.

———. "From Antagonism to Assimilation: Syriac Attitudes to Greek Learning." In *East of Byzantium: Syria and Armenia in the Formative Period*, edited by Nina G. Garsoïan, Thomas F. Mathews, and Robert W. Thomson, 17–34. Washington, DC: Dumbarton Oaks, 1982.

———. "Isaac of Nineveh." *Sobornost* 7, no. 2 (1975): 79–88.

———. "L'apport des pères grecs à la littérature syriaque." In *Les pères grecs dans la tradition syriaque*, edited by Andrea B. Schmidt and Dominique Gonnet, 9–26. Etudes syriaques 4. Paris: Geuthner, 2007.

———. "Towards a History of Syriac Translation Technique." In *III° Symposium Syriacum, 1980: Les contacts du monde syriaque avec les autres cultures; Goslar 7–11 Septembre 1980*, edited by René Lavenant, 1–14. Orientalia Christiana analecta 221. Roma: Pont. Institutum Studiorium Orientalium, 1983.

Brown, Peter. *The Body and Society: Men, Women, and Sexual Renunciation in Early Christianity*. Lectures on the History of Religions, N.s.r. 13. New York: Columbia University Press, 1988.

Budge, E. A. Wallis. *The Book of Paradise, Being the Histories and Sayings of the Monks and Ascetics of the Egyptian Desert by Palladius, Hieronymus and Others: The Syriac Texts, According to the Recension of 'Ânân-Îshô of Bêth-'Âbhê*. London, 1904.

———, ed. *The Discourses of Philoxenus, Bishop of Mabbôgh, A.D. 485–519*. London: Asher, 1893.

Bundy, David. "The Philosophical Structures of Origenism: The Case of the Expurgated Version (S1) of the Kephalaia Gnostica of Evagrius." In *Origeniana Quinta: Historica, Text and Method, Biblica, Philosophica, Theologica, Origenism and Later Developments; Papers of the 5th International Origen Congress, Boston College, 14–18 August 1989*, edited by Robert J. Daly, 577–84. Bibliotheca Ephemeridum Theologicarum Lovaniensium 105. Leuven: Leuven University Press, 1992.

Bunge, Gabriel, ed. *Briefe aus der Wüste*. Sophia 24. Trier: Paulinus-Verlag, 1986.

Busse, Adolf, ed. *In Porphyrii Isagogen et Aristotelis Categorias commentaria*. Commentaria in Aristotelem Graeca 18.1. Berlin: typ. et impensis G. Reimeri, 1900.

Butler, Cuthbert. *The Lausiac History of Palladius*. 2 vols. Cambridge: Cambridge University Press, 1898; rpt. Whitefish, MT: Kessinger Publications, 2012.

Butler, Judith. *Gender Trouble: Feminism and the Subversion of Identity*. New York: Routledge, 1999.

———. *Undoing Gender*. New York: Routledge, 2004.

Butterworth, G. W., ed. *Origen on First Principles, Being Koetschau's Text of the De Principiis Translated into English, Together with an Introduction and Notes*. London: Society for Promoting Christian Knowledge, 1936.

Büttner, Elmar. *Erzbischof Leon von Ohrid (1037–1056): Leben und Werk; Mit den Texten seiner bisher unedierten asketischen Schrift und seiner drei Briefe an den Papst*. Bamberg: [s.n.], 2007.

Casiday, Augustine, ed. *Evagrius Ponticus*. New York: Routledge, 2006.

———. "Gabriel Bunge and the Study of Evagrius Ponticus: A Review Article." *St. Vladimir's Theological Quarterly* 48, no. 2 (2004): 249–97.

———. "On Heresy in Modern Patristic Scholarship: The Case of Evagrius Ponticus." *The Heythrop Journal* 53, no. 2 (2008): 241–52.

Cassian, John, and Michael Petschenig. *Iohannis Cassiani De institutis coenobiorum et de octo principalium vitiorum remediis libri XII*. Corpus scriptorum ecclesiasticorum latinorum 17. Vienna: F. Tempsky, 1888.

Ceresa-Gastaldo, Aldo, ed. *Capitoli sulla carità*. Verba seniorum (Rome, Italy), n.s. 3. Rome: Editrice Studium, 1963.

Chadwick, Henry. *The Sentences of Sextus: A Contribution to the History of Early Christian Ethics*. Texts and Studies 5. Cambridge: Cambridge University Press, 1959.

Chialà, Sabino. "Evagrio il Pontico negli scritti di Isacco di Ninive." *Adamantius* 15 (2009): 73–82.

Chin, Catherine. "Rufinus of Aquileia and Alexandrian Afterlives: Translation as Origenism." *Journal of Early Christian Studies* 18 (2010): 617–47.

Çiçek, J. J., ed. *A Commentary on the 100 Theses of Evagrius Ponticus*. Bar Ebroyo Kloster Publications 10. Piscataway, NJ: Gorgias Press, 2011.

Clark, Elizabeth A. *The Origenist Controversy: The Cultural Construction of an Early Christian Debate*. Princeton, NJ: Princeton University Press, 1992.

Contreras, Enrique. "Evagrio Pontico en los catalogos de varones ilustres." *Salmanticensis* 33 (1986): 333–43.

Conybeare, F. C. *The Ring of Pope Xystus: Together with the Prologue of Rufinus*. London: Williams and Norgate, 1910.

Corrigan, Kevin. *Evagrius and Gregory: Mind, Soul and Body in the 4th Century*. Ashgate Studies in Philosophy and Theology in Late Antiquity. Burlington, VT: Ashgate, 2009.

———. "Simmias' Objection to Socrates in the *Phaedo*: Harmony, Symphony and Some Later Platonic/Patristic Responses to the Mind/Soul-Body Question." *The International Journal of the Platonic Tradition* 4, no. 2 (2010): 147–62.

Costache, Doru. "Queen of the Sciences? Theology and Natural Knowledge in St Gregory Palamas' *One Hundred and Fifty Chapters*." *Transdisciplinarity in Science and Religion* 3 (2008): 27–46.

Cyril of Scythopolis. *Kyrillos von Skythopolis*. Texte und Untersuchungen zur Geschichte der altchristlichen Literatur 49.4. Leipzig: J. C. Hinrichs, 1939.

Daley, Brian E. "Divine Transcendence and Human Transformation: Gregory of Nyssa's Anti-Apollinarian Christology." *Studia Patristica* 32 (1997): 87–95.

———. *Gregory of Nazianzus*. The Early Church Fathers. New York: Routledge, 2006.

———. "'Heavenly Man' and 'Eternal Christ': Apollinarius and Gregory of Nyssa on the Personal Identity of the Savior." *Journal of Early Christian Studies* 10 (2002): 469–88.

———. *The Hope of the Early Church: A Handbook of Patristic Eschatology.* Cambridge: Cambridge University Press, 1991.

———. "Leontius of Byzantium: A Critical Edition of His Works, with Prolegomena." PhD dissertation, Oxford University, 1978.

———. "Nature and the 'Mode of Union': Late Patristic Models for the Personal Unity of Christ." In *The Incarnation: An Interdisciplinary Symposium on the Incarnation of the Son of God*, edited by Stephen T. Davis, Daniel Kendall, and Gerald O'Collins, 164–96. Oxford: Oxford University Press, 2002.

———. "'One Thing and Another': The Persons in God and the Person of Christ in Patristic Theology." *Pro Ecclesia* 15 (2006): 17–46.

———. "The Origenism of Leontius of Byzantium." *The Journal of Theological Studies*, n.s., 27 (1976): 333–69.

———. "What Did 'Origenism' Mean in the Sixth Century?" In *Origeniana Sexta: Origène et La Bible = Origen and the Bible; Actes Du Colloquium Origenianum Sextum, Chantilly, 30 Août–3 Septembre 1993*, by Gilles Dorival and Alain Le Boulluec, 627–38. Bibliotheca Ephemeridum Theologicarum Lovaniensium 118. Leuven: Leuven University Press, 1995.

———. "Who Is the Real Bishop of Constantinople? A Reconsideration of Gregory of Nazianzus's Will." *Studia Patristica* 47 (2010): 147–52.

Declerck, José H. "Encore une fois Léonce et Pamphile." In *Philohistōr: Miscellanea in honorem Caroli Laga septuagenarii*, edited by A. Schoors and Peter van Deun, 199–216. Orientalia Lovaniensia Analecta 60. Leuven: Departement Oriëntalistiek, 1994.

Declerck, José H., and Pauline Allen. *Diversorum postchalcedonensium auctorum collectanea*, vol. 1, *Pamphili Theologi opus; Eustathii Monachi opus.* CCSG 19. Turnhout: Brepols, 1989.

de Goeje, M. J., ed. *Catalogus codicum Orientalium Bibliothecae Academiae Lugduno Batavae*. Vol. 5. Leiden: Brill, 1877.

Dennis, George T., ed. *The Taktika of Leo VI.* Corpus Fontium Historiae Byzantinae, Series Washingtonensis 49. Washington, DC: Dumbarton Oaks Research Library and Collection, 2010.

Diekamp, Franz. *Die origenistischen Streitigkeiten im sechsten Jahrhundert und das fünfte allgemeine Concil.* ATLA Historical Monographs Collection. Series 2 (1894–1923). Münster i. W.: Aschendorff, 1899.

Draguet, René, ed. *Les formes syriaques de la matière de l'Histoire lausiaque*. 4 vols. CSCO, 389–90, 398–99, Scriptores Syri 169–70, 173–74. Louvain: Secrétariat du CorpusSCO, 1978.

Driscoll, Jeremy, ed. *Evagrius Ponticus: Ad Monachos*. Ancient Christian Writers 59. New York: Newman Press, 2003.

Driver, Steven D. *John Cassian and the Reading of Egyptian Monastic Culture*. Studies in Medieval History and Culture 8. New York: Routledge, 2002.

Durand, Georges-Matthieu de, ed. *Traités*. 2 vols. Sources Chrétiennes 445, 455. Paris: Éditions du Cerf, 1999.

Dysinger, Luke. *Psalmody and Prayer in the Writings of Evagrius Ponticus*. Oxford: Oxford University Press, 2005.

Ehrhard, A. "Review of Papadopoulos-Kerameus, *Varia graeca sacra*." *Byzantinische Zeitschrift* 20 (1911): 260.

Elm, Susanna K. "Evagrius Ponticus' *Sententiae ad virginem*." *Dumbarton Oaks Papers* 45 (1991): 97–120.

———. "The *Sententiae ad virginem* by Evagrius Ponticus and the Problem of Early Monastic Rules." *Augustinianum* 30 (1990): 393–404.

Emminger, Kurt. *Studien zu den griechischen Fürstenspiegeln: Programm des K. Luitpold-Gymnasiums in München*. Munich: Buchdruckerei von J. B. Lindl, 1906.

Eustratiades, Sophronios. *Michael tou Glyka: Eis tas aporias tes Theias Graphes kephalaia*. Athens: P. D. Sakellariou, 1906.

Ferguson, Everett. *Forms of Devotion: Conversion, Worship, Spirituality, and Asceticism*. Recent Studies in Early Christianity 5. New York: Garland, 1999.

Frankenberg, W., ed. *Euagrius Ponticus*. Abhandlungen der Königlichen Gesellschaft der Wissenschaften zu Göttingen. Philologisch-Historische Klasse, n. F., 13, no. 2. Berlin: Weidmannsche Buchhandlung, 1912.

Frankenberry, Nancy, and Hans H. Penner. *Language, Truth, and Religious Belief: Studies in Twentieth-Century Theory and Method in Religion*. Texts and Translations Series (American Academy of Religion) 19. Atlanta: Scholars Press, 1999.

Frohne, Renate. *Agapetus Diaconus: Untersuchungen zu den Quellen und zur Wirkungsgeschichte des ersten byzantinischen Fürstenspiegels*. St. Gallen: OK Druck, 1985.

Frothingham, Arthur L. "Letter of Mar Xenaias of Mabûg to Abraham and Orestes, Presbyters of Edessa, Concerning Stephen Bar Sudaili the Edessene." In *Stephen Bar Sudhaili, the Syrian Mystic, and the Book of Hierotheos*, 28–48. Leiden: Brill, 1886.

———. *Stephen Bar Sudhaili, the Syrian Mystic, and the Book of Hierotheos.* Leiden: Brill, 1886.

Gain, Benoît. *L'église de Cappadoce au IVe siècle d'après la correspondance de Basile de Césarée (330–379).* Orientalia Christiana Analecta 225. Roma: Pontificium Institutum Orientale, 1985.

Gallay, Paul, ed. *Discours.* Sources Chrétiennes 250. Paris: Éditions du Cerf, 1978.

———, ed. *Grégoire de Nazianze: Lettres.* 2 vols. Collection des universités de France. Paris: Les Belles lettres, 1964.

Gamble, Harry Y. *Books and Readers in the Early Church: A History of Early Christian Texts.* New Haven: Yale University Press, 1995.

Gebhardt, Oscar von, and Ernest Cushing Richardson, eds. *Hieronymus liber* De viris inlustribus*; Gennadius liber* De viris inlustribus. Texte und Untersuchungen zur Geschichte der altchristlichen Literatur 14.1. Leipzig: J. C. Hinrichs, 1896.

Géhin, Paul, ed. *Chapitres des disciples d'Évagre.* Sources Chrétiennes 514. Paris: Éditions du Cerf, 2007.

———. "Les collections de *kephalaia* monastiques: Naissance et succès d'un genre entre création originale, plagiat et florilège." In *The Minor Genres of Byzantine Theological Literature*, edited by Antonio Rigo, 1–50. Studies in Byzantine History and Civilization 8. Turnhout: Brepols, 2013.

———. "D'Égypte en Mésopotamie: La réception d'Évagre le Pontique dans les communautés syriaques." In *Monachismes d'Orient: Images, échanges, influences; hommage à Antoine Guillaumont; cinquantenaire de la chaire des "Christianismes orientaux," EPHE SR*, edited by Florence Jullien and Marie-Joseph Pierre, 29–49. Bibliothèque de l'École des hautes études. Section des sciences religieuses 148. Turnhout: Brepols, 2011.

———. "En marge de la constitution d'un repertorium Evagrianum Syriacum: Quelques remarques sur l'organisation en corpus des oeuvres d'Évagre." *Parole de l'Orient* 35 (2010): 285–301.

———. "Fragments patristiques syriaques des Nouvelles découvertes du Sinai." *Collectanea Christiana Orientalia* 6 (2009): 67–93.

———. "La place de la *Lettre sur la foi* dans l'oeuvre d'Evagre." In *L'epistula fidei di Evagrio Pontico: Temi, contesti, sviluppi; Atti del III convegno del gruppo italiano di ricerca su "Origene e la tradizione alessandrina,"* edited by Paolo Bettiolo, 25–58. Studia Ephemeridis Augustinianum 72. Rome: Institutum Patristicum Augustinianum, 2000.

———. "La tradition arabe d'Évagre le Pontique." *Collectanea Christiana Orientalia* 3 (2006): 83–104.

———. "Le Filocalie che hanno preceduto la 'Filocalia.'" In *Nicodemo l'Aghiorita e la Philocalia*, edited by Antonio Rigo, 83–102. Magnano: Edizioni Qiqajon-Monastero di Bose, 2002.

———. "Les versions syriaques et arabes des *Chapitres sur la prière* d'Évagre le Pontique: Quelques données nouvelles." In *Les Syriques transmetteurs de civilisations: L'expérience du Bilâd El-Shâm à l'époque omeyyade*, Al-Ṭabʿah 1., 181–97. Actes du Colloque 9. Anṭilyās: Markaz al-Dirāsāt wa-al-Abḥāth al-Mashriqīyah, al-Jāmiʿah al-Anṭūnīyah, 2005.

———. "Nouveaux fragments grecs des lettres d'Évagre." *Revue d'Histoire des Textes* 24 (1994): 117–47.

———. "Reconstitution et datation d'un recueil syriaque melkite (Ambr. A 296 inf., ff. 22-224 + Sinaï syr. 10)." *Rivista di Studi Byzantini e Neoellenici* 42 (2005): 51–68.

———, ed. *Scholies aux Proverbes*. Paris: Éditions du Cerf, 1987.

Géhin, Paul, Claire Guillaumont, and Antoine Guillaumont, eds. *Sur les pensées*. Sources Chrétiennes 438. Paris: Éditions du Cerf, 1998.

Gill, Christopher. *The Structured Self in Hellenistic and Roman Thought*. Oxford: Oxford University Press, 2006.

Goehring, James E. "Monastic Diversity and Ideological Boundaries in Fourth-Century Christian Egypt." *Journal of Early Christian Studies* 5, no. 1 (1997): 61–84.

Golitzin, Alexander. "'Earthly Angels and Heavenly Men': The Old Testament Pseudepigrapha, Niketas Stethatos, and the Tradition of 'Interiorized Apocalyptic' in Eastern Christian Ascetic and Mystical Literature." *Dumbarton Oaks Papers* 55 (2001): 125–53.

———. "Hierarchy versus Anarchy? Dionysius Areopagita, Symeon the New Theologian, and Nicetas Stethatos, and Their Common Roots in Ascetical Tradition." *St. Vladimir's Theological Quarterly* 38 (1994): 131–79.

———. "The Vision of God and the Form of Glory: More Reflections on the Anthropomorphite Controversy of AD 399." In *Abba: The Tradition of Orthodoxy in the West; Festschrift for Bishop Kallistos (Ware) of Diokleia*, edited by John Behr, Andrew Louth, and Dimitri E. Conomos. Crestwood, NY: St. Vladimir's Seminary Press, 2003.

Gonnet, Dominique. "Liste des oeuvres patristiques traduites du grec en syriaque." In *Les pères grecs dans la tradition syriaque*, edited by Andrea B. Schmidt and Dominique Gonnet, 195–212. Etudes syriaques 4. Paris: Geuthner, 2007.

Gouillard, J. "L'acrostiche spirituel de Théognoste (XIVe s.?)." *Echos d'Orient* 39 (1940): 126–37.

Graf, Georg. *Geschichte der christlichen arabischen Literatur*, vol. 1, *Die Übersetzungen*. Studi e testi 118. Vatican City: Biblioteca apostolica vaticana, 1944.

Gregg, Robert C. "Form in Consolatory Letters, Orations and Sermons." In *Consolation Philosophy: Greek and Christian Paideia in Basil and the Two Gregories*, 51–80. Patristic Monograph Series 3. Cambridge, MA: Philadelphia Patristic Foundation, 1975.

Gribomont, Jean. "Ps.-Basil, Epistula 8." In *Le lettere*, edited by Marcella Forlin Patrucco, 84–112. Corona Patrum 11. Torino: Società editrice internazionale, 1983.

Griffith, Sidney. "Asceticism in the Church of Syria: The Hermeneutics of Early Syrian Monasticism." In *Asceticism*, edited by Vincent L. Wimbush and Richard Valantasis, 220–45. New York: Oxford University Press, 1995.

Grillmeier, Alois. *Jesus der Christus im Glauben der Kirche*, vol. 2.2, *Die Kirche von Konstantinopel im 6. Jahrhundert*. Freiburg im Breisgau: Herder, 1989.

———. *Jesus der Christus im Glauben der Kirche*, vol. 2.3, *Die Kirchen von Jerusalem und Antiochien*. Freiburg im Breisgau: Herder, 2002.

Grosdidier de Matons, Jean. "Trois études sur Léon VI." *Travaux et Mémoires* 5 (1973): 181–242.

Guillaumont, Antoine. "Le rôle des versions orientales dans la récupération de l'oeuvre d'Évagre le Pontique." *Comptes rendus des séances de l'Académie des inscriptions et belles-lettres* 129 (1985): 64–74.

———. *Les "Képhalaia gnostica" d'Évagre le Pontique et l'histoire de l'origénisme chez les grecs et chez les syriens*. Publications de la Sorbonne série Patristica Sorbonensia 5. Paris: Éditions du Seuil, 1962.

———, ed. *Les six centuries des "Kephalaia gnostica": Édition critique de la version syriaque commune et édition d'une nouvelle version syriaque, intégrale, avec une double traduction française*. Patrologia Orientalis 28. Paris: Firmin-Didot, 1958.

———. "Les versions syriaques de l'oeuvre d'Évagre le Pontique et leur rôle dans la formation du vocabulaire ascétique syriaque." *Orientalia Christiana Analecta* 221 (1983): 35–41.

———. *Un philosophe au désert: Evagre le Pontique*. Textes et Traditions 8. Paris: Vrin, 2004.

Guillaumont, Antoine, and Claire Guillaumont, eds. *Le gnostique, ou, A celui qui est devenu digne de la science*. Sources Chrétiennes 356. Paris: Éditions du Cerf, 1989.

———. "Les versions orientales et le texte grec des Lettres d'Evagre le Pontique." *Langues orientales anciennes philologie et linguistique* 3 (1991): 151–62.

Guillaumont, Claire. "Fragments grecs inédits d'Évagre le Pontique." In *Texte und Textkritik: Eine Aufsatzsammlung*, edited by Johannes Irmscher, Franz Paschke, Kurt Treu, and Jürgen Dummer, 209–21. Texte und Untersuchungen zur Geschichte der altchristlichen Literatur 133. Berlin: Akademie-Verlag, 1987.

Guillaumont, Claire, and Antoine Guillaumont, eds. *Traité pratique, ou, Le moine*. 2 vols. Sources Chrétiennes 170–71. Paris: Éditions du Cerf, 1971.

Guy, Jean-Claude, ed. *Les Apophtegmes des Pères: Collection systématique*. 2 vols. Sources Chrétiennes 387 and 474. Paris: Éditions du Cerf, 1993 and 2003.

Haas, Christopher. *Alexandria in Late Antiquity: Topography and Social Conflict*. Baltimore: Johns Hopkins University Press, 1997.

Hage, Wolfgang. *Syriac Christianity in the East*. Mōrān᾽ Eth᾽ō 1. Kottayam: St. Ephrem Ecumenical Research Institute, 1997.

Haldon, John F. "The Works of Anastasius of Sinai: A Key Source for the History of Seventh-Century East Mediterranean Society and Belief." In *The Byzantine and Early Islamic Near East*, vol. 1, *Problems in the Literary Source Material*, edited by Averil Cameron and Lawrence I. Conrad, 107–47. Studies in Late Antiquity and Early Islam 1. Princeton, NJ: Darwin Press, 1992.

Halleux, André de. *Commentaire du prologue johannique (ms. Br. Mus. Add. 14, 534)*. CSCO 380–81, Scriptores Syri, 165 (text), 166 (trans.). Louvain: Secrétariat du CorpusSCO, 1977.

———. *Philoxène de Mabbog: Sa vie, ses écrits, sa théologie*. Dissertationes ad gradum magistri in Facultate Theologica vel in Facultate Iuris Canonici consequendum conscriptae / Universitas Catholica Lovaniensis, ser. 3, no. 8. Louvain: Impr. orientaliste, 1963.

Hammond-Bammel, Caroline P. "The Last Ten Years of Rufinus' Life and the Date of His Move South from Aquileia." *Journal of Theological Studies* 28, no. 2 (1977): 372–429.

Hansbury, Mary, ed. *The Letters of John of Dalyatha*. Texts from Christian Late Antiquity 2. Piscataway, NJ: Gorgias Press, 2006.

Hansen, Günther Christian, ed. *Kirchengeschichte*. Die griechischen christlichen Schriftsteller der ersten Jahrhunderte, n. F. 1. Berlin: Akademie Verlag, 1995.

Harb, Paul. "La conception pneumatique chez Philoxène de Mabbūg." *Meltho* 5, no. 1 (1969): 5–16.

———. "La vie spirituelle selon Philoxène de Mabbūg." Dissertation, L'Université de Strasbourg, Faculté de Théologie Catholique, 1968.

———. "Le rôle exercé par Philoxène de Mabbūg sur l'evolution de la morale dans l'église syrienne." *Parole de l'Orient* 1 (1970): 27–48.

Harb, Paul, and Gabriel Khouri-Sarkis. "L'Attitude de Philoxène de Mabboug à l'égard de la spiritualité 'savante' d'Évagre le Pontique." In *Mémorial Mgr Gabriel Khouri-Sarkis, 1898–1968, fondateur et directeur de l'Orient syrien, 1956–1967: Revue d'étude et de recherches sur les églises de langue syriaque*, 135–55. Louvain: Impr. orientaliste, 1969.

Harmless, William. *Desert Christians: An Introduction to the Literature of Early Monasticism*. Oxford: Oxford University Press, 2004.

———. *Mystics*. Oxford: Oxford University Press, 2008.

Hausherr, Irénée. "Aux origines de la mystique syrienne: Grégoire de Chypre ou Jean de Lycopolis?" *Orientalia Christiana Periodica* 4 (1938): 497–520.

———. "Centuries." *Dictionnaire de Spiritualité*. Paris: G. Beauchesne et ses fils 1932.

———. "Contemplation et sainteté, une remarquable mise au point par Philoxène de Mabboug." *Revue d'Ascétique et de Mystique* 14 (1933): 171–95.

———. "Eulogios—Loukios." *Orientalia Christiana Periodica* 6 (1940): 216–20.

———. "Ignorance infinie ou science infinie?" *Orientalia Christiana Periodica* 25 (1959): 44–52.

———. "Le *De Oratione* d'Évagre le Pontique en Syriaque et en Arabe." *Orientalia Christiana Periodica* 5 (1939): 7–71.

———. "Les grands courants de la spiritualité orientale." *Orientalia Christiana* 11 (1935): 114–38.

———. "Les versions syriaque et arménienne d'Évagre le Pontique, leur valeur, leur situation, leur utilisation." *Orientalia Christiana* 22, no. 2 (1931): 69–118.

———. "L'influence du *Livre de saint Hiérothée*." In *De doctrina spirituali christianorum orientalium: Questiones et scripta*, edited by Irénée Hausherr, 176–211. Orientalia Christiana, 30.3 (no. 86). Rome: Pont. Institutum Orientalium Studiorum, 1933.

———. *Penthos: The Doctrine of Compunction in the Christian East*. Cistercian Studies Series 53. Kalamazoo, MI: Cistercian Publications, 1982.

———. "Spiritualité syrienne: Philoxène de Mabboug en version française." *Orientalia Christiana Periodica* 23, nos. 1–2 (1957): 171–85.

———. "Un grand auteur spirituel retrouvé: Jean d' Apamée." *Orientalia Christiana Periodica* 14 (1948): 3–42.

Henry, René, ed. *Bibliothèque*. 9 vols. Collection des Universités de France. Paris: Société d'édition Les Belles lettres, 1959.

Hermann, Theodor. "Die armenische Überlieferung der Sextussentenzen." *Zeitschrift für Kirchengeschichte* 57 (1938): 217–26.

Hilberg, Isidorus, ed. *Sancti Eusebii Hieronymi Epistulae*. Editio altera supplementis aucta. Vol. 3. Corpus scriptorum ecclesiasticorum latinorum 56. Vienna: Verlag der Österreichischen Akademie der Wissenschaften, 1996.

Holmes, Catherine. "Byzantine Political Culture and Compilation Literature in the Tenth and Eleventh Centuries: Some Preliminary Inquiries." *Dumbarton Oaks Papers* 64 (2010): 55–80.

Hombergen, Daniël. *The Second Origenist Controversy: A New Perspective on Cyril of Scythopolis' Monastic Biographies as Historical Sources for Sixth-Century Origenism*. Studia Anselmiana 132. Rome: Centro studi S. Anselmo, 2001.

Hubler, J. N. "Moderatus, E. R. Dodds, and the Development of Neoplatonist Emanation." In *Plato's Parmenides and Its Heritage: History and Interpretation from the Old Academy to Later Platonism and Gnosticism*, edited by John Douglas Turner and Kevin Corrigan, 115–28. Writings from the Greco-Roman World Supplement Series 2. Atlanta: Society of Biblical Literature, 2010.

Hunter, Erica C. D. "Interfaith Dialogues: The Church of the East and the Abbassids." In *Der christliche Orient und seine Umwelt: Gesammelte Studien zu Ehren Jürgen Tubachs anlässlich seines 60. Geburtstags*, edited by G. Sophia Vashalomidze and Lutz Greisiger, 289–302. Studies in Oriental Religions 56. Wiesbaden: Harrassowitz Verlag, 2007.

Iamblichus. *Iamblichus on the Mysteries*. Edited by Emma C. Clarke, John M. Dillon, and Jackson P. Hershbell. Writings from the Greco-Roman World 4. Atlanta: Society of Biblical Literature, 2003.

Isaac, Bishop of Nineveh. *On Ascetical Life*. Translated by Mary Hansbury. Crestwood, NY: St. Vladimir's Seminary Press, 1989.

Joest, Christoph, ed. *Ad monachos; Ad virginem; Institutio ad monachos = Der Mönchsspiegel; Der Nonnenspiegel; Ermahnungen an Mönche*. Fontes Christiani 51. Freiburg im Breisgau: Herder, 2012.

John Climacus. *Opera Omnia*. Edited by Matthäus Rader. Lutetiae Parisiorum: Sumptibus Sebastiani Cramoisy, 1633.

Julianus the Theurgist, and Ruth Dorothy Majercik. *The Chaldean Oracles: Text, Translation, and Commentary*. Studies in Greek and Roman Religion 5. Leiden: Brill, 1989.

Kalvesmaki, Joel. "Canonical References in Electronic Texts: Rationale and Best Practices." *Digital Humanities Quarterly* 8, no. 2 (2014). http://www.digitalhumanities.org/dhq/vol/8/2/000181/000181.html.

———. "The *Epistula Fidei* of Evagrius of Pontus: An Answer to Constantinople." *Journal of Early Christian Studies* 20, no. 1 (2012): 113–39. doi:10.1353/earl.2012.0001.

———. "The Soul's Cure in Letters: The Death of Gregory of Nazianzus and the Consolation of Evagrius of Pontus." *The American Benedictine Review* 65, no. 2 (June 2014): 135–44.

Kazhdan, Alexander P. *The Oxford Dictionary of Byzantium.* 3 vols. New York: Oxford University Press, 1991.

Kessel, Gregory, Françoise Briquel-Chatonnet, and Muriel Debié. "Sinai Syr. 24 as an Important Witness to the Reception History of Some Syriac Ascetic Texts." In *Sur les pas des araméens Chrétiens: Mélanges offerts à Alain Desreumaux*, edited by F. Briquel Chatonnet and M. Debié, 207–18. Cahiers D'études Syriaques 1. Paris: Geuthner, 2010.

King, Daniel. *The Syriac Versions of the Writings of Cyril of Alexandria: A Study in Translation Technique*. Louvain: Peeters, 2008.

King, Karen L. "Social and Theological Effects of Heresiological Discourse." In *Heresy and Identity in Late Antiquity*, edited by Eduard Iricinschi and Holger M. Zellentin, 28–49. Texte und Studien zum antiken Judentum 119. Tübingen: Mohr Siebeck, 2008.

Kitchen, Robert A. *The Discourses of Philoxenos of Mabbug: A New Translation and Introduction.* Collegeville, MN: Liturgical Press, 2013.

———. "Yoḥannan Iḥidaya." In *The Gorgias Encyclopedic Dictionary of the Syriac Heritage*, 1st ed., edited by Sebastian P. Brock et al., 442. Piscataway, NJ: Gorgias Press, 2011.

Klimkeit, Hans-Joachim, and Ian Gillman. *Christians in Asia before 1500.* Richmond: Curzon, 1999.

Koetschau, Paul, ed. *Origenes Werke*, vol. 5, *De principiis.* Die griechischen christlichen Schriftsteller der ersten drei Jahrhunderte 22. Leipzig: J.C. Hinrichs, 1913.

Konstantinovsky, Julia. "Evagrius in the Philocalia of Sts Macarius and Nicodemus." Forthcoming.

———. *Evagrius Ponticus: The Making of a Gnostic.* Ashgate New Critical Thinking in Religion, Theology, and Biblical Studies. Burlington, VT: Ashgate, 2009.

———. "Evagrius Ponticus on Being Good in God and Christ." *Studies in Christian Ethics* 26, no. 3 (2013): 317–32.

Krausmüller, Dirk. "Aristotelianism and the Disintegration of the Late Antique Theological Discourse." In *Interpreting the Bible and Aristotle: Christian and Late Platonist Commentary between Rome and Bukhara*, edited by Josef Lössl and J.W. Watt, 151–64. Farnham: Ashgate, 2011.

———. "Conflicting Anthropologies in the Christological Discourse at the End of Late Antiquity: The Case of Leontius of Jerusalem's Nestorian Adversary." *Journal of Theological Studies* 56 (2005): 413–47.

———. "Dating John of Carpathus to the Sixth Century: A Textual Parallel Between His Capita Hortatoria and the Pandectes of Antiochus of St. Sabas." *Gouden Hoorn* 7, no. 1 (1999): 7–13.

———. "Divine Genus—Divine Species: John Philoponus' Impact on Contemporary Chalcedonian Theology." In *The Mystery of Christ in the Fathers of the Church: Essays in Honour of D. Vincent Twomey SVD*, edited by Janet Elaine Rutherford and David Woods, 94–105. Dublin: Four Courts Press, 2011.

———. "Human Souls as Consubstantial Son of God: The Heterodox Anthropology of Leontius of Jerusalem." *Journal of Late Antique Religion and Culture* 4 (2010): 43–67.

———. "Leontius of Jerusalem, a Theologian of the Seventh Century." *Journal of Theological Studies* 52 (2001): 637–57.

———. "Origenism in the Sixth Century: Leontius of Byzantium on the Pre-Existence of the Soul." *Journal of Late Antique Religion and Culture* 8 (2014): 46–67.

Lackner, Wolfgang. "Zu Quellen und Datierung der Maximosvita (BHG3, 1234)." *Analecta Bollandiana* 86 (1968): 285–316.

Lamberton, Robert. *Homer the Theologian: Neoplatonist Allegorical Reading and the Growth of the Epic Tradition.* Transformation of the Classical Heritage 9. Berkeley: University of California Press, 1986.

Lang, Uwe Michael. *John Philoponus and the Controversies over Chalcedon in the Sixth Century: A Study and Translation of the Arbiter.* Spicilegium Sacrum Lovaniense. Etudes et Documents 47. Louvain: Peeters, 2001.

Larchet, Jean-Claude. *La divinisation de l'homme selon Saint Maxime le Confesseur.* Cogitatio Fidei 194. Paris: Éditions du Cerf, 1996.

Lavenant, René. *La lettre à Patrikios de Philoxène de Mabboug.* Patrologia Orientalis 30.5. Paris: Firmin-Didot, 1963.

Leclercq, Henri, and Fernand Cabrol, eds. *Dictionnaire d'archéologie chrétienne et de liturgie.* 15 vols. Paris: Letouzey et Ané, 1907.

Leclercq, Jean. "L'ancienne version latine des Sentences d'Évagre pour les moines." *Scriptorium* 5 (1951): 195–213.

———. *The Love of Learning and the Desire for God: A Study of Monastic Culture.* New York: Fordham University Press, 1961.

Lemoine, Eugène. *Philoxène de Mabboug, Homélies.* Nouv. éd. revue / par René Lavenant. Sources Chretiénnes 44. Paris: Éditions du Cerf, 2007.

Leutsch, Ernst von, and Friedrich Wilhelm Schneidewin. *Corpus Paroemiographorum Graecorum.* Göttingen: Vandenhoeck et Ruprecht, 1839.

Lewis, Agnes Smith. *Catalogue of the Syriac Mss. in the Convent of S. Catharine on Mount Sinai.* Studia Sinaitica 1. London: C. J. Clay, 1894.

Liddell, Henry George, Robert Scott, Henry Stuart Jones, and Roderick McKenzie. *A Greek-English Lexicon.* 9th ed., rev. and augm. Oxford: Clarendon Press, 1996.

Lloyd, A. C. *The Anatomy of Neoplatonism.* Oxford: Clarendon Press, 1990.

Lollard, Joshua. *To See into the Life of Things: The Contemplation of Nature in Maximus the Confessor and His Predecessors.* Monothéismes et Philosophie: Collection Diregée par Carlos Lévy. Turnhout: Brepols, 2013.

Loofs, Friedrich. *Leontius von Byzanz und die gleichnamigen Schriftsteller der griechischen Kirche: Erstes Buch, das Leben und die polemischen Werke des Leontius von Byzanz.* Leipzig: J. C. Hinrichs, 1887.

Lossky, Vladimir. *The Mystical Theology of the Eastern Church.* London: J. Clarke, 2005.

Luibheid, Colum, and Norman Russell, trans. *John Klimakos, The Ladder of Divine Ascent.* Classics of Western Spirituality. New York: Paulist Press, 1982.

MacIntyre, Alasdair C. *After Virtue: A Study in Moral Theory.* 3rd ed. Notre Dame, IN: University of Notre Dame Press, 2007.

Marchini, Diego. "La tradizione latina del *De octo spiritibus malitiae* di Evagrio Pontico." In *Origeniana nona: Origen and the Religious Practice of His Time; Papers of the 9th International Origen Congress, Pécs, Hungary, 29 August–2 September 2005*, edited by György Heidl and Róbert Somos, 565–75. Bibliotheca Ephemeridum Theologicarum Lovaniensium 228. Louvain: Peeters, 2009.

Markopoulos, A. "Autour des chapitres parénétiques de Basil 1er." In *Eupsychia: Mélanges Offerts à Hélène Ahrweiler*, edited by Michel Balard. Publications de la Sorbonne. Série Byzantina Sorbonensia 16. Paris: Publications de la Sorbonne, 1998.

Marsili, Salvatore. *Giovanni Cassiano ed Evagrio Pontico: Dottrina sulla carità e contemplazione.* Studia Anselmiana philosophica, theologica 5. Rome: Herder, 1936.

Maximus the Confessor. *The Ascetic Life: The Four Centuries on Charity.* Translated by Polycarp Sherwood. Ancient Christian Writers 21. Westminster, MD: Newman Press, 1955.

McGuckin, John Anthony. *St. Gregory of Nazianzus: An Intellectual Biography.* Crestwood, NY: St. Vladimir's Seminary Press, 2001.

Méhat, André. *Étude sur les "Stromates" de Clément d'Alexandrie.* Patristica Sorbonensia 7. Paris: Éditions du Seuil, 1966.

Michelson, David A. "A Bibliographic Clavis to the Works of Philoxenos of Mabbug." *Hugoye* 13, no. 2 (2010): 273–338.

———. "'It Is Not the Custom of Our Syriac Language . . .': Reconsidering the Role of Translation in the Polemics of Philoxenos of Mabbug." In *Shifting Cultural Frontiers in Late Antiquity*, edited by David Brakke, Deborah Deliyannis, and Edward Watts, 7–21. Burlington, VT: Ashgate, 2012.

———. *The Practical Christology of Philoxenos of Mabbug*. Oxford: Oxford University Press, 2014.

Migne, J.-P., ed. *Patrologiae cursus completus, Series graeca*. Paris, 1857.

Moffett, Samuel H. *A History of Christianity in Asia*, vol. 1, *Beginnings to 1500*. American Society of Missiology Series 36. San Francisco: Harper-San Francisco, 1992.

Montgomery, James A. *The History of Yaballaha III, Nestorian Patriarch, and of His Vicar, Bar Sauma, Mongol Ambassador to the Frankish Courts at the End of the Thirteenth Century*. Records of Civilization, Sources and Studies 8. New York: Columbia University Press, 1927.

Mortley, Raoul. *From Word to Silence*. Theophaneia 30–31. Bonn: Hanstein, 1986.

Mühmelt, Martin. "Zu der neuen lateinischen Übersetzung des Mönchsspiegels des Euagrius." *Vigiliae Christianae* 8 (1954): 101–3.

Munitiz, Joseph A. "Anastasios of Sinai's Teaching on Body and Soul." In *Desire and Denial in Byzantium: Papers from the 31st Spring Symposium of Byzantine Studies, University of Sussex, Brighton, March 1997*, edited by Liz James, 49–56. Publications (Society for the Promotion of Byzantine Studies) 6. Aldershot: Ashgate, 1999.

———. "Leo of Ohrid: The New *Kephalaia*." *Orientalia Christiana Periodica* 76, no. 1 (2010): 121–44.

Muravjev, Alexej. "Macarian or Evagrian: The Problem of Origenist Legacy in Eastern Syriac Mystical Literature." In *Origeniana octava: Origen and the Alexandrian Tradition = Origene E La Tradizione Alessandrina: Papers of the 8th International Origen Congress, Pisa, 27–31 August 2001*, edited by Lorenzo Perrone, P. Bernardino, and D. Marchini, 1185–91. Bibliotheca Ephemeridum Theologicarum Lovaniensium 164. Leuven: Leuven University Press, 2003.

Murre-van den Berg, Heleen. "The Church of the East in Mesopotamia in the Mongol Period." In *Jingjiao: The Church of the East in China and Central Asia*, edited by Roman Malek and Peter Hofrichter. Collectanea Serica. Sankt Augustin: Institut Monumenta Serica, 2006.

Muyldermans, Joseph. "Evagriana." *Le Muséon: Revue d'Études Orientales* 44 (1931): 37–68.

———, ed. *Evagriana syriaca: Textes inedits du British Museum et de la Vaticane*. Bibliothèque du Muséon 31. Louvain: Publications universitaires, 1952.

———. "Le discours de Xystus dans la version arménienne d'Évagre le Pontique." *Revue des Études Arméniennes* 9 (1929): 183–201.

———. "*Sur les séraphins* et *Sur les chérubins* d'Évagre le Pontique dans les versions syriaque et arménienne." *Le Muséon: Revue d'Études Orientales* 59 (1946): 367–79.

———. "Une nouvelle recension du *De octo spiritibus malitiae* de S. Nil." *Le Muséon: Revue d'Études Orientales* 52 (1939): 235–74.

Neil, Bronwen. "The Lives of Pope Martin I and Maximus the Confessor: Some Reconsiderations of Dating and Provenance." *Byzantion* 68 (1998): 91–109.

Nicodemus the Hagiorite and Saint Makarios, eds. *The Philokalia: The Complete Text*. Translated by G. E. H. Palmer, Philip Sherrard, and Kallistos Ware. London: Faber and Faber, 1979.

———. *Φιλοκαλία τῶν νηπτικῶν συνερανισθεῖσα παρὰ τῶν ἁγίων καὶ θεοφόρων πατέρων ἡμῶν ἐν ᾗ διὰ τῆς κατὰ τὴν Πρᾶξιν καὶ Θεωρίαν Ἠθικῆς Φιλοσοφίας ὁ νοῦς καθαίρεται, φωτίζεται, καὶ τελετοῦται*. 3rd ed. 5 vols. Athens: Ἀστήρ, 1957.

Niculescu, Vlad. "Coping with the Grief of Ignorance: Evagrius Ponticus's Hermeneutics of the Distance between God and Humanity." *Arches: Revue internationale des sciences humaines* 7 (2004). http://www.arches.ro/revue/no07/no7art10.htm.

Nutton, Vivian. *On My Own Opinions*. Corpus Medicorum Graecorum 5, pt. 3, fasc. 2. Berlin: Akademie Verlag, 1999.

Odorico, Paolo. "Les miroirs des princes à Byzance: Une lecture horizontale." *Autour de Byzance* 1 (2009): 223–46.

O'Laughlin, Michael. "Origenism in the Desert: Anthropology and Integration in Evagrius Ponticus." PhD dissertation, Harvard Divinity School, 1987.

O'Meara, Dominic J. *Pythagoras Revived: Mathematics and Philosophy in Late Antiquity*. Oxford: Clarendon Press, 1989.

Origen. *Commentaire sur le Cantique des cantiques*. Edited by Luc Brésard, Henri Crouzel, and Marcel Borret. Sources Chrétiennes 375–76. Paris: Éditions du Cerf, 1991.

———. *Traité des principes*. Edited by Henri Crouzel. 5 vols. Sources Chrétiennes 252–53, 268–69, 312. Paris: Éditions du Cerf, 1978.

———. *Vier Bücher von den Prinzipien*. Edited by Herwig Görgemanns and Heinrich Karpp. 1. Aufl. Texte zur Forschung 24. Darmstadt: Wissenschaftliche Buchgesellschaft, 1976.

Otis, Brooks. "Cappadocian Thought as a Coherent System." *Dumbarton Oaks Papers* 12 (1958): 97–124.

Papadopoulos-Kerameus, Athanasios. *Varia graeca sacra: Sbornik grečeskich neizdannych bogoslovskich tekstov IV–XV vekov*. Editionem phototypicam. Subsidia Byzantina lucis ope iterata 6. Leipzig: Zentralantiquariat der Deutschen Demokratischen Republik, 1975.

Parmentier, M. "Evagrius of Pontus' *Letter to Melania*." *Bijdragen* 46 (1985): 2–38.

Payne Smith, Jessie, and Robert Payne Smith. *A Compendious Syriac Dictionary: Founded upon the Thesaurus Syriacus of R. Payne Smith*. Oxford: Clarendon Press, 1903.

Perczel, István. "The Earliest Syriac Reception of Dionysius." *Modern Theology* 24, no. 4 (2008): 557–71.

Petschenig, Michael, ed. *Iohannis Cassiani Conlationes XXIIII*. Corpus scriptorum ecclesiasticorum latinorum 13. Vienna: C. Geroldi filium, 1886.

Philothea, Mother. *Nouveaux manuscrits syriaques du Sinaï*. Athens: Fondation du Mont Sinaï, 2008.

Phrantzolas, Konstantinos G. *Ὁσίου Ἐφραίμ τοῦ Σύρου ἔργα*. 6 vols. Thessalonica: To Perivoli tis Panagias, 1988.

Pinggera, Karl. *All-Erlösung und All-Einheit: Studien zum "Buch des heiligen Hierotheos" und seiner Rezeption in der syrisch-orthodoxen Theologie*. Sprachen und Kulturen des christlichen Orients 10. Wiesbaden: Reichert, 2002.

Pitra, J. B. *Analecta Sacra Spicilegio Solesmensi Parata*. Paris: A. Jouby et Roger, 1876.

Price, Richard. *The Acts of the Council of Constantinople of 553: With Related Texts on the Three Chapters Controversy*. 2 vols. Translated Texts for Historians 51. Liverpool: Liverpool University Press, 2009.

Rapp, Claudia. *Holy Bishops in Late Antiquity: The Nature of Christian Leadership in an Age of Transition*. Berkeley: University of California Press, 2005.

Rashīd al-Dīn Ṭabīb. *The Successors of Genghis Khan*. Translated by John Andrew Boyle. Persian Heritage Series 10. New York: Columbia University Press, 1971.

Rasimus, T. "Porphyry and the Gnostics: Reassessing Pierre Hadot's Thesis in Light of the Second- and Third-Century Sethian Treatises." In *Plato's "Parmenides" and Its Heritage: Reception in Patristic, Gnostic, and Christian Neoplatonic Texts*, edited by John Douglas Turner and Kevin Corrigan, 81–110. Writings from the Greco-Roman World Supplement Series 3. Atlanta: Society of Biblical Literature, 2010.

Rawls, John, and J. L. Mackie. *Ethics: Inventing Right and Wrong*. Harmondsworth: Penguin, 1977.

Refoulé, François. "La date de la lettre à Évagre (P. G. 46, 1101–1108)." *Recherches de Science Religieuse* 49 (1961): 520–48.

Reiter, Siegfried, ed. *Sancti Evsebii Hieronymi In Hieremiam prophetam libri sex*. Corpus scriptorum ecclesiasticorum latinorum 59. Vienna: F. Tempsky, 1913.

Rich, Antony D. *Discernment in the Desert Fathers: Diákrisis in the Life and Thought of Early Egyptian Monasticism*. Studies in Christian History and Thought. Milton Keynes: Paternoster, 2007.

Richard, Marcel, and Joseph A. Munitiz. *Anastasii Sinaitae Quaestiones et responsiones*. CCSG 59. Turnhout: Brepols, 2006.

Riedinger, Rudolf, ed. *Der Fürstenspiegel für Kaiser Iustinianus*. Kentron Ereunēs Vyzantiou 4. Athens: Hetaireia Philōn tou Laou, 1995.

Roey, A. van, Lionel R. Wickham, and R. Y. Ebied. *Peter of Callinicum: Anti-Tritheist Dossier*. Orientalia Lovaniensia Analecta 10. Leuven: Departement Oriëntalistiek, 1981.

Rorty, Richard. *Consequences of Pragmatism: Essays, 1972–1980*. Minneapolis: University of Minnesota Press, 1982.

———. *Philosophy and Social Hope*. New York: Penguin Books, 1999.

Rossabi, Morris. *Voyager from Xanadu: Rabban Sauma and the First Journey from China to the West*. 1st ed. Tokyo: Kodansha International, 1992.

Roth, Catharine P., ed. *The Soul and the Resurrection*. Crestwood, NY: St. Vladimir's Seminary Press, 1993.

Roueché, Charlotte. "The Literary Background of Kekaumenos." In *Literacy, Education and Manuscript Transmission in Byzantium and Beyond*, edited by Catherine Holmes and Judith Waring. Medieval Mediterranean 42. Leiden: Brill, 2002.

———. "The Place of Kekaumenos in the Admonitory Tradition." *Autour de Byzance* 1 (2009): 129–44.

Rufinus of Aquileia. *Historia monachorum, sive, De vita sanctorum patrum*. Edited by Eva Schulz-Flügel. Patristische Texte und Studien 34. Berlin: W. De Gruyter, 1990.

Russell, Norman. *The Doctrine of Deification in the Greek Patristic Tradition*. Oxford Early Christian Studies. Oxford: Oxford University Press, 2004.

———. *Theophilus of Alexandria*. The Early Church Fathers. London: Routledge, 2007.

Rutherford, Janet Elaine, ed. *One Hundred Practical Texts of Perception and Spiritual Discernment from Diadochos of Photike*. Belfast Byzantine Texts and Translations 8. Belfast: Belfast Byzantine Enterprises, Institute of Byzantine Studies, the Queen's University of Belfast, 2000.

Samir, Khalil. "Évagre le Pontique dans la tradition arabo-copte." In *Actes du IVe Congrès copte: Louvain-la-Neuve, 5–10 septembre 1988*, edited by Marguerite Rassart-Debergh and Julien Ries, 2:125–53. Publications de l'Institut Orientaliste de Louvain 40. Louvain-la-Neue: Université catholique de Louvain, 1992.

Sargisean, Barsegh, ed. *Vark' ew matenagrut'iwnk': T'argmanealk' i hunē i hay barbaṙ i E. daru [The Life and Works of the Holy Father Evagrius Ponticus in an Armenian Version of the Fifth Century, with Introduction and Notes].* Venice: S. Ghazar, 1907.

Scher, Addai. "Joseph Hazzâyâ écrivain syriaque du VIIIe siècle." *Rivista degli Studi Orientali* 3 (1910): 45–63.

———. "Notice sur les manuscrits syriaques et arabes conservés à l'Archevêché Chaldéen de Diarbékir [part 1]." *Journal Asiatique*, ser. 10, vol. 10 (1907): 331–62.

———. "Notice sur les manuscrits syriaques et arabes conservés à l'Archevêché Chaldéen de Diarbékir [part 2]." *Journal Asiatique*, ser. 10, vol. 10 (1907): 385–432.

Schwartz, Eduard. *Collectio Sabbaitica contra acephalos et origeniastas destinata: Insunt acta synodorum Constantinopolitanae et Hierosolymitanae A. 536*. Acta Conciliorum Oecumenicorum 3. Berlin: W. de Gruyter, 1940.

Simeon the New Theologian. *Chapitres théologiques, gnostiques et pratiques.* Edited by Jean Darrouzès and Louis Neyrand. 2nd ed. Sources Chrétiennes 51bis. Paris: Éditions du Cerf, 1980.

Sims-Williams, Nicholas. *The Christian Sogdian Manuscript C2*. Schriften zur Geschichte und Kultur des alten orients. Berliner Turfantexte 12. Berlin: Akademie-Verlag, 1985.

Sinkewicz, Robert E., ed. *Evagrius of Pontus: The Greek Ascetic Corpus*. Oxford: Oxford University Press, 2003.

Slaveva-Griffin, Svetla. *Plotinus on Number*. Oxford: Oxford University Press, 2009.

Sorabji, Richard. *Emotion and Peace of Mind: From Stoic Agitation to Christian Temptation*. Oxford: Oxford University Press, 2000.

Stählin, Otto, ed. *Clemens Alexandrinus*. 3., durchgesehene Aufl. Die griechischen christlichen Schriftsteller der ersten Jahrhunderte 12, 15, 17, 39. Berlin: Akademie-Verlag, 1936.

Stefaniw, Blossom. *Mind, Text, and Commentary: Noetic Exegesis in Origen of Alexandria, Didymus the Blind, and Evagrius Ponticus*. Early Christianity in the Context of Antiquity 6. Frankfurt am Main: Lang, 2010.

Stewart, Columba. "Another Cassian?" *Journal of Ecclesiastical History* 66 (2015): 372–76.

———. *Cassian the Monk*. Oxford Studies in Historical Theology. New York: Oxford University Press, 1998.

———. "Evagrius Ponticus and the Eastern Monastic Tradition on the Intellect and the Passions." *Modern Theology* 27, no. 2 (April 2011): 263–75. doi:10.1111/j.1468-0025.2010.01675.x.

———. "Evagrius Ponticus on Monastic Pedagogy." In *Abba: The Tradition of Orthodoxy in the West; Festschrift for Bishop Kallistos (Ware) of Diokleia*, edited by John Behr, Andrew Louth, and Dimitri E. Conomos, 241–71. Crestwood, NY: St. Vladimir's Seminary Press, 2003.

———. "Imageless Prayer and the Theological Vision of Evagrius Ponticus." *Journal of Early Christian Studies* 9, no. 2 (2001): 173–204.

———. "John Cassian's Schema of Eight Principal Faults and His Debt to Origen and Evagrius." In *Jean Cassien entre l'orient et l'occident: Actes du colloque international organisé par le New Europe College en collaboration avec la Ludwig Boltzman Gesellschaft, Bucarest, 27–28 Septembre 2001*, edited by Cristian Bădiliță and Attila Jakab, 205–19. Paris: Beauchesne, 2003.

Straw, Carole. "Gregory, Cassian, and the Cardinal Vices." In *In the Garden of Evil: The Vices and Culture in the Middle Ages*, edited by Richard Newhauser, 35–58. Papers in Mediaeval Studies 18. Toronto: Pontifical Institute of Mediaeval Studies, 2005.

Takahashi, Hidemi. *Barhebraeus: A Bio-Bibliography*. 1st ed. Piscataway, NJ: Gorgias Press, 2005.

Taylor, Charles. *A Secular Age*. Cambridge, MA: Belknap Press of Harvard University Press, 2007.

———. *Sources of the Self: The Making of the Modern Identity*. Cambridge, MA: Harvard University Press, 1989.

Teule, Herman. "L'Échelle du Paradis dans la tradition syriaque: Premières investigations." *Parole de l'Orient* 20 (1995): 279–93.

———. "Les compilations monastiques syriaques." In *Symposium Syriacum VII: Uppsala University, Department of Asian and African Languages, 11–14 August 1996*, edited by René Lavenant, 249–64. Orientalia Christiana Analecta 256. Rome: Pontificio Istituto Orientale, 1998.

Thomas, John, and Angela Constantinides Hero. *Byzantine Monastic Foundation Documents: A Complete Translation of the Surviving Founders' Typika and Testaments.* 5 vols. Dumbarton Oaks Studies. Washington, DC: Dumbarton Oaks Research Library and Collection, 2001.

Thunberg, Lars. *Microcosm and Mediator: The Theological Anthropology of Maximus the Confessor.* 2nd ed. Chicago: Open Court, 1995.

Tollefsen, Torstein. *The Christocentric Cosmology of St. Maximus the Confessor.* Oxford: Oxford University Press, 2008.

Törönen, Melchisedec. *Union and Distinction in the Thought of St. Maximus the Confessor.* Oxford Early Christian Studies. Oxford: Oxford University Press, 2007.

Tugwell, Simon, ed. *Praktikos and On Prayer.* Oxford: Faculty of Theology, 1987.

Turner, John Douglas. "The Platonizing Sethian Treatises, Marius Victorinus's Philosophical Sources, and Pre-Plotinian *Parmenides* Commentaries." In *Plato's Parmenides and Its Heritage: History and Interpretation from the Old Academy to Later Platonism and Gnosticism*, edited by John Douglas Turner and Kevin Corrigan, 131–72. Writings from the Greco-Roman World Supplement Series 2. Atlanta: Society of Biblical Literature, 2010.

Uthemann, Karl-Heinz. *Anastasii Sinaitae Sermones duo in constitutionem hominis secundum imaginem Dei: Necnon, Opuscula adversus monotheletas.* CCSG 12. Turnhout: Brepols, 1985.

Van Rompay, Lucas. "Sṭephanos bar Ṣudayli." In *The Gorgias Encyclopedic Dictionary of the Syriac Heritage*, 1st ed., edited by Sebastian P. Brock, Aaron Michael Butts, George Anton Kiraz, and Lucas Van Rompay, 384. Piscataway, NJ: Gorgias Press, 2011.

Vaschalde, Arthur Adolphe, ed. *Mar Babai: Liber de unione.* CSCO, Scriptores Syri 34–35. Rome: K. de Luigi, 1915.

Vitestam, Gösta. *Seconde partie du traité, qui passe sous le nom de "La grande lettre d'Évagre le Pontique à Mélanie l'Ancienne."* Scripta minora Regiae Societatis Humaniorum Litterarum Lundensis 3. Lund: Gleerup, 1964.

Vivian, Tim. *Four Desert Fathers: Pambo, Evagrius, Macarius of Egypt, and Macarius of Alexandria: Coptic Texts Relating to the Lausiac History of Palladius.* Popular Patristics. Crestwood, NY: St. Vladimir's Seminary Press, 2004.

Vogüé, Adalbert de. "Un morceau célèbre de Cassien parmi des extraits d'Évagre." *Studia Monastica* 27 (1985): 7–12.

von Ivánka, E. "ΚΕΦΑΛΑΙΑ: Eine Byzantinische Literaturform und ihre antiken Wurzeln." *Byzantinische Zeitschrift* 47 (1954): 285–91.

Vosté, J.-M. "Recueil d'auteurs ascétiques nestoriens." *Angelicum* 6 (1929): 143–206.

Warner, Michael, Jonathan VanAntwerpen, and Craig J. Calhoun. *Varieties of Secularism in a Secular Age*. Cambridge, MA: Harvard University Press, 2010.

Watt, John W. "Philoxenus and the Old Syriac Version of Evagrius' *Centuries*." *Oriens Christianus* 64 (1980): 65–81.

———. *Philoxenus of Mabbug: Fragments of the Commentary on Matthew and Luke*. CSCO 392–93, Scriptores Syri, 171 (text), 172 (translation). Louvain: Secrétariat du CorpusSCO, 1978.

———. "The Syriac Adapter of Evagrius' *Centuries*." *Studia Patristica* 17, no. 3 (1982): 1388–95.

Wensinck, Arent Jan. *Bar Hebraeus's Book of the Dove: Together with Some Chapters from His Ethikon*. Leiden: Brill, 1919.

Westerink, Leendert Gerrit, ed. *Arethae archiepiscopi Caesariensis Scripta minora*. 2 vols. Bibliotheca scriptorum Graecorum et Romanorum Teubneriana. Leipzig: Teubner, 1968.

Wilmart, André. "La fausse lettre latine de Macaire." *Revue d'ascetique et de mystique* 3 (1922): 411–19.

Wright, William. *Catalogue of Syriac Manuscripts in the British Museum Acquired since the Year 1838*. London: British Museum, 1870.

Young, Robin Darling. "The Armenian Adaptation of Evagrius' *Kephalaia Gnostica*." In *Origeniana Quinta: Historica, Text and Method, Biblica, Philosophica, Theologica, Origenism and Later Developments; Papers of the 5th International Origen Congress, Boston College, 14–18 August 1989*, by Robert J. Daly, 535–41. Bibliotheca Ephemeridum Theologicarum Lovaniensium 105. Leuven: Leuven University Press, 1992.

———. "Cannibalism and Other Family Woes in Letter 55 of Evagrius of Pontus." In *The World of Early Egyptian Christianity: Language, Literature, and Social Context; Essays in Honor of David W. Johnson*, edited by James E. Goehring and Janet Timbie, 130–39. CUA Studies in Early Christianity. Washington, DC: Catholic University of America Press, 2007.

———. "Evagrius the Iconographer: Monastic Pedagogy in the *Gnostikos*." *Journal of Early Christian Studies* 1 (2001): 53–71.

———. "The Influence of Evagrius of Pontus on the Early Monastic Thought of Philoxenos of Mabbug." In *To Train His Soul in Books: Syriac Asceticism in Early Christianity*, edited by Monica J. Blanchard and Robin Darling Young, 157–75. CUA Studies in Early Christianity. Washington, DC: Catholic University of America Press, 2011.

———. "The Path to Contemplation in Evagrius' Letters." *Studia Patristica* 57 (2013): 75–86.

Zonta, Mauro. "Syriac, Hebrew and Latin Encyclopedias in the Thirteenth Century: A Comparative Perspective." In *Was ist Philosophie im Mittelalter? = Qu'est-ce que la philosophie au Moyen Âge? = What Is Philosophy in the Middle Ages? Akten des X. Internationalen Kongresses für mittelalterliche Philosophie der Société Internationale pour l'Étude de la Philosophie Médiévale, 25. bis 30. August 1997 in Erfurt*, edited by Jan Aertsen and Andreas Speer. Miscellanea mediaevalia 26. Berlin: W. de Gruyter, 1998.

CONTRIBUTORS

GREGORY COLLINS, OSB, is the abbot of Dormition Abbey in Jerusalem. A scholar in Byzantine studies, Collins previously taught at the Benedictine university of Sant' Anselmo in Rome. Among his publications are *The Glenstal Book of Icons* (2002) and *Meeting Christ in His Mysteries: A Benedictine Vision of the Spiritual Life* (2011).

KEVIN CORRIGAN, Director of the Emory University Graduate Institute of the Liberal Arts and the Samuel Candler Dobbs Professor of Interdisciplinary Humanities, specializes in ancient philosophy, particularly Neoplatonism. Among his writings are *Evagrius and Gregory: Mind, Soul, and Body in the Fourth Century* (2009) and *Reason, Faith and Otherness in Neoplatonic and Early Christian Thought* (2013). He co-edited *Gnosticism, Platonism and the Late Ancient World: Essays in Honour of John D. Turner* (2013); *Religion and Philosophy in the Platonic and Neoplatonic Traditions: From Antiquity to the Early Medieval Period* (2012); and *Plato's Parmenides and Its Heritage* (2011).

BRIAN E. DALEY, SJ, is the Catherine F. Huisking Professor of Theology at the University of Notre Dame, where he teaches patristic theology, focusing on the subject of Christology and the thinkers Gregory of Nazianzus and Maximus the Confessor. Among his chief writings are *The Hope of the Early Church: A Handbook of Patristic Eschatology* (1991) and two collections of translated texts, *On the Dormition of Mary: Eastern Patristic Homilies* (1998) and *Gregory of Nazianzus* (2006).

LUKE DYSINGER, OSB, is a Benedictine monk of Saint Andrew's Abbey, Valyermo, California, and a scholar of Evagrius and early monasticism; his *Psalmody and Prayer in the Writings of Evagrius Ponticus* appeared in 2004. He is professor of church history and moral theology at St. John's

Seminary in Camarillo and also serves as adjunct faculty and teaches at the School of Theology of Saint John's Abbey in Collegeville, Minnesota, and at Loyola-Marymount University. He has published a translation of the Rule of Benedict, as well as articles on Evagrius Ponticus, *lectio divina*, Christian contemplative practices, and other subjects in monastic spirituality.

Joel Kalvesmaki is editor in Byzantine studies at Dumbarton Oaks. His research and scholarship covers intellectual history in late antiquity, with a specific focus on ancient number symbolism and the writings of Evagrius Ponticus. He is the author of *The Theology of Arithmetic: Number Symbolism in Platonism and Early Christianity* (2013) and is the general editor of the reference work *Guide to Evagrius Ponticus*, http://evagriusponticus.net/.

Julia Konstantinovsky's interests are in the thought of Evagrius and of Maximus the Confessor. She is a British Academy Research Fellow at Christ Church, Oxford, and a tutor for the Faculty of Theology. She has written *Evagrius of Pontus: The Making of a Gnostic* (2008), and was assistant editor for *The Encyclopedia of Eastern Orthodox Christianity* (2011).

Dirk Krausmüller is a professor at Mardin Artuklu University with interests in theological and cosmological speculation in early medieval Byzantium; Byzantine concepts of the human person, gender, self-determination, the afterlife, and the communication between the living and the dead; Byzantine hagiography and monasticism; and many other topics of Byzantine intellectual, spiritual, and cultural life. Among his many recent publications is "Biography as Allegory," *Byzantine and Modern Greek Studies* 37 (2013): 161–75.

David A. Michelson is assistant professor of the history of Christianity at Vanderbilt University. As a historian of Middle Eastern and Mediterranean Christianity, he is interested in how the methods of the digital humanities can aid the study of late antiquity. Michelson is the author of *The Practical Christology of Philoxenos of Mabbug* (2014) and co-editor of The Syriac Gazetteer (2014). He is currently preparing a book titled *Diligent and Angelic Readers: A History of Syriac Christian*

Literature. He also serves as general editor of Syriaca.org, an online reference work.

BLOSSOM STEFANIW has been, since April 2011, junior professor of ethics in Antiquity and Christianity at the Evangelisch-Theologische Fakultät at Johannes-Gutenberg-Universität Mainz. Her interests lie in the fields of early Christian ethics, asceticism, and biography. She has written *Mind, Text, and Commentary: Noetic Exegesis in Origen of Alexandria, Didymus the Blind, and Evagrius Ponticus* (2010). She is currently writing a book titled *Sages and Their Custodians in Late Antiquity.*

COLUMBA STEWART, OSB, is the current executive director of the Hill Museum and Manuscript Library (HMML) in Collegeville, Minnesota, where he supervises the digitization of largely Christian manuscript collections from Europe, Africa, the Middle East, and India. Stewart has published extensively on Eastern spirituality, with a focus on Evagrius, most notably in his monographs *Working the Earth of the Heart: The Messalian Controversy in History, Texts and Language to 431*, Oxford Theological Monographs (1991) and *Cassian the Monk* (1998).

ANTHONY J. WATSON is associate director of Middle East studies at the Watson Institute for International Studies, and adjunct assistant professor in history (Christian and Islamic history) at Brown University. His recent publications include "Evagrius and the History of Mar Yahaballa: Preliminary Findings on a Virtue Tradition in the Church of the East," in *From the Oxus River to the Chinese Shores*, edited by Li Tang and Dietmar W. Winkler (2013).

ROBIN DARLING YOUNG is associate professor at the Catholic University of America. Her interests lie in the history of Eastern Christianity; she has translated works from Armenian and Syriac, and is currently preparing an annotated translation of the *Letters of Evagrius of Pontus* from the surviving Syriac translation for the Fathers of the Church series, and convening a translation team (with Luke Dysinger, Joel Kalvesmaki, Charles Stang, and Columba Stewart) to produce English translations from the Greek texts and Syriac translations of the same author's gnostic trilogy (*Praktikos*, *Gnostikos*, *Kephalaia gnostika*) for Oxford University Press.

INDEX

Non-Evagrian works are listed under the name of the author. The writings of Evagrius are listed under "Evagrius of Pontus, works" and as separate entries by title. Since multiple titles are used for Evagrian writings, please check "Evagrius of Pontus, works" for the titles used in this index. Manuscripts will be found under their specific location by city (e.g., "London, British Library"). Italic *t* after a page number indicates a table. Italic *f* after a page number indicates a figure.